CW00808424

VIOLENCE, CUSTOM AND LAW

Violence, Custom and Law

The Anglo–Scottish Border Lands in the
Later Middle Ages

Cynthia J. Neville

Edinburgh University Press

© Cynthia J. Neville, 1998

Edinburgh University Press
22 George Square, Edinburgh

Typeset in 10 on 12pt Monotype Ehrhardt
by Hewer Text Limited, Edinburgh, and
printed and bound in Great Britain

A CIP record for this book is available
from the British Library

ISBN 0 7486 1073 1

The right of Cynthia J. Neville to be identified as author of this
work has been asserted in accordance with the Copyright, Designs
and Patents Act 1988.

A University of Edinburgh Award for
Distinguished Scottish Scholarship

Contents

Acknowledgements

This book has been several years in the making. I would not have been able to undertake lengthy searches for pertinent source materials without the assistance of the Social Sciences and Humanities Research Council of Canada and the support of its officers. I am also indebted to members of the staff of several British archives, in particular those of the Public Record Office in London, Durham University Library and the Cumbria Record Office (Carlisle). Their helpful suggestions on occasion led me to records that shed valuable light on my examination of the peculiarities of border law. To the following persons or corporations I owe thanks for permission to cite manuscripts in their possession or custody: the Keeper of the Records of Scotland, the Bishop of Carlisle, the Bishop of Durham, the Earl of Lonsdale, the Earl of Northumberland, Judge F. J. Aglionby, Carlisle City Council and Mr Browne-Swinburne. The staff of the Document Delivery office of the Killam Library at Dalhousie University deserves mention here too for its assistance in responding to my numerous requests for inter-library loan materials.

My intellectual debts are more onerous. I wish first to thank Professor John Bellamy for instilling in me a serious interest in English law, and Dr Grant G. Simpson for willingly sharing with me his knowledge of medieval Scotland. The research of other border historians has been invaluable in helping me to understand the context in which Anglo–Scottish march lords operated; my respect for their work is abundantly apparent in the endnotes of this book. At regular intervals parts of my research were presented at seminars and colloquia held at Dalhousie University. The comments and queries of several of my colleagues, especially Daniel Woolf and Jack Crowley, helped me to identify problems in my arguments, and to ask new questions of my source materials. If there are errors in this work, they are mine alone, and are committed despite the assistance of all these people. Finally, I wish to thank most sincerely my friend and husband, Stephen. This book could not have been written without his patience, forbearance and support during my prolonged absences abroad.

Abbreviations

Acts of Council	*The Acts of the Lords of Council in Civil Causes*
APS	*Acts of the Parliaments of Scotland*
BL	British Library
CCR	*Calendar of Close Rolls*
CDS	*Calendar of Documents relating to Scotland*
Chron. Bower	*Joannis de Fordun Scotichronicon cum Supplementis et Continuatione Walteri Boweri*
CPR	*Calendar of Patent Rolls*
CRO	Cumbria Record Office (Carlisle)
DCD	Dean and Chapter, Durham Cathedral
Historia Anglicana	*Thomae Walsingham quondam monachi S. Albani Historia Anglicana*
NLS	National Library of Scotland
NRO	Northumberland Record Office
PPC	*Proceedings of the Privy Council of England*
PRO	Public Record Office
Reg. Mag. Sig.	*The Register of the Great Seal of Scotland*
Reg. Sec. Sig.	*The Register of the Privy Seal of Scotland*
SRO	Scottish Record Office
Treasurer Accts.	*Accounts of the Lord High Treasurer of Scotland*

Preface

The last two decades have seen a vigorous revival in the study of the medieval origins of English law. The seminal research into early legal procedure and the painstaking scrutiny of a wealth of contemporary record materials begun by the late nineteenth- and early twentieth-century legal historians T. F. T. Plucknett and F. W. Maitland have become the basis of renewed scholarly investigation of such varied fields as common law jurisprudence, the emergence of the professional lawyer and the evolution of the complex system that governed the settlement of disputes in medieval England. More recently, the work of S. F. C. Milsom has encouraged historians to explore the social history of English law. Interest in the workings of the common law has brought to light the immense value of the hundreds of plea and assize rolls available for the English counties. In studies based on these records historians have examined such topics as the origins and evolution of particular offences, the interaction between Westminster legal theorists and the juries who gave the law effect, and recourse to extra-curial settlements of disputes.

If the study of English medieval law has benefited tangibly from recent trends in the social sciences, it has been less heavily influenced by the strong tradition of regionalism in English historical enquiries. Yet the work of scholars interested in local aspects of medieval history has made it abundantly clear that in the realms of politics, the economy and even religious sensibilities, regional differences were crucial in the making of the English polity. Arguably, nowhere were these peculiarities of greater import and relevance than in the north where, by 1066, there existed 'a pronounced consciousness' of the divide between north and south and the border counties themselves were becoming part of a 'far north'.[1]

The distinct nature of northern English society is as pertinent to the study of legal institutions as it is to that of other features of medieval governance. The history of the north is dominated in all its aspects by the open hostility that characterised relations between the English and Scottish crowns. Although the bitter conflict of the years between the outbreak of war in 1296 and the sealing of a comprehensive treaty of peace and friendship in 1502 was relieved by long periods of truce and the suspension of military campaigns, the Anglo-Scottish conflict profoundly disturbed the political and economic stability of Lancashire, Cumberland, Westmorland and Northumberland. Wartime conditions contributed in marked fashion to the crown's enduring difficulties in maintaining law and order in the frontier region and, in periods of acute tension, as far south as Durham and Yorkshire. More important still, the ever-present danger of open conflict with Scotland played a crucial role in the development and operation of legal institutions there.

For much of the fourteenth and fifteenth centuries intercommunion between subjects of England and Scotland was prohibited, yet the fluctuation of the border line delimiting English lordship (in the west march chiefly in Annandale and in the east around Berwick) bedevilled royal efforts to distinguish clearly men and women in the English allegiance from 'the king's enemies'. Small-scale trade occurred between the English and the Scots during periods of truce, and families continued to intermarry. Throughout the lands of the north Scottish aliens lived and sometimes prospered as servants, labourers and merchants, but among their numbers were also to be found thieves, robbers, murderers and spies. The proximity of the king's enemies and their ubiquitousness in the border counties were aspects of northern society that no medieval king could afford to ignore. More than in any other part of the kingdom the unique conditions of the frontier region in the period after 1296 compelled the English crown to adapt its institutions to meet special requirements.

Historians have long been aware of the existence in the north of a body of law designed specifically to deal with offences involving both English and Scottish subjects. Detailed examination of its substance and procedure, however, has been impeded by the assumption that the law administered in the medieval border tribunals is too rudimentary to merit systematic consideration. Tudor records, by contrast, are plentiful and generally more accessible in printed form. Thus, while much is known about sixteenth- and seventeenth-century border law the reluctance of historians to search vigorously for and to analyse a wide diversity of primary source materials dating from the pre-Tudor period has left in remarkable obscurity the medieval origins and functions of that system of law. Despite recent efforts to focus critical attention on the earliest written 'code' of border custom (1249) and the context of legal practices peculiar to the border,[2] the observation of the late Professor Rae that 'the earlier laws . . . have not yet been adequately studied in themselves' still holds true.[3]

Long before Henry VIII established conciliar government in the north, the English crown had developed a body of law designed specifically to cope with the endemic, and diplomatically dangerous, problem of cross-border crime that troubled the frontier region. Indeed, the Tudor monarchs succeeded in fashioning an effective method for the governance of the border lands thanks largely to the efforts of their medieval predecessors and to the failures that sometimes accompanied innovations. Several expedients were tried, most notably the establishment of the office of warden of the march which, from the time of Edward I, combined the military, administrative and judicial authority required to safeguard the northern counties from the ravages of an enemy people. Edward III bestowed on the wardens the authority to make and enforce truces and endowed his warden-conservators with the broad punitive powers they needed to give credible expression to this authority. From the mid-fourteenth century onwards the king of England increasingly permitted his northern officials to make law, too. The days of march, which brought representatives of the English and Scottish crowns together at traditional border meeting places, became regular fora for the sealing of comprehensive truces. It was in the stuff of these written agreements that the procedures, process and substance of border law were elaborated.

The history of the medieval origins of border law has been neglected largely because there exists no single body of legal record related to its workings comparable to the vast corpus of documents that makes it possible to trace the development of the common law. The source materials used in this study are scattered among several collections, private and public, including central records of the chancery, the exchequer, the privy council, the itinerant courts of common law and the court of King's Bench, as well as local manuscript collections from medieval Cumberland, Northumberland, the duchy of Lancaster and Durham. The variety of documentation is itself an indication of the experimental nature of the medieval crown's attempts to deal effectively with border-related offences in a period of well-nigh perpetual war with neighbouring Scotland.

Valuable materials concerning individual incidents of cross-border crime are combined here with a careful examination of the texts of dozens of truces that, from the death of Edward I on, constituted the business of hundreds of meetings between ambassadors, messengers and wardens of the two kingdoms. Collectively, they reveal that the evolution of border law between the thirteenth and the early sixteenth centuries followed several distinct stages. The reign of Henry III, when relations between the crowns were generally amicable, saw the first attempt by the English crown to impose uniformity on a body of customary practice that was as yet inchoate and irregular. This brief period of cooperation was brought to an abrupt end by Edward I, whose ambitions to dominate Scotland demanded the suppression of a body of law that gave distinct status to the marches of either kingdom. By the middle of the fourteenth century, continued war with Scotland focused the crown's attention on the need to adapt northern legal institutions to suit the specific requirements of a hostile frontier; there was no longer any doubt that the normal machinery of the common law was inadequate to meet conditions there. From this period on royal justices began to share their judicial authority with the king's wardens, and border law came to supplement, complement – and occasionally override altogether – the common law in Cumberland, Westmorland and Northumberland. Edward's successors, from Richard II to Henry VII, built on foundations laid in the mid-fourteenth century. Over 100 years after the death of Edward III, the days of march had evolved into a sophisticated series of courts boasting their own procedural rules, administering a comprehensive body of substantive law and rendering unique sentences of redress, reparation and compensation.

One of the premises of this study is that while each of the kings of later medieval England brought new perspectives to the 'problem of the north', each built on the successes and failures of his predecessors. The book is therefore divided into a chronological study of the stages by which the English crown developed then refined the system of border law. The introductory chapter examines the customs that governed cross-border dispute settlement in the period before 1296. The thirteenth century is portrayed here as something of a 'golden age', both in general diplomatic terms, and in respect of the more specific matter of border law. The text of an indenture of 1249 – often referred to by historians as the first code of march law – is seen as the culmination of several years of fruitful cooperation and discussion with the Scots. An analysis of its several clauses is provided, and their implementation down to the mid-1290s traced in a variety of legal records.

The year 1296 saw the outbreak of war between Edward I and the Scots; although this first phase of the Wars of Independence drew to a close in 1328 with the Treaty of Edinburgh–Northampton, the Anglo-Scottish conflict endured until the end of the Middle Ages. Chapter 1 examines the efforts by Edward I and his son and successor, Edward II, to suppress the ancient laws and customs of the marches. It argues that the existence of a system of law that had as its basis recognition of the sovereignty of the smaller kingdom was fundamentally inimical to the English crown's claim to overlordship of Scotland. Legal practices peculiar to the border region nevertheless survived the attempt at suppression, and the earliest indentures of truce quickly came to include provision, at least in principal, for the revival and implementation of these procedures and customs. This chapter thus introduces the theme (found throughout the work) that the notion of Anglo-Scottish cooperation in the prosecution of cross border offences remained strong despite the fact of war, because it responded in meaningful and effective fashion to the unique social and legal circumstances of the borderers.

Chapter 2 studies the gradual but steady development of border law in the period between 1328 and the treaty of Berwick of 1357. The treaty of Edinburgh–Northampton included formal acknowledgement of the laws and customs of the march lands; in the course of the next thirty years there was shaped a body of legal 'precedent' according to which the crowns of either realm agreed to adjudicate cross-border grievances. The period is seen as one of important experimentation, both with the office of warden of the march (the crown's chief agent in the region) and with the substance of border law. Edward III had to weigh several considerations at once, including the need for a securely defended frontier, the wishes of his northern subjects, and the ambitions of an increasingly powerful northern nobility. Not least among his concerns, moreover, was the relationship between the common law and the newer system of border law. This chapter discusses these concerns, and examines evidence of the interaction of the two legal traditions.

The Treaty of Berwick of 1357, sealed at the time of the release from English captivity of the Scottish king, David II, initiated a new phase in the history of Anglo-Scottish relations. With the drawing of the smaller realm firmly into the orbit of the Hundred Years War as an ally of France, English diplomacy became more complex, and the matter of cross-border dispute settlement acquired a new dimension. Chapter 3 examines the elaboration of procedures for apprehending march criminals, the growing administrative and judicial burden assumed by the wardens, and the increasingly lengthy and detailed texts of indentures of truce, in which the principles governing the laws and customs of the march were regularly set out. Here again, special attention is devoted to the means by which the wardens, acting under commissions to keep the truce, shared with the royal justices of assize and justices of the peace the task of maintaining peace and order in the region.

In Chapter 4 the reign of Richard II is portrayed as a period in which border laws and customs continued to flourish and develop. Written evidence for the operation of the northern courts is abundant and permits a careful scrutiny of the subtle but important changes that occurred in the areas of procedural and substantive law. The years 1377–99 also witnessed a crucial period in the history of the English crown's relations with its northern magnates. This theme is explored through an examination of the alterations and improvements effected to the office of warden–conservator, and the creation of the office of lieutenant of the marches. The consequences of these changes, and of the troubled reign in general, on the workings of border law are reviewed and assessed.

The steady development of border legal principles that was characteristic of the fourteenth century was abruptly halted by the early Lancastrian rulers, Henry IV and Henry V. Anxious to consolidate the position of the new dynasty on the English throne, Henry IV suddenly revived claims to lordship over Scotland; in so doing, he reverted, of necessity, to Edward I's policy of denying the legitimacy of border legal customs and practices. His son, preoccupied with the war against France, devoted little attention to the judicial problems peculiar to the border region. Chapter 5 explores the effects of neglect on a system of law that, by the late fourteenth century, had begun to cope effectively and efficiently with the problem of cross-border crime. A significant collection of correspondence between the warden of the east march, John of Lancaster, and the English royal council, together with surviving assize records and various privy council documents, all suggest that the borderers were ill served by the early Lancastrians, and that the problem of disorder in the north increased significantly.

The minority of Henry VI saw not only a reversion to the crown's reliance on the customs of the march for the settlement of cross-border disputes, but clear and formal acknowledgement by the English government of the diplomatic advantages to be gained by encouraging the further growth and elaboration of the system of border law. Chapter 6 argues that the years 1424–61 were of tremendous importance in the increasing sophistication of march procedures and in the development of notions of 'international' law in the north. Special attention is given to noting the similarities between the newly revived march tribunals on the one hand and, on the other, the courts of admiralty and chivalry, and to the role of the king's council and Chancery in shaping the law administered in those tribunals. Here again, the texts of indentures of truce are closely examined for the evidence they reveal of changes to procedure and substance. The study of extant assize records suggests that, by the third decade of the fifteenth century, the warden-conservators had begun to compete with the king's common law justices for the prosecution and punishment of many northern offenders.

Chapter 7 examines late medieval developments in the history of border law from the accession of Edward IV to the year 1502, when England and Scotland sealed their first treaty of peace since 1328. It explores the continued elaboration of border procedures, and traces in these the origins of the sophisticated (and well-documented) system of Tudor border law. It examines also the origins of the

Council of the North and the important innovations of Richard III in the general administration of the frontier region. Henry VII effected something of a 'revolution' in the office of warden of the marches. The chapter studies the changes made to the office, their influence on the northern nobility and their consequences on the ways in which cross-border offenders were pursued and punished.

In the conclusion an effort is made to place the medieval system of border law in several general contexts. It explores the similarities and differences between the concept of the 'northern marches' on the one hand and, on the other, the Welsh and Irish frontiers. Special attention is paid here to the work of R. R. Davies with respect to Wales and of Robin Frame, Steven Ellis and others with respect to Ireland. The place of border legal procedure in the history of English common law is also addressed anew, as is the argument that the two systems of law were in competition in the north. The evidence of the records of assize is summarised and the place of the warden-conservators in relation to the justices of the peace in the northern shires assessed. The concluding chapter ends with general comments on the links between the medieval system of border law and its better-known Tudor successor.

Cynthia J. Neville
Halifax, N.S.
March 1998

Notes

1. Jewell, *North-South Divide*, pp. 5, 24.
2. Scott, 'The March Laws Reconsidered', pp. 114–30; Summerson, 'Early Development', pp. 29–42.
3. Rae, *Administration of the Scottish Frontier*, p. 69, note 28.

Introduction

The Thirteenth Century: A 'Golden Age' of Border Custom

In the spring of 1249 a group of English and Scottish knights convened in the border lands of southern Scotland to set down in writing the 'laws and customs of the march'. The sheriff of Northumberland was present as a representative of the English crown; the sheriffs of Berwick, Edinburgh and Roxburgh presided on behalf of the Scottish king, Alexander II. A mixed jury of twelve landholders from the border region of each realm reported, in unanimous fashion, the customs and practices that they agreed had long governed disputes between subjects of the kingdoms. The fruit of their efforts, often referred to subsequently as 'the first code of border law', quickly infiltrated the legal culture of the English and Scots inhabitants of the area, and in its written form became part of the collective memory of the borderers. Though its provisions would eventually be altered beyond recognition, the codification of 1249 thus became the basis of a system of law that remained unique to the border lands throughout the later medieval period.

The code of 1249 has proven of abiding interest to historians. It was at once a venerable curiosity and a manifest Scottish hoax to eighteenth-century antiquarians,[1] but earlier in the twentieth century one scholar opined that it was 'genuine and beyond challenge',[2] and the text has since been acknowledged as a 'very authoritative view' of what local men believed were practices that had obtained in the region beyond living memory.[3] Later medieval Scotsmen certainly regarded it as a reliable statement of contemporary custom, for they included it among their earliest royal muniments and had translated it into the vernacular by the early fifteenth century.[4] Edward I, too, accorded it sufficient importance to include it in an inventory of Scottish records that he ordered to be compiled when he presided over the Great Cause in 1292.[5]

The origins of the code of 1249, however, are shrouded in obscurity, and the antiquity of the practices described by the jurors has been the subject of wide and varied discussion. In 1913 Howard Pease asserted cautiously that 'the whole procedure derives from an earlier epoch';[6] a few years later, Rachel Reid suggested more confidently that the origins of the customs lay, more precisely, in the tenth-century laws of Athelstan and Edgar.[7] In 1971 the Stair Society published a manuscript completed in 1902 by George Neilson, which included a fully annotated edition and a lengthy discussion of the code. In his survey of the antecedents of the laws of the march, Neilson argued that the existence of a formal system for the adjudication of border-related disputes before the mid-twelfth century was merely 'hypothetical', and that 'the core of March Law is clearly post-

Norman'.[8] A recent work repeats Neilson's warnings against dating the origins of the code in the too distant past.[9] Yet Neilson himself was intrigued by the existence of much older elements in the jurors' findings. He commented at length on the tradition, already ancient in 1249, of convening meetings in specific border sites for the settlement of disputes involving the two realms, and his suggestions have been amply borne out by the research of the Scottish scholar, Geoffrey Barrow.[10] Wager of battle as a method of proof (identified in the text of 1249 as *handwarsil*), a hallmark of the thirteenth-century code, similarly argues for a pre-Norman origin.[11] A recent essay traces in scrupulous detail the origins of the pledges distrainable in both countries required of both plaintiffs and defendants (the *inborch* and *utborch* of articles 4 and 13), and demonstrates that these may have been in use as early as the first half of the eleventh century.[12] Taken together, these findings strongly suggest that, as Neilson suspected, 'the 1249 text is really a mosaic of provisions from different periods'.[13]

In this respect the form of the 'code' of 1249, together with the notions that inspired its authors to commit to writing the ancient customs of the march, bore a striking resemblance to contemporary developments elsewhere. Throughout western Europe the thirteenth century was the period *par excellence* of the redaction of legal treatises, texts and codes, each of which sought ultimately to impose order and coherence on a bewildering variety of local customs and practices, some of genuinely ancient provenance, others of more spurious descent. The spirit that prompted these attempts was a complex one: it was in many places both an expression of a nascent sense of 'national' identity and a reaction to the growing intrusion of princely and royal governments into the everyday lives of their subjects.[14] The trend toward the refinement of law and custom was particularly marked in the British Isles. The treatises attributed to Glanvill and Bracton constitute only the most famous manifestation of the systematisation of law in Britain: the latter in particular represented an affirmation that 'English law was by this time recognized as distinctively English, and Englishmen were proud of it'.[15] But among the Welsh and the Scots, too, the thirteenth century was a period during which legal thinkers laboured to define in coherent fashion the customs and laws according to which their peoples lived, held their lands, and settled their disputes. In Wales, the years between 1218 and 1277 saw the native princes of Gwynedd create and promote a powerful myth around their authority, using native law 'to foster an ideology of political unity and national identity';[16] an assize of 1244 formally acknowledged the existence of a distinct body of law and custom peculiar to the men of Galloway.[17] In 1249, then, the men of the march lands were doing little more than following contemporary fashion in wishing to set down in comprehensive and definitive form the customs which had prevailed in the region since 'time immemorial'.

The need to establish a distinct legal tradition was particularly pressing among the Celtic peoples of thirteenth-century Britain. While scholars of the English common law hail the age of Bracton as a crucial stage in the development of the English crown's authority over its subjects and as a manifestation of the increasing confidence of royal government, historians of Ireland, Wales and Scotland view the period in a considerably different light. For many of them, the thirteenth century saw the Celtic peoples of Britain thrown on the defensive in reaction to the imperialist tendencies and ambitions of the English crown. In the attempts of the Welsh in particular to resist domination by the English, distinctive legal traditions became a potent weapon in 'the armoury of national identity' that was launched against 'an intrusive officialdom and an alien governance'.[18] The Anglo-Scottish march lands were not, it is true, a distinct 'nation' in the same sense as were the Scots, the Irish and the Welsh, and their efforts to commit to writing their ancient laws and customs were not borne of the same urgency to defend their region from the territorial ambitions of the English crown. But insofar as the impulse to codify custom can be interpreted as a reaction to the uniformity of legal, administrative and financial institutions so cherished by the kings of thirteenth-century England, the compilation of 1249 was as determined a statement of regional identity and independence as were the efforts of the princes of Gwynedd or the Scottish king, Alexander III.

The notion of the border lands as a part of the kingdom geographically as well as culturally distinct from the rest of the realm (as well as the rest of Scotland) was one the mid-thirteenth-century conditions rendered not merely predictable, but timely. The formal settlement of the Anglo-Scottish political boundary in 1237, and generally amicable relations thereafter between England and Scotland provided fertile ground for the elaboration of procedures that would provide redress in disputes between subjects of two distinct and independent allegiances. This introduction examines the conditions under which the first steps were taken in the elaboration of those procedures, and the means by which they came to achieve recognition among the northern English borderers as 'the custom of the march'.

The evidence that survives with respect to Anglo-Scottish dispute settlement in the late twelfth and the thirteenth-centuries is patchy and difficult to interpret. Indeed, it is of such a varied and irregular nature that it is difficult to know whether or not the English crown itself was conscious of a clear tradition of dealing with problems that arose in the march lands. In 1280, old and experienced borderers would speak confidently of customs dating 'from a time whereof no memory exists',[19] but before the middle of the century mentions of legal practice relating to the region and its judicial peculiarities are rare. These are confined largely to a general consensus on the part of the kings of England and Scotland concerning the appropriate treatment of fugitives. Thus, in 1174 the Treaty of Falaise stated that

the king of Scots and his men shall hereafter receive no one into Scotland, or into their other territory, who is fleeing as a felon from the realm of the king [of England], unless he is willing to come to trial in the court of the king and to submit to the judgment of the court, but the king of Scots and his men shall take him as soon as they can, and render him to the king, or his justices or bailiffs of

England. But if anyone from the land of the king of Scots is a fugitive in England, on account of felony, unless he is willing to come to trial in the court of the king of Scots or of the king, and to submit to the judgment of the court, he shall not be received in the realm of the king, but shall be delivered to the men of the king of Scots, by the bailiffs of the king, where he is found.[20]

Just what this general extradition agreement entailed was made clearer in a bull of Pope Innocent III issued in 1216. The bull *Contra duellum religiosi* was issued in response to a complaint by members of the English and Scottish church that, in defiance of ecclesiastical privilege, clerics were required to submit to judicial duel in the settlement of all cross-border disputes 'as was customary between laymen'.[21] The papal prohibition, however, went unobserved. In 1237 angry English clerics reported to the visiting papal legate, Otto, that local custom continued to compel clerics of all ranks in the diocese of Carlisle to answer charges laid against them by subjects of the Scots crown 'with spears and swords', that is, by recourse to trial by combat. Thus, 'an abbot or prior, whatever his dignity or order, must either undergo the duel in person or, himself a prisoner on the scene of the duel, must have a champion. If his champion fall he is slain and the abbot or prior himself likewise is beheaded'.[22] Lamenting the recent fate of one of their fellows, they sought exemption for all clerics from this 'abominable abuse'.

As interesting as these allusions to cross-border dispute settlement may be, they make little explicit reference to a recognisable body of border custom, designed to apprehend offenders, put them to trial, secure the punishment of convicted persons, and ensure restitution of any stolen goods. On the contrary, they attest more clearly than anything else the inability of the kings of England and Scotland to agree on a system for providing remedy in a region over which both claimed jurisdiction. No workable solution to the difficulties represented by cross-border offenders was possible until the matter of royal authority in the march lands themselves had been unequivocally decided. It was only in that same year, 1237, that a resolution of the territorial question was effected. In the Treaty of York, Alexander II offered formal defeasance of all Scottish claims to the counties of Northumberland, Cumberland and Westmorland.[23] The terms of the treaty were concerned chiefly with setting out the legal authority that the king of Scots would exercise within the English territories assigned to him in the northern counties in exchange for the renunciation of his claim.[24] It made no mention of border customs or practices; clearly, Henry III intended to focus the negotiations of 1237 on the fact of the defeasance, rather than on its potential consequences in the matter of march-related dispute settlement. Yet it was not long before questions centred on the customs of the border required the attention of the English crown, and that the elucidation of a system that represented 'ancient custom' became pressing.

Less than a decade after the sealing of the Treaty of York, a squabble erupted between the canons of the little priory of Carham and the Scotsman Bernard de Hadden, concerning lands claimed by both. At issue was the delineation of the 'true and ancient marches' between the kingdoms, but overshadowing the dispute was the larger matter of jurisdiction in the settlement of cross-border grievances. In October 1245 Henry III dispatched the sheriff of Northumberland, Hugh de Bolbec, to Reddenburn,[25] where arrangements were made to perambulate the territory and to determine the junction of the English lands belonging to Carham, and the Scottish lands claimed by Hadden. A mixed jury of six English and six Scottish knights was assembled, but appears to have accomplished little, and the exercise degenerated into undignified argument. According to Bolbec, the Scottish jurors 'entirely disagreed . . . and contradicted' the findings of their English fellows, and neither side would submit to the resolution offered by the other.[26]

A second perambulation was undertaken on 1 December 1246, when the English knights returned the same findings as had their predecessors.[27] In 1248 Alexander II raised anew the question of border custom when he sent envoys to the English court with a complaint that the laws and customs of the march, 'hitherto used, are not being observed at present'.[28] The grievance concerned a Scotsman of some rank, Nicholas de Soules, who, it was alleged, had been unlawfully appealed of larceny in an English court by Robert de Gressop. At the command of Henry III six English knights were sent to the banks of the River Tweed to meet with an equal number of Scottish representatives. After sober consultation with 'old and discreet' persons in both allegiances, this mixed panel of recognitors returned the verdict that Soules had, indeed, been brought unlawfully before justices of the king of England. Its members concluded that, in accordance with 'ancient and approved custom', offences committed by the men of one kingdom within the territories of the other must not be impleaded 'other than at the march'. The ambiguities of this assertion are manifest, but the implication was that the tribunals held in the marches would be presided over by justices from either realm; in 1245 and 1246 this function had been assumed by the sheriffs of Northumberland and Roxburgh. It is also evident that the adjudication of questions concerning border custom and usage was intended to fall to a mixed panel of English and Scottish recognitors. Here, too, the perambulations of 1245 and 1246, despite their failure to engender unanimity of opinion, provided guidance.

In 1248, however, neither Henry III nor Alexander II appears to have been familiar with the precise nature of border law and custom to which each had to date given tacit approval. The following year, therefore, a jury was once again assembled on the marches, composed of twenty-four English and Scottish knights, some of them veterans of the failed perambulations of 1245 and 1246.[29] Here, in the formulation of the code of march law and custom, they achieved the consensus that had earlier proved so elusive. The code of 1249 set out in more systematic and lucid fashion ancient usage in the border lands of either realm, as the twenty-four local men believed this to be. In the second half of the thirteenth century, the findings of the recognitors were further elucidated and adapted as specific circumstances required.

Quite apart from its preservation of legal customs long superseded or unknown elsewhere in the kingdom, the text of 1249 is noteworthy in many respects. Several of the articles note the use of personal pledges as an effective means of ensuring the appearance of both plaintiff and defendant before march officials: these were to be produced by a lord seeking to recover a fugitive bondsman, by debtors in respect of their obligations, and in all claims involving life and limb.[30] As Neilson noted, the requirement that oaths of accusation and denial be supported by six compurgators recalled the use, in 1245 and 1246, of an equal number of English and Scottish participants;[31] the presence of jurors from both realms also anticipated by more than a century the presence of mixed juries in English courts of law.[32] The code reveals great concern on the part of the borderers for the payment of compensation in matters justiciable under march law. In cases of homicide the compilers provided for the payment of *manbote*, a form of wergild, to the family of the slain man.[33] In cases of proven theft restitution in full was to be made. However, as Neilson remarked, 'from first to last the assessment of damages was a serious difficulty of March Law',[34] and despite alterations to the requirements governing compensation and restitution, for the remainder of the medieval period the resolution of border disputes was bedevilled by the failure of both sides to agree on this aspect of the law.

The method of proof in all contested disputes was wager of battle, a feature of border legal procedure that survived to the end of the medieval period, despite the mistrust of the crown and the censure of the church. The reasons for the borderers' preference for judicial duel were many and varied. It has been noted that in 1249 trial by jury had only recently begun to replace the duel in English courts of law.[35] Moreover, in the fourteenth and fifteenth centuries judicial combats provided northerners steeped in generations of warfare with licit means of expressing their belligerence. But the survival of this method of proof meant that the role of the mixed jury in border tribunals remained, for many years, ambiguous at best. The text of 1249 was compiled by a mixed body of English and Scottish commissioners, and the mixed jury was mentioned again in cross-border disputes of the later thirteenth century and beyond, but for much of the medieval period the settlement of grievances was hampered by the tendency of border customs to confine jurors to the role of declaring an ever-shifting body of law and custom. As with respect to the disappearance of the personal pledges identified as the *inborch* and *utborch* in the code, inimical relations between England and Scotland after 1296 made this aspect of march law largely unworkable.

The text of 1249 was never interpreted by the kings of England as a rigid set of procedures, incapable of alteration. Indeed, its development, or, rather, its metamorphosis, in the course of the next century demonstrated the flexibility of the notion of march law under conditions of prolonged warfare. Although cross-border pledges disappeared soon after the outbreak of war in 1296, and the role of the mixed jury was similarly circumscribed by war, the belief remained strong in the collective mind of northern Englishmen that the march lands were the proper locus for the settlement of border-related disputes. The unique circumstances under which they lived and worked, together with their respect for what they believed was ancient custom, ensured the survival of a body of rules and regulations designed to answer the special needs of the region.

Despite the optimistic and cooperative mood that produced the compilation of 1249, problems in implementing its provisions began almost immediately. In November 1249 Henry III commanded the sheriff of Cumberland to proceed with the case of Gressop vs Soules 'according to the custom of the march',[36] but the dispute remained unresolved more than six months later. During this interval Soules apparently launched an appeal of his own against Gressop, and there is no indication that this hearing was ever brought to the march.[37] Of greater significance is the fact that, for the remainder of the thirteenth century, the customs enunciated in 1249 competed with the strong influence of English common law in the north. In 1251 and again the following year, for example, Henry III issued charters of pardon to the Scotsmen Patrick son of Constantine of Goswick and Geoffrey de Prestwick after they had been outlawed according to common-law procedure.[38] At assize sessions held in Newcastle-upon-Tyne in 1256 the Scot Gilbert de Nithsdale was put to trial for assaulting and robbing a wandering hermit. After confessing his misdeeds he was summarily executed (by the hermit himself!), not according to the law of the march, but, rather, in keeping with 'the custom of the county of Northumberland, which is such that, when any one is taken in possession of stolen goods (*manuopere*) he is immediately beheaded, and the person who pursued the thief in order to recover his stolen goods is to have the return of his chattels after performing the beheading'.[39] Nithsdale was one of more than a dozen Scotsmen who appeared, both as plaintiffs and defendants, at this session; several more were present at assize sessions convened in 1272 and 1279.[40]

On some occasions complaints against alleged Scottish felons were heard *coram rege*. Ralph de Bethum of Cumberland appeared in February 1266 against a large gang of border outlaws and accused them of carrying off animals and other goods worth £100.[41] Writs originating in Chancery also initiated inquests into alleged incidents of cross-border crime. One such inquiry was held in 1266, when a Newcastle man was charged with killing a Scot whom he discovered breaking into his house.[42] Several years later another inquest was ordered when a band of Scotsmen robbed and slew two servants of the Englishman Henry Sturmy.[43] Despite the findings of the jurors in the case of Gressop vs Soules, which had required that all offences involving subjects of the two realms be heard at the march, the customs and practices enunciated in 1249 did not exert unchallenged influence over all border-related grievances. Throughout the thirteenth century plaintiffs involved in incidents of cross-border crime had recourse to English common law and the remedies of English justice in their actions against alleged Scottish offenders. Resort to English law remained a constant, and competing, feature of the settlement of such disputes for the entire later medieval period. This was a result of several different factors, chief among which must have been a mistrust by English northerners of the impartiality or goodwill of their Scottish neighbours. But the border counties also reflected developments characteristic of thirteenth-century English legal history generally, including preference for the testimony of jurors as a method of proof, and the efforts of the English crown to effect and maintain firm control over the realm through the vehicle of the common law.[44]

Despite these pressures, the years after 1249 by no means witnessed the withering away of the distinctive features of border custom. The elucidation and development of march law proceeded apace, and it did so, for a time at least, with the overt encouragement of the English crown. A border tribunal was convened in the middle years of the 1260s, when a judicial duel successfully settled a grievance involving a tenant of the abbot of Jedburgh.[45] An inquest of 1272 reiterated the custom governing fleeing bondsmen set out in the code of 1249. Roger le Lung, the villein of William de Leversdale, fled to Scotland, where he confessed to having committed homicide and other felonies, and where he sought refuge 'according to the custom of the march of both countries'. An inquest returned that Roger was innocent of any slaying, but by then he was secure in Scottish territory, and, although invited back to Cumberland, he was not compelled to return to his lord.[46] In 1279, when two Englishmen were detained for the homicide of a Scot, Edward I commanded that the sheriff of Northumberland make inquiry into the custom of the march with respect to fugitive felons.[47] The matter of suspects who took flight into the opposite realm had been fully rehearsed in the code of 1249, but the incident provided the opportunity to restate current practice in the border shires. The king's missive noted the outcome of the inquiry that had brought the question into practice, and sought to ensure merely that the two men had been granted royal protection as required by the law.

March custom was at the centre of another legal argument in 1279, when a Cumberland man sought remedy in Chancery after being appealed of stealing a horse that he claimed had been lawfully purchased in Carlisle. Henry Scot noted that the appeal against him had been made 'according to the law of the march of Scotland at Solway', and complained that custom required to him to find sureties and to submit to judgement 'as though legally convicted'.[48] He sought, rather, to prove his case on the verdict of a jury, and the king, 'desiring to do justice and to be further informed on the law and custom of the March,' ordered the sheriff to hold an inquest.

The jury empanelled several weeks later from among knights and other landholders of Cumberland restated in no uncertain terms the customs they believed obtained in cases such as Henry Scot's: as previous recognitors had done, they hearkened back to the code of 1249. They argued that 'from a time of which no memory exists', plaintiffs pursuing stolen goods must cross the border within one day of the alleged theft and proclaim the crime. If the defendant was located within forty days, writs were to be exchanged between the English and Scottish sheriffs (in this case officials in Cumberland and Dumfriesshire), giving notice that *handwarcelle* (that is, wager of battle), had been offered.[49] Thereafter, the onus of proof lay with the defendant by means of the judicial duel. If he failed to better his opponent in battle his sureties remained responsible for making reparation; this was set, as it had been in 1249, at two-thirds of the damages claimed. Complaints were sometimes made about delays in obtaining justice in the marches,[50] and the old dispute concerning the lands of the Hadden family was still unresolved in the 1280s.[51] But in the later years of the thirteenth century the English crown continued to have recourse to the testimony of mixed panels of English and Scottish juries.[52] A letter of Bishop Anthony Bek, dated March 1287, shows that meetings at traditional border sites – in this case, ironically, the priory of Carham – continued to be held.[53]

There were signs in the air, however, of a shift of attitude on the part of the English crown in respect of the legal customs peculiar to the march lands. Edward I, in particular, grew increasingly suspicious of the challenge to common-law procedure represented by border procedures. Initially, his concern probably reflected little more than a determination to reserve to the crown the profits of justice arising from border-related offences, for Edward was always a careful steward of prerogative revenues. But political developments at the very end of the thirteenth century provided the opportunity for him to effect vigorous reform in the north and ultimately to suppress practices he considered inimical to English royal interests.

The first indications of a wish to impose some limitations on the traditional workings of march law date from the earliest years of the reign. Richard de Creppings, sheriff of Cumberland, wrote the king lamenting the number of robberies and homicides committed daily in the county. He blamed these crimes on the impunity with which the Scots crossed the border, but he also noted that the warrant under which he operated did not empower him to compel the local inhabitants to appear at inquests.[54] A more definitive sign of royal concern in respect of march custom is evident in a writ sent in 1279 to the sheriff of Northumberland concerning two Scotsmen detained in Newcastle gaol.[55] Although he acknowledged that it was customary to offer the king's peace to fugitives from Scotland who had confessed their misdeeds, Edward I made it clear that the inquest in this case must also ensure that 'traditional practice' did not prejudice the rights of the crown.[56] The hearing of disputes customarily justiciable in border tribunals in courts presided over instead by English justices of assize was still another aspect of the king's attempts to challenge a system he considered too competitive with his own.

Other considerations, too, influenced the shift in English royal policy away from support for the peculiarities of border custom. Chief among these was the dramatic series of events that occurred north of the border in the last years of the thirteenth century. The aftermath of the sudden demise, in 1286, of Alexander III of Scotland, then of his nearest heir, the Maid of Norway, saw the first attempts by Edward I to assert his superiority over Scotland. Those efforts culminated in the homage performed by John Balliol in December 1292. Thereafter, Edward determined to make real his lordship, and one of the most powerful means by which he chose to do so was in the exercise of judicial authority. The quarrel of the Gascon merchant, John le Mazun, with his Scottish creditors, the grievance of the nobleman MacDuff of Fife, and the complaints of several other Scottish plaintiffs were removed into the king's hands and their adjudication set in motion in English courts of law.[57] Edward's assumption of judicial superiority over Scottish appeals has much preoccupied historians of the Anglo–Scottish wars. Scottish scholars argue that concern with this aspect of the king's designs in the early 1290s 'has filled a disproportionately large place in Scottish history',[58] and that in the months after Balliol's act of homage 'there followed no flood of appeals from Scotland to England'.[59] They note, nevertheless, that the appeals were 'significant'. English scholars, by contrast, stress the fact that, for the English king, 'overlordship . . . was not a mere legal fiction', and that the matter of appeals 'was the first test of Edward's strength'.[60]

Edward I's claims to jurisdiction over Scottish causes have not, however, been examined in the light of a related shift away from the toleration that he and his predecessors had demonstrated for the customary adjudication of border-related disputes by mixed tribunals of English and Scottish jurors. The king's change of heart was made manifest in the courts of the general eyre that began its visitation of the northern counties in the autumn of 1292. At sessions convened in Carlisle in November Cumberland jurors were asked to declare the ancient custom of the march with respect to the homicide of an Englishman committed in Scotland.[61] Once again, the jury restated the clauses of the code of 1249 governing the pursuit of fugitive felons, including the requirement that the alleged offence be publicly proclaimed on either side of the border, the obligation of both plaintiff and defendant to find pledges, the duty to submit all claims to trial by battle, and the guarantee of sanctuary to suspects who confessed their misdeeds. These customs, the jurors noted, had been observed 'of ancient times'. When pressed, however, they added: 'until the time of the present king, who condemned them about the ninth year of his reign'.[62] They nevertheless insisted that 'they have never seen or heard that any other English king had the suit of any felonies committed in Scotland'.

The recollections of the Cumberland jurors were echoed just a few weeks later, when they royal eyre moved on to Newcastle. On this occasion, too, when queried about the custom regulating larceny cases in which subjects of the two realms were involved, the jurors informed the presiding justices that, according to march law, fugitive felons must not be impleaded in English courts, but must be left unmolested once they had come to the king's peace.[63] But these jurors, too, proved meek in the face of royal pressure. When the justices sternly reminded them that 'the king of England is the lord superior of the king of Scots', they returned that the defendant had failed to come to the peace of the Scottish king in due course, and that therefore the English crown must have suit of the case. The visitation of this eyre saw several other incidents of cross-border crime put to trial at English common law, without regard for march custom.[64] In another incident of cross-border larceny the crown allowed, in ambiguous fashion, that the case be put to an inquiry 'as elsewhere has been determined customary with respect to felonies committed in the kingdom of Scotland', but the dispute remained unsettled because the plaintiff failed to appear.[65] In still another, a Scottish fugitive was required to place himself on the verdict of an English jury, and his captor, who had attempted to return him to Scotland, was charged with trespass.[66]

The suppression of the customs of the northern border lands occurred against the backdrop of two competing, though complementary, forces. Edward I's efforts to impose procedural and substantive legal uniformity over the northernmost reaches of his kingdom meant that customs and practices that competed with common-law procedure must be discouraged, and eventually eradicated. As Maitland noted long ago, while not overtly hostile to local custom, royal judges in the late thirteenth century increasingly circumscribed regional peculiarities by imposing limits on their application: 'especially in matters of procedure, the king's court, which is now obtaining a thorough control over all other courts, is apt to treat its own as the only just rules'.[67] Of greater significance still was Edward's determination, as early as the year 1290, to impose his authority over the Scottish kingdom. The existence of a body of custom peculiar to the frontier region, one which accorded the Scottish crown a voice in march affairs equal to that of the English, was bound to be viewed as profoundly inimical to a king who subscribed wholeheartedly to current notions of the inherent superiority of a single body of law, and one that was, necessarily, English.[68]

Edward's intention of abolishing the customary practices of the border lands was given practical expression in his disposition of the written record attesting those customs. Included among the several hundred Scottish muniments carefully listed and collected by the king in 1291 and 1292, then removed for safekeeping, were not only a copy of the codification of 1249, but also documents relating to perambulations made of disputed march territories by mixed panels of English and Scottish recognitors, and a letter of the sheriff of Northumberland 'concerning a march matter'.[69] These were not the actions of a king whose motives bespoke merely 'a new spirit of precision in organization and a concern for detailed reform';[70] more accurately, they foreshadowed the imperialist designs that Edward would soon implement in respect of Scotland. In the early 1290s the king had not yet come to view the smaller realm as the 'kingdom in abeyance' that it would become in his eyes after 1296.[71] But in exerting his authority over border-related matters once acknowledged as most appropriately justiciable in 'international' tribunals, he made abundantly clear to English- and Scotsmen alike that the 'golden age' of border custom was fast drawing to a close.

Notes

1. Nicolson, *Leges Marchiarum*; Nicolson and Burn, *History and Antiquities of Westmorland and Cumberland*, i.ix.
2. Neilson, 'The March Laws', p. 68.
3. Scott, 'The March Laws Reconsidered', p. 118. See also the authorities cited in notes 6, 7, 9 and 10 below.
4. The earliest version of the text is printed in *APS*, i.413–16; a Scots vernacular text is found in NLS Adv. Ms. 7.1.9.

5. *APS*, i.114.
6. Pease, *The Lord Wardens*, p. 77.
7. Reid, 'Office of Warden', pp. 480–1.
8. Neilson, 'The March Laws', pp. 12, 24.
9. Summerson, 'Early Development', pp. 29–30.
10. Neilson, 'The March Laws', p. 17; Barrow, *Kingdom*, pp. 153–60. For an early discussion of the pre-Norman antecedents of the code, see Graham, 'Border Tenure', pp. 92–4.
11. Neilson, 'The March Laws', articles 7 and 11.
12. Scott, 'The March Laws Reconsidered', pp. 123–8.
13. Ibid., p. 123.
14. See, in general, Van Caenegem, *English Common Law*, pp. 85–110; Reynolds, *Kingdoms and Communities*, pp. 39–66, and Clanchy, 'Literacy, Law and the Power of the State', pp. 25–34.
15. Pollock and Maitland, *History of English Law*, i.188.
16. Davies, 'Law and National Identity', p. 57.
17. MacQueen, 'Laws of Galloway', pp. 131–43. See also the discussion of the so-called Laws of the Brets and Scots in Barrow, *Robert Bruce*, pp. 135–6. On Scottish legal thought generally in the thirteenth century see, most recently, Walker, *Legal History of Scotland*, pp. 252–63.
18. Davies, 'Law and National Identity', pp. 53, 60. More generally, see Davies, *Domination and Conquest*, pp. 142–68; Davies, 'Lordship or Colony?', pp. 155–60.
19. PRO C 145/39(5).
20. Stones, *Anglo-Scottish Relations*, pp. 5–7.
21. Innes, *Registrum episcopatus Glasguensis*, i.94.
22. Luard, 'Annales de Burton', i.256–7. Also printed, with annotations, in Powicke and Cheney, *Councils and Synods*, i.283–4.
23. Stones, *Anglo-Scottish Relations*, pp. 38–53. The negotiations that preceded the drafting of the treaty are reviewed in Duncan, *Making of the Kingdom*, pp. 533–4.
24. See Moore, *Lands of the Scottish Kings*, pp. 6–8, 40–7.
25. The use of Reddenburn as a traditional meeting place on the borders is discussed in Barrow, *Kingdom*, pp. 155–8.
26. PRO SC 1/2(166A), edited and translated in Stones, *Anglo-Scottish Relations*, pp. 54–7. This letter reports the perambulation described in PRO C 47/22/12(3), calendared in *CDS*, i. no.1676.
27. PRO C 47/22/12(4), calendared in *CDS*, i. no.1699.
28. PRO C 145/3(15). A Latin transcript of the complaint is printed in CDS, i.559–60, and an English translation in *Cal. Inqu. Misc.* 1219–1307, no.71.
29. These included the English knights Roger FitzRalph, Robert Malenfant, Robert de Ulster and William de Scremerston. The names of the Scottish jurors of 1245 are unknown, but Ralph de Bonkill, Robert de Bernham and Robert de Durham had represented Scotland before Henry III in 1248. The sheriffs of Northumberland and Berwick had also been present in 1248. The antecedents of the jurors named in the complaint of 1248 are reviewed in Scott, 'The March Laws Revisited', pp. 114–20.
30. Neilson, 'The March Laws', articles 3, 4, 8, 9, 12, 13.
31. Ibid., p. 18. Neilson misdated the inquest of 1245 to 1222.
32. Constable, *Law of the Other*, pp. 96–102.
33. Neilson, 'The March Laws', p. 21.
34. Ibid., p. 21.
35. Summerson, 'Early Development', p. 30.
36. *CCR*, 1247–51, p. 345.
37. Ibid., pp. 256–7.

38. *CPR*, 1247–58, pp. 122–3, 154.
39. PRO JUST 1/642 m.13.
40. PRO JUST 1/1216 m.3; JUST 1/645 m.11. For another beheading, see *Cal. Inqu. Misc.*, 1219–1307, no.600.
41. PRO KB 26/175 m.21; KB 26/128 m.10. See also KB 26/186 m.23d, and JUST 1/1216 m.3, for the case of a Scotsman who appealed another Scot for the death of the former's cousin.
42. PRO C 145/13(21).
43. PRO C 145/40(34).
44. Pollock and Maitland, *History of English Law*, ii.630–6.
45. *Exch. Rolls*, 1264–1359, p. 29.
46. PRO C 66/90 m.11, calendared in *CPR*, 1266–72, p. 658. The relevant clause in the code of 1249 read as follows: 'Item. They say unanimously that if any liege man or bondsman shall take flight from the kingdom of Scotland, with his chattels or without, into the kingdom of England seeking thus to escape his lord, and if he shall be pursued by his lord within forty days after he has crossed the march he shall be taken back into Scotland without any opposition by the kingdom of England upon his [his lord's] personal oath: and similarly as regards England. But if he shall be pursued after forty days the lord shall never recover his man unless by a brieve of the king in whose realm he shall be . . .'. Neilson, 'The March Laws', pp. 17–18.
47. PRO SC 1/13(156, 162).
48. PRO C 145/39(15), calendared in *Cal. Inqu. Misc.*, 1219–1307, no.1208.
49. See Neilson, 'The March Laws', p. 20.
50. See, for example, PRO SC 1/7(84); SC 8/277(13807).
51. In 1277–8 the priory of Kirkham raised afresh its claim to lands in Wark Common against those of Aymer de Hadden, son and heir of the priory's opponent in 1245 and 1246. PRO SC 8/332(15793), JUST 1/645 m.16. Despite a heated exchange between the crowns the grievance remained unresolved at Alexander III's death in 1286. *CCR*, 1281–92, p. 211; PRO C 47/22/9(16); C 47/22/1(3).
52. See, for example, *CPR*, 1281–92, p. 211, an inquest entrusted to 'twelve knights and other good men of Northumberland, and the like number of Scotland'.
53. PRO SC 1/29(185).
54. PRO SC 1/29(185).
55. PRO SC 1/13(156, 162).
56. PRO SC 1/13(156).
57. The records concerning John le Mazun are found in *CCR*, 1279–88, p. 412, CPR, 1281–92, pp. 249, 329, 344, 365; STEVENSON, *Documents*, i.71–7, 121–2, 157–8; PRO C 47/22/5(27); C 47/22/9(9); SC 1/13(158). The suits of MacDuff and the other Scottish plaintiffs are reviewed in Nicholson, *Later Middle Ages*, pp. 45–6 and Barrow, *Robert Bruce*, pp. 58–9. See also PRO C 47/22/5(28) (complaint regarding the seizure of a ship's cargo), and C 47/22/1(41) (complaint regarding the seizure of Scottish goods).
58. Barrow, *Robert Bruce*, p. 57.
59. Nicholson, *Later Middle Ages*, p. 45.
60. Prestwich, *Edward I*, pp. 366, 371.
61. PRO JUST 1/137 m.13.
62. Perhaps in 1280, following the trial of Henry Scot, noted above. The case is reviewed in Summerson, 'Early Development', pp. 30–1.
63. PRO JUST 1/653 m.37.
64. See, for example, PRO JUST 1/653 mm.3, 14d; JUST 1/137 mm.26, 31.
65. PRO JUST 1/137 m.30.
66. PRO JUST 1/137 m.31. The captor, Richard de Soules, was pardoned his trespass. See *CPR*, 1281–92, p. 511.

67. Pollock and Maitland, *History of English Law*, i.184.
68. Ellis, *Tudor Frontiers*, p. 259; Jones, 'England Against the Celtic Fringe:', pp. 168–71; Frame, *Political Development*, pp. 142–4; Davies, *Domination and Conquest*, pp. 120–6.
69. See the various lists of muniments compiled by Edward's agents in *APS*, i.109–10, 112, 114.
70. Smith, 'Statute of Wales', p. 137; Prestwich, *Edward I*, p. 288.
71. Nicholson, *Later Middle Ages*, p. 51.

I

The War Years, 1296–1328

The years between 1296 and the end of Edward I's reign in 1307 mark the beginning of a long 'dark age' in the history of border law. The conflict that began in 1296 extended, with only a few periods of truce, until 1328. Even then, the 'true, final and perpetual peace'[1] agreed to in the Treaty of Edinburgh–Northampton brought little respite to the hostility between England and Scotland, and the 1330s saw renewed warfare. Amid such conditions there was no opportunity for a return to the relatively cordial meetings that had taken place in the border lands in the thirteenth century, or for the continued development of a body of custom that encouraged mutual cooperation between the inhabitants of a region now divided by a hostile political boundary. Indeed, it was not until the middle years of the fourteenth century that the English crown made any real effort to address the troublesome problem of cross-border crime. By then, however, longstanding wartime conditions necessitated a whole new approach to the resolution of such incidents.

John Balliol's inability to counter effectively Edward I's ambitions to dominate Scotland led to the deposition of the king of Scots in 1295, his replacement with a body of Guardians, the forging of a Franco–Scottish alliance and, ultimately, the outbreak of open war in 1296. For all intents and purposes, cooperation between the crowns in the apprehension of cross-border offenders and the settlement of border disputes was halted. The English conquest of 1296 was quickly followed by the establishment of a government for Scotland, headed by a keeper (John earl of Warenne), a treasurer, a chancellor and justices. Among the latter was a veteran of the northern assize circuit, William of Ormsby.[2] Border-related disputes became the concern of the new administration, but one charged now with making the recent conquest real and forceful by means of English justice and English law. The question of punishment for offences done by Englishmen against the Scots became, almost by definition, redundant, and violence committed against the king's enemies was pardoned, if not actively encouraged. In the autumn of the year 1300, for example, the king ordered an inquest into the imprisonment in Newcastle of the Englishmen Henry Tod and Hugh son of Robert, detained for the homicide of the Scotsman William of Bulthorp. The record of the gaol delivery sessions before which their case was tried provides revealing testimony of the tension that now pervaded the border lands as a consequence of war, and of the unlikelihood that a mixed jury would be able to function effectively in this kind of setting. The Northumberland jurors informed the justices that

> William was born in Scotland, and was living in England until the war broke out, when he left the kingdom and returned to Scotland as an enemy of the king. But

once he saw that the English king had the victory he returned to England, even though he was still an enemy. He came to Alnmouth with two swords, where Henry and Hugh found him. They asked him if he was in the king's allegiance, and demanded that he deliver himself into their hands. William replied that he would never return to the peace or allegiance of the English king and brandished his swords in the manner of an enemy refusing to submit himself to the king's peace. Henry and Hugh slew him as such an enemy and felon.[3]

The actions of the culprits were excused in light of the victim's infamy, and were fully pardoned.[4]

Requests by Scotsmen for the redress of injuries were treated in notably casual fashion. Incidents that occurred within Scotland were merely assigned to the king's lieutenant in Scotland, in whose hands, more often than not, they were left to languish. Thus, when the abbot of Jedburgh complained that a gang of Cumberland men had carried off animals worth £100, his petition went unanswered.[5] Scots apprehended for offences committed in England, however, were subjected to English justice in sessions of gaol delivery and were treated there in the same fashion as English suspects.[6] In the tense atmosphere of the north, moreover, short shrift was given to persons believed to sympathise, however remotely, with the Scots.[7]

Despite a strong (and, for a time, successful) resistance movement in Scotland, a second English conquest was effected in 1304.[8] An ordinance drawn up the following year was unequivocal: 'As for the laws and customs to be used in the governance of the land of Scotland, it is ordained that the customs of the Scots and the Brets be henceforth forbidden, so that it is never used . . . And the king's lieutenant, in concert with the council which shall be there . . . shall reform and amend the laws and customs which are clearly displeasing to God and to reason'.[9] The practice thus summarily condemned appears to have been a system of wergilds, already forgotten throughout much of the northern kingdom, and long abandoned in those parts of Cumbria in which it had once been known.[10] It has been suggested that this aspect of Edward's legal reforms in Scotland never became a matter of controversy among the Scots, for the system in which the wergilds survived was itself 'long overdue for abolition'.[11] But when viewed in conjunction with the suppression of the northern border customs, the king's actions assumed a different complexion. Like the survival (however vestigial) of blood prices in parts of Celtic-speaking Scotland, the persistence of mixed tribunals of English and Scots in the border lands of England and Scotland challenged the rule of a king such as Edward I, who now claimed to govern a territory subject to his feudal overlordship, and over whose laws he now exercised control. In his references to Scotland after 1296 Edward left the status of the realm and crown deliberately vague, and neither he nor his son ever acknowledged Robert Bruce as king. While the Scots fought what they considered a war of independence the English crown claimed to be engaged in a conflict against its feudal superiority.[12]

The king's treatment of border custom echoed in many respects the policy he had followed when initiating reforms to Welsh law, aspects of which had been suppressed after the conquest of 1284. Here, too, although many local customs survived, the practices that Edward considered most prejudicial to the royal prerogative – in particular, the customs governing felonious offences – were summarily abolished and replaced with English law.[13] There were parallels, too, between the legal and constitutional position of Ireland in respect of the English crown in the late thirteenth century which must have coloured Edward's attitudes in respect of the Scots.[14] His death in 1307 put an end to the attempt to initiate the widespread reform of Scottish law he had envisaged in 1305. But far more effectively than any royal decree, ongoing war and the frequency of cross-border raids by both English and Scottish armies in the years 1296 to 1307 prevented the resumption of mixed English and Scottish tribunals and the revival of border custom.

The question of a return to the thirteenth-century customs and usages of the border lands was never addressed by either the Scots or the English in the closing years of Edward's reign. Neither of the truces sealed in October 1300 and January 1302 made any reference to tribunals of mixed jurors.[15] It would have been fruitless for the Scots to attempt raise the issue, for Edward made it clear to them that the truces were intended to be no more than intervals in a war of total conquest. In the early 1300s, despite the setbacks he had suffered, the king remained firm in his resolve to crush his Scottish enemies. The preservation of a body of march custom remained as incompatible with his designs over the smaller realm in 1305 as they had in 1292. In the estimation of both parties, it must have appeared as if the heyday of border law had come and gone.

The conflict with Scotland occupied the energies of Edward II to a much lesser extent than it had those of his father, but firm peace with the northern kingdom was not achieved until after his deposition in 1327. Ongoing hostilities continued to render cordial meetings on the borders at best impracticable. In the autumn of 1317, for example, papal legates seeking to impose a truce succeeded in making contact with Robert Bruce only with great difficulty; when they did eventually reach him, they were summarily rebuffed.[16] The first significant truce of the reign was not sealed until Christmas 1319,[17] and was secured only after the northerners had endured a period of devastating raids by Scottish armies.[18] It is hardly surprising that unambiguous evidence of the recourse to the 'ancient customs' of the border lands should be almost completely lacking for these years. That these traditions appear to have survived despite war is, then, all the more remarkable.

Yet survive they did. At sessions of gaol delivery held in Newcastle in 1309, a Northumberland man was appealed and convicted of the theft of two oxen at the suit of Mariota, a servant of the son of the Scottish earl of Dunbar. After the jury had pronounced its verdict the culprit was duly led off to be hanged, but the earl's son stepped forward to demand the return of the animals 'according to the custom of the march between England and Scotland in use until now'.[19] The presiding justices queried the matter, and summoned a second jury of men 'from beyond and from this side of Coquet'. These jurors supported the claim by reciting local practice in such cases. They did so in terms that closely echoed the relevant clauses of the code of 1249:

> They say that the custom of the said march is such that if anyone from the march of Scotland steals horses, cows or other animals or any other goods and brings them into the march of England, and is there condemned before justices at the suit of the man to whom the animals belong, or at the suit of his servant, he who owns the animals or goods shall recover them. And the same custom exists for persons living in the march of England whose animals or goods are stolen and taken into Scotland.

The court ruled that the animals should be restored to the earl's son.[20] The case was a highly unusual one, not merely because it upheld customs that had allegedly long been suppressed. The earl of Dunbar was in the allegiance of the English crown in 1309, and the justices of gaol delivery were no doubt aware of the king's need to maintain the goodwill of this important Scottish magnate. Recourse to the customs that had governed similar incidents in more peaceful times served the purpose of appeasing a disgruntled plaintiff and of preventing a breach of good relations with his family.

There are, however, further indications that adherence to customs and practices peculiar to the marches remained a living aspect of cross-border dispute settlement in the north. In the autumn of 1310, while he was in Berwick, Edward II presided over an inquest convened to hear a dispute concerning the revenues arising from the operation of a ferry service. Despite the tensions generated by the presence of the English expeditionary force in the town, the inquiry sought, and received, the advice of a mixed jury of English and Scottish recognitors, who returned that the plaintiff's claim was genuine.[21] In 1319 the inhabitants of Carlisle sent a long list of grievances to Edward II relating to the conduct of their sheriff, Andrew de Harcla, and his brother, John. These ranged far and wide, from accusations of misappropriation of monies and victuals, to charges of collusion with the Scottish enemy. One of the complaints stated that, in the absence of the warden of the march, John carried off two Scottish prisoners from Carlisle castle and took them 'to the Solway water', where he put them to ransom for ten and twelve marks respectively. On another occasion, John de Harcla's groom was said to have been found 'with others, buying beasts and other goods from the Scots at Solway water'.[22] Reference to the traditional meeting place on the borders is significant, as is the involvement of a representative of the sheriff in the deliberations with the Scots; both recalled thirteenth-century practice. Another interesting allusion to meetings on the borders was made in 1324, when it was reported to King Edward II that Scottish prisoners had been arrested at Solway and handed over to the sheriff of Cumberland.[23] Edward I might have effected the abolition of border custom *de jure*, but their tenacity in local practice was strong.

Andrew de Harcla's efforts as warden to pacify the march and to establish a *modus vivendi* with the Scots culminated in an unlawful treaty sealed with Robert

Bruce early in 1323.[24] Edward II, informed of the agreement just days after its negotiation, ordered the arrest of Harcla, and condemned him to death as a traitor for presuming to acknowledge Bruce as king of Scotland.[25] Yet the earl of Carlisle's negotiations 'helped pave the way' for the truce talks that were subsequently held.[26] In May 1323, when a long armistice was concluded, one of the items specifically mentioned was the agreement that 'in all things touching the law of the march, let that law be observed in all matters, as it was between the realms in times of peace'.[27] This clause was more than merely perfunctory or symbolic. A month before the conclusion of the truce talks the newly appointed warden in Cumberland, Anthony de Lucy, informed the king that a court had been held on the march, and 'all those who wished to make plaint from one side or the other' had been present.[28]

Despite the vicissitudes of war and an attempt at suppression by Edward I, border tribunals and the operation of border customs and practices once more became matters for discussion between the realms. The formal treaty of peace eventually sealed in 1328 at Edinburgh and Northampton made explicit acknowledgement of the revival of these customs: 'it is settled and agreed that the laws of the marches between the realms be well kept, and that strict right and justice be done against trespasses which take place on one side and the other'.[29] Just what the newly revived 'laws' were was left deliberately vague, for neither side was naive enough to envisage a ready return to the mixed tribunals of the thirteenth century. But in providing for the amendment of any 'defects' found in the laws, the treaty explicitly acknowledged the English crown's acquiescence to the partial revival of customs that Edward I had found abhorrent.

It is significant that the truce of 1323 and the treaty of 1328 should both have referred to border customs collectively as 'the laws of the march'. Despite a long period of bitter war and the suppression of those customs by Edward I, belief in the appropriateness of a body of rules and procedures designed to meet the unique requirements of the north remained strong, not only among the northerners, but also in the minds of the crown and the officials who lived and worked among them. It remained to be seen whether the newly revitalised body of law, especially one as yet so ill defined, could function effectively against the backdrop of continuing warfare that troubled the region throughout the reign of Edward III and beyond.

Both the vicissitudes and the exigencies of the Anglo-Scottish war drastically altered the shape of cross-border dispute settlement in the first years of the fourteenth century. As noted above, even before the outbreak of war in 1296 the crown had begun to assign to justices of assize the adjudication of offences committed by Scotsmen in England, and English plaintiffs used the common-law process of indictment, without reference to the ancient custom of the realm, in order to prosecute Scottish defendants. The adjudication of individual incidents of cross-border crime, however, because these were local in nature, was not a chief preoccupation of Edward I in the last years of his life. Nor did Edward II much care about them during his reign. Of much more immediate concern to both was the stability of the border region as a wartime front and the maintenance of a strong line of defence against the Scots. It was in order to ensure the safety of the northern frontier from attack that the crown created the office of warden of the march. From *ad hoc* beginnings the wardens became, and remained, the most important and influential royal agents in the border lands for well over three centuries.

The origins and early history of the office of warden of the marches were long ago elucidated by Rachel Reid.[30] In its initial form the office entailed purely military duties, some exercised formerly by the sheriff. These were altered and expanded as the changing needs of the northern border region required. In April 1297, preparatory to an expedition to Scotland, Edward I issued a commission to Robert de Clifford to 'keep the marches' that had been established by English forces in southern Scotland following the conquest of 1296. To this end, he was assigned several hundred armed men, and empowered to take hostages from among Scottish landholders who had come to the royal peace.[31] Within two months Henry Percy had joined Clifford in Scotland, and both were commanded to 'arrest, take, imprison and otherwise do justice' to all disturbers of the peace there.[32] In addition, both were empowered to receive into the king's peace all who wished to avail themselves of the royal grace, and several Scottish noblemen did so.[33] The events of the summer and autumn of 1297, which culminated in the defeat of an English army at the battle of Stirling Bridge, made it imperative that the northern counties be placed on a permanent war footing. Commissions dated 12 July appointed Ralph FitzWilliam, Robert de Clifford and Brian FitzAlan 'captains for the defence' of Northumberland, Cumberland and Westmorland, respectively.[34] Slightly altered commissions in October and November transformed these officials into 'captains of the custody of the Scottish marches', and 'captains and wardens for the defence' of the march regions of the border counties.[35]

Despite the differing terminology of these, and subsequent, commissions, the responsibilities of the wardens remained fundamentally unchanged for the duration of Edward I's reign. Within the conquered Scottish border territories they exercised a broad authority to accept all manner of persons into the king's peace, and to distrain and amerce all who disobeyed their orders.[36] Within England, they were charged with overseeing the provisioning and defence of the key fortresses of Carlisle and Newcastle under the lieutenancy of John earl of Warenne, and arraying the men of the region for forays into Scotland.[37] When in 1300 Warenne informed the crown that the inhabitants of the English border counties were evading or abandoning military service and refusing to join armed expeditions, the lieutenant and the wardens were given power to arrest, imprison and fine offenders.[38] But they exercised judicial authority solely in matters arising from their military authority; as Reid argued, they never enjoyed civil powers comparable to those of royal justices, nor did their work constitute a challenge to the workings of the common law in the north.[39]

Continuing warfare throughout the reign of Edward II transformed the office of the warden into a permanent feature of the royal administration in the border region. It was, however, one of the consequences of the king's difficulties at home that the importance of minimising tensions between the kingdoms was first linked clearly to the resumption of a regular machinery of justice for dealing with cross-border disputes. The sealing of indentures of truce, which began to suspend open war for increasingly long periods after 1319, the elaboration of the office of warden, and the related need to preserve the peace during those truces became the means by which the settlement of such grievances was accomplished. Early fourteenth-century developments in border law, then, were closely tied to the fortunes of the war, and reflected the crown's effectiveness in responding to the changing conditions of the conflict. Despite his failure to govern with much success at home, Edward II established the genesis of the system of border law that regulated Anglo-Scottish disputes for many years to come. Of crucial importance during this period was the distinction that the crown increasingly began to make between the purely military duties attached to the office of warden, and the judicial respon-sibilities of conservators of the truce. By the end of the reign the crown was learning to deal with march-related matters in terms of both their strategic and their legal requirements.

The powers of the wardens of the march remained largely unaltered throughout the first decades of the fourteenth century. They retained the power to array the fencible men of the northern counties in defence of the marches, and to punish anyone who refused to obey them. The text of the commission issued to Andrew de Harcla in September 1315, for example, was comprehensive: it bestowed 'full powers to do everything required to repulse the Scots, our enemies and rebels, and to ensure the safe and secure custody of our said city [Carlisle] and its surrounding parts'.[40] A commission of 1318 to Anthony de Lucy was more precise; it concluded with the clause: 'We also give to the said Anthony by virtue of these letters full power to distrain all men from the said county, both within and outwith its liberties . . . and to punish them . . . as he sees fit'.[41] Just what was understood by the 'full powers' thus conveyed is well illustrated in surviving record. John de Grey, a small landholder in Heton, Northumberland, had his lands confiscated by the warden in 1311 when he became an 'enemy and rebel of the king'.[42] John de Newbiggin was similarly punished in 1314, and was able to secure a pardon only after the warden had intervened with the king on his behalf.[43] When the receiver of the king's victuals at Carlisle was charged with the cost of replacing goods that he alleged had been stolen in a raid by the Scots, the warden held an inquest into the matter.[44] When he was warden, Henry Percy ordered the arrest and imprisonment at Newcastle of one John de Rodom, probably on a charge of spying. The latter petitioned the king when he was refused the opportunity to answer the charge.[45] None of these offences, however, was clearly justiciable at common law, and the wardens' authority arose merely from their duties as military agents of the crown in the north.

The sealing of a long truce in 1319 was welcomed by Edward II. His envoys, who included Aymer de Valence earl of Pembroke and the chancellor, John bishop of Ely, were sent to Newcastle with instructions to negotiate as long an armistice as possible. Their commissions also empowered them to appoint keepers of the truce, if one was made, from among the chief landholders in the north.[46] The sealing of the truce of 1323 was similarly preceded by the appointment of conservators, this time specifically nominated by the king himself: Anthony de Lucy in the march of Cumberland, and Ralph de Neville and Roger de Horsley in the march of Northumberland.[47] It was in this capacity that Lucy wrote to the king in April 1323 about the state of the marches and a border tribunal then in session.[48] The conclusion of the truce on 30 May was quickly followed by the formal appointment of new conservators. Anthony de Lucy, now warden of the march, was replaced by three local noblemen, Ralph de Dacre, John de Haverington and Adam de Skelton.[49] In Northumberland Ralph Neville and Roger de Horsley were joined by Richard de Emeldon.[50] In both regions it was felt necessary to separate the wardenial office from that of conservator, a feature of border administration that had obtained for some twenty years. The division of responsibilities was intended primarily to leave the wardens the freedom of movement throughout the march regions that their military duties required, but the crown also sought to ensure a modicum of impartiality in the settlement of truce-time disputes by investing the comprehensive judicial authority inherent in the conservators' functions in officials other than its military captains.

The bestowal of truce-keeping duties on men other than the wardens may also have been effected more immediately in response to the unpopularity of these officials among the northerners. From Cumberland only a month earlier had come a long list of complaints concerning the conduct of Andrew de Harcla,[51] and for several years already the wardens had been deeply resented in the border region generally for their heavy-handedness in keeping the northern counties properly arrayed for war. Many considered them at least partially responsible for the widespread devastation wrought by Robert Bruce's raids in the previous decade. The author of the *Vita Edwardi Secundi*, for example, made explicit reference to the contempt in which the wardens were held in Northumberland:

> In past years the king had been in the habit of strengthening the March with wardens throughout the winter, but their oppression was more injurious to the people than the persecution of their enemies. For the Scots used to spare the inhabitants of Northumbria for a time in return for a moderate tribute, but those who were supposed to be set over them for their protection were constantly at leisure to oppress them every day.[52]

The men appointed as conservators in 1323 were by no means newcomers to royal service in the north. Though unpopular, Horsley had been constable of Bamburgh castle, and active in the king's service in the marches since Bannock-burn.[53] Emeldon had been mayor of Newcastle, a position he was to occupy for several years, as well as a royal purveyor, victualler and a member of numerous commissions of inquiry.[54] Haverington, Dacre and Skelton were familiar with the military and administrative requirements of the region,[55] and Ralph Neville was already a veteran of the Anglo-Scottish wars.[56] All were well placed to investigate the circumstances surrounding alleged violations of the truce, but also to gauge the tenor of local sentiment when they determined the punishment of suspects.

The armistice of 1323 made only a general reference to the means by which the new officials should 'keep' the truce.[57] Mutual mistrust between Edward II and Robert Bruce, and a marked conservatism on the part of the English crown mitigated against a clear declaration of jurisdictional privilege and authority in the marches. But Edward made more than a nominal gesture in acknowledging the importance of the new office by making efforts to appoint conservators of the truce on a regular basis.[58] In the later 1320s these men responded to local conditions as circumstances required, and thus began, by practice rather than policy, to define the duties of the office. In June 1323, for example, conservators of the truce in Northumberland acting under a commission of oyer and terminer held an inquest into the attempted seizure of Norham castle the previous year by a gang of rebel Englishmen and enemy Scots.[59] When rumours reached the king early in October that large numbers of Scotsmen were roaming about the northern counties committing depredations against the terms of the truce, conservators in Northumberland and Cumberland were ordered to make every effort to arrest them, and to report their names to the king's council.[60] A similar round-up was ordered in Cumberland in June 1326, when news of widespread collusion with the Scots was sent south. The keeper of the truce, Anthony de Lucy, was instructed to compile a list of Englishmen alleged to have adhered to the enemy. His enquiries netted a significant number of culprits, most of whom were reported to have committed homicides in England with the assistance of Scottish accomplices.[61] All were granted the king's peace on Lucy's authority, and all were formally pardoned within a month, probably in return for promises to serve in the king's army.[62]

The Lanercost chronicler noted that the truce of 1323 empowered conservators of the truce to grant safe conducts to subjects wishing to travel across the border, and to Scotsmen coming to England.[63] This privilege was jealously guarded by the crown, only reluctantly bestowed,[64] and one over which Edward II exercised close supervision. When he felt that the letters permitted too much freedom of movement within the border territories for suspicious Scotsmen, he did not hesitate to take his conservators to task.[65] Despite his concerns, the king quickly came to appreciate the importance of the new privilege, for the ability of the conservators to organise meetings with their Scottish counterparts on short notice had been greatly enhanced. Frequent exchanges between officials of the two realms, it was hoped, would prove valuable in diffusing tensions generated by isolated incidents of cross-border raiding.

Despite the ambiguity of their position in the handling of truce-related disputes, Edward II's conservators performed their multifarious functions effectively, and their importance in Anglo-Scottish diplomatic relations was quickly acknowledged by the crown. In June 1324 Edward ordered the release of several Scottish suspects from the custody of the sheriff to whom they had been entrusted, and their delivery to the conservator, 'who will deal with them appropriately, according to the terms of the current truce'.[66] The courts of the conservators, where redress and reparation for acts committed in violation of the truce were discussed, were to have a long history in the administration of the northern border shires. The peace treaty of 1328, like the truce of 1323, made only general reference to these tribunals, but despite the difficulties caused by war, the origins of these courts lie firmly in the decade after 1319. Robert Bruce complained that breaches of the truce were not being adequately redressed by English officials,[67] but the Scots were themselves responsible for disrupting some of the earliest efforts to secure redress. The bailiff of Wark castle petitioned the crown in 1328, for example, when he was charged with the loss of £13 worth of rent stolen by the Scots. He was instructed to sue for recovery with the conservator of the truce, but his suit was suspended when the Scots renewed their raids.[68]

Hostilities between the realms continued to hamper the efforts of the conservators to establish regular and effective communication with the Scots, but within the northern border counties themselves the first attempts to create an office specifically designed to deal with march-related disputes in a wartime setting were successful. The role of the sheriff in border affairs, already circumscribed in the early fourteenth century, was now further reduced to that of mere assistant to the keepers of the truce. Although the crown continued, in the course of the next two centuries, to experiment with the powers assigned to the offices of both warden and conservator, their fundamental authority in matters that had once been the purview of the sheriff remained unchanged. For many years after 1328 the crown required a corps of officials whose commission enabled them above all to respond to the unique requirements of war in the north. Ongoing tensions in Anglo-Scottish relations in the reign of Edward III ensured that these officials would occupy an important – and now a permanent – place in march-related matters.

Notes

1. Stones, *Anglo-Scottish Relations*, p. 339.
2. Barrow, *Robert Bruce*, p. 75.
3. PRO C 81/22(2162A-E).
4. *CPR*, 1292–1301, p. 576.
5. PRO SC 8/117(4432). See also the cases of Evota of Stirling and John of Laysingby, in *Rot. Parl.*, i.469; SC 8/57(2812).
6. See, for example, PRO JUST 3/53/1 mm.1, 1d, 5d.
7. PRO JUST 1/226 mm.4d, 5d. These trials were held, ironically, before Justice William Ormsby, whose experience in conquered Scotland made him particularly antagonistic towards its people.
8. Barrow, *Robert Bruce*, pp. 128–30.
9. Stones, *Anglo-Scottish Relations*, p. 251.
10. Barrow, *Robert Bruce*, p. 136; Duncan, *Making of the Kingdom*, pp. 531–2; Black, 'Delictual Liability', pp. 49–50.
11. Barrow, *Robert Bruce*, p. 136. See also Prestwich, *Edward I*, p. 504. The survival in Galloway of the custom known as *surdit de sergaunt* and its manifestation in nearby Carrick are reviewed in Dickinson, 'Surdit de Sergaunt', pp. 170–5; MacQueen, 'Laws of Galloway', pp. 133–5; MacQueen, 'Kin of Kennedy', p. 281.
12. See the discussion of Edward I's refusal to observe the laws of war in hostilities with the Scots; to have done so would have been tantamount to acknowledging the sovereign authority of his opponents. Prestwich, 'England and Scotland', pp. 181–97.

13. Smith, 'Statute of Wales', pp. 151–2.
14. Barrow, *Robert Bruce*, p. 186; Otway-Ruthven, *History of Medieval Ireland*, pp. 188–9; Davies, *Domination and Conquest*, esp. pp. 120–6.
15. The texts of those truces are found in *Foedera*, I.iv.4, 13.
16. Hill, 'Belief and Practice', pp. 135–7.
17. *Chron. Lanercost*, p. 228; *Vita Edwardi Secundi*, p. 103; PRO C 47/22/12(19), C 47/22/13(6).
18. *Chron. Lanercost*, pp. 212–16; Stevenson, *Illustrations*, p. 4; 'Ypodigma Neustriae', xii.252; *Historia Anglicana*, i.155–6; 'Adae Murimuth continuatio chronicarum', p. 30; *Chron. Melsa*, ii.333; *Chron. Harding*, pp. 308–9. The devastation and poverty caused by the Scottish raids of the 1310s are discussed in Scammell, 'Robert I and the North of England', pp. 385–403, and McNamee, 'Buying Off Robert Bruce', pp. 77–89.
19. PRO JUST 3/53/2 mm.4/1d-4/2.
20. It has been suggested that members of the plaintiff's entourage, which was probably considerable, acted in the capacity of pledges, as required by the provisions of the code of 1249. Summerson, 'Early Development', pp. 31–2.
21. PRO C 81/293(15737). The incident is mentioned in a document dated October 1343. Richard Bernard, the plaintiff, charged that Richard de Bury bishop of Durham continued to enjoy the profits of the ferry service in violation of the findings of the inquest of 1310. Edward II was in Berwick from November 1310 until late June 1311. See *Vita Edwardi Secundi*, p. 13.
22. PRO C 47/22/10(35).
23. *Foedera*, II.ii.100.
24. The text of the treaty is reprinted in Stones, *Anglo-Scottish Relations*, pp. 308–15.
25. *Brut*, i.227; *Chron. Lanercost*, pp. 241–5; Bellamy, *Law of Treason*, pp. 52–3; Mason, 'Sir Andrew de Harcla', pp. 120–37.
26. Barrow, *Robert Bruce*, p. 248.
27. PRO C 47/22/13(3) (conditions proposed by both parties for the truce); C 47/22/13(4), printed in *Foedera*, II.ii.74 (text of the truce).
28. PRO SC 1/38(165).
29. Stones, *Anglo-Scottish Relations*, p. 315.
30. Reid, 'Office of Warden', pp. 479–96.
31. PRO C 47/22/2(2).
32. *CPR*, 1292–1301, p. 315.
33. PRO C 47/22/12(41).
34. *CPR*, 1292–1301, p. 315.
35. *Parl. Writs*, i.294–6, 301, 305.
36. See, for example, *CPR*, 1292–1301, pp. 315, 372; PRO E 101/7/1; SC 1/25(41); C 47/22/2(51); C 47/22/9(112).
37. See, for example, PRO E 159/71 m.109; *Parl. Writs*, i.294–5, 318; PRO E 101/7/21, E 101/7/20; *CCR*, 1296–1302, p. 367.
38. *Parl. Writs*, i.344.
39. Reid, 'Office of Warden', pp. 497–8.
40. *Rot. Scot.*, i.149.
41. Ibid., i.189.
42. Fraser, *Ancient Petitions*, pp. 23–4.
43. PRO C 81/88(3043).
44. PRO C 145/92(29).
45. PRO SC 8/136(6800).
46. *Foedera*, II.i.187.
47. Ibid., II.ii.65, 71.
48. PRO SC 1/38(165).

49. *Foedera*, II.ii.74–5.
50. Neville and Emeldon were replaced in July by Robert de Umfraville and Roger Heron. *CPR*, 1321–4, p. 292.
51. PRO C 47/22/10(35). See above, p. 18.
52. *Vita Edwardi Secundi*, p. 103.
53. *CPR*, 1313–17, p. 309; *CPR*, 1317–21, pp. 22, 158–9, 201, 205.
54. *CPR*, 1313–17, pp. 208, 247, 403; *CPR*, 1321–4, pp. 48, 49, 58, 158–9, 205, 207, 231–2, 317.
55. *CPR*, 1313–17, pp. 21, 22, 23, 685, 688; *CPR*, 1321–4, pp. 55, 130.
56. *CPR*, 1321–4, pp. 92, 100, 205, 212, 227, 261, 264, 268.
57. *Foedera*, II.ii.73.
58. *CPR*, 1324–7, p. 113; *Foedera*, II.ii.133–4 (April 1325); II.ii.134 (May 1325); II.i.139 (July 1325); II.ii.154 (before 25 March 1326).
59. *CPR*, 1321–4, p. 318; *CCR*, 1323–7, p. 26.
60. *CCR*, 1323–7, p. 25; *Foedera*, II.ii.536–7. See also a commission of oyer and terminer issued to the conservators of Cumberland in June 1324, *CPR*, 1321–4, p. 422.
61. Twenty-five men were named in Lucy's report. PRO SC 1/45(209, 210).
62. *CPR*, 1324–7, p. 307.
63. *Chron. Lanercost*, p. 247. See, for example, *CPR*, 1323–7, p. 85, the case of a Scotsman on pilgrimage to Canterbury who was assaulted in violation of a conservator's safe conduct, and PRO C 145/123(12), in which the heirs of a portrait painter challenged the accusation that the latter had used letters of safe conduct to defect to the Scots.
64. Keen, *Laws of War*, pp. 197–206.
65. *Foedera*, II.ii.154.
66. Ibid., II.ii.100.
67. Ibid., II.ii.164. See also Barbour, *Bruce*, ii.144–5.
68. Fraser, *Ancient Petitions*, p. 92; *CCR*, 1327–30, p. 342.

2

Experimentation, 1328–57

The Treaty of Edinburgh–Northampton, in which Queen Isabella and Roger Mortimer acknowledged the independence and sovereignty of the kingdom of Scotland, was deeply disappointing to Englishmen great and small. Several chroniclers denounced it as cowardly and ill-conceived.[1] To Geoffrey le Baker it was a 'shameful peace', concluded without the consent of the young king.[2] Within less than three years of its sealing Edward III himself declared that peace with the Scots had been made without his consent.[3] The claims of the so-called 'disinherited' – English noblemen who lost lands in Scotland as a consequence of the treaty – and Edward's support for the client king, Edward Balliol, became the focus of renewed warfare in the 1330s. The conflict with Scotland greatly preoccupied English royal energies until well into the 1340s. Hostilities also erupted with France, and the remainder of the reign saw English armies fighting on two fronts.

The continued exposure of the northern border shires to the dangers of Scottish invasion compelled the crown to devote increasingly close attention to the matter of cross-border dispute settlement. During the reign of Edward III the mechanisms for coping with this problem that had first been established by the government under Edward II were subjected to a great deal of experimentation. The office of warden of the march was enhanced, and, as before, the powers allotted to these men were modified to meet the changing circumstances of the conflict. The sealing of increasingly lengthy truces required the development of more elaborate provisions for the maintenance of these fragile periods of peace within the border counties, and for the exchange of compensation and redress on behalf of injured parties in both the English and the Scottish allegiances. Ultimately, the persistence of hostile relations between the crowns demanded a fundamental reappraisal of the English government's perceptions of the 'ancient customs and usages' of the marches, one that no longer took for granted the peaceable conditions that had prevailed in the thirteenth century.

The volume of records generated by the central government in respect of border-related matters beginning in the 1340s suggests that Edward III and his council came to take very seriously the problems caused by endemic warfare in the north. They attest, too, a great variety of approaches to these problems. From a sometimes bewildering array of Exchequer, council and, especially, Chancery records, it is possible to discern several stages in the crown's policy of dealing with the matter of cross-border dispute settlement, but also a clear sense of purpose. During the heyday of Edward Balliol's attempt to rule Scotland beginning in 1332, and until 1346, the English government confined its efforts in the north to maintaining the region on a war footing; as a result, the focus of royal policy was little more ambitious than the provision of adequate men to fill the office of warden of the marches and of the numerous fortresses of the border lands. During periods of armistice (although these were few) the king made the conventional gesture of appointing conservators of the truce, but as long as Balliol's claims to the throne remained tenable little energy was expanded on encouraging frequent or regular meetings between these officials and representatives of the Scottish patriotic party. The capture in 1346 of the Scots king, David II, at the battle of Neville's Cross tipped the scales in the conflict decidedly in favour of the English. David's long captivity at Edward III's court signalled a shift of royal opinion in respect of border law and border tribunals; the future of the customs of the marches became a matter of negotiation, closely allied, like the status of the Scottish realm and crown, to diplomatic concerns. By the time the Scottish king returned home in 1357 a new system of border administration had been established, one which now reflected the realities of ongoing warfare, but which also bespoke Edward's willingness to acknowledge the Scottish realm as something more than the 'kingdom in abeyance' that it had been under Edward I.

In the last decade of Edward III's reign, then, frequent and regular meetings on the borders were arranged between the kingdoms. The laws and customs in operation in the northern marches in the 1370s would have been virtually unrecognisable to the borderers of the previous century. But among contemporaries they were widely respected and heartily lauded, for in common with their earlier versions, they more than adequately performed the essential function of bringing together plaintiffs and defendants from two distinct allegiances. Redress for injuries done in violation of the truce or in conflict with lawfully prescribed border custom was seldom achieved in harmonious circumstances, and the mills of justice ground very slowly indeed in the cross-border tribunals. But by the end of Edward III's reign a long period of experimentation and elaboration had produced a system of law that was able to cope in more than merely adequate fashion with the competing claims of neighbouring peoples separated by a hostile political border.

Despite his distaste for the Treaty of Edinburgh-Northampton, Edward III delayed renewing war with the Scots until the latter had completed payment of £20,000 negotiated as one of the terms of the peace of 1328.[4] The final instalment was made in mid-summer 1331; thereafter, Edward began to exert diplomatic pressure on the Scots for the restoration of the Scottish territories formerly belonging to Thomas Wake, Henry Beaumont and several other disinherited English noblemen.[5] That same summer Edward Balliol sailed from Picardy to England, where he performed homage to the English king for Scotland and sought the king's assistance in his bid for the throne of the northern realm. For a time, Edward III gave little overt support to Balliol or to the cause of the disinherited. Anxious not to rupture prematurely the peace treaty, he played a role of 'benevolent neutrality' in the expedition that Beaumont led to Scotland in the summer of 1332.[6] Although he made no attempt to discourage a sea-borne campaign of harassment launched from the Humber, or to prevent the disinherited from landing in Fife, he maintained as late as January 1333, both before his own parliament and in a missive to the pope, that he was committed to observing the terms of the peace.[7]

Edward's motives were entirely self-serving. While he must have welcomed news of the victory won by Balliol at Dupplin Moor in August 1332, he was also extremely wary of provoking the French king into a resumption of the Auld Alliance.[8] Whether or not his reticence to endorse the activities of Balliol and the disinherited arose in fact from an 'obsession' with the first Franco–Scottish alliance of 1295,[9] Edward was meticulous, between 1330 and the first weeks of 1333, in his attempts to convey to the Scots a spirit of cautious goodwill. In the first parliament convened after the execution of Roger Mortimer in the autumn of 1330 the by now hoary issues surrounding the territorial claims of the Hadden family to lands belonging to the priory of Kirkham were raised afresh. The fact that the dispute remained unsettled after almost a century was not lost on Edward III, who championed the sovereignty of the English crown in the border region as tenaciously as had his grandfather. But by now it had also come to be closely identified with the whole matter of border law, and its political value was high. In a skilfully orchestrated public display Edward III ordered the wardens of Northumberland to convene with representatives of the Scottish king and, once more, to undertake a perambulation of the area.[10] In January 1331 the bishop of Durham petitioned for assistance in settling another dispute with the Scots in respect of the vill of Upsettlington West.[11] The king referred this disagreement to the conservators of the truce, and made a show of easing their task by ordering that the 'rolls and remembrances' of thirteenth-century perambulations be searched for guidance.[12]

Clear and unambiguous references to the substance of the laws and customs of the marches are lacking for most of the decade of the 1330s: there occurred no revival of the optimism that had brought together twenty-four men from either realm in 1249. But it is equally clear that Edward III saw in the preservation of the notion of a living body of border custom an important way of ensuring that the northern region remained, at least on the surface, peaceable. In February 1331 he appointed several men *justiciarios nostros* in the counties of Northumberland and Cumberland, charged with keeping the peace made with the Scots in the treaty of 1328. These commissions, though they bore some resemblance to those that had empowered conservators of the truce under Edward II, were unusually broad in scope. The new conservators (who included the archbishop of York and the prior of Durham) were directed to undertake several tasks. In association with Scottish officials they were to make perambulations of disputed border territories, and to hear and determine all cross-border incidents 'according to the laws and customs of the marches'.[13] Further gestures of goodwill included the appointment of commissioners in October 1332 and January 1333, in response to complaints of unlawful ransom-taking by aggrieved Scottish petitioners.[14]

By the spring of 1333, however, Edward III had decided that the pretence of Anglo–Scottish cooperation was no longer necessary. Abruptly abandoning his policy of abiding by the terms of the Treaty of Edinburgh–Northampton, he now moved openly against the Scots. Balliol's victory at the battle of Halidon Hill in July was followed by the cession of eight of the lowland Scottish counties to the

English crown, and the imposition of English rule there. From 1334 until his departure for France in 1337, Edward conducted a costly defensive war in the north, where his energies were directed solely towards maintaining his hold over the newly-won border fortresses and their hinterland. The need for cross-border tribunals became obsolete, and the notion of border law fell once again into abeyance. As had occurred under Edward's grandfather in the decade following the conquest of 1296, the crown concentrated instead on strengthening the office of warden in the marches of England, to facilitate the arrest of any of the inhabitants now under English rule who collaborated with the patriotic party, still strong north of Forth.

The English occupation of southern Scotland diminished steadily between 1335 and 1342. Truces sealed in 1335 and 1340 were of brief duration,[15] and Edward made no attempt to appoint conservators. The Scottish resistance movement gathered momentum after 1341, when the Scottish king, David II, returned from France to assume personal control of his government. By the summer of the following year English possessions in Scotland had been reduced to Lochmaben and Berwick.[16] The English government, more interested now in a continental campaign, was content to allow a period of uneasy peace to descend on the border region.

The protracted war against the Scots in the years between 1330 and 1342 exacted a heavy toll, not merely on the material possessions of the English borderers,[17] but also on levels of lawlessness and disorder in the region. The crown sought to cope with the problem with a modicum of effort, and adopted a series of strategies designed to keep the region as peaceable as possible under tremendously difficult circumstances. Despite the confusion caused by war it maintained a clear division of responsibility between its military agents, the wardens of the marches, and officials whose duties were purely civil. Throughout the period, the wardens' commissions emphasised the need to keep the marches of Northumberland, Cumberland and Westmorland fully arrayed for war, and gave them full authority to punish desertion and opposition to their directives.[18] Rumours of unlawful communication with the Scottish enemy were met with a flurry of commissions in which royal justices were ordered to disband 'confederations, leagues, congregations and conventicles', and to root out the names of those who sustained and comforted Scottish patriots.[19] Within the conquered Scottish territories the keepers of border fortresses were most often entrusted with these duties, but in England the king's agents in dealing with such offenders were local noblemen, and occasionally county sheriffs, whose authority remained distinct from that of the wardens. Persons found guilty of such potentially treasonable activities were forfeited, though several were pardoned their misdeeds when they offered to perform military service in exchange for their lives.[20]

The key fords of the Solway Firth, because of their strategic importance on the borders, were accorded separate consideration. In April 1340 they were entrusted to a faithful servant of the royal household, John de Stratford, who was instructed to arrest all Scotsmen trying to enter England without safe conduct.[21] The earl of

Northampton, keeper of Lochmaben castle, complained that Stratford's deputies were impeding the lawful movement of Annandale Scots into Cumberland,[22] but custody of the fords and the attendant responsibility for preventing the sale of arms and foodstuffs to the enemy remained in Stratford's hands.[23]

The regulation of unlawful cross-border activity by the inhabitants of the bishopric of Durham proved a more difficult problem to resolve. In October 1341 Edward III wrote to Bishop Richard de Bury expressing grave concern about the existence of gangs from the neighbouring counties of Yorkshire and Northumberland whose chief purpose was to hold their countrymen to ransom. Their activities, he alleged, were greatly assisted by the inability of sheriffs and their agents to enter the lands of the liberty in pursuit of such felons.[24] The difficulty was resolved in December, when the bishop entered into an unusual extradition agreement with the crown that allowed for the freer exchange of suspects who fled into the liberty from the surrounding district, or from the liberty into royal territory.[25] From the abbey of Melrose, where he spent Christmas, Edward III issued a proclamation making explicit the terms of the agreement.[26] A year later, when the liberties of Hexham and Tyndale were similarly said to be infested with ransom takers 'feigning to be Scots', special powers were granted to royal agents to apprehend and punish suspects.[27] Bishop Richard Bury of Durham participated actively in the detection and apprehension not only of notorious felons who colluded in crime with the Scots, but also of men whose dealings with the king's enemies were matters of local suspicion. Thus in 1340, the sheriff of Durham was ordered to hold an inquest into the circumstances surrounding the homicide of the Scot Robert Mallard; in 1341 a jury of Durham men informed the sheriff and one of the bishop's coroners of the lengthy history of cross-border crime of their neighbour Hugh Carter.[28]

Ad hoc arrangements such as these proved adequate in responding to the periodic waves of unease experienced by the borderers in specific localities. But they did not address the grave problem of isolated incidents of collusion with the Scottish enemy, which occurred on an intermittent basis throughout the march lands, when troublemakers took advantage of local disruptions caused by enemy incursions. In the absence of long periods of truce between 1330 and 1343, and given its failure to appoint conservators even when hostilities were temporarily suspended, the crown fell back almost entirely on the machinery of the common law for the apprehension and punishment of cross-border offenders. As had occurred in the two decades after 1296, felonies committed in collusion with the Scots were subsumed into the business of the itinerant courts of assize. The wardens' commissions made it clear that in respect of such offences their powers were limited to the arrest of suspects; they were expressly forbidden to put them to trial without royal warrant.[29] It was, then, at the sessions of gaol delivery convened in Carlisle in 1335 that a local man was charged with leading a gang of Scots into the vill of Carleton, from where they led off all the inhabitants' oxen.[30] In Newcastle in 1338 three local collaborators were put to trial, and two sentenced to death.[31]

The inclusion within the common law of offences that had once been tried at the march proved an effective means of dealing with felons who were able to avoid the periodic sweeps of suspected collaborators ordered by the crown. Early in 1343 an English truce with France was extended to the latter's Scottish allies, then prorogued until the autumn of 1346.[32] The lengthy suspension of hostilities envisaged in the agreement offered the first opportunity since the beginning of Edward's reign for the English crown to resume regular communication with the Scottish government in the matter of unlawful cross-border activity. In 1342 Richard earl of Arundel had been appointed warden of the entire march region.[33] That commission was now permitted to lapse,[34] and a new emphasis was placed on the resolution of grievances arising from depredations committed by both sides in the previous decade. A series of commissions issued in May, August, November and December bestowed broad powers on a large body of conservators of the new truce, and in so doing anticipated the joining of the offices of warden and conservator that would take place formally just three years later, in 1346.

The commissions of 1343 were entirely novel in virtually all their aspects. Yet each varied sufficiently from the others to suggest that the crown was keenly interested in experimenting with the office of conservator. In the early part of the fourteenth century two, three or at most four, officials had been considered sufficient to undertake the business of keeping the truce. Henceforth, their numbers were considerable larger, ranging from sixteen for the entire march region (in a commission of 20 May), down to ten in August, then back to seventeen in November.[35] The bishops of Carlisle and Durham joined the roster of noble laymen, a shrewd move designed to ensure that the church be given a stake in the preservation of peaceable conditions in the north. Bishop Kirkby of Carlisle had been conspicuously absent from his diocese in the spring. His appointment, first as a conservator, then as keeper of Carlisle castle,[36] suggests that the crown placed great importance on his presence in the north.[37]

Royal experimentation with the powers of arrest, detention and trial granted to its officials has long been recognised as characteristic of the peace commissions issued in the middle years of the fourteenth century,[38] but Bertha Putnam's detailed exploration of the transformation of the keepers of the peace into regularly appointed justices did not take into account the place of conservators of the truce within the context of the many changes that were effected in the office. On 17 May 1343 four conservators were associated with four other northern noblemen in a general commission to hear and determine in the three border counties 'all felonies and trespasses', and also to put to trial all who unlawfully sold food or armour to the Scots.[39] The crown, however, superseded that commission almost immediately, concerned, perhaps, that too much authority had been vested in the conservators that belonged more properly to the keepers of the peace. Indeed, from the 1340s on, commissions of the peace and commissions appointing conservators, although they were often issued to the same individuals, were always careful to distinguish between the truce-related offences these men were to adjudicate and others of a more general nature. Thus, the commission of 20 May directed the conservators to punish breaches of the truce by Englishmen, to pursue and prosecute similar offences by Scotsmen and, more generally, to 'cause to be done all that is necessary for the preservation of the truce'.[40]

The crown's failure to address clearly the procedures according to which the conservators were to undertake such prosecutions immediately proved troublesome, as indeed it had done earlier in respect of peace commissions. In August 1343 Edward received a long petition from the common folk of Cumberland.[41] The northerners complained of the absence from the march of Bishop Kirkby of Carlisle and his fellow conservators, and suggested that, as a consequence of their disregard, Scottish commissioners were 'refusing to offer redress or to do justice on known truce-breakers'. More significantly, they requested that notaries public be put to the task of drafting protocols of march-related disputes, so that the adjudication of breaches might proceed. This demand was highly unusual. The use of notaries for the authentication of royal records occurred only rarely in fourteenth-century England; their services were intended chiefly to lend credence to documents which might be queried in foreign courts.[42] Significantly, Edward I had commanded that the proceedings leading up to the award of the Scottish crown to John Balliol, known as the Great Cause, be authenticated formally by the notary John of Caen;[43] the so-called 'Ragman Rolls', which listed the names of the Scottish landholders who made formal submission to Edward in 1296, were similarly drawn up in the form of notarial instruments.[44] Some years ago Professor Cheney remarked upon the appeal to the services of notaries coincident with Anglo-French negotiations during the Hundred Years War;[45] the same sort of impulse that motivated the crown on these occasions no doubt informed its negotiations with the Scots, too. But the use of notarial instruments by corporate bodies, be they municipal governments, monastic establishments or the commons of an English county, remained rare, for they had no acknowledged status at common law. To the borderers of the mid-fourteenth century the gravity of the current débâcle over the matter of march tribunals, and perhaps more particularly the still ambiguous place of these courts within the general framework of the common law warranted the perceived weight of notarial authentication.

Edward III thought otherwise, but the appeal nonetheless bore fruit, for on the same day as it was presented a new commission was issued to conservators of the truce. This one commanded the crown's agents to arrange meetings with Scottish representatives to 'treat and come to an agreement concerning the forms and conditions under which the truce shall be kept'.[46] These instructions were given added weight in December, when the crown specifically ordered the bailiffs of the great northern liberties to assist the keepers in their tasks.[47] For the time being, prosecution was to continue under the purview of the laws and customs of England. Despite the innovations they included, then, the commissions of 1343 still assumed that the customs that had once governed the adjudication of march-related offences were for all intents and purposes a dead letter. A revival of such customs would have to await the establishment of a greater feeling of security in the north, and a much warmer feeling of amity on the part of the English crown for its Scottish enemy.

As it had done in respect of the instructions issued in the previous decade to the wardens, the crown remained reluctant to delegate significant judicial authority to the conservators. The commissions of 1343, as well as others issued in 1344 and 1345, all restricted the activities of the crown's northern agents to the arrest and detention of suspects.[48] On occasion, the keepers' expertise in local affairs made it expedient for them to participate in the trial of suspects accused of committing border offences, but when they presided over judicial sessions they did so only under the authority of commissions of oyer and terminer. It was eminently practicable, for example, for the crown to include three conservators in a commission of June 1344, which was ordered to investigate allegations of cattle theft said to have been committed by English suspects within Scottish territory.[49] The conservators' familiarity with local conditions were again employed in an inquest convened in Northumberland in February 1346 in response to rumours that Englishmen were providing arms and provisions to a notorious Scottish gang.[50] Accusations made against a resident of Newcastle in the late summer of 1345, however, were heard and determined in a session of oyer and terminer in which the conservators played no role.[51] The justices of assize bore the brunt of prosecuting most suspects accused of committing cross-border felony or of colluding with the Scots. Sessions of gaol delivery held in Carlisle in 1344 and 1345 dealt with several such cases,[52] and, indeed, these continued to be regular venues for the trial of border-related crime for the remainder of Edward's reign.

In the early 1340s the distinction between offences justiciable in the newly reconstituted conservators' courts and those liable to trial at common law was still blurred. The crown had not yet defined clearly which misdeeds constituted breaches of the truce *tout court*, and which were to be considered common-law felonies. The Carlisle gaol delivery sessions of 1344 and 1345 heard and determined a variety of border-related offences, including the theft of livestock, unlawful ransom-taking and collusion with the Scottish enemy. Many of these were said to have occurred in 1342, before the Scots were included in the truce of Malestroit (1343), and so before conservators had been appointed. Strictly speaking, then, the common-law courts were the proper venues for the presentment and trial of these crimes. But other indictments alleged unlawful activity involving the Scots within the period covered by the truce of 1343 and its prorogation. As such, they might have been regarded as lying within the scope of the conservators' responsibilities for 'keeping' the truce.

The conservators' courts were certainly in operation in something more than merely notional form as early as 1344. In July of that year four of the crown's recently appointed northern agents convened in Carlisle to 'keep the truces in the march of Scotland and to arrest and punish those infringing the same'. Their proceedings were disrupted when Robert de Mulcastre and several confederates assaulted them and prevented them from conducting their business.[53] Another session of the conservators' court was held around the same time, when Henry Percy and Ralph Neville presided over an inquest into an act of piracy committed by the Scots off the coast of Bamburgh. The court ruled that the incident had occurred during a period of truce, and ordered the chamberlain of Berwick to distrain merchandise from other Scottish merchants in the town.[54]

The crown was, in effect, still experimenting with the office of conservator, and uncertain about its future role. Some of this ambiguity was a reflection of the traditional royal policy of reserving to the common-law courts as much business as possible, a policy which, under various guises, had governed attitudes towards the northern border tribunals since the time of Edward I. But it was also a consequence of the uneasy peace that prevailed in the region in the aftermath of the truce of 1343. In June 1344 parliament was warned of the Scots' lukewarm attitude towards the truce,[55] and in August commissions of array were ordered to ready the northern levies in the event of an invasion.[56] The threat was real enough to compel the bishop of Durham to levy a tax within his lands with which he intended to pay tribute to a hostile army.[57] A similar scare in the summer of 1345 constituted the main item of business at councils of war convened by the archbishop of York and the bishops of Carlisle and Durham.[58] Until the truce was prorogued indefinitely, or a formal peace was achieved, there was little reason to believe that meetings between English and Scottish conservators could be anything but intermittent, and even less chance that they might be anything more than superficially cordial. As late as the autumn of 1346 the Scots showed little inclination to favour the establishment of an enduring armistice. The month of July saw them descend into Cumberland and Westmorland in a sudden raid.[59] The victory of the English army over the French at Crécy on 26 August triggered a more massive invasion, when, according to the Lanercost chronicler, 'the Scots assembled, children of accursed Belial, to raise war against God's people, to set a sword upon the land, and to ruin peace'.[60] The western border counties were left harried, burned and pillaged before David II's army was defeated at Neville's Cross and the king himself taken captive.[61]

During the armistice years of 1343 to 1346 the policies of the English crown in the settlement of cross-border disputes was tempered by conservatism and caution. The customary *leis des marches* received no mention in the numerous commissions in which the king and his advisors experimented with the conservators' authority. To have admitted the validity of traditional march customs would have undermined Edward III's claim to the lowland counties of Scotland ceded by Balliol in 1342, and would have amounted to a recognition of the jurisdiction of the Scottish crown in those territories.[62] Throughout this period the English crown was at pains to emphasise the jurisdiction of English common law in the region.[63] Among the borderers themselves, however, the memory of customary law remained remarkably strong, as did the collective belief that some cross-border disputes were most appropriately the business of mixed juries meeting in march tribunals. The chronicler Robert de Avesbury recorded in some detail the terms of the truce made with the Scots in 1335. He noted the agreement made: that when the earl of Atholl submitted himself and his lands to the English king he reserved the opportunity to defend himself from charges of treason 'by his body, according to the laws and customs of Scotland and on the march'.[64]

The persistence of custom is still more clearly illustrated in the protracted resolution of an incident that occurred in 1344.[65] In May of that year the plaintiff,

John Mons, reported to the conservators of the truce in Northumberland, Henry Percy and Ralph Neville, that his cargo of wheat, beans and fish had been lost *en route* to Berwick when the ship that was carrying it was attacked by Scottish pirates off the coast of Bamburgh. The conservators convened an inquest in Berwick, and jurors from the town confirmed that the offence had taken place during a time of truce. The chamberlain of Berwick, Peter Greathead, was ordered to distrain goods to the value of £45 (the amount that Mons claimed had been lost) from among Scottish merchants then lawfully resident in Berwick, and to deliver the goods to Mons. The chamberlain went about his task with some vigour (he seized Scottish coin and merchandise in excess of £192). But he refused to give Mons the sum awarded by the conservators, arguing that the plaintiff could show no warrant to certify his claim. Frustrated by Greathead's persistent stubbornness, Mons went on to sue his case before the treasurer and barons of the Exchequer, where he sought, and eventually won, not only restitution of his original loss (though reduced to the sum of £43 4d), but also £5 in damages. But in the interim, the Exchequer inquest revealed that customary practices had by no means disappeared in the northern reaches of the kingdom. Greathead's refusal to make restitution to Mons from among the distrained Scottish goods was based not only on the alleged absence of a properly authorised warrant, but on his argument that the conservators had acted *ultra vires* when they made that award. He told the treasurer and barons of the Exchequer that 'when an offence is committed on the march between England and Scotland it must be determined before justices of the said marches, that is, before six men of England and six of Scotland, and not elsewhere', and he shrewdly pointed out that the Exchequer had no authority to compel the men of Scotland to appear before it. The challenge was sufficiently intriguing to give pause to the crown's officials, who ordered a further, and final, inquest, this one in Berwick. The names of the jurors present at this inquest are not recorded. But it is possible that Henry Percy, who in 1335[66] had been awarded lands once belonging to the earl of March, exercised in vestigial fashion the authority formerly vested in those lands (the *inborch* and *utborch* of the thirteenth century) to call upon the testimony of both English and Scottish recognitors.

The conclusion of Mons's case in Exchequer to the satisfaction of the plaintiff enabled the crown to avoid addressing directly the several important issues it had raised. Quite apart from the general problem of piracy – a problem which increasingly preoccupied a government at war with both Scotland and France[67] – the incident demonstrated the need for the government to act with a firmer resolve in the settlement of Anglo-Scottish disputes, and, more particularly, to clarify the role of the conservators in that process. Edward's decision to lead an expedition to Normandy in the summer of 1346 provided the impetus for the crown to make adequate provision not only for the defence of the north, but also the preservation of the truce there. In December 1345 commissions were issued to Henry Percy, Ralph Neville, Thomas de Lucy and Thomas de Musgrave authorising them to extend indefinitely the current truce with the Scots.[68] This was the first time since the period of Andrew de Harcla's wardenship that the king had demonstrated his readiness to invest his agents in the borders with such extensive authority. More significant still was the grant of this power for an unspecified period. Within a few months, the importance of the maintenance of good relations with the Scots was recognised when the authority to negotiate brief truces became a regular feature of the wardens' commissions.

Further changes were still to come. In March 1346 new commissions were issued in which, for the first time, the crown distinguished between the east and the west marches.[69] The new designations acknowledged that each of the regions had specific requirements and that each demanded separate attention. The old march of Northumberland was a land of liberties, episcopal and baronial, through much of which the king's writ did not run.[70] Recent experience had shown that jurisdictional squabbles might too easily allow these territories to become havens for truce-breakers, and it was essential that the crown's agents work in concert with bailiffs and other liberty officials in the apprehension and punishment of offenders.[71] The problems experienced by the borderers of Cumberland and Westmorland were of a different sort. The lordship of Annandale and the castle of Lochmaben in south-western Scotland had been in English hands since their grant to the Bohun family in 1334.[72] Cultural links between Dumfriesshire and Cumberland were strong,[73] but the war years had effected profound hardship in the region, and poverty exacerbated relations between the peoples.[74] Attempts to promote peaceful intercommunion were still proving only partly successful,[75] and it was evident that if the west march was to remain peaceful its particular problems must be addressed. The division of the march region into clearly defined territories remained a feature of border administration for the remainder of the medieval period, though a third area, known as the middle march, was occasionally accorded a distinct status in the fifteenth century. The commissions issued after 1346 in respect of each of the marches in turn reflected the political conditions which characterised the eastern and western regions as the war years progressed.

The commissions of March 1346 were also novel because they combined the duties of the office of warden with those that had to date been assigned to the conservators of the truce. The sudden reversal of the crown's practice of clearly separating military authority and quasi-judicial responsibilities was no mere matter of convenience. It reflected, rather, a profound change in the government's policy towards the border region. In the mid-1340s the conflict with France increasingly occupied the energies of Edward III. The escalation of the French war effort was matched by the strengthening of the Auld Alliance. The young king of Scots had been offered shelter and assistance at the French court during the war of the disinherited, and since his return to Scotland in 1341 had been active in maintaining close ties with Philip VI.[76] The previous decade had shown that an offensive war on two fronts was impossibly expensive, and that the conflict with the Scots must perforce be defensive. In 1346 Edward III sought, therefore, to secure the northern border lands from a possible Scottish invasion during his absence, but also to establish there an effective means of ensuring that local incidents of cross-border crime did not assume regional proportions. The enhancement of the military authority of the wardens accomplished the first of these goals: in addition to their traditional responsibilities of arraying the men of the region and the punishment of deserters the new commissions gave them authority to remove and replace the custodians of key northern fortresses whenever necessary. The second goal was achieved in the broad powers to keep the truce that were added to the commissions: henceforth, the wardens were to act as conservators of these precious periods of peace, to compel the delivery of truce-breakers into their own hands, and to punish such offenders at the king's discretion.

The assimilation of the conservators' duties within the office of warden was also, however, the consequence of other, collectively significant factors related to the governance of the border region, and in some ways the union of the offices had been anticipated before 1346. The conservators' tribunals, especially those in the west march, brought these officials in contact with Scotsmen who, for a variety of reasons, wished to become subjects of the English crown. The authority to accept such persons into the king's peace, and to secure pardons for their adherence to the enemy had traditionally belonged to the wardens, but in April 1344 it was granted to the conservator in Cumberland,[77] and in March 1346 to the newly reconstituted wardens of the east and west marches.[78] From Northumberland in September 1346 there came to the king a long letter of complaint alleging that assize sessions had not been held in the county for some time because the northern lords had been too busy preparing for the defence of the region to see to the business of the courts.[79] In vesting the conservators' judicial functions in the office of warden, itself held by magnates who had a vested interest in protecting the region, the crown facilitated the arrest and punishment of at least some offenders, notably those involved in unlawful incidents of cross-border activity.

Edward's fear of the political dangers represented by the Franco-Scottish alliance were realised in the autumn of 1346. In September the wardens were ordered once again to attempt to negotiate a truce with the enemy,[80] but those efforts proved fruitless, and in October a large Scottish army marched into Durham. The northern levies had been well prepared,[81] and the Scots were soundly defeated at Neville's Cross on 17 October. The capture of David II proved a watershed in the development of late-medieval border administration in general, and march law in particular, chiefly because the king's long captivity provided Edward III with the time he needed to implement real and significant change to that body of law. David remained in England until 1357. While those years were not always peaceful in the border lands – in 1355 the town of Berwick was assaulted and its castle besieged[82] – the Scots remained nonetheless aware that the life of their king depended ultimately upon their willingness to maintain good relations with England. The capture of several noblemen and their removal to English prisons left the Scots in no position to avenge themselves by seeking a renewal of hostilities, and an uneasy peace descended once again on the borders. In April 1347 the Scots were formally included in a truce sealed with the French,[83] and the armistice was thereafter renewed as required until the Treaty of Berwick of October 1357.

Negotiations for the ransom and release of David II proceeded only slowly, frustrated on several occasions by the intransigence of both Edward III and the Scottish government. The progress of the talks and the complex issues of dynasty and sovereignty that underlay them have been examined in great detail by scholars,[84] but very little notice has been taken of the significance of the years of captivity to the history of Anglo-Scottish dispute settlement. While Edward III haggled for eleven years, determined to exact as favourable an agreement as possible in exchange for David's person, he was nevertheless astute enough to recognise the tremendous opportunities offered by a long cessation of hostilities. He used those opportunities not only to assess the recent changes he had effected in border administration in the experimental period between 1343 and 1346, but also to establish more clearly the shape of border law and legal procedure. The years before 1346 had shown that the military duties of the office of warden could profitably be combined with the judicial powers of the conservators. The crown now began to consider more carefully how the wardens might be employed in future as a permanent feature of the legal administration of the north, and how border law might be made to work in complementary fashion with the existing machinery of the common law. The goal was a system of Anglo-Scottish dispute management that would endure beyond the temporary diplomatic advantage represented by David's captivity in England.

In April 1348, on the same day as a new truce was proclaimed,[85] the crown appointed justices to punish the large numbers of criminals said to be roaming the border counties. In contrast to the ambiguity of previous commissions, this commission distinguished clearly subjects who were subject to the jurisdiction of the common-law courts from those whose transgressions were justiciable at march law.[86] The former included English subjects, the latter 'Scottish enemies' who resided outside English-held territories in lowland Scotland and who had not come to the peace of the English king.[87] The justices were authorised to hold inquests and to put to trial persons suspected of committing breaches of the truce, in the former case according to the laws of England but, where appropriate, in accordance with the law and custom of the march. A new commission, issued in July, clarified the ambiguities of the earlier orders, and sought to ensure that the work of the new border justices did not interfere with the business of the common-law courts. It appointed the wardens, Henry Percy and Ralph Neville, justices to hear and determine allegations of truce-breaking, and defined these more narrowly as the unlawful ransom taking of Scotsmen by English subjects, theft of animals and foodstuffs from the Scots, and the receiving or harbouring of persons guilty of such offences.[88]

The judicial powers bestowed on the wardens in 1348 remained largely unchanged through 1357. That the crown was satisfied, at least for the time being, with their function in the border lands is amply illustrated in its frequent renewal of their commissions, despite the sometimes hostile diplomatic wrangling that continued to impede the release of King David, and even in the bitter aftermath of Edward's destructive 'Burnt Candlemas' campaign of 1356.[89] The early work of the wardens' courts, however, has left little trace in extant record.

Unlike the rolls of the justices of assize, which had been required from at least 1336 to be deposited at Westminster,[90] the proceedings of the wardens' tribunals remained for much of the medieval period the property of the king's agents in the borders, and thus subject to the vagaries of time and poor storage. After 1352 commissions issued to the wardens made explicit their authority to condemn persons found guilty of breaking the truce to indefinite periods of imprisonment, but it is evident that in the mid-fourteenth century the wardens competed for business only modestly with the common-law courts of the north. Their commissions continued to emphasise that they had authority to act only when a breach of the truce had been committed, and it was to be several years yet before the crown itself had clarified the meaning of this offence. In the 1340s and 1350s most incidents of cross-border crime and of collusion with the Scottish enemy were still brought to trial as a consequence of indictment in sheriffs' tourns or before coroners and justices of the peace. Sessions of gaol delivery in Carlisle and Newcastle, presided over by itinerant justices of assize, remained the chief venue for the adjudication of such offences, as they had been in the earlier fourteenth century. Virtually all the accused felons who appeared there to answer charges of unlawful cross-border activity were subjects of the English crown, but at least one Scotsman confessed his misdeeds and was sentenced to death.[91] As before, the crown enacted measures to ensure that the great liberties of the north did not escape the vigilance of its agents. In June 1356 a commission to keep the truce made special provision for the arrest and punishment of violators who attempted to shelter there.[92] The surrender of Berwick castle to the Scots in 1356 by Sir Robert Ogle was a matter too grave to be adjudicated by the wardens: its keeper was tried in parliament, and sentenced to loss of life and limb.[93]

From the period of David II's captivity, the wardens' courts functioned alongside the common-law tribunals. The procedures in use there included vestiges of thirteenth-century custom, but they also reflected the strong influence of current common-law practice. From the outset, the system of border law had acknowledged the suitability of trial by battle as a means of settling grievances between subjects of hostile realms. Recourse to the sword helped to offset the profound mistrust that inevitably characterised disputes between subjects whose governments were at war; it also provided licit means of giving expression to the belligerence that had so long been a feature of border life. The practice had been noted by one chronicler as customary in the marches in 1335;[94] twenty years later, the king granted William Heron license to hold a judicial duel to prove the accusation of theft he had brought against two Scottish defendants.[95] A royal writ of 1357 which ordered the suspension of proceedings in a wager of battle did not condemn the practice, but sought merely to prevent the occasion from jeopardising the final stages of the negotiations for David II's release.[96] Trial by combat remained a feature of border legal practice well into the fifteenth century, fully sanctioned (if never entirely applauded) by the crown.[97]

The wardens' courts of the mid-fourteenth century were not, however, impervious to the influence of the common law. The commission of July 1348 which authorised Henry Percy and Ralph Neville to punish violators of the truce, directed them to uncover the names of suspects by means of 'the oaths of the honest and lawful men of those parts, and by other expedient means in accordance with the laws and customs of the said marches'.[98] One scholar has suggested that this passage should be interpreted as making reference to English jurors alone.[99] In 1348, when the Scottish knight, William Lidell, brought a complaint of unlawful ransom-taking before the warden of the west march, he did so before a jury composed solely of Westmorland men,[100] and a wardenial court held in Carlisle in 1350, though it met in order to hear the accusations of Scottish plaintiffs, appears to have been attended by Cumberland men alone.[101] But there is other evidence to suggest that mixed juries of Englishmen and Scotsmen had not disappeared altogether in the border region, and that the commission of 1348 made allowance for their use in appropriate circumstances. In 1345 the king's chamberlain in Berwick certainly believed that mixed juries had an important role to play in cross-border disputes, and the treasurer and barons of the Exchequer readily admitted that wartime conditions alone had prevented the distraint of Scottish jurors in the settlement of John Mons's complaint.[102] Lidell's grievance was not, in fact, remedied until after it had been submitted to an inquest composed of both English and Scottish recognitors.[103]

In the middle years of the fourteenth century there was room enough in the border lands for a system of tribunals whose work would both complement and supplement the business of the common-law courts. The detention of the Scottish king in England brought only a temporary respite to the war; indeed, the persistence of hostile relations necessitated the continued vigilance of royal justices in the north, because isolated incidents of cross-border felony might precipitate the abandonment of the precarious condition of peace achieved in the sealing of truces. In the absence of cordial relations between the realms in the eleven years between 1346 and 1357 Edward III was wise to enhance the opportunities for Scottish plaintiffs to present their grievances before properly appointed officials under the safety of letters of safe conduct, but a more immediate concern was to ensure that breaches of the truce committed by his own subjects were punished in condign fashion. The changes wrought in the wardens' commissions accomplished those twin goals in satisfactory fashion. Further alterations to the office would have to await the resolution of the dynastic issues that surrounded negotiations for the release of David II. Only then would the course of future diplomatic relations between England and Scotland become clearer.

Notes

1. See, for example, *Brut*, i.257–8; *Chron. Lanercost*, p. 261; 'Adae Murimuth Continuatio Chronicarum', pp. 57, 283; *Scalacronica*, p. 83.
2. *Chron. Baker*, p. 40.
3. Nicholson, *Edward III and the Scots*, pp. 55–6.
4. Stones, *Anglo-Scottish Relations*, pp. 337–8.
5. Nicholson, *Edward III and the Scots*, pp. 59–60; Nicholson, *Later Middle Ages*, p. 124.

6. Nicholson, *Later Middle Ages*, p. 125.
7. Nicholson, *Edward III and the Scots*, pp. 76, 102; *Rot. Parl.*, ii.69; *Foedera*, II.iii.75, 81–2, 86; PRO C 81/192(5699).
8. McKisack, *The Fourteenth Century*, p. 117; Campbell, 'England, Scotland and the Hundred Years War', pp. 187–91; Ormrod, *Reign of Edward III*, pp. 8–9.
9. Nicholson, *Edward III and the Scots*, p. 105.
10. *Rot. Parl.*, ii.42.
11. PRO SC 8/145(7233).
12. PRO C 81/182(4602).
13. *Foedera*, II.iii.58.
14. *CPR*, 1330–4, pp. 387, 440, 499.
15. *Rot. Scot.*, i.335; *Foedera*, II.iv.83–4.
16. Campbell, 'England, Scotland and the Hundred Years War', p. 191; Nicholson, *Later Middle Ages*, pp. 143–4.
17. The losses suffered by the inhabitants of Carlisle in particular during this period are reviewed in some detail in Summerson, *Medieval Carlisle*, i.263–78.
18. See, for example, the commissions issued in April 1333, August 1333, August 1334, September 1334, November 1334, February 1335, August 1335, January 1336, July 1336, in *Rot. Scot.*, i.228, 257, 276, 277, 281, 282, 287, 318, 376, 398, 436.
19. *Rot. Scot.*, i.278; *Foedera*, II.iii.160. See also *CPR*, 1330–4, p. 501; *Rot. Scot.*, i.381, 463, 491, 495, 518, 523–4, 531, 590, 598–9; *CPR*, 1338–40, p. 555; *CPR*, 1340–3, p. 319, 320–1, 322, 544; *CCR*, 1341–3, p. 490.
20. See, for example, *CPR*, 1340–3, pp. 528, 533; *Rot. Scot.*, i.282, 571.
21. PRO C 81/265(12998).
22. *CPR*, 1340–3, p. 363.
23. *Rot. Scot.*, i.648, 658; *CPR*, 1345–8, p. 240. The strategic importance of the Solway region during the Anglo-Scottish wars is discussed in McIntire, 'Fords of the Solway', pp. 152–70.
24. *Reg. Pal. Dunelm.*, iii.141–2 (fragment of Richard de Bury's register, 1338–43). More generally, see Lapsley, *County Palatine of Durham*, pp. 305–6.
25. *Reg. Pal. Dunelm.*, iv.244–7; *CCR*, 1341–3, pp. 353–4.
26. *CCR*, 1341–3, p. 364.
27. Fraser, *Northern Petitions*, pp. 100–1; *CPR*, 1343–5 pp. 67, 88.
28. *Reg. Pal. Dunelm.*, iii.243; DCD Misc. Ch. 1611.
29. See, for example, the commission of April 1333 issued to Anthony de Lucy, in *Rot. Scot.*, i.228.
30. PRO JUST 3/128 m.4d.
31. PRO JUST 3/132 m.13d. See also m.14d for the trial of a suspect who, among other offences, was charged with selling a stolen mare in Dunbar.
32. Foedera, II.iv.145; Rot. Scot., i. 638–9; PRO C 47/22/4(45).
33. PRO E 101/68/3(51, 57).
34. In August 1343 it was not the warden, but conservators of the current truce, who were commanded to array the men of Cumberland and Westmorland in defence of Lochmaben castle. *Rot. Scot.*, i.640.
35. *Foedera*, II.iv.145, 149–50; *Rot Scot.*, i.644.
36. *Calendar of Fine Rolls*, 1337–47, p. 334.
37. The crown's attempts to compel Kirkby's attendance on local matters, however, were only partly successful, and the people of Cumberland had more than one occasion to complain of his absence. In July 1344 the bishop was commanded yet again to remain in the north to see to the defence of the region. CRO DRC 1/1 (Register of Bishop Kirkby), fo.247.
38. Putnam, 'Transformation', pp. 19–48; Putnam, *Proceedings Before the Justices of the Peace*, pp. xxii–xxix; Putnam, 'Keepers of the Peace', pp. 185–217.

39. *CPR*, 1343–5, p. 93.
40. *Foedera*, II.iv.145.
41. PRO SC 1/42(19).
42. Cheney, *Notaries Public*, pp. 55, 61, 69–70; Pollock and Maitland, *History of English Law*, i.218.
43. Stones and Simpson, *Edward I and the Throne of Scotland*, i.77–100.
44. Ibid., i.92, 209–10.
45. Cheney, *Notaries Public*, p. 62.
46. *Foedera*, II.iv.149–50.
47. Ibid., II.iv.156, also printed in *Rot. Scot.*, i.644.
48. *Foedera*, II.iv.166–7; *Rot. Scot.*, i.656, 661.
49. *CPR*, 1343–5, p. 387. The case remained unresolved two years later, when a new inquiry was ordered. This one, too, included current conservators. See *CCR*, 1346–9, p. 59. The conservators were also included in a commission of February 1344 to investigate unlawful collusion between Scottish enemies and subjects of the English crown in Cumberland and Annandale. *CPR*, 1343–5, p. 280.
50. *CPR*, 1343–5, p. 105.
51. PRO C 260/56(43). Thomas de Greathead was accused of unlawfully putting to death a man who had attempted to deliver Newcastle into Scottish hands, and who was a known collaborator with the enemy.
52. PRO JUST 3/135 mm.8, 8d, 10, 10d, 13. The assumption of cross-border offences within the body of the common law is discussed in detail in Neville, 'Law of Treason', pp. 1–30.
53. *CPR*, 1343–5, pp. 383, 392.
54. PRO E 13/71 m.40.
55. *Rot. Parl.*, ii.147.
56. Edward Balliol was appointed captain of the defence of the north. The anticipated incursion, however, did not occur. *Rot. Parl.*, ii.148; *Foedera*, II.iv.166–7; *Rot. Scot.*, i. 648–9; *Chron. Knighton*, ii.30.
57. *Reg. Pal. Dunelm.*, iv. 273–7; PRO DURH 3/29 m.13d.
58. *Rot. Scot.*, i.663.
59. *Chron. Lanercost*, p. 326; 'Adae Murimuth Continuatio Chronicarum', p. 202; *Chron. Knighton*, ii.33.
60. *Chron. Lanercost*, p. 330. The priory of Lanercost suffered especial hardship at the hands of the Scots in the course of the invasion.
61. *Chron. Lanercost*, pp. 330–42; *Chron. Melsa*, iii.60–2; *Chron. Knighton*, ii.41–6; *Chron. Baker*, pp. 86–9. The extent of the damage inflicted on the region in the course of this expedition was revealed in a series of inquests held in 1347, PRO C 145/159(15).
62. In the 1340s Edward continued to refute David II's claim to the Scottish throne. His support of Edward Balliol, though lukewarm, was not formally withdrawn until 1356. See Campbell, 'England, Scotland and the Hundred Years War', pp. 197–200; Nicholson, *Later Middle Ages*, p. 161.
63. *CPR*, 1343–5, p. 67; *Rot. Scot.*, i.658.
64. 'The Chronicle of Robert de Avesbury', p. 302. Avesbury's access to newsletters and to the testimony of eye witnesses renders his account of Edward's campaigns particularly trustworthy. See Gransden, *Historical Writing*, pp. 68–70.
65. PRO E 13/71 mm.41, 41d.
66. Nicholson, *Edward III and the Scots*, p. 190.
67. See the discussion of early piracy cases and their venues, in *Select Pleas in the Court of Admiralty*, Introduction.
68. *Rot. Scot.*, i.667.
69. *Rot. Scot.*, i.670.

70. The great liberties of Northumberland included Tynedale, Redesdale, Hexham, Norham with Bedlington, Tynemouth and the entire county of Durham, which was subject directely to the bishop of Durham. There were a few baronial and episcopal liberties in Cumberland and Westmorland, but collectively they were not as significant as those of the east march.

71. See above, p. 31 and notes 25–7.

72. Nicholson, *Edward III and the Scots*, p. 170; *Rot. Scot.*, i. 280–1, 399.

73. McIntire, 'Historical Relations between Dumfriesshire and Cumberland', pp. 64–80.

74. Much of south-western Scotland, including Annandale, was burned and pillaged by the English in 1337, and again in December 1345. The castle of Lochmaben was besieged in 1343. See *Chron. Lanercost*, pp. 305–6, 326; *Rot. Scot.*, i.640; Duncan, 'A Siege of Lochmaben Castle', pp. 74–7; Webster, 'The English Occupation of Dumfriesshire', pp. 64–80.

75. In December 1344 the crown initiated an inquest to discover the names of Cumberland residents who hindered the lawful passage of goods across the fords of the Solway Firth. Just a few months later the conservators of the truce were specifically ordered to treat the Annandale tenants of the earl of Northampton 'as subjects of England'. *Rot. Scot.*, i.658. See also above, notes 21–3, and a commission of January 1343, in which Gilbert de Umfraville earl of Angus and lord of Redesdale was directed to arrest and punish Annandale Scots who plundered their English neighbours in Cumberland and Westmorland. *CPR*, 1343–5, p. 67.

76. McKisack, *Fourteenth Century*, pp. 118–19, 124–5; Campbell, 'England, Scotland and the Hundred Years War', pp. 187–91.

77. *Rot. Scot.*, i.647. Thus in April 1346 John the clerk of Galloway secured a pardon for his adherence from one of the conservators in Cumberland. *CPR*, 1345–8, p. 72.

78. *Rot. Scot.*, i.671.

79. PRO C 46/F7 no.20.

80. *Rot. Scot.*, i.674.

81. On the same day as he had issued new commissions to the wardens of the marches the king ordered that a conference of northern magnates be held to discuss the defence of the region. *Rot. Scot.*, i.670, 671–3.

82. The assault precipitated an expedition into Scotland led by Edward III himself. *Chron. Fordun*, i.372; *Chron. Bower*, ii.351, 354–6; *Chron. Knighton*, ii.85; *Scalacronica*, p. 120. Norham Castle was also taken in a raid led by Patrick earl of March; *Scalacronica*, p. 119.

83. *Rot. Scot.*, i.713.

84. Duncan, '*Honi soit qui mal y pense*', pp. 113–41; Nicholson, *Later Middle Ages*, pp. 156–63; Campbell, 'England, Scotland and the Hundred Years War', pp. 196–200.

85. *Rot. Scot.*, i.713.

86. Ibid., i.713–14.

87. A brief but successful campaign led by Edward Balliol in the spring of 1347 had resulted in the occupation by the English of Berwickshire, Roxburghshire and Peeblesshire, and the forests of Ettrick, Selkirk and Jedburgh. Nicholson, *Later Middle Ages*, p. 148. The commission also made provision for Scotsmen resident in those lands; they were to be subject to 'the laws of those parts'. But the English hold on the lowland region was short-lived, and ended formally with the treaty of Berwick. See the text of an indenture for the governance of lowland Scotland dated 30 October 1346 in *APS*, i.180.

88. *Rot. Scot.*, i.718–19.

89. Commissions to keep the truce were renewed in September 1351, July 1352, June 1354, October 1354, June 1356, May 1357 and July 1357. *Rot. Scot.*, i.744–5, 752, 766, 794, 808; *Foedera*, III.i.104, 134.

90. 9 Edw III, stat. 1, cap. 5.

91. PRO JUST 3/135 m.3.
92. *Rot. Scot.*, i.794.
93. *Rot. Parl.*, iii.11–12. The castle was left by Lord Greystoke in the charge of Sir Robert Ogle. Although Ogle died defending the fortress, Greystoke was held responsible for the loss 'because he had undertaken to safeguard the said town and castle'. He was eventually pardoned at the behest of the queen. *CPR*, 1358–61, p. 18.
94. 'The Chronicle of Robert de Avesbury', p. 302.
95. *Foedera*, III.i.105.
96. *CCR*, 1354–60, p. 411.
97. Neville, 'Keeping the Peace', pp. 14–15.
98. *Rot. Scot.*, i.718.
99. Summerson, 'Early Development', p. 37.
100. PRO SC 8/244(12171); *CPR*, 1348–50, p. 152.
101. *CPR*, 1348–50, p. 588. See also another reference to a Cumberland wardenial court, *CPR*, 1350–4, p. 202.
102. PRO E 13/71 mm.41, 41d.
103. *Rot. Scot.*, i. 835. An account of William Lidell's double ransoming is found in Wilson, 'Border Incidents: A Prisoner', pp. 32–4.

3

Elaboration, 1357–77

The English victory at Poitiers in September 1356 proved a turning point in the negotiations for the release of David II. Deprived, for several years to come, of the hope of French assistance in the ongoing war, the Scots renounced their internal squabbles and began to discuss terms for the release of the king and for a long period of truce. An armistice to run until Michaelmas was arranged in May 1357, and in England the wardens were ordered to ensure that the truce was kept.[1] There is little doubt that Edward III was now operating from a position of strength in his dealings with the Scots. Nevertheless, he displayed real interest in promoting English goodwill in the negotiations, and in ensuring that outstanding grievances did not jeopardise the restoration of cordial diplomatic relations with Scotland. A commission issued in July commanded Henry Percy and Ralph Neville to make diligent inquiry into all alleged violations of the current truce;[2] in September, even as Scottish and English ambassadors were convening in Berwick to discuss the final stages of David's release, that commission was renewed and the wardens prompted to offer more generous provisions to their Scottish counterparts in the settlement of outstanding grievances.[3]

The Treaty of Berwick, duly sealed on 3 October, and ratified in Scotland a month later,[4] has been carefully examined by both English and Scottish historians. Perhaps predictably, both view the agreement as a victory of sorts for each of the warring parties. To Ranald Nicholson, the omission of concessions other than the heavy ransom of 100,000 marks was 'a setback to Edward's cherished ambitions' of dominating the smaller realm as his grandfather had done, however temporarily;[5] the king's English biographers, on the other hand, suggest that the sums extracted from the Scots and the peace that followed the drafting of the treaty represented a triumph of English diplomacy.[6] Although he may indeed have harboured disappointment and frustration at his failure to settle clearly the claims he maintained over the lowland shires, Edward III was not one to brood over lost opportunities. His interests remained primarily focused, as they had been since 1337, on the continental theatre of war, and for the time being a temporary suspension of hostilities with Scotland permitted him to concentrate on that front.

Despite the Scots' failure to remit the sums they had promised for David's ransom, and even in the midst of the tortuous negotiations that resulted from their default,[7] the decade following the treaty proved an important period in the development of border law. During this period, the numerous experiments begun during David's captivity with the offices of warden and conservator saw tangible results in the northern border lands, and the march tribunals, which had only tentatively begun to convene there, became permanent and regular features of the legal landscape. The time for experimentation was passing; instead there began a period in which march customs were elaborated and refined. The decade of the 1370s would witness the renewal of open warfare with Scotland, but the system of border law created in the aftermath of the Treaty of Berwick survived the deterioration of diplomatic relations with remarkable success.

Edward III's goodwill in the negotiations leading up to the meeting of English and Scottish ambassadors at Berwick was not merely empty gesture. It was given concrete expression, during the several months after David returned to Scotland, in the careful attention the king devoted to the settlement of truce-time acts of aggression and violence. Barely before the ink had dried on the treaty parchment William lord Douglas complained to the English council of depredations committed against the men of Eskdale by a band of English marauders and their leader, Robert Tilliol. Douglas maintained that in a recent incident several thousand animals and £20 in coin had been carried off, allegedly with the collusion of the warden of the west march, Thomas de Lucy. He also noted that on an earlier occasion the truce of May 1357 had been violated by Tilliol and Lucy, who had ridden 'with banners displayed' and taken dozens of his people to ransom. Although he had been willing to purchase observance of the truce for the hefty sum of £20, Tilliol, 'not wishing to be at truce', had refused; Lucy, he said, had informed him that he had neither the will nor the power to redress these grievances.[8]

Just a few weeks after Douglas's letter had been delivered to the English council another complaint reached the king's ears, concerning a second violation of the May truce. In this one Archibald Douglas and several other Scots claimed that they had been unlawfully taken prisoner by men of the English march, detained in prison and set to ransom.[9] Neither Edward nor his council was inclined to sympathise with either petition: they no doubt noted with particular interest William lord Douglas's casual reference to the reprisals his own 'poor men' had taken in Cumberland and Westmorland over the course of that same summer, and they were certainly aware of the recent seizure, by Douglas himself, of the English-held stronghold of Hermitage castle.[10] The allegations of Archibald Douglas and his companions were also sufficiently suspicious for the king to order that manucaptors be secured from them pending judgement of their case.

But Edward was quick to recognise the advantages represented by these complaints. He saw in them at once vehicles for demonstrating his intention of abiding by the terms of the new truce; more important still, their settlement in the border lands themselves by representatives of both the English and Scottish crowns pointed the way for the future resolution of truce-time grievances. In June 1358 the warden-conservators, Thomas de Musgrave, Thomas de Grey and William Heron, were ordered to assemble a panel of English and Scottish jurors, to hold an inquiry into the circumstances of William Douglas's capture of Hermitage castle, and to resolve the matter of restitution and compensation as they saw fit.[11] On the same day, however, that commission was abruptly supplemented and revised. A new commission directed Henry Percy and Ralph Neville – the same men who had been singled out to hold inquests into truce-time violations back in July 1357 – to act as arbiters in both outstanding disputes, and to resolve the matters in cooperation with representatives of the Scottish crown 'according to the custom of those parts'. This inquiry, too, was to rest on the testimony of a mixed panel of recognitors.[12]

The favourable atmosphere engendered by Edward's handling of the complaints of William and Archibald Douglas very quickly encouraged other borderers, English and Scottish, to bring their grievances before the wardens' tribunals. The records of these hearings reveal a great deal about the procedures adopted by the crown's officials in the resolution of disputes, and also about the ways in which border-related procedures were becoming part of the legal framework of four-teenth-century England. In the winter of 1359 Simon Chaudy, burgess of Berwick, sent a petition to the king and council praying remedy in respect of a debt of 500 marks, which he had incurred some months earlier, when he and two other burgesses had stood surety for two Scottish prisoners taken and detained by John de Clifford, constable of the castle. The Berwick men had agreed to present the Scots at the castle on an unspecified date.[13] The prisoners, temporarily released, travelled to Billymire, where they appeared in a court convened by the warden-conservators,[14] and sought judgement in respect of their capture. In accordance with recently established procedure the wardens of both realms agreed to become each others' debtors 'to make restitution as should be adjudged'. A second day of march was planned for the hearing of the particulars of the dispute. At this tribunal, a mixed jury of six English and six Scottish jurors returned the verdict that the Scotsmen had been unlawfully taken prisoner. As a result of this finding they were relieved of the onus of returning to prison and of paying ransom to their gaoler, John de Clifford. All this had happened, however, before the day on which Chaudy and his fellows had agreed to bail the prisoners and to present them before Clifford. The latter was now withholding the 500 marks, to Chaudy's prejudice, and although an inquest of March 1358 had been convened to hear Chaudy's complaint, Clifford had refused to appear before the chamberlain of Berwick to answer for his misdeeds.[15]

Simon Chaudy's case disappears from record on February 1359, after the king had initiated a new investigation into Clifford's alleged misappropriation of funds, but the concern that the crown had demonstrated to resolve a grievance that was supposed to have been satisfactorily settled in a border tribunal was not lost on local observers. That same month the Scotsman Sir William Lidell was emboldened to come forward with a complicated tale of his own experience in the border courts. A decade earlier he had sent to Edward III a petition seeking redress for the injury that he had suffered when he had been subjected to a double ransom.[16] The king had ordered the wardens to hold an inquest into the allegations,[17] but several years later Lidell remained unsatisfied. He was granted another hearing of his complaint in February 1359, when Edward directed the wardens to summon a jury of English and Scottish men-at-arms to examine the incident anew.[18] The results of the inquest are unknown, but it was significant, in that it foreshadowed the influence that the law of arms would come to exert on border laws and customs in the years to come.

An old dispute concerning the vill of Upsettlington West in Norham was similarly examined afresh in 1359. Tenure of the land had been the subject of disagreement for many years already: in 1331, when Edward III had referred the matter to his conservators, the English claim to title had lain with the bishop of Durham.[19] A generation later the title was championed by Henry de 'Esshelynton', though the grievance remained unchanged. The vill was situated on the north bank of the Tweed and, as Patrick earl of March complained, 'ought to belong to the realm of Scotland'.[20] Bishop Thomas Gray had held an inquest of Durham men, which had found that the vill lay firmly within English territory. In maintaining that the earl's occupation of the lands was 'contrary to the truce', 'Esshelynton' now sought to have the matter brought to a border tribunal, where he hoped that it would be definitively resolved.

The prosecution of claims in the wardens' courts in the first few years after the treaty of 1357 was generally a procedure of several months' duration, but plaintiffs appear to have considered the effort worthwhile. In the summer of 1359 Archibald Douglas was still complaining that the grievance he had made in respect of his capture had not yet been settled. Edward III once again assigned the matter to his warden-conservators, but his instructions this time were explicit. Henry Percy and Ralph Neville were to summon a mixed jury, composed (as had been that of the earlier session) of local men-at-arms, and, if it was found that Douglas had indeed been unlawfully taken, they were to compel the guilty parties to make full restitution of the money, on pain of distraint of their goods and imprisonment of their persons.[21] This inquest appears, finally, to have had tangible results. Several months later Douglas recovered the 40 marks he had been charged as ransom, though his fellow captives were still attempting to do the same. On this occasion the king reiterated his grant of the powers of distraint and arrest of recalcitrant debtors to the wardens.[22]

Douglas's complaint appears to have set a precedent of sorts: a wardenial commission of July 1359 bestowed similar authority to compel restitution on the officials newly appointed. Thereafter the wardens – and their deputies, formally recognised in November 1359 – exercised it as a regular feature of their commissions.[23] In the atmosphere of cooperation that characterised the border tribunals in these early years of truce even a minor Scottish cleric felt sufficiently optimistic about his chances as a plaintiff to bring his case before the wardens.[24]

By 1360 the English crown appears to have been won over to the usefulness of the border tribunals in the settlement of truce-related matters. Edward's projected absence in France in the autumn and winter of 1359–60 was preceded by royal orders to maintain the kingdom in a state of war readiness,[25] and the wardens considered it prudent to increase the vigilance of the arrayed men of the west march.[26] But despite heightened tension in the region the truce held, and the grievances of Scottish plaintiffs remained a matter of ongoing business in the border courts. The wardenial commissions of July 1359 included the bishops of Durham and Carlisle, as had earlier commissions, an indication of the crown's firm conviction that the most important ecclesiastical landholders in the region played as important a role in its border-related administration and in diplomatic encounters with the Scots as did lay noblemen. The bishops continued to share responsibility for the office until 1385. Some, at least, brought real vigour and efficiency to the office: Bishop Welton of Carlisle, for example, summoned meetings of the fighting men of the west march to discuss strategies for defending the region against Scottish incursions, and was actively involved in wardenial business throughout his episcopal career.[27]

Edward and his council were also growing increasingly accustomed to the place of the wardens and their tribunals within the larger context of English local administration. In part this was a purely pragmatic response to regional requirements: the border lands were situated hard by an enemy who was all too ready to form an alliance with a hostile continental power, and those lands had to be kept in a state of near-permanent war footing. The military duties of the wardens' office were therefore of paramount importance. To the already extensive powers relating to the array and deployment of the fensible men of the region, the commission of July 1359 added authority to seize the goods and chattels of persons who were sufficiently wealthy to contribute to the expense of local defence, but whose age or infirmity made them unfit for service. It also granted them authority to supervise the garrisoning of key castles and to replace constables at will.[28] The November commission, in which the crown made arrangements for the wardens to be replaced by deputies during the former's absence from the marches, acknowledged the need for a permanent military figurehead in the region, though for some years the crown would insist on its right to authorise such replacements. Already long-recognised as crucial figures in northern defence, the wardens had become the most important of the crown's military resources in the north.

The sense of optimism generated in the years after 1357 persisted in the northern tribunals, despite the diplomatic wrangling caused by the Scots' refusal to continue payment of David II's ransom. A second treaty of 1365 burdened them with heavier payments still than that of 1357,[29] but a third agreement, sealed in 1369, was made against the background of a renewal of the Anglo-French conflict, and restored the ransom to the sum that had been settled at Berwick.[30] Although payment of the monies had been halted in 1360 after only two instalments, Edward III remained impassive; hopeful, for a while, that the Scots might be moved to accept his offer to succeed to the Scottish throne should David die without issue, but consistent in his determination to maintain the split in the Franco-Scottish alliance that had been effected by events at Poitiers. One of the prices paid for his pacific attitude was the slow but steady encroachment on English-held territory in Scotland by David and his border magnates: revenues from the lowland shires were now being diverted to Scottish coffers, including those of Annandale.[31] But within the English march lands the suspension of open hostilities had valuable consequences. Though they note the frequent shuttling of Scottish ambassadors back and forth across the border in the decade of the 1360s, the normally voluble English chroniclers are remarkably silent about atrocities or depredations committed by the enemy.

The wardens used the long period of quiet to summon meetings among the northern magnates to initiate discussions concerning local defence,[32] and to effect badly needed repairs to border strongholds.[33] For much of the period 1360 to 1371 their commissions were unaltered, and were issued rather as a matter of course than in response to specific incidents.[34] In 1362 the crown turned its attention to the great northern liberties which, in the later fourteenth century, were notorious havens for truce-breakers and cross-border felons. Although the legal dilemma represented by the traditional independence of the liberties had been mitigated in the past by appointing the lords of these territories to the wardenial commissions,[35] the king now made explicit the jurisdiction of his northern officials in truce-related matters.[36]

The seemingly endless negotiations for the payment of David II's ransom were themselves turned to advantage in these relatively quiet years. In August 1360, after the second instalment had been remitted only belatedly, Edward III directed several of the northern magnates (including the wardens) to meet with Scottish ambassadors both to treat for a permanent peace and to discuss all dissensions, discords and disputes then outstanding between the realms.[37] Similar commissions followed in the summer of 1362.[38] The 'dissensions, discords and disputes' undoubtedly related to the scheme designed to set Edward III himself (or one of his sons) on the Scottish throne following David's death,[39] and to the disposition of the few lands still held by England in the lowland counties.[40] They must also, however, have included frank discussions of the operation of border laws and the functions of the march tribunals. Despite the abandonment of the matter of the succession and the failure of the ambassadors to settle the future of Annandale, the tenor of the negotiations was, on the surface, cordial and occasionally even festive.[41]

The linking of broad diplomatic issues with more particular questions of redress for truce-time offences proved a shrewd and successful move on the part of Edward III, and set a pattern for the future. Henceforth, meetings between royal ambassadors charged with extending the truce or attempting to forge a permanent peace with Scotland frequently included the discussion of specific violations of the armistice. A direct relationship was thus established between the 'national' concerns of the central governments and the localised grievances of individual borderers. In forging that link Edward hoped to ensure that regional conflict of the sort that had characterised Anglo-Scottish relations for so many years – the raids and counter raids so vilified by the chroniclers – would not escalate into open war and send the Scots back into alliance with the French. In later years meetings between ambassadorial parties were referred to as 'great days of march', to distinguish them from the smaller *jours de marche*, that is, sessions of the border tribunals presided over by the warden-conservators. The great days of march never became courts of appeal, for judgements rendered by the conservators were always intended to be final and binding. But they did become important fora for the airing of notorious acts of violence. And, because the grievances of individual plaintiffs were represented and championed by the wardens of either side (as had occurred, for example, when Simon Chaudy appeared in the Billymire court of law), their inclusion on the agenda of ambassadorial negotiations augured well for the settlement of these disputes.[42]

In the late 1360s Edward III was shrewd enough to perceive the opportunities offered by the linking of regional and central concerns. In efficient and typically businesslike fashion he set about facilitating the means by which his wardens might convene with their Scottish counterparts, and clarifying the procedures by which they might present English complaints and seek redress for Scottish depredations. Commissions issued in February 1367 appointed new wardens in the east and west marches, and granted them authority to keep the truce by doing 'speedy justice' on all English violators. They were also to seek redress from, and the punishment of, Scotsmen found guilty of doing the same.[43] In July the wardens were joined by Thomas de Beauchamp earl of Warwick in a commission that granted extensive powers of arrest and punishment over English truce-breakers, and the authority to make redress to the Scots for their misdeeds.[44] This commission signalled two significant changes in the administration of the border lands, a further indication that Edward III had developed a clear notion of the role his officials should play in the legal fabric of the north. The inclusion of Warwick, one of the most powerful of his barons, and a man of wide military and diplomatic experience suggests that border tribunals were now considered the highest expression of royal jurisdiction on the northern frontier, and no longer merely informal and irregular fora for low-level dealings between the local officials of either crown, however useful these had proved.

Just as the English government had experimented with 'supervisors' (occasionally referred to as *les grantz*) and charged them with overseeing the work of the keepers of the peace when the latter office was in its early stages of development,[45] so did Edward envisage Warwick acting as a 'supervisor' of the judicial work of the wardens. In the lengthy and complicated process by which keepers of the peace were transformed into the justices of the peace in fourteenth-century England the 'supervisors' disappeared. In northern England, however, they could not so easily be dispensed with. Here, the diplomatic dimension of proceedings added weight to the deliberations held in march tribunals. The crown invested them accordingly with symbols of that added weight. From the later 1360s the warden-conservators' commissions included the names of important household figures and military officers of state, notably the steward and the marshal.[46] The commission of July 1367 also presaged a change in the legal complexion of the border courts in that it named a quorum of two to the judicial bench, to include the earl of Warwick. Quorum numbers would vary in future, and soon ceased to identify specific individuals, but they, too, became a permanent feature of wardenial commissions, as they had by then become of peace commissions.[47]

The commissions of 1367 equipped the wardens with the kind of authority they required to act as royal justices in the settlement of cross-border disputes. But they lacked a clear framework within which to exercise that authority. Although some of the procedures used in the border tribunals – most notably, recourse to the testimony of a mixed panel of recognitors – had a venerable tradition behind them, the Anglo–Scottish wars had rendered unworkable much of the substance of thirteenth-century custom and practice. Those in current use were based largely, but still tenuously, on the cooperation that the Scots had demonstrated since the 1340s, and consisted of little more than an informal undertaking by the wardens of either side to present alleged truce-breakers at chosen border sites. To date, these meetings had sometimes resulted in the redress of injuries and the award of compensation to plaintiffs, and Edward III had good reason to be pleased with the modest success of the courts. But the doubts expressed by one of the king's own wardens, Bishop Appleby of Carlisle, about the efficacy of the days of march were symptomatic of the problems that continued to bedevil them.[48] It was evident that if these tribunals were to become truly effective, a concerted effort must be made to clarify the way in which they conducted their business.

An indenture sealed at Moorhouselaw in Roxburghshire in September 1367 was designed to provide some of the structure that border customs and border tribunals lacked.[49] It set out the sites where, later that autumn, English and Scottish warden-conservators would meet for the discussion of current disputes: Moorhouselaw in the east march (13 October) and Gretna in the west (18 October); both sides agreed that further days would be set aside as required. The wardens undertook to present there felons who had been 'properly attaint' of theft, a reference to a two-tiered process in which it was envisaged that both English and Scottish juries would play a preliminary role in determining which of their fellow subjects would proceed to the border tribunals. Persons accused but not yet proven guilty of theft were to undergo trial at a day of march itself, before 'an assize of [men of] both parts, lawfully elected and appointed'. All guilty persons were to make full restitution to their victims within fifteen days, though as yet there was no provision for the payment of damages. The lords of those who were adjudged by the same mixed panel incapable of offering appropriate restitution were themselves made responsible for the debt; men who had no goods to offer and no lord to vouch for them were to be handed over to the plaintiff and set to lawful ransom. The indenture retained a vestigial role for the sheriffs in the legal process of the march courts by directing them to assist the wardens in the apprehension of suspects who took flight. It also strictly forbade the recourse to self-help that had been so characteristic a feature of dispute settlement on the frontier. Finally, it stated that persons currently held on suspicion of unlawful cross-border activity be released after finding sureties for their appearance at the days of march scheduled for October; likewise, chattels stolen in raids were to be restored to plaintiffs pending judgement of the courts.

The Moorhouselaw indenture was quickly followed by a commission granting judicial powers to several conservators in the east and west marches.[50] Here, once more, the crown effected a subtle change in the tenor of the office: associated with the roster of magnates were members of the lesser nobility (such as Thomas de Grey and Richard Tempest in Northumberland, and Thomas de Ros and Thomas Strickland in Cumberland and Westmorland), landholders of more modest standing in their respective counties, but no less intimately familiar with local conditions. This time, the quorum was set at six. The meetings at Moorhouselaw and Gretna were duly held, and although the business discussed there took many months to resolve, both sides demonstrated a commendable level of cooperation. Flood conditions prevented a meeting early in January 1368,[51] but sessions were convened throughout the summer and autumn.[52] In October, when King David complained that the settlement of disputes was proceeding too slowly, Edward ordered one of the wardens, Bishop Thomas Appleby, to devote a greater effort to resolving the Scots' grievances, and in particular to ensure his presence at scheduled days of march.[53] The crown also thought it advisable to remind the bishop that raids of reprisal across the border were unlawful,[54] but this warning was more in the nature of a pre-emptive admonition than it was a reaction to actual incidents of truce-breaking. In fact, the framework for the conduct of border tribunals set out in the indenture of 1367 was functioning in effective fashion, and wardens from both sides were beginning to view the days of march as Edward III had wished, that is, as properly constituted venues for the resolution of cross-border disputes.

The troubled lands of Annandale, situated in a kind of no man's land deep in enemy territory, proved the greatest threat to the stability of the border region in the last years of Edward III's reign, and, by extension, to the integrity of the border tribunals. The years since David II's return to Scotland in 1357 had seen friction in the region as the Scots king made steady advances into the English-held territory, largely at the expense of the families of Bohun and Dacre.[55] Both sides had been guilty of contributing to the chronic disorder of the region; as has been very capably argued by J.A. Tuck, the English crown was well aware that the very men to whom it entrusted the safe custody of the border lands 'themselves had an interest in perpetuating disturbed conditions'.[56] But even in turbulent Annandale, Edward's determination to promote the march tribunals prevailed over local rivalries and enjoyed a measure of success. Although an indenture of 1366, which divided the revenues of the lordship of Annandale equally between the king of Scots and Humphrey de Bohun earl of Hereford, must have been viewed by the English crown as a diplomatic and military concession to the enemy, the agreement went some way towards establishing an atmosphere in which incidents of violence might be settled amicably. It made provision for the free movement of persons of both allegiances between Annandale and the English marches; more important still, it required that violations of the 'great truce' of 1357 be submitted to the border courts and the laws and customs of the marches.[57]

In 1369 Henry Percy and Archibald Douglas set their seals to another agreement in which each undertook to present before the other persons accused of committing truce-time violations, and to offer specific redress for unlawful 'trespasses and damages' done in the region.[58] Eventually, a mixed jury returned a verdict against Hugh Dacre, and he was ordered to make restitution of £100 to the earl of Douglas. When he defaulted Percy, as warden of the march, remitted the sum, and in so doing probably averted a new series of raids of reprisal. The crown fully supported his subsequent efforts to retrieve his money by ordering the arrest and imprisonment of the recalcitrant debtor and the seizure of £100 of his goods.[59]

A shift in the tide of the Anglo-French war caused Edward to grant concessions to the Scots when a third ransom treaty was negotiated in 1369, chief among which was a long truce of fourteen years.[60] But in the north the border tribunals continued to operate,[61] and commissions to the warden-conservators were regularly issued.[62] Indeed, the tenor of relations between the wardens of either side was sufficiently cordial to permit both crowns to expend some energy in the pursuit of such minor infractions as the unlawful trade in woolfells and animals that had sprung up in the lull between phases of open war.[63] The accession of Robert II, weak and almost chronically cautious in his dealings with England, and the beginning of Edward III's decline into decrepitude should have augured well for the continued health of the border tribunals. The English crown had a vested interest in keeping a watchful and protective eye on their operation: the northern march lands remained, after all, a war front. Thus, when Robert's resolve to observe the truce apparently wavered when belligerents among his council convinced him to renew the alliance with France in October 1371,[64] Edward responded by ordering the wardens to remain in the marches, and to make ready to defend the region against an enemy incursion.[65] Incidents of violence continued to engage the attention of the king's northern officials: several Northumberland men were murdered by a Scottish gang, and another carried off to ransom, while a clerk from Carlisle suffered similar rough handling.[66] Despite the tension generated by the unlawful activities of the borderers the English crown sought to ensure that the border courts functioned as effective fora for the punishment of cross-border offenders. The king responded to a complaint made in the late summer of 1372 by Archibald earl of Douglas concerning the postponement of planned days of march because of Henry Percy's absence by arranging for the holding of a court on a new date, and promising to order another some months hence.[67]

That disorder should once again have become endemic, as it did in 1373, was in no wise a reflection of poor resolve on the part of either Edward III or Robert II. It was, rather, the result of the English crown's failure, as far back as the 1330s, to address clearly the grievances of the disinherited in Scotland. Almost two generations after the vain attempt to set Edward Balliol on the Scottish throne the claims of most of those who had benefited from his rule had lapsed; the course of Scottish politics, especially since 1357 had all but nullified the territorial gains made in the brief heyday of Balliol's power. Chief among the few, however, who remained determined to maintain their lands in the Scottish lowlands was the Percy family, and the quarrel of Henry Percy with William earl of Douglas over the lands of Jedburgh and Jed Forest erupted into open war in 1373.

Lordship over Jedburgh had been granted to the Percy family in 1334, in compensation for the territory of Annandale and the castle of Lochmaben, awarded to Edward Bohun.[68] The aggrandisement of the Douglas family in the borders in the last years of David II's reign had occurred largely at the expense of these families. The latter had come to a *modus vivendi* with the Scots crown by agreeing to share the revenues of Annandale, and by and large the Douglases had observed a truce sealed in respect of these territories in August 1364.[69] But the lands of

Jedburgh and its surrounding forest, deep in the heart of Douglas territory, proved a more troublesome bone of contention. The castle was still in English hands and its strategic location meant that it was of great importance to the crown. The Percies had no wish to relinquish the revenues they derived from their Scottish estates. When discord sprang up between the two important border families, Edward III was compelled to take notice. A commission of February 1373 instructing three local noblemen to hear and settle the dispute noted grimly that it endangered the peace of the marches, because both Percy and Douglas were wardens;[70] underlying those concerns were also the stability and effectiveness of the border tribunals presided over by these officials. Another commission, this one appointing a more distinguished group of noblemen (including the earl of Stafford and the steward of the king's household), proved no more successful in satisfying either party.[71]

Eventually, the rivalry between Percy and Douglas degenerated into open warfare, beginning in 1377, when Roxburgh was pillaged and burned.[72] But despite the tension generated by the dispute, both Robert II and Edward III worked to maintain the integrity of the border tribunals, and their efforts were largely successful. Commissions of May and July 1373, and January, February and July 1375 directed the warden-conservators to exercise their judicial authority in the apprehension and punishment of violators of the truce,[73] and the orders of 1375 facilitated the summoning of jurors, defendants and plaintiffs alike by authorising the wardens to issue letters of safe conduct for all Scots wishing to travel across the border in pursuance of march suits. The bitterness between the earl of Douglas and Henry Percy was sufficiently alarming to move Robert II to assure Edward of his sincerity in wishing to maintain the truce,[74] but a rich variety of Exchequer records reveals that days of march (or days of truce, as they were also known) were convened on both sides of the border with near flawless regularity right down to the death of Edward III.[75] Scottish wardens grumbled as frequently as they always had about delays in obtaining restitution for offences committed against Scottish subjects, but the earl of March's demand that the English warden reciprocate the payment of damages he had made in respect of a series of truce violations suggests that the system of exchanging compensation was functioning, however imperfectly.[76] Incidents of blatant ruptures of the truce occasionally drew the attention of the English chroniclers, such as the capture in 1376 of the wealthy Scottish burgess, John Mercer.[77] But the complaints of lesser folk were settled in the border courts with much less animosity: a monk of Dunfermline was sent to a day of march in the autumn of 1376, where his accuser confronted him before a jury of English- and Scotsmen.[78]

When Edward III died in June 1377 the peace that had been maintained in the border lands for two decades was about to come to an end. But the respite afforded by the long period of truce had seen the system of border tribunals gain strong currency among the northerners, and especially with the crown, as the appropriate venue for the airing and settling of march-related grievances. Those courts had shown evidence of functioning in efficient and effective fashion irrespective of the state of diplomatic relations between the crowns. In focusing his attention as closely as he had on the structure of the courts as well as on the judicial authority of the warden–conservators, Edward transformed border law from a loose amalgam of ancient custom and *ad hoc* measures into a system well–equipped to deal with the unique problems of a people divided by a hostile political boundary.

Wartime exigencies contributed in significant fashion to the urgency of establishing the border tribunals, but they also played an important role in determining the kind of justice that would obtain in the courts. Before the outbreak of the Hundred Years War the law of arms was ill-defined in England, and incidents that occurred in the context of war, ranging from trespasses committed within the ranks of royal armies to notorious acts of treason, had been tried in a variety of tribunals, according to several different criteria.[79] The war, however, gave 'a new prominence to legal problems arising out of state [*sic*] of war',[80] and was indeed the genesis of a complex and sophisticated body of law that governed the resolution of wartime disputes for the rest of the Middle Ages, and well beyond.

The involvement of England and its allies on French soil played a singular role in shaping martial law. Disputes concerning Scottish ransoms and the taking of Scottish prisoners and spoil were no doubt resolved by applying principles that had recently been found appropriate and satisfactory on the continent. But historians of the laws of war have seldom appreciated the unique legal problems that characterised the northern border lands, and that in turn influenced the development of the legal response to wartime conditions there. Unlike the province of Gascony or any other lands in France conquered and held by Edward III in the course of the mid-fourteenth century, the northern marches were, and had always been, an integral part of the English realm. Border law could not be permitted to infringe on the workings of the common law, for the crown had never wished to establish in the north a march zone such as it knew with respect to Wales in the west. The English government had long acknowledged that the cases brought to trial at the days of march were, by their very nature, unusual. But Edward III in particular sought to make provision for these cases with a minimum of risk and cost to the royal prerogative in the border counties. In constructing a legal framework for the resolution of cross-border disputes he drew, then, not merely on the principles of the law of arms then current on the French war front, but also, and, indeed, heavily, on the experience he and his predecessors had gained while reshaping the common law of England. In particular, the experiments made in the course of developing the office of justice of the peace were applied also to the wardens' office. The lessons learned in respect of the former were used to good effect in apportioning the duties and responsibilities of the latter.

Some resemblances in the development of the two offices have already been noted, namely the use of 'supervisors' and provision for a quorum.[81] But there are other parallels, sufficiently numerous to suggest that some of the same problems that bedeviled the crown's efforts to clarify the role of the justices of the peace were experienced with that of the warden-conservators. In her studies of the keepers' transformation into justices, Bertha Putnam noted the 'confusion in administrative machinery' that occurred when three sets of commissions were issued in March 1322, all virtually identical in personnel.[82] A similar indecision marked the appointment of wardens and conservators throughout the 1330s and 1340s, until 1346, when the crown decided that the functions of both offices were most efficiently combined in a single commission.

The strategic importance of the border lands required that the king's military commanders be men of high social standing, experienced in the kind of leadership in war that was still so important an aspect of the baronial class. By the middle years of the fourteenth century a position at the apex of northern landed society had been secured by Henry Percy, though the Nevilles, Cliffords and Dacres were also significant figures in the region.[83] The onerous fiscal demands of the wardenship also meant that only the wealthiest magnates could assume the cost of garrisoning key strongholds and paying soldiers when the Exchequer failed to deliver the sums it had agreed to in indentures of service.[84] The 'institutionalisation' of the Anglo-Scottish wars, as one historian has aptly noted, ensured that the office of warden should be monopolised by the great families.[85]

But in judicial matters the fourteenth-century crown had embarked on what was to be a centuries-long reliance on the lesser nobility, the elusive 'gentry' of so many studies of the administration of the common law in the localities.[86] In his early years Edward III had been wary of endowing the keepers with the authority to put to trial persons 'notoriously suspected' of committing felony, and had restricted them largely to the imprisonment of suspects.[87] A similar hesitancy marked the limited authority granted to the conservators before 1346.[88] By the end of the reign the crown had come to a decision. Although they ceded to the justices of assize the power to hear and determine felonies, the gentry had secured a permanent place on the judicial bench of the peace sessions. The king and his council experimented in similar fashion with the judicial expertise (and perhaps the objectivity) of lesser noblemen in its search for effective means by which to govern the border region. On several occasions in the 1370s, for example, Henry le Scrope, Thomas de Musgrave and Ralph Hastings joined the likes of Percy, Neville and the bishops of Carlisle and Durham in keeping the truce,[89] and in 1373, when Henry Percy and the earl of Douglas began to quarrel, it was to the judgement of three lesser local figures that the crown entrusted the first hearing of the dispute concerning the lands of Jedburgh.[90] In the later fourteenth and the fifteenth centuries the dispensing of justice in respect of truce-time acts of violence remained the responsibility primarily of the northern magnates, but the crown never abandoned altogether its policy of including lesser noblemen among the ranks of the conservators. And, just as the justices of the peace became the workhorses of the English government in the administration of the shires, the gentry of northern England, among them the families of Musgrave, Heron, Scrope and, later still, Eure, Mitford, Ogle and Moresby, became prominent and invaluable agents in the later medieval and early modern administration of the marches.

The middle years of the fourteenth century saw the first appointment to the peace commissions of men 'learned in the law' and the introduction of the professional lawyer into all matters involving life and limb.[91] A similar development occurred in respect of border law slightly later, in 1373, when the warden-conservators' commissions began to include as a matter of course at least one man 'learned in the law'.[92] In the north the expertise sought was not that of persons trained in the common-law courts, but rather of men well versed in the Roman civil tradition. The link between the substance of border law and the laws of war, emerging already in the late 1350s, could hardly have been made more explicit. On the continent treatises that dealt at length with concepts of the just war were influencing to a significant degree the business of the military courts.[93] The changes effected by Edward III and his council in the resolution of cross-border disputes required a rigorous appreciation of the subtleties of civil law upon which these works were based that would only become more pronounced as the century (and the wars) wore on. The first lawman appointed to the conservators' commissions was Master John de Appleby, Dean of St Paul's, London and doctor of civil law trained in Oxford.[94] The contribution of the technical expertise of the civil lawyers was as yet minimal in the northern courts – they did not, for example, regularly sit as members of the quorum – but their inclusion presaged the important role they would come to play in a variety of border-related legal and diplomatic matters.

The period 1357 to 1377 saw the march courts firmly established within the administration of the northern shires. Among the myriad concerns of the crown in this crucial phase of the development of border law was the relationship between the newly elaborated system and the common law of the realm. In some respects that relationship was already clear, but in others the changes wrought by Edward III would not be accommodated until later in the fourteenth century. Despite their broad military powers and the jurisdiction they now exercised in the border courts, the warden-conservators posed little threat to the justices of the peace in the northern parts. The latter conducted the same variety of legal and administrative business in the peace sessions of Northumberland, Cumberland and Westmorland as did their fellows elsewhere in the kingdom. If, on occasion, members of a wardenial commission acted simultaneously in both capacities, they were nevertheless in no doubt about the limitations imposed by each of these grants of royal authority, as Rachel Reid observed many years ago.[95] Over criminal offences committed within English territory, as distinct from the march lands, the wardens exercised virtually no jurisdiction. In the second half of the century, as occurred throughout the realm, the delivery of county gaols fell overwhelmingly (if not exclusively) to the itinerant justices of assize. The wardens may even have lost ground in some felony cases to the professional judges. Since the early years of Edward III's reign they had been empowered to convene, within the march lands they controlled, courts for the trial of persons suspected of breach of the truce. As has been seen, those tribunals began to function at least intermittently from the 1330s. The indenture sealed in 1367 at Moorhouselaw made explicit mention of the wardens' responsibility to preside over such courts in advance of scheduled days of march, so that suspects presented in the former venues might be dealt with at the latter. This was still one of their duties in 1377.

But at the end of Edward's reign the definition of breach of the truce was still fluid. The Percy-Douglas indenture of 1367 made specific reference to incidents of larceny, but other offences, including homicide, arson, robbery and burglary, were ambiguously subsumed under such terms as 'grievances', 'damages', and 'injuries'.[96] In the absence of a clear notion of the offences that constituted breach of the truce the indictment and trial of most incidents involving Scottish subjects appear, rather, to have been assumed by the common-law courts, as they had been in previous years. At sessions of gaol delivery held in Carlisle and Newcastle numerous presentments were made of collusion with the Scottish enemy for the purpose of extracting ransoms from English captives (offences, ironically, that were not clearly acknowledged at common law) or in acts of burglary.[97] Only rarely did a clash of jurisdiction openly halt proceedings, but when it did, the questions that gave pause to the royal judges highlighted the problems represented by the existence of an alternate system of law in the borders. In 1359 a local troublemaker who had been indicted before the sheriff of Cumberland appeared before justices of assize, and was charged with seditiously adhering to the Scots and stealing several head of kine.[98] When asked how he wished to plead he claimed to be a Scot, born in Scotland, and so beyond the jurisdiction of the common law. In support of his plea he produced a letter of safe conduct bearing the seal of the warden of the west march, Thomas de Lucy. Irrespective of what ought to have been a guarantee of immunity, he placed himself on the verdict of the country and, in a gesture he thought would bolster his chances of avoiding punishment, also claimed benefit of clergy. The assembled jurors rejected his story and argued that John de Ayton had been born in England but had gone over to the enemy. The justices were clearly uncertain about how to dispose of him, and remitted him to gaol under the watchful eye of the sheriff until such time as the crown advised them on the matter. Ayton disappears from record a year after the trial, when he was again remitted to prison;[99] perhaps he was one of the many who escaped the law to live the life of the numerous 'outputters' who moved back and forth across the border conducting an illicit trade in stolen goods.[100]

Other, less specific, allusions to the functions of the wardens' courts suggest that the crown's failure to define offences considered breach of the truce was causing some confusion for its agents. In 1362 a criminous clerk refused to put himself on the verdict of a jury comprised solely of Northumberland men, and after rejecting no fewer than thirty-six of them was condemned to *peine forte et dure*.[101] His intransigence may have been founded on the belief that a jury of Englishmen only was inappropriate in the adjudication of a march-related offence. Other cases, such as the trial of John Yele of Cumberland and two associates, reveal that the line between common law and border law was sufficiently ill-defined as to blur the differences between them. Yele was indicted before the sheriff for burglary and presented before justices of gaol delivery at Carlisle in 1376, where the jury returned a verdict of guilty.[102] The enrollment of the case is typically brief, but the calendar entry, fortuitously preserved, notes that he had appeared previously at sessions of the peace, on the bench of which sat one of the warden-conservators. Here he and his colleagues were said to be 'common thieves, burglars and communicators with the Scots for the purpose of committing robbery and burglary in England'.[103] The peace sessions may have been used on this occasion, as well as on others, as a convenient venue for hearing border-related presentments, as well as accusations of common-law wrongdoing.

At least one of Yele's accomplices benefited from the straightforward legal differentiation of laymen from clerics that characterised all matters at English law. William of Rockcliff claimed clergy after his condemnation in Carlisle, and was released from confinement in the episcopal prison when he successfully purged himself before an ecclesiastical court.[104] The distinction between offences justiciable in the wardens' march courts and those liable to presentment and trial in common-law courts was not yet so clear. The task of elucidating and delimiting that jurisdiction was one of the challenges that Edward III bequeathed to his successor, Richard II.

Notes

1. *Foedera*, III.iii.138–9.
2. *Rot. Scot.*, i.808.
3. *Rot. Scot.*, i.811. The commission of September 1357 authorised the wardens to offer reparations for offences done against the Scots as far back as September 1355.
4. The text of the treaty is found in *Foedera*, III.ii.151–3; its ratification by David II, various magnates and prelates and, finally, the Scottish royal council, is enrolled in ibid., III.ii.155–9. See also *APS*, i.518–21.
5. Nicholson, *Later Middle Ages*, p. 163.
6. Campbell, 'England, Scotland and the Hundred Years War', p. 201; Ormrod, *Reign of Edward III*, p. 29; Packe, *King Edward III*, p. 227.
7. Nicholson, *Later Middle Ages*, pp. 174–8; Balfour-Melville, *Edward III and David II*, pp. 18–21.
8. PRO E 36/190 fo.1.
9. *Rot. Scot.*, i.817; *Foedera*, III.i.159–60.
10. Fraser, Douglas Book, i.233.
11. *Rot. Scot.*, i.826; *Foedera*, III.i.166.
12. *Rot. Scot.*, i.826.
13. PRO SC 8/209(10443).
14. Henry Percy and Ralph Neville, appointed in July and September 1357 to undertake inquests into violations done against the truce of May 1357.
15. PRO C 145/178/23, calendared in *Cal. Inqu. Misc. (Chancery)*, iii. no.343.
16. PRO SC 8/244(12171).
17. *CPR*, 1348–50, p. 152.
18. *Foedera*, III.i.178.
19. PRO SC 8/145(7233); C 81/182(4602).
20. *CPR*, 1354–60, p. 550.
21. *Rot. Scot.*, i.838–9.
22. Ibid., i.848.
23. Ibid., i.839, 843; *Foedera*, III.i.189.
24. In June 1360 the clerk David Stupy sought the verdict of a mixed jury in the settlement

of his claim regarding an unlawfully extracted ransom. *Rot. Scot.*, i.849.

25. *CPR*, 1358–61, pp. 414–15. See also a writ of September 1359 urging several northern magnates to remain in the marches for the defence of the region against Scottish incursions. *Rot. Scot.*, i.841.

26. CRO DRC 1/2 fos.42, 61d (Reg. Welton); D/Lons/L5/1 no.D20.

27. CRO DRC 1/2 fos.42, 42d (Reg. Welton). A few years later, Bishop Fordham of Durham demonstrated similar care for the custody and the state of repair of the strongholds in his lands. PRO DURH 3/32 m.4. More generaly, see Rose, 'Bishops and the Diocese of Carlisle', pp. 90, 93–4; Lapsley, *County Palatine of Durham*, pp. 304–7.

28. *Rot. Scot.*, i.839; CRO DRC 1/2 fo.42d (Reg. Welton).

29. *Rot. Scot.*, i.894–5.

30. *Rot. Scot.*, i.933–5, 938–9. The circumstances surrounding the drafting of these treaties are concisely reviewed in Nicholson, *Later Middle Ages*, pp. 167–73.

31. Nicholson, *Later Middle Ages*, p. 173; PRO DL 36/3(86,222); Rot. Scot., i.939.

32. *Rot. Scot.*, i.844.

33. *Rot. Scot.*, i.856; Summerson, *Medieval Carlisle*, i.311; *Foedera*, III.ii.163–4.

34. *Rot. Scot.*, i.857, 903, 906–7, 910–11, 923, 935, 939–40, 945, 946.

35. Reid, 'Office of Warden', p. 487 and note 56.

36. *Rot. Scot.*, i.862.

37. *Foedera*, III.i.214; *Rot. Scot.*, i.851–2.

38. *Foedera*, III.ii.63; *Rot. Scot.*, i.864.

39. *Rot. Scot.*, i.871; PRO E 39/2/17; *APS*, i.494–5; *Foedera*, III.ii.82–3; PRO E 39/2/2; E 39/4/18; *Foedera*, III.ii.97–9; *Rot. Scot.*, i.894–5; PRO SC 1/56(35).

40. *Rot. Scot.*, i.957; PRO DL 36/3(86). The unfortunate situation of Annandale made it vulnerable to the attacks of Scots and English alike. See PRO DL 34/11; *Rot. Scot.*, i.875–6, 887–8.

41. In the autumn of 1363 a total of £76 12s 3d was expended on the purchase of gifts for the Scottish ambassadors, ranging from £10 18d for a gilt cup presented to the earl of Douglas, to £4 15s 8d for a silver cup given to an esquire. PRO E 403/417 mm.24, 25. Other sums, spent in 1364, are enrolled at E 101/314/37 and E 364/9 m.1d.

42. These developments are summarised in Neville, 'Keeping the Peace', p. 16.

43. *Rot. Scot.*, i.910–11. The commissions also granted the wardens the broad military authority characteristic of earlier orders.

44. *Rot. Scot.*, i.913.

45. Putnam, 'Transformation', pp. 26, 34–8; Putnam, 'Keepers of the Peace', pp. 188, 205.

46. Neville, 'Keeping the Peace', p. 10.

47. Putnam, 'Transformation', p. 42; Holdsworth, *History of English Law*, i.289–90. Further parallels between the development of the office of justice of the peace and that of the wardens are discussed above, pp. 59–61.

48. In 1367 Bishop Appleby felt compelled to write to David II of Scotland urging him to make better and more dutiful provision for the observance of the truce. He claimed that violations had become 'more usual than in a long time'. CRO DRC 1/2 fo.8 (Reg. Appleby).

49. *Rot. Scot.*, i.913–14; *Foedera*, III.ii.137–8.

50. *Rot. Scot.*, i.915; *Foedera*, III.ii.139.

51. *Rot. Scot.*, i.918.

52. Sums disbursed by the Exchequer in respect of a series of march days held between August and November 1368 are enrolled in PRO E 101/29/26.

53. CRO DRC 1/2 fo.41d (Reg. Appleby). The bishop found his involvement in the secular affairs of march administration both onerous and distasteful to a man of the cloth, and had to be reminded again to perform his duties. Ibid., fo.37.

54. CRO DRC 1/2 fo.29.

55. Webster, 'English Occupation of Dumfriesshire', pp. 64–80; PRO DL 36/3(222); DL 25/99.
56. Tuck, 'Richard II and the Border Magnates', pp. 29–30.
57. PRO DL 36/3(86). See also Gladstone, 'The Early Annandale Charters', pp. 141–2.
58. CRO DRC 1/2 fo.41d.
59. PRO SC 1/40(188); CCR, 1369–74, p. 338.
60. Nicholson, Later Middle Ages, p.173; Foedera, III.ii.158–9, 161–3.
61. See, for example, PRO E 101/316/11; E 364/5 m.3d.
62. Foedera, III.ii.171; Rot. Scot., i.940, 945, 946.
63. CPR, 1367–70, pp. 353, 422; APS, i.547.
64. Foedera, III.ii.186–7.
65. Foedera, III.ii.192; CRO DRC 1/2 fos.56–7. Arrays were ordered in August. Rot. Scot., i.951–2.
66. CCR, 1369–74, p. 296; PRO C 269/16/11/1.
67. Stevenson, Illustrations, pp. 72–3; Parliamentary Records, p. 128. The second meeting was planned for March 1373. Rot. Scot., i.953; Foedera, III.ii.967–8.
68. Nicholson, Edward III and the Scots, pp. 141, 147–8, 151, 170; Bean, 'The Percies and their Estates', pp. 91–9; Bean, Estates of the Percy Family, pp. 6–7.
69. Rot. Scot., i.957.
70. Rot. Scot., i.955; Foedera, III.iii.3–4; PRO E 403/447.
71. Rot. Scot., i.965; Foedera, III.iii.20. In 1376 the commons of Teviotdale in nearby Roxburghshire complained in parliament that Edward III's failure to defend them adequately had led to their disherison and impoverishment. The most that the king could do was to order the march lords and prelates to discuss these grievances with the Scottish wardens. Rot. Parl., ii.353.
72. Chron. Angliae, p. 165; Historia Anglicana, i. 340; Chron. Bower, ii.383–4; PRO C 47/2/11(3).
73. Foedera, III.iii.6; Rot. Scot, i.960, 967, 971, 983.
74. BL MS Cotton Tit. A XIX, fo.87.
75. PRO E 364/7 mm.2, 2d, 4, 5; E 101/316/23, 24, 26; Exch. Rolls, 1359–79, p. 433 (1373); PRO E 364/8 m.7; E 364/9 mm.4d, 6d; E 364/10 m.3; E 101/317/4–9 (1375); Exch. Rolls, 1359–79, pp. 554, 587 (1376–77); PRO E 364/11 m.3d; E 364/12 m.7; E 101/317/28 (1377).
76. BL MS Cotton Faust. A VI, fo.87 (DCD Registrum Parvum I).
77. Historia Anglicana, i.396. See also below, pp. 71–2.
78. CCR, 1374–7, p. 389.
79. See, for example, Neville, 'Plea Roll of Edward I's Army', pp. 7–133; the cases of David ap Gruffydd (1282) and William Wallace (1305), in Bellamy, Law of Treason, pp. 24–30, 32–9; Andrew de Harcla (1323), in Keen, 'Treason Trials', pp. 88–90; and Walter de Selby (1346), in Keen, Laws of War, pp. 45–6.
80. Keen, 'Jurisdiction and Origins of the Constable's Court', p. 167.
81. See above, p. 52.
82. Putnam, 'Transformation', p. 29.
83. Tuck, 'Emergence of a Northern Nobility', pp. 9–17.
84. Reid, 'Office of Warden', pp. 490–2.
85. Tuck, 'Northumbrian Society', p. 35. The problems experienced by the crown in making adequate arrangements for arraying the fensible men of England were, ironically, most satisfactorily and efficiently resolved in the north. While it was undecided for many years about the role the keepers of the peace should play in commissions of array, responsibility for organising the men of the marches fell naturally to the wardens. See Putnam, 'Transformation', pp. 34–5, 39, 43, 45; Putnam, Proceedings Before the Justices of the Peace, pp. xxviii, xliv-xlvi.

86. Studies of the role of the gentry in local administration have proliferated in recent years. See, for example, Acheson, *Gentry Community*, pp. 107–34; Payling, *Political Society*, pp. 109–85; Saul, *Scenes from Provincial Life*, 28–97; Carpenter, *Locality and Polity*, pp. 263–77; Clayton, *Administration of the County Palatine of Chester*, pp. 132–277.
87. Putnam, 'Transformation', p. 31.
88. See, for example, the commission of April 1345, in which the conservators were directed to arrest and imprison suspected truce-breakers, and to hold them 'until the king shall order otherwise'. *Rot. Scot*, i.661.
89. *Rot. Scot.*, i.946 (1371); ibid., i.960; *Foedera*, III.iii.6 (1373); *Rot. Scot.*, i.967, 971 (1375); ibid., i.983 (1377).
90. *Rot. Scot.*, i.955.
91. Putnam, 'Transformation', p. 42.
92. *Foedera*, III.iii.6.
93. Coopland, 'The Tree of Battles', pp. 189–202; Keen, *Laws of War*, pp. 7–22; Wright, 'The *Tree of Battles* of Honoré Bouvet', pp. 12–31; Contamine, 'War Literature of the Late Middle Ages', pp. 102–14.
94. Emden, *Biographical Register*, i.40–1.
95. Reid, 'Office of Warden', pp. 483–4.
96. *Rot. Scot.*, i.914.
97. See, for example, PRO JUST 3/145 m.25. These incidents of cross-border crime are examined in Neville, 'Law of Treason', pp. 3–10.
98. PRO JUST 3/143 m.1d.
99. PRO JUST 3/145 m.10.
100. The term is discussed in Neville, 'Law of Treason', p. 29n.
101. PRO JUST 3/145 m.24.
102. PRO JUST 3/165A m.3.
103. PRO JUST 3/165B m.16.
104. CRO DRC 1/2 fos.92, 96 (Reg. Appleby).

4

Consolidation, 1377–99

The reign of Richard II has almost always been viewed by historians as an exercise in failure, deeply troubled by the young king's inability to establish and maintain good relations with the great men of the realm.[1] One of the many manifestations of Richard's ill judgement was his effort to alter the tenor of border administration by appointing men from outside the northern region to the key position of warden-conservator. In the course of implementing this policy he alienated the most powerful of the northern magnates, the Percy family, and, as one historian has suggested, virtually drove them into rebellion.[2] One of the many consequences of that same lack of judgement was the resumption of open war with the Scots and a return to the devastation of the border lands which Edward III had succeeded so ably in curbing. The years 1377 to 1399 witnessed a larger proportion of parliamentary petitions by the commons of Northumberland and Cumberland complaining piteously of wartime poverty and want than in any other period in the fourteenth century. Most of these the crown failed adequately to remedy.

At first glance, there appears to have been little in Richard II's methods of governance to commend king and council to a people against whom, one chronicler lamented 'not for the past hundred years, indeed, had so much mischief been done'.[3] Yet difficult as were the twenty-two years of the reign, they were also a period in which the system of border law so carefully constructed by Edward III continued to flourish. From a northern point of view, denunciation of Richard's failures must be at least partially tempered by an acknowledgement of the tremendous success with which the border tribunals functioned, even in the midst of war, as fora for the satisfactory settlement of cross-border disputes. It is ironic, but indisputable, that the two decades for which the greatest volume and variety of border-related materials survive are those that suffered more hardship at the hands of the enemy than they had since the heyday of Robert Bruce's reign. Richard II was interested chiefly in the French theatre of war, and Anthony Goodman's recent study of John of Gaunt has left little doubt that the machinations of the duke of Lancaster were instrumental in embroiling the English in the Iberian peninsula.[4] But the ever-present dangers represented by the Scoto-French alliance ensured that the affairs of the northern region remained of vital interest to the English government. In permitting frequent and regular meetings between English and Scottish wardens, Richard achieved a measure of success that eluded him in so many other endeavours, and it was only in the last years of the fourteenth century that the border tribunals finally achieved the level of competence that Edward III had foreseen.

The consolidation of the march courts occurred against a background of bitter raids and counter raids. The first dozen years of Richard's proved a particularly trying testing ground. As Edward III lay dying, the rivalry between Henry Percy and the Douglas family began to manifest itself in violent fashion. In the summer of 1377 a squire of the earl of Dunbar was killed while in Roxburgh, and the Scots retaliated by sacking the town and setting it ablaze.[5] Percy, now earl of Northumberland, led an expedition of his own across the border, and even the Scottish chronicler John Fordun, normally so hostile to the English, was moved to comment: 'in this way the truce was broken, and all and sundry from all parts of the marches committed massacres, depredations, ravages, burnings and captures . . . and so acrimonious was the strife of the marchers that not a single day passed that some damage was not done by one side or the other'.[6] The government of the new king sought to diffuse tension in the north by arranging a conference between John of Gaunt and Robert II's son, the earl of Carrick.[7] Despite the sealing of a truce, the tension remained high[8], and overt hostilities were renewed in the autumn of 1378, when a small marauding party from Scotland seized Berwick castle, murdered the constable, then held out for several days in defiance of their own warden.[9] The culprits were put to death,[10] but ferocious raids continued throughout 1379. A petition directed to the king and council by the men of Wark and Redesdale in Northumberland complained that they were paying tribute money to the enemy, as were the inhabitants of Berwick, Roxburghshire, Tweedmouth, Cumberland and Dumfriesshire.[11] The pressure abated only when the Scots began to fear that the plague which was then sweeping the region would be carried home with their booty.[12] The wardens were nonetheless strictly enjoined to compel all substantial landholders 'to reside constantly in defence of the marches'.[13]

A more durable truce was sealed at Berwick in November 1380, and hastily renewed in June 1381 in the aftermath of the Peasants' Revolt.[14] The author of the *Anonimalle Chronicle* charged that the armistice was 'badly kept' by the Scots.[15] This opinion is given some credence by the ordinance made for the defence of the borders in the parliament that met in 1382, but English borderers were not entirely blameless either: even as parliament agreed to grant broad authority to the wardens to array the fensible men of the region, the king's council was actively pursuing a band of renegades accused of robbing Scottish subjects.[16] In the summer of 1383 the English crown was forced to turn its attention more closely to the north, when the Scots attacked the stronghold of Sir Thomas Montague at Wark.[17] Despite the renewal of the truce and a humble letter from the Scots king, in which Robert II affirmed his own wish to observe the armistice, the borders remained unsettled.[18] The key castle of Lochmaben was taken in February 1384, never to be recovered,[19] and in November, despite a punitive raid by John of Gaunt, it appeared that the same fate would befall Berwick.[20]

The chroniclers are unanimous in accusing the Scots of continuing to violate truces sealed in the summer and autumn of 1384,[21] and their animus was manifested among the English royal counsellors. It was only in 1385, when Robert II openly welcomed to Scotland a French expeditionary group led by Jean de Vienne, and a combined force of French and Scottish soldiers marched into

Northumberland,[22] that Richard II's council responded with a decisiveness that it had hitherto lacked. The king himself led a campaign into lowland Scotland at the head of a sizeable army, and although the expedition was marred by deep mistrust between Richard and the duke of Lancaster, at its conclusion the Scots were themselves quarrelling with their allies and were prepared to observe a suspension of hostilities.[23]

Despite the sealing of truces in September 1385 and June 1386,[24] Scottish raids continued to disrupt the border region: the east and west marches were assaulted in simultaneous strikes in October 1385 and again in the spring of 1386.[25] Another series of armed incursions by two separate raiding parties into the east and west marches in July 1388 precipitated a new period of crisis. Richard II's discomfiture at the hands of the Lords Appellant rendered the likelihood of a second royal campaign unlikely; John of Gaunt was abroad, and in the borders themselves, the earl of Northumberland and his son were at odds with the lords Neville and Clifford over the recent disposition of the wardenship of the marches.[26] The Scottish victory at the battle of Otterburn signalled another year of hardship for the inhabitants of the north,[27] and it was only at the urging of the French that the Scots agreed to abide by the Treaty of Leulinghen of 18 June 1389 which imposed a three-year truce in the marches.[28]

The persistence of such intense hostility with the Scots had a profound effect on the military preparedness of the frontier region, and on the responsibilities assumed by the wardens. Within weeks of Edward III's death the new government issued commissions appointing wardens in the east and west marches, and nominating Thomas Percy, youngest son of Henry Percy, constable of the disputed castle of Jedburgh.[29] The imminence of Scottish attack resulted in the reorganisation of the office just a few months later: although their military authority was in no way diminished, the wardens were reduced in number and, in order to facilitate ease of communication among them, all were jointly entrusted with supervision of the marches.[30] But raids by the Scots continued to endanger the stability of the entire frontier, and in February 1379 John of Gaunt was appointed king's lieutenant in the north. The commission under which he first assumed his new authority was succinct (it commanded him to do everything he considered 'necessary and suitable' for the defence of the marches), and unambiguous: it subordinated all royal officials in the north, including the wardens, to his command.[31] Lest any of the secular or ecclesiastical magnates currently holding wardenial commissions have any doubt about the breadth of Gaunt's authority, a second set of orders was issued in September 1380, in which the duke of Lancaster's position in the border hierarchy was made abundantly clear. He was to exercise full royal powers in all things military, ranging from the array of the fensible men of the north to the garrisoning of fortresses, as well as in all matters relating to the conservation of the truce. Thus, he could extend the armistice for as long as he required (or suspend it altogether), and was expected to oversee the work of the conservators in their march days.[32]

In the course of the five years in which Gaunt acted as lieutenant, the terminology of the commissions in which his duties were set out became increasingly lengthy and elaborate.[33] In part, the tendency towards complexity was a reflection of the crown's intention to invest the office with the full weight of the royal dignity, a response dictated in turn by the disintegration of stability in the north. But the commissions may also have been rendered more elaborate at Gaunt's request, in reaction to the jealousies expressed by Henry Percy at the duke's intrusion into a region the former had come to regard as his own. For some two generations the Percy family had enjoyed a prominence in the defence of the north and presidency over the tribunals in which cross-border disputes were adjudicated. The animosity that grew between Gaunt and the earl of Northumberland, which reached a peak at the time of the Peasants' Revolt, was not soon forgotten by the king's lieutenant,[34] and the wide-ranging commissions were blatant reminders to his rival that he was the crown's most trusted agent in the borders. Nevertheless, both men were aware that the tension between them was inimical to the security of the region, and the earl was partly mollified by Gaunt's tendency to leave much of the day-to-day business of march administration to the wardens.

The duke insisted on attending in person several days of truce with the Scottish earl of Carrick, where he represented the crown in discussions concerning the still unpaid ransom of David II and lands claimed by the English within Scottish territories.[35] In meetings such as these it was appropriate that the English ambassadorial party should be headed by a member of the royal family. When circumstances dictated the abandonment of amicable diplomacy, the duke was also prominent in the deployment of military operations against the Scots. The campaign he led into the eastern lowlands in the spring of 1384, while it failed to secure a new truce or to deter further attacks on the remnants of English-held lands there, did at least demonstrate to the Scots the crown's determination to punish enemy incursions.[36] Similarly, in spite of a quarrel with Richard II during the royal expedition of 1385, he took care to remain in the north in order to be seen to safeguard the region against retaliation.[37]

But by 1384, Gaunt was fast losing interest in the problematic north. The lieutenant's commission of May 1382 was not renewed; instead, supervision of the garrisons of the border castles and the maintenance of the men of the region in armed readiness were delegated almost entirely to the wardens.[38] The Westminster chronicler disapproved strongly of the duke's performance as lieutenant. Writing about the events of November 1383 (which opened with a Scottish attack on the county of Northumberland), he commented wryly that Richard II's council had made a wise choice in assigning the defence of the north to 'certain persons of rank and prominence who were to have the keeping of the countryside and to enjoy the foremost position in the region concerned', rather than to John of Gaunt.[39] The monk displayed a marked preference for the northern magnates as the appropriate champions of the borderers against the Scottish foe: when he described the raid in which Jean de Vienne joined forces with the Scots, he attributed the enemy's ease of passage through English territory to the dissension that Gaunt had raised among the great families, and elsewhere he reserved especial praise for the Percies.[40]

Modern scholars do not unanimously share the chronicler's opinion that the duke's decisions at days of march were unjust,[41] but most agree that the region was well-nigh impossible to govern in the absence of Percy support.[42]

The duke of Lancaster's wishes were fulfilled when he was relieved of the lieutenancy in 1384. Thereafter, defence of the marches devolved solely on the wardens. For the remainder of the decade their military duties remained unaltered, and they exercised their responsibilities with the same kind of extensive authority as had their Edwardian predecessors. The changes that were effected occurred, rather, in the organisation of the march territories, the place of the office within the administration of the north, and in personnel. A middle march came into existence in 1381, following the death of the last Umfraville earl of Angus. The new division consisted of the lands of Tyndale, Redesdale and Hexham, with a stretch of unstable territory running westward from Newcastle to Roxburgh; the east march was accordingly reduced in extent.[43] The creation of the new administrative unit is sometimes portrayed as one aspect of Richard II's determination to challenge the Percy dominance of the north, as the appointment of Gaunt as lieutenant had been.[44] If this was the crown's intention, it was poorly executed, for the third march enjoyed only a precarious existence. It was dissolved and reconstituted several times in the late Middle Ages, and assigned variously to the Percies in the east march or the Nevilles in the west. The geography of the border region militated against the preservation of a territory so haphazardly created. There existed no natural boundary line here, and no sites traditionally associated with either the English or the Scottish kingdoms, such as were known in both the east and west marches, even if these were identified only after bitter wrangling. Until the sixteenth century, then, control over a distinct middle march was never as highly contested as it was over the other two.

The wardens' commissions underwent considerable structural change in the course of Richard II's reign. Professor Storey has argued convincingly that by the end of the 1380s the disturbed state of the border lands had permanently altered the office: 'the warden had become a paid officer, appointed under certain conditions. Before the war of 1384-86, he had been a commissioner. If he had been retained to maintain a body of soldiers, this was an additional and extraordinary measure. After 1388, a man became a warden by force of his indenture; he did receive a commission, but this was no longer the foundation of his authority'.[45] Indentures of service issued in 1389 became the standards by which wardens were engaged for the next hundred years, and while rates of pay and terms of service fluctuated, 'the principles remained the same'. Although Richard II preferred, from 1386, to appoint only one warden for each of the marches,[46] this practice was abandoned by his Lancastrian successors.

Under Richard II the wardenship was used as a political tool to a much greater extent than it had been earlier. The rise of the Neville family to prominence in the north at the expense of the Percies – much as Gaunt had been used in the early 1380s – is a familiar theme in the historiography of the region, and needs no emphasis. To his dismay Richard found that in the absence of a standing army, the border lands could adequately be defended only by magnates who had the status to command local forces, the private wealth to support their endeavours and the vested interest to preserve a modicum of peace. After 1388, the king's choices were limited to the Percies and the Nevilles. In the first decade of the reign, however, the personnel of the wardenship was frequently manipulated. In the months following Gaunt's appointment as lieutenant Henry Percy and John lord Neville were overlooked entirely, and a series of lesser men shared the duties of the office. In the strangest of these commissions, dated 7 December 1379, the east march was governed by a clique of seven small Northumberland landholders; the west by a similar group of six Cumberland and Westmorland men.[47] The duke of Lancaster's ascendancy in the north saw the temporary eclipse of Henry Percy from the wardenial office, but from 1384, with his interest in the north on the wane, Gaunt was aware that he could compete with the earl's ambitions only from a distance, by having his friends and retainers included in the commissions. Thus he kept in touch with border affairs through such men as John lord Neville, Richard Scrope and Hugh Dacre.[48]

The effects of these alterations to the personnel of the warden's office on the level of disorder in the border lands are difficult to ascertain. The Westminster chronicler criticised the northern lords for making it possible for the enemy to harry the region with apparent abandon, but the Scots must also have been greatly emboldened by Richard II's discomfitures at home with the Lords Appellant, and by the waning, after 1377, of the grim determination with which Edward III had sought to crush their realm. In the parliament held in the spring of 1379 there were vociferous complaints from the commons of Northumberland about the hardships suffered at the hands of the Scots, including an accusation that the Scottish wardens were refusing to abide by truce-time regulations for the ransom of prisoners, and a request for exemption from taxation based on widespread loss.[49] The council agreed, eventually, to the latter,[50] but did little more than assign the former to a forthcoming meeting of ambassadors of the realms, 'at which day, if it please God, reasonable remedy will be ordained'. A request that a competent warden 'demurrant as Coustages du Roi' be appointed until the duke of Lancaster should travel north to assume the lieutenancy, was met with the equally vague reply that the king would do 'le mieltz que lui semblera a faire'.[51] Repeated calls from the northerners, not only in 1379, but thereafter almost annually, that the lords of the march should be commanded to remain in the region prepared to defend its people were answered with varying degrees of urgency,[52] and the major expeditions of 1384 and 1385 were undertaken only in response to particularly severe breaches of the truce. Richard II could not afford to ignore altogether his northern frontier, but for the better part of his reign he was more than content to leave the resolution of its problems as well as its defence to others.

Situated close to a newly resurgent enemy, bedeviled by a lack of royal commitment to its defence, and sensitive to the rivalry between the Percy family and its competitors, the northern marches knew very little peace in the years between 1377 and 1389.[53] It is therefore remarkable that the system of border law should have emerged relatively unscathed from this unsettled period, and noteworthy, too, that even against a background of profound violence, improvements should have been effected to the means by which border disputes were resolved. That both survival and consolidation should have occurred was a reflection of the devotion the warden–conservators demonstrated to the system, and the skills they used to shape legal principles to suit difficult circumstances.

After the comparative peace of the last few years of Edward's reign, the violence committed by the Scots at the Roxburgh fair in the summer of 1377 profoundly antagonised the English wardens. When a vigorous letter of protest to the Scottish warden, William earl of Douglas, failed to elicit a response, Henry Percy took his grievance to the Scots king himself. Robert II, anxious to avert further trouble, promised to compel his officials to justify their actions, and arrangements were made for the wardens of both realms to meet in September at Fairnington Crags.[54] Sentiment was still running high when Percy and Douglas came together. Given that the personal involvement of the wardens in the incident for control over Jedburgh and its surrounding territory was still a matter of dispute between them, both agreed to defer arbitration and settlement to the 'greater lords of the realms'. A second meeting was planned for January 1378, at the traditional site of Lilliot Cross in the west march. In the meantime, both sides agreed to extend the current truce.[55]

Percy prepared assiduously for the January meeting, well aware that the two sides would be contending highly volatile issues. Chief among these was bound to be the capture at sea in 1376 of the wealthy Scottish merchant, John Mercer, and the recent attack on Roxburgh. Mercer was transferred from London to Alnwick,[56] although the earl of Douglas continued to claim that the merchant had been taken in violation of the truce and should be released forthwith.[57] Other members of the English delegation headed by Gaunt, and including Edmund Mortimer earl of March, the wardens and two civil lawyers, set out for Lilliot Cross armed with a commission that gave them broad powers to punish English violators of the truce.[58] The great day of march was duly convened at the end of January,[59] and while there was much posturing on both sides, there began the slow process of reparation for damages inflicted by the subjects of either realm since the previous summer. In conformity with the arrangements made more than a decade earlier at Moorhouse-law, Percy agreed temporarily to release all Scotsmen captured and imprisoned since the previous July, and in particular to restore all merchandise and chattels taken since that date to the plaintiffs who came forward to claim them. Persons who had wilfully destroyed or wantonly consumed goods lost in shipwrecks were to be sent to trial at the next day of march.[60]

The resolution of the Roxburgh incident and competing claims concerning the capture of Mercer, however, proved as contentious as they had promised to be, and only some progress was made in settling these matters. The English accepted responsibility for the slaying that had precipitated the Scottish attack on the fair and a jury of borderers identified Sir Thomas Musgrave as one of the culprits. The Scots, for their part, conceded that John Mercer had been lawfully taken at sea and should be compelled to pay ransom to his captors. Both defendants undertook to present themselves to their captors at an agreed date some four months hence under a heavy penalty of 10,000 marks, and each provided surety for the performance of his obligations in the shape of personal pledges.[61]

The march day revealed both the problems and the promises characteristic of the border tribunals of Richard II's early reign. The appointment of pledges hearkened back to the 1249 code of march law, and suggested that despite the tensions generated by war, the borderers were reluctant to dispose entirely of poinds (as they were known in the region). The practice had been adapted to the more difficult circumstances of the mid-fourteenth century when the Moorhouse-law indenture had made the northern lords responsible for the discharge of their tenants' debts, and, though destined soon to disappear, these were still regularly sought by plaintiffs. Indeed, the earl of Douglas himself had stated clearly to Richard II his wish to have the circumstances of Mercer's capture adjudicated 'according to the customs of the days of march'.[62] The obligations of equal value imposed on the Englishman Musgrave and the Scot Mercer represented an attempt to break the impasse and to cancel out the redress owed by one side to the other. The notion of reciprocal awards, too, was to be of lasting importance in the marches, and served to create a careful balance between perceived reparation accounts still outstanding, and those that had been discharged.[63]

In the absence of a machinery capable of enforcing the decisions made in the courts, however (and in 1378 the political climate rendered impossible the erection of such a machinery), the successful resolution of disputes depended not only on the cooperation of the warden–conservators, but on the willingness of the borderers themselves to submit to the judgements made there. Satisfactory results there were: in the months after the January meeting Henry Percy set about implementing some of the decisions made at Lilliot Cross in respect of merchant property seized in march-related incidents.[64] But there were grave problems, too. As early as April the earl of Douglas was threatening to levy a distress of 10,000 marks on the inhabitants of Berwick should Sir Thomas Musgrave default on his obliga-tion.[65] Although he took pains to meet with Douglas in order to reassure him that Musgrave would indeed abide by the tribunal's judgement, Percy was unable to compel the recalcitrant debtor. When Musgrave made it clear that he had no intention of surrendering himself into the enemy's custody on the appointed date, the wrath of the Scots descended on the region.[66] Musgrave's sureties sought the assistance of the king's council, lamenting the dire consequences should the debtor refuse to honour his promise, and the crown dutifully ordered the wardens to seize the person of Musgrave and return him to the custody of the Scots.[67] In the end, John Neville of Raby, one of the wardens, made satisfaction of Musgrave's debt from his own revenues. He was still awaiting repayment of the sum by the crown several years later.[68]

The border tribunals were nevertheless crucial organs of border administration, and despite the difficulties involved in enforcing their decisions the wardens continued to believe that they were the most appropriate venues for the resolution of cross-border disputes. Thus, despite the animosity that had marred deliberations in January 1378, another day of march was planned for June.[69] The commissioners agreed here to exchange suspects taken in violation of the current truce, and set two dates in October and November for sessions of the border tribunals. More important from the Scottish perspective was the undertaking by the English wardens to halt the seizure of enemy ships in retaliation for acts of truce-breaking,[70] a concession intended to demonstrate their determination to preserve the integrity of the days of march and perhaps to dissolve lingering resentments about the assault on John Mercer. Richard II's council in turn gave expression to its tacit agreement with the wardens' show of goodwill by issuing a steady stream of commissions to keep the truce, and Exchequer clerks were kept busy recording the expenses incurred by frequent sessions of the days of march.[71] A prohibition laid on Henry Percy forbidding the overzealous extension of his wardenial authority to the men of the liberty of Durham probably dates from this period, when the earl was seeking by every means possible to ensure the smooth functioning of the border courts.[72]

In the spring and summer of 1380 two incidents threatened to destroy the truce and to undo the work of the march tribunals. The first began with the wreck off the coast of Northumberland of a Scottish merchant vessel laden with goods worth 7000 marks; according to the chronicler Thomas Walsingham an alliance of men from Newcastle and Hull seized the merchants and threatened to rise in rebellion when Henry Percy, acting under the authority of his wardenial commission, attempted to claim the goods.[73] The earl's failure to secure the merchandise, says Walsingham, was the trigger for a savage invasion of the west march which inflicted widespread damage on Cumberland.[74] The chronicler notes that the warden himself despaired of an orderly resolution of this débâcle, for he was commanded by the king to refrain from retaliating in forceful fashion until a day of march should be held to discuss the matter in peaceable fashion.[75] The second source of friction involved an assault on the person of Ralph lord Greystoke who, together with a retinue of 120 men, was captured by the Scots while on his way to Roxburgh to assume command of the castle, and held for the considerable ransom of 1000 marks.[76] In a complaint addressed to parliament in 1381 he argued that his seizure had been effected in retaliation for English assaults on two Scottish vessels by the Northumberland magnate, William lord Hilton. An inquest into the matter subsequently found that Hilton's prizes were worth no less than £10,000,[77] and Greystoke, perhaps justifiably, held him in large measure responsible for the ruin and poverty he had suffered.[78]

It has been suggested that the crown's reluctance in 1380 to sanction violent reprisals in respect of both incidents may have been the result of the duke of Lancaster's machinations. At the very least, his interests in faraway Castile and his jockeying for a position of supremacy in the north at the expense of Henry Percy made him 'eager to procure redress for breaches of the truce at sea as well as on land',[79] despite the fact that previous Scottish attacks had elicited a strong English response. Anxious to join Edmund of Langley's expedition to the Iberian peninsula,[80] he went through the motions of ordering an English expeditionary force to muster at Newcastle, but, to the disgust of the chroniclers and the dismay of the inhabitant of Northumberland, he postponed belligerent action in favour of a peaceful meeting with Scottish ambassadors.[81] The resulting truce, sealed at Berwick on 1 November, became something of a model for future Anglo-Scottish agreements. Henceforth indentures of truce served a dual purpose: they were concerned not only with defining the terms and duration of a general armistice, but, more important, with refining the procedures according to which the border tribunals would function.

The agreement of 1380 (which established an armistice of twelve months' duration) dealt with two specific matters. It established that within a month of committing breach of the truce offenders must be attached by their respective wardens, handed over to the warden of the opposite march, and imprisoned until put to trial; meanwhile, full restitution of stolen goods would be made. The indenture also enumerated specific border sites where, in future, formal accusations of violation of the truce would be exchanged, including Melrose Abbey, the castle of Jedburgh, the priory of Canonbie, and Lochmaben castle.[82] The meeting of November 1380 was followed by the assignment of a day of march where recent depredations might be discussed and amended. Gaunt was aware of several outstanding disputes: just days before meeting with the earls of Douglas and March and Sir Archibald Douglas, he wrote to the king of a new incident at Roxburgh, and suggested that a raid carried out by Sir Robert de Vaux had been committed in retaliation for an attack by Scotsmen of Annandale.[83] Nevertheless, he acknowledged that these and other allegations of violence were best left to the determination of conservators, and the wardens of the English marches were ordered to present themselves for a day of march, once again at Lilliot Cross.[84]

The border tribunal that convened at Berwick in November 1380 disposed of several outstanding disputes, including that of two Scottish merchants, who were awarded the sums of £133 6s 8d and £75 15s in compensation for goods seized from their ships in Newcastle.[85] Another Scottish plaintiff duly appeared, prepared to defend his claim to a cargo of fish and cloth, but was later released when no one came forward to challenge him.[86] At Gaunt's behest the crown commissioned an inquiry into the seizure of still another Scottish vessel and cargo worth £244.[87] An assize returned that the recent incident at Roxburgh had been the fault of the duke of Lancaster's retainer, Sir William Tunstall, and several other 'evildoers', who, while staying in the town, became involved in an altercation and did £50 worth of damage.[88] The warden, Henry Percy, assumed responsibility for Tunstall's debt, and later sought Gaunt's assistance in recovering it.[89] At another series of border tribunals, held at Ebchester in June 1381, the Scottish commissioners complained loudly that acts of violence by English truce-breakers were not being punished in accordance with recent agreements. Several English subjects were nevertheless found guilty of truce-time atrocities and subjected to heavy fines.[90] Relations between Lancaster and Carrick were, indeed, sufficiently smooth to enable them to extend the current armistice until February 1384.[91] The agreement made it possible for further sessions of the border courts to be held in the next two years, where once again several outstanding grievances saw satisfactory settlement. Judicial revenues accrued to John of Gaunt's treasury in 1382 were sufficient to underwrite expenses and gifts for several of his household officials;[92] the following year further progress was made when the Scots agreed to offer redress for the 1380 raid on Wark castle and for an assault on Billymire by the earl of March. The English, for their part, accepted liability for a raid into Scottish territory by a gang of armed men, and although Gaunt proved unable to lay hands on the culprits (who fled to the wilds of the Cheviot hills) the armistice held.[93]

The royal council found good reason, in the turbulent 1380s, to be grateful not merely to its lieutenant, John of Gaunt, but more particularly to the efforts of its northern warden-conservators. Lancaster deliberately maintained a high profile throughout the period of his lieutenancy, arranging for his meetings with the earl of Carrick to be lavish and grandiose affairs,[94] and keeping the royal council closely apprised of the results of these encounters. The indentures made at Berwick in 1380 and Ebchester in 1381, for example, were forwarded to the crown for formal exemplification and were ordered to be proclaimed as far away as Ireland.[95] The agreement to summon a panel of jurors from England and Scotland for the purpose of assessing the damage done to the castle of Wark in the Scottish attack of 1380 was made the subject of an elaborately worded indenture, which Gaunt promised to take to the king as well as to parliament for certification.[96] But it was the warden-conservators who managed the day-to-day business of ensuring that the judgements of the border tribunals were executed. The great days of march attended by the duke of Lancaster and his impressive retinue were far outnumbered by smaller, less ostentatious meetings, in which men such as Percy, Neville and Scrope worked at the minutiae of border legal administration: the summoning of plaintiffs and defendants, the organisation of panels of jurors, and the payment of sums awarded in compensation to those who had suffered the effects of truce violations.[97] When Gaunt was relieved of the lieutenancy, they resumed direction of the tasks for which, until 1379, the crown had considered them its most appropriate agents.

On occasion, they acted entirely on their own initiative. As Richard II and Robert II were preparing for war in the spring of 1385, Henry Percy and Archibald Douglas lord of Galloway met at the Water of Esk to seal an indenture of 'special Trewe and Assurance' for the west march. Both sides agreed to release prisoners currently held in their respective custody, as well as the latter's pledges. The indenture was novel in two respects: the death penalty was specifically invoked for persons who deliberately committed cross-border theft in breach of the truce, and the matter of restitution in cases of theft was clearly addressed, and set at double the value of the goods carried off.[98]

Under the management of Henry Percy first earl of Northumberland and John Neville lord of Raby in particular, the role of the wardens in shaping the substance and practice of border law was greatly intensified. Edward III had intended that these officials exercise a wide-ranging judicial authority in the march tribunals, and by the end of his reign royal commissions had provided them with the wherewithal to do so. But the old king, anxious to preserve the royal prerogative, had kept a close and controlling eye on the development of the warden-conservators' powers. His grandson, Richard II, was less concerned to do so. Virtually all the significant changes effected in the workings of border law in the last fifteen years of the fourteenth century originated in the north, in the meetings held between the English and Scottish wardens. The indentures of agreement which became, and remained, the written basis of the law were regularly and dutifully submitted to the crown for ratification, but until the very end of the reign, neither the king nor the varied counsellors who advised him demonstrated a keen interest in actively assisting the wardens in their endeavours. On occasion Richard made a half-hearted effort to curb what he considered the excessive zeal of the wardens in imposing their jurisdiction over too broad a spectrum of border troublemakers. This kind of concern underlay, for example, the sharply worded order to Henry Percy to respect the regalian prerogative of the bishop of Durham, cited above, and the crown's attempts to secure the goods of a border fugitive in opposition to the warden's claims.[99]

Ironically, a marked lack of royal interest proved the most valuable of Richard's contributions to the system of border law. In permitting the wardens great latitude to refine and improve the practices of the march tribunals and enabling them to take full advantage of their local expertise, he made it possible for them to complete a process begun by Edward III and to shape a body of law that was responsive to the unique conditions of the frontier region. The jurisdictional obstacles to the administration of border justice represented by the liberty of Durham were overcome by the simple expedient of appointing Bishop Fordham to the warden-ship of the east march.[100] The episcopal lands lost much of their appeal to fugitive border felons such as Thomas Tylliof, whose arrest was ordered by the bishop in the autumn of 1384,[101] and although the bishops remained jealous of their prerogatives they had good reason to appreciate the benefits of close association with the conscientious warden-conservators.[102]

A truce of 1386, sealed between John lord Neville and the earls of Douglas and March, restated some of the terms of agreement made the previous year, but it also included some innovations.[103] A clause prohibiting communication of any kind between the peoples of either realm (save in the environs of Jedburgh, Roxburgh and Berwick, where it was impossible to prevent) was of symbolic importance in positing the march courts as the only acceptable venues of cross-border inter-course. As the wardens now enjoyed virtually unlimited authority to grant letters of safe conduct, provision was made for plaintiffs to pursue stolen goods by 'hand and horn', that is, according to the northern version of the hue and cry.[104] One of the important corollaries of this provision was the resumption in the marches of trial by combat, now frequently invoked in cases in which mixed juries were unable to agree on ownership of stolen property.

Judicial combat had been the normal method of proof in border tribunals in the thirteenth century, and had never completely disappeared: in 1335, for example, Edward III had tacitly recognised the practice in the Scottish lowlands, and in

1354 had permitted the Northumberland lord, William Heron, to defend his claim to a number of stolen horses by challenging his opponent in the lists.[105] More recently, the crown had sanctioned recourse to judicial ordeal in the autumn of 1380, and again a year later, when the Scottish plaintiff John de Chatton met the English defendant William Badby.[106] Richard II's attitude toward the procedure was ambivalent. In 1383 he insisted that the wardens seek royal licence – either from the king himself, or from his lieutenant, John of Gaunt – for all wagers of battle in march-related disputes,[107] but thereafter judicial duels were organised with some frequency.[108] In the early years of the 1390s Richard may well have begun to employ the Court of Chivalry as a political tool within England, as some scholars have suggested,[109] but his agents also made effective use of its appeal and traditions in the exercise of foreign policy. A series of splendid tournaments sponsored by the crown served the dual purpose of settling cross-border disputes under the guise of chivalric display, but also tacitly underscored the appropriateness of recourse to judicial combat in the border tribunals.[110] Wager of battle remained from the 1390s to the late fifteenth century a popular aspect of march law.[111]

The truce of 1386 formally abolished the practice of distraining, known in the north as poinding, and transferred responsibility for all debt and compensation to the wardens alone. In one sense, it completed a process begun in 1367 with the Moorhouselaw indenture.[112] But the change also signalled recognition by the officials of both realms that their reliance on the goodwill of the northern nobility for the timely payment of monetary penalties and compensation, as well as for the strict observance of the letter of march law, had been misplaced. Too often, Dacres, Musgraves, Nevilles and Redmans had reneged on their obligations to discharge the sums imposed on them by the march tribunals; too often, moreover, they had tried to cloak violations of the truce under the mantle of lawful distraint. The agreement of 1386 merely acknowledged that this aspect of the law was unenforceable across a national boundary line as hotly contested as were the Anglo-Scottish marches, and thus unworkable.

Finally, the indenture was novel in that it made clear reference to the kinds of offences that constituted breach of the truce and were justiciable in the border courts. To date, although the texts of royal commissions in England and of brisk letters exchanged between the wardens had noted the unlawful carrying off of persons, ransom-taking and homicide, only the theft of livestock, grain and chattels had merited specific mention in truce agreements. In the indenture of 1386 the warden-conservators agreed to allow 'nouthir the brynnyng, ne Slaghter of Men Takyng and Ransonyng of Prisoners, Takyng of Castelx, of Forteresses and Walled Townes na nane othir harmes, in onykyn manere for to done', and to forbid the *chivanches* (armed and mounted raids), and the *ref* (cattle reiving, the border term for cattle theft) that had hitherto disturbed the fragile peace of the region. Although subsequent events were to belie the sincerity with which both sides set their seals to the agreement, each continued to consider these offences as the chief concerns of the border courts for the remainder of the medieval period.

The alterations made to the law in 1386 helped to smooth the function of the march tribunals in the difficult years ahead. Despite the tensions generated by frequent violations of the truce, days of march were convened with remarkable regularity in the later 1380s. The range of the warden-conservators' activities is well illustrated in surviving record materials; it includes the summoning of defendants, grants of letters of safe conduct to litigants, and restitution offered to the Scottish wardens on behalf of English subjects found guilty of truce-time infractions.[113] The outrages committed by the Scots in the summer of 1388 and the disaster suffered by the English at Otterburn temporarily suspended sessions of the border tribunals, but they resumed a year later, when English ambassadors were sent north to discuss the inclusion of Scotland in the Treaty of Leulinghen.[114] The earl of Fife (who acted as effective ruler of the Scots from 1388, in place of the now enfeebled Robert II) delayed accepting the three-year armistice with England until the autumn of 1389.[115] But discussion of outstanding cross-border grievances began in late summer,[116] and the English crown was assiduous in ensuring that a large number of conservators of the new truce were appointed in the marches.[117]

The last decade of the fourteenth century opened with a great deal more promise than had the 1380s. However reluctant the Scots might have been to observe the terms of the recent treaty, the death of Robert II in 1390 and the succession of his weak son as Robert III prevented them from taking advantage of the victory won at Otterburn. The new king swore, even before his coronation, to abide by the three-year truce, then agreed to two subsequent extensions, arranged in May 1392 and June 1393.[118] Robert's complaisance was not lost on the English king, who now decided to inject more substance into his policy towards the Auld Enemy; more particularly, he now sought 'to isolate Scotland, deal with her directly, and thus obtain more favourable terms from her'.[119] In the end, Richard failed to win the (surely excessive) concessions he expected of the Scots – the abandonment of the Franco-Scottish alliance – and the treaty of amity he hoped for proved elusive. But he did succeed in establishing a level of fragile peace in the region that had been so markedly absent in previous years. More important to his own designs, while keeping Scottish ambassadors occupied with negotiations for a lasting territorial settlement and a proposal of marriage between the royal houses, he bought himself the opportunity to strike once more at the power of the earl of Northumberland within the marches.[120] From 1396 to 1399 Percy supremacy in the north was challenged by the appointment to the office of warden of Ralph Neville and several other courtiers, by the detachment from that office of the truce-keeping duties of the conservators, and by the resurrection of the lieutenancy in the marches, to which John of Gaunt was once more assigned in March 1398.[121]

As had occurred in the previous decade, royal attempts to interfere in the administration of the frontier region had mixed results. In the political sphere they proved disastrous: by 1399, Richard had isolated both the earl of Northumberland and Ralph Neville (now earl of Westmorland) to the extent that each supported the rebellion of Henry of Bolingbroke in an effort to win back the wardenial office and dominance of the military and social governance of the border lands. There is evidence to suggest, moreover, that Richard's northern policy had a deleterious effect on the regular functioning of the march tribunals. During the years of Northumberland's wardenship of the east march (1391–6),[122] days of march were convened at least annually, sometimes in conjunction with negotiations for an armistice, at other times for the sole purpose of discussing redress in march-related incidents.[123] Percy's experienced hand is clearly visible in the records of dispute settlement: for example, in ordering the seizure of the goods of Scottish merchants in distant Yarmouth pending the satisfaction of English merchants robbed in Edinburgh, and in the building of lists in Berwick, preparatory to a judicial battle.[124] It was Percy, moreover, who undertook to clear up a host of unfinished wardenial business left by his predecessor in the east march, the earl of Nottingham,[125] and who made elaborate arrangements for a judicial duel staged at Rulehaugh.[126]

After the earl was excluded from the wardenial and conservator's offices, however, the smooth running of the courts appears to have suffered interruption. Commissions to punish violators of the truce were issued throughout the last years of Richard II's reign,[127] but accounts enrolled in the Exchequer suggest that, with the notable exceptions discussed below, the meetings that were convened in the borders were concerned more with efforts to convince the Scots to make a permanent peace than with the more delicate business of dispute settlement.[128] A letter of Robert III, undated but probably written in the later 1390s, suggests that the exchange of prisoners and the return of stolen goods that had been normal features of earlier pre-trial procedures in the marches were no longer in operation, leaving Scottish wardens bewildered and Scottish plaintiffs unsatisfied.[129] The duke of Albemarle, thrust into the wardenial office, himself criticised the king's lack of wisdom in attempting to govern the north without Percy. In the summer of 1399 he wrote to Richard II, urging him to appoint the earl to a newly revived middle march, in order to facilitate the resumption of the border tribunals for the resolution of grievances that the earl of Douglas claimed were too long unsettled.[130] Deprived of Percy's experience and authority the most that Richard II's northern officials could win from the Scots during these years was general agreement that days of truce were the appropriate venues for the redress of wrongs.[131] If there were significant settlements of individual disputes during the last years of the reign they have left few traces in surviving record materials.[132]

While the courts proved incapable of offering the resolution of outstanding grievances, the Scots remained willing to discuss the substance of border law. Here again, the influence of the earl of Northumberland's years as keeper of the truce in the shaping of legal procedure is manifest. An indenture sealed at Dunfermline in October 1397 was important, for it explicitly required, for the first time, the submission of written bills of complaint by aggrieved parties, to be deposited at Roxburgh (English bills) and Kelso Abbey (Scottish plaints), then forwarded to the conservators of either realm.[133] The introduction of written pleas to border procedures has been linked to a similar development in respect of accusations made in the Court of Chivalry.[134] Provision for the formal notification of outstanding grievances had in fact been included in indentures made between English and Scottish warden-conservators for several years already and, more particularly, during the period of Gaunt's lieutenancy in the early 1380s.[135] It is perhaps no coincidence that in the 1390s Scottish officials accustomed in the interim to treating in informal fashion with the earl of Northumberland, should once more have requested the implementation of structured and clearly defined pre-trial procedures under a new regime. Written bills did not disappear from the border tribunals in the fifteenth century, when the Percy family regained its prominence in the north, but they were never the sole, nor even the necessary, foundations for trial at march law. Neither side regarded them as needful until the last years of Richard II's reign. Under the administration of inexperienced northern appointees, such as those whom Richard introduced, written bills of complaint were a means of assuring Scottish plaintiffs that the business of seeking redress for truce-time outrages would be brought to the attention of their opponents.

The great days of march that Richard II and Robert III had hoped would be held in the spring of 1398 were, however, postponed for several months. Frustrated, perhaps, by delays in obtaining justice in the matter of two ships allegedly seized in contravention of the current truce,[136] the Scots agreed only to an extension of the armistice. The indenture in which its terms were set out included only points of law that had been established in earlier written agreements. Thus it made provision for the speedy execution of justice by the conservators of either side, the immediate release of prisoners and stolen property, the awarding of double the value of items found to have been unlawfully taken, and the death penalty in cases of cross-border homicide.[137]

Richard II awakened only belatedly to the need to oversee closely and carefully the administration of border law. The establishment of a firm peace with Scotland would be secured only if both realms had in place an efficient and proven machinery for the resolution of cross-border disputes. Equally important, if, as he hoped, the rule of the earl of Northumberland was to end in the north, it was essential that both the crown and its inexperienced body of new wardens and conservators be apprised of current legal practice. Richard's appointment of John of Gaunt to the newly revived office of lieutenant in March 1398 was intended in part to endow the duke with the authority needed to negotiate a permanent peace with Scotland, but it also signalled the king's intention to impose 'long-term supervision' over march affairs.[138] With the armistice now safely extended, he was able next to arrange for the drafting of a kind of protocol of border law which would provide a definitive statement of custom and procedure to guide those who would administer it in future. Early in October four of Richard II's favourites were appointed conservators of the truce and sent north with commissions granting them comprehensive powers to punish and make restitution for all violations committed since 1389.[139] In the instructions that Richard sent after them a few days later he specifically required them to ensure that sealed copies of any indentures of agreement made on this occasion be deposited in a permanent location in the north, presumably in order that they be readily available for consultation. He also required that all such agreements be written in English.[140] This unusual request was perhaps an acknowledgement that future conservators would need to familiarise themselves with terms used in the northern tribunals, but not generally encountered elsewhere, and, indeed, the new men (John Bushy, Henry Green, William Ferriby and Lawrence Dru) were introduced in the course of their discussions to legal terms to which they can only have had little previous exposure.

The indentures drawn up in October and November 1398 were by no means legal treatises in the tradition of Britton or Bracton, nor did they much resemble the tract that would become so influential in the mid-sixteenth century, Sir Robert Bowes's comprehensive *Order and Form of Days of Truce*.[141]But collectively they were the descendants of the code of 1249 in their breadth and depth, and they were periodically brought up to date in the course of the fifteenth century, in several subsequent indentures of truce. Although both were drafted under the authority of the duke of Lancaster, acting for the English crown, and David Stewart duke of Rothesay (the son of Robert III) representing the Scots, they revealed clearly the imprimatur of Percy's years and experience as conservator.

The first meeting, convened at Haddenstank on 26 October, addressed grievances originating in the east marches of either realm.[142] Gaunt and Stewart agreed to the release of all men unlawfully taken prisoner since 1389, and to restore to them before Candlemas all monies paid in ransom. Both sides offered guarantors (identified in the indenture as *borowis*), who bound themselves to abide by the release terms. Persons who failed to secure their freedom were to be *assithed*, that is, recompensed, by payment of double the value of their ransoms, and their captors fined. All *borowis* were similarly to be released by Candlemas. The Scottish conservators identified three men, Adam Gordon, Willie Barde and Adam French, as grievous offenders against the most recent armistice who 'unmesurit Harmes has done within the tyme of this Trewe', and undertook to present these men at a future day of march for adjudication.[143] Arrangements were also made to begin the trial of two outstanding disputes, one concerning the unlawful taking of Scottish merchandise in English ports, the other regarding the burning and pillaging of Roxburgh by Scottish brigands.[144]

The commissioners turned next to a general review of the procedures that would govern truce-time relations in future. Both Lancaster and Rothesay noted that the frequency of the movements of their respective subjects across the ill-defined boundary line 'ar principale Cause of distroublance of the quiet of bath the Reaumes', and agreed that, temporarily at least, they would halt the practice of granting the king's peace to wanderers. Both further admitted that delays in obtaining justice in the border tribunals had been a matter of contention of late; henceforth, days of march were to be convened on a monthly basis, either under the presidency of the warden-conservators themselves, or their duly appointed deputies. Harsh penalties were decreed for truce-breakers found guilty by a border assize: 'he or thai sal be deliverit to the Partie that has sustenit the scath, to Sla or Raunson at thair lykyng'. Dates and sites were nominated for forthcoming days of march where all unsettled grievances were definitively to be addressed: business relating to the middle marches would be settled at Gamelspath on 12 November next, and that of the east march ten days later at Haddenstank or some other suitable place. Both sides agreed once again to limit communication between members of the English garrisons situated in the lowlands and the Scots who lived nearby, but all aggrieved parties were to be free to pursue stolen goods with hand and horn, without threat of 'distrouble'.

A similar meeting, concerned with the affairs of the west march, was held a week later at Lochmaben.[145] The provisions set out in an indenture of agreement were similar in nature and scope to those drafted at Haddenstank, with only minor differences regarding the dates of future meetings: prisoners and *borowis* were to be released by 11 November, and ransoms restored by Shrovetide. The west march in England was smaller in extent that the east, but on the Scottish side was divided among many lords, including the English crown. In order to accommodate these conditions, four distinct sites were allotted for future tribunals: Lochmabenstone (for disputes involving the inhabitants of Galloway, Nithsdale and Annandale), Kirkandrews (for the tenants of Eskdale and Liddesdale), Kirkandrews or Kersop Brig (for Tyndale and Redesdale) and Kersop Brig again (for Teviotdale and the Jedburgh area). Mutual accord on such a mundane matter as border meeting places was no mean feat; it represented, rather, the culmination of several years' worth of diplomacy on the part of the wardens. As far back as the autumn of 1380 the king of Scots had written to Richard II charging that under Gaunt's orders the English wardens had refused to agree to several sites, which the Scots nevertheless held were traditional meeting places.[146] He noted that the vill of Rulehaugh in particular had been rejected, and was still protesting several weeks later that it had been a place of meeting since 'beyond the memory of the wardens and the people of your own marches'.[147] The dispute simmered unresolved for almost a decade, and it was only in 1389 that both kings conceded that the selection of trial sites was most appropriately left to the warden–conservators.[148] The vills incorporated into the terms of the truce of 1398 were the sites where, for some years, Percy and Neville had become accustomed to convening with Scottish officials.

The second indenture differed from the first in including in its text a blunt assessment of the recent performance of English officials. Douglas noted that 'the Commissairs of Scotland has Allegyt that Due Reformacion and Redress of Attemptatz has nocht bene done before this tyme, for that, on the party of England, has been gret changyng of Wardanys on the West Marche syn the tyne of this Trewis, the qwilk wil nocht Redress bot ilke man for his awne tyme', and suggested, as a remedy for the problem, that the crown permit its wardens and conservators to appoint deputies conversant in march legal procedures to carry out the business of the courts. A clearer indictment of Richard's officials, and a more pointed demonstration of support for the restoration of the earl of Northumberland, could hardly have been made. Richard ignored Douglas's advice – as he did that of the duke of Albemarle several months later[149] – and continued to exclude

Percy from all border-related duties. But the advice was not lost on Henry IV. One of his first acts as king was the reinstatement of the earl as warden-conservator, under a commission that henceforth granted all wardens permission to appoint fully authorised deputies.[150]

The optimism which characterised the compilation of current border legal practices in the autumn of 1398 did not bear much fruit. Richard II was careful to make new appointments to the office of conservator in both marches in the winter of 1398–9, and again the following spring,[151] but in instructions that he issued to his officials in April he emphasised the matter of a prolonged peace, rather than the need to provide redress for English acts of violence.[152] A day of march held in May has left no written record of any compensation paid or redress made by the conservators to Scottish plaintiffs,[153] and if an early letter of the newly enthroned Henry IV to his rival, Robert III, can be read as anything more than conventional grumbling, truce-time violations may even have increased during the unsettled summer of 1399.[154]

Richard's abrupt removal from the English throne was something of a fortuitous event in the development of border laws and customs. In the years since the dismissal of John of Gaunt from the office of lieutenant in 1384, the crown had demonstrated little commitment to assisting the warden-conservators in the difficult task of maintaining the cross-border tribunals in good functioning order, and manipulation of the wardenial office between 1396 and 1399 appears to have actually impeded their effectiveness. The sudden interest Richard displayed in 1398, when he directed that written protocols of march-related legal procedures be drafted at Haddenstank and Lochmaben held out the promise of tangible results in future, but he failed utterly to comprehend that the full cooperation of the Scottish wardens in the resolution of cross-border disputes depended ultimately on the respect that the earl of Douglas and his fellows felt for their counterpart on the English frontier, the Percies. Ralph Neville, newly raised to the dignity of earl, was unable to command a similar degree of approval, and there was little chance that other men – the duke of Exeter or the duke of Albemarle, appointed as wardens, or Bushy, Green and Dru, named as conservators of the truce – would be able to do so. Henry Bolingbroke would exhibit no hesitation in reversing his predecessor's mistake.[155] Fortunately for the inhabitants of the border lands, the brevity of Richard's experimentation with the offices of warden and conservator in the end exerted little harm on the integrity of the march courts. The immediate resumption of regular days of truce was the subject of discussion between the crowns as early as October 1399, and the tribunals were in operation again by January 1400.[156]

The indifference to the activities of his warden-conservators that was so evident throughout much of Richard II's reign was also manifested in a lack of attention to the exercise of wardenial authority within the marches of England proper. Edward III had been concerned to ensure that the powers exercised by his northern officials in the pursuit and punishment of truce-breakers did not infringe on the operation of the common law in Northumberland, Cumberland and Westmorland. Thus, while he had granted them significant jurisdiction over offences that were clearly related to the keeping of the truce, he had been careful to protect the purview of the common law, for example by distinguishing clearly between commissions that required wardenial experience and authority and those in which the northern expertise of a Percy, Neville or Dacre was seen as desirable, but not necessary. The common-law sessions of gaol delivery, moreover, remained a source of strong competition for the border tribunals. One of the manifestations of the old king's concern is that the business that was undertaken by the wardens' courts has left relatively little trace in extant judicial record.

There is some evidence that, beginning in the 1380s, the wardens' tribunals were beginning to compete more aggressively with the common-law courts in the north, and that the crown failed to maintain a clear division between their respective jurisdictions. Between 1379 and 1384 several suspects charged with committing offences that were clearly breach of the truce were indicted before justices of the peace, sheriffs and coroners, and sent to trial at gaol delivery in Carlisle and Newcastle before justices of assize.[157] From the 1390s on, moreover, trial juries at gaol delivery began to make use of a clause in the Statute of Treasons of 1352 relating to adherence to the king's enemies to charge notorious border trouble-makers with the most serious of offences known to the common law.[158]

A significant number of incidents, however, were handled solely by the warden-conservators. In 1382, when several inhabitants of the west march were accused of cattle reiving, it was to the warden that the crown entrusted the responsibility of holding an inquest into their activities and those of their accomplices.[159] The following year Henry Percy was commanded to apprehend English subjects said to be committing breach of the truce with impunity throughout the east march; his counterparts were issued similar orders in respect of known felons there.[160] On these occasions the king's lieutenant himself was expected to submit to the authority of the warden.[161] Between 1384 and 1390 the disruptions caused in the border counties by Scottish raids were so frequent and severe that royal justices of assize refused outright to travel beyond Yorkshire. In their absence, the wardens assumed increasing responsibility for the punishment of a wide variety of infractions that occurred in the marches. The crown was not only prepared to accept their assistance, but may tacitly have encouraged it. In August 1384 Henry Percy's commission as warden included the duty of taking cognisance of all plaints relating to prisoners, spoil, plunder and rapine, but also of accusations of revealing secret counsel to the Scots, and of incidents of treasonable collusion with the enemy 'according to the laws and customs of the marches'.[162] The offence of spying had to date fallen almost exclusively under the jurisdiction of the courts of gaol delivery.[163] Further intrusion by the wardens into the sphere of the common law occurred in 1386, when the royal council directed Henry Percy to put to trial and punish persons suspected of initiating 'unlawful conspiracies' with the Scots.[164] The close relationship between border legal customs and practices current in continental military tribunals was made clear in still another commission of February 1386: here, Percy was ordered to punish persons who released

Scottish prisoners without wardenial permission 'according to the law of arms and the customs of the marches'.[165] Just a month later these newly expanded powers were included in a wardenial commission.[166]

The punitive powers of the crown's northern officials varied according to the venue in which they were exercised. In the tribunals over which they presided in the company of their Scottish counterparts, the death penalty was not unknown. The earliest reference to the execution of men condemned by a border assize dates to the year 1401,[167] but there is no reason to believe that it was not practised in Richard II's reign. Provision for the imposition of sentence of life and limb in cases of breach of the truce was made as early as 1385, and surviving evidence indicates that in virtually all other aspects of march-related justice these agreements closely reflected actual practice. More frequently, however, the Anglo-Scottish border courts imposed financial penalties, for the *raison d'être* of these sessions was 'to amend damages done on both sides' for the preservation of peace in the region.[168] Truce-time agreements throughout the reign stipulated that redress and compensation for stolen goods be made in money or moveable goods, and that the wardens be responsible for the discharge of all obligations imposed by the courts. The need to maintain the cooperation of the Scottish wardens made English officials take this responsibility very seriously, and during their tenure of the office Henry Percy, John and Ralph Neville and Richard Scrope paid substantial sums to Scottish plaintiffs in accordance with awards made by the courts.[169]

Within England proper, the wardens' punitive authority was more restricted. The wardenial commissions of the 1380s and 1390s empowered them to punish English subjects involved in violations of the armistice, once again 'according to the laws and customs of the marches', implying that they had powers of life and limb. But unambiguous evidence for the exercise of these powers is difficult to find. Most obviously, it was hardly likely that the wardens would attempt to make use of the death penalty in respect of offences committed by the 'better sort' of truce-breakers, and it has long been known that the northern noblemen themselves played the most significant roles in perpetuating late medieval disturbances in the border lands.[170] In the punishment of lesser fry, men such as the notorious Northumberland truce-breaker, Thomas of Lidell, the wardens appear to have deferred to the authority of the justices of assize, at least when the latter were on circuit.[171] In such cases they may consciously have preferred the unchallenged powers of life and limb exercised by the common-law courts to their own, more questionable punitive authority. It is apparent, however, that in the late fourteenth century, in truce-related matters, there was still some confusion between the jurisdiction of the common-law courts and that of the wardens. In addition to the men (and women) who appeared in sessions of gaol delivery, at least one suspect was presented before justices of the King's Bench; two others were indicted before justices of the peace, and a fourth before the coroner in Northumberland.[172] Conflicts of jurisdiction occurred, for example when the sheriff of Yorkshire refused to deliver to the warden a man indicted of homicide in Henry Percy's wardenial court,[173] and when another plaintiff sought a writ of *certiorari* to remove to the King's Bench a case that had originated in a wardenial tribunal.[174]

The limitations of the wardens' authority were perhaps most vividly experienced in cases in which the interests of these officials clashed with those of the crown or other great northern lords. In 1380, for example, Henry Percy's attempt to claim the estates of a local man forfeited for adhering to the Scots met with opposition by Richard II, who maintained that the lands should revert to the crown.[175] The following year Percy was likewise unable to prevent the escalation of reprisals in a border incident that began when two Scottish ships laden with some £10,000 of merchandise were seized in English waters by Sir William de Hilton and a band of marauders. In retaliation, the Scots descended into the east march, where they captured Ralph baron Greystoke (himself a warden) and 120 of his retainers. Hilton remained at large and the stolen goods were distributed amongst his friends and clients. Petitions presented to the crown in the spring of 1381, then again in parliament later that summer, gained the aggrieved parties only the comfort of knowing that the incident would be referred both to a day of march and a special commission of inquiry. But the grievance was still outstanding in the autumn, when the crown ordered John of Gaunt to convene another inquiry and to return its finding into Chancery.[176] In the end, Greystoke and his men were compelled to purchase their freedom, and Hilton presumably made a separate peace with the crown.[177] The resolution of the dilemmas posed by a multiplicity of jurisdictions was a long process, one that had only begun to be addressed in the reign of Richard II.[178]

Richard's reign nevertheless saw the wardens take decisive action when challenges to their authority threatened to disrupt the border tribunals or, more seriously, the stability of the frontier region itself. Among the many impediments to speedy process in the north, as indeed it was in all English courts of law, was the problem of non-appearance by defendants. Edward III and his grandson were sufficiently astute to recognise that a warden deprived of the authority to compel parties to a suit to appear at trial was an official with very little power at all, but despite the punitive sanctions granted them by the crown the warden–conservators found it as difficult as did their common-law brethren to guarantee that accused persons would duly present themselves in court. In the early 1380s the earl of Northumberland warned a recalcitrant Sir William Swynburn that failure to attend the forthcoming day of march would be severely punished. One letter stated: 'We charge you on behalf of the king our sovereign to be there [at Kersop Brig] on the said day to do and receive as right requires, and we wish to compel you to do right and justice'. A second missive was more admonitory: 'And know, indeed, in case you are unwilling [to come] that we shall distrain your body and goods to recompense ourself'.[179] In the Easter term of 1381 Swynburn failed to appear in King's Bench to answer an appeal of felony, because he had been summoned to present himself in person at the day of truce planned for 16 May.[180] The wardenial letters enjoining Swynburn's attendance at the march tribunal suggested that Percy considered the accusation of border-related crime the more pressing of Swynburn's problems. The king's justices agreed, and postponed the appeal of felony until the defendant's march business should have been dispatched.

Wardenial authority came into conflict with a local attempt at self-help at the height of the Appellant crisis, when Sir William Heron of Ford sought to remedy losses he had incurred in Scottish raids without benefit of the conservators' assistance.[181] He claimed that in the previous two years he had been repeatedly attacked by the enemy and had seen more than £100 of animals carried off. When march tribunals failed to provide adequate compensation, he initiated a judicial raid into the Scottish east march. Far from approving his actions, the earl of Northumberland compelled him to make restitution to the Scots of 320 oxen and horses, 1006 sheep and £100 in money. Heron complained in parliament that the earl had also assaulted his castle at Ford and taken property he found there 'in the manner of the king's enemies'. Preoccupied with the demands of the Appellants, and anxious to retain the neutrality of the earl of Northumberland, the crown supported Percy's fierce response to Heron's raid and ordered merely that arbitrators be assigned 'to treat between the parties and to reconcile them'.[182]

Equally problematic, although less frequent, were incidents of violence at the border tribunals between English subjects who sympathised with the Scots or who were unwilling to submit their disputes to the lengthy process of march law. In the autumn or winter of 1380–1, for example, the widow of a Cumberland landowner sought the assistance of the crown in prosecuting the gang of local troublemakers who had murdered her husband. The latter, she alleged, had peacefully attended a day of march at Gretna, where he was killed in an affray led by Thomas de Blenkinsop and his Scottish adherents.[183] In the late 1390s the mother of William Cawood similarly complained that her son had been murdered while acting as bailiff of the wardenial court by Sir Ralph Bulmer.[184] John of Gaunt's apparently genuine wish to abide by the judgement of a cross-border tribunal was thwarted when the felons he sought to attach fled the region.[185]

In the late fourteenth century, despite the troubles attendant on them, the broad military and judicial powers exercised by the warden–conservators in the northern marches ensured that the office remained a highly valued and jealously guarded prize. But the prestige it bestowed on families such as the Percies and Nevilles must also have been offset by the tremendous financial burdens it represented. Some years ago, Professor Storey explored in great detail the crown's payment of the English wardens.[186] His careful examination of extant Exchequer records, together with other, more general studies of royal fiscal policy under Richard II, have made it abundantly clear that the warden–conservators were among the most poorly paid of the crown's numerous servants. Anthony Steel estimates, for example, that of all the substantial fictitious loans made by the Exchequer in the first part of the reign, 'the principal sufferer was John Neville of Raby . . . followed by the earl of Northumberland and his son, Hotspur', that is, the wardens of the west and east marches, respectively.[187]

Less often appreciated in examinations of the financial onus borne by these officials is the role they played as what might be termed 'brokers' in cross-border dispute settlement. At a day of march held in the summer of 1384, John Neville paid to the Scottish warden the sum of £113 6s 8d, in reparation for robberies committed in Scotland by the nobleman Sir Peter Tylliof.[188] Neville sought to recover the debt from the king, who immediately turned the matter over to Tylliof's lord, Bishop John Fordham of Durham. Richard II's orders to the bishop enabled him to put the matter out of his own mind; it was left to Neville to sue his debtor in the episcopal court, and it is not known how long he was compelled to wait for his money. Neville's experience was shared by all who held the wardenial office, and Henry Percy's assault on Sir William Heron becomes understandable in light of the crown's failure to reward adequately the officials upon whom it relied so heavily for the stability of the frontier region. On rare occasions the wardens did succeed in wresting hard cash from the king, but usually only at some loss. Thus, in 1386 the earl of Northumberland was able to shame Richard II into sealing an indenture of payment for services he had rendered on the marches, but the agreement compelled him to renounce all outstanding royal debts in return for the relatively paltry sum of £100, and to accept only a promise of an unspecified future payment of £500 for a prisoner whose ransom the crown had set at £700.[189]

The wardens of the marches, then, operated very much at risk to their personal fortunes. Richard II's government was no less remiss than Edward III's had been at rewarding its servants in condign fashion, or than the Lancastrian crown would be in the fifteenth century. The families who sought office in the marches did so knowing that the financial obligations they assumed would be heavy. In this sense, the changes effected to the substance and operation of border legal practices were dictated not by some abstract admiration for ancient and revered northern custom, but by a real and hard-headed desire to ensure that the payment of heavy sums in redress and compensation for truce-time atrocities did not come out of their own purses. In the last two decades of the fourteenth century, they succeeded in transforming the legacy of Edward III's interest in march affairs into a coherent and effective system of law. The Scottish chronicler Hector Boece later condemned Henry Percy's efforts as warden-conservator when he recounted the earl of March's attempts treatment at a day of march:

To mak redres als far as tha had faillit.
Richt oft the Persie so he hes assaillit,
Askand redres of all wes done beforne,
And he agane gat na ansuer bot scorne,
With greit derisioun ilk da moir and moir.[190]

But to the English author of the *Chronicon Angliae*, the days of truce were civilised and productive venues, 'where it is the custom for the English and the Scottish wardens to meet annually'.[191] The assiduous work of the wardens, sometimes in despite of Richard II's interference, ensured that the border tribunals remained for the next century the most important of the crown's institutions in the north.

Notes

1. See Goodman, *Loyal Conspiracy*; Tuck, *Richard II and the English Nobility*. For a rigorous and illuminating assessment of the relations between Richard II and the earl of Lancaster, see Goodman, *John of Gaunt*.

2. Tuck, 'Richard II and the Border Magnates', p. 27; Tuck, *Richard II and the English Nobility*, p. 202.

3. *Westminster Chron.*, pp. 344-5.

4. Goodman, *John of Gaunt*.

5. *Chron. Bower*, i.384; *Historia Anglicana*, ii.340.

6. *Chron. Bower*, ii.384.

7. *Rot. Scot.*, ii.3; *Chronicon Angliae*, pp. 194-5.

8. In April 1378 the earl of Northumberland warned the king of the perilous state of both marches and of the belligerent activities of Archibald earl of Douglas. PRO SC 1/57(7), printed in *CDS*, iv., App.I, no.18. Petitions sent to the archbishop of York by the canons of Hexham priory and by the commons of Cumberland to the king in parliament are found in Raine, *Priory of Hexham*, ii.149-51, *Rot. Parl.*, iii.30, 33, 34.

9. *Historia Anglicana*, i.373, 387-9; *Chron. Angliae*, pp. 219-20; *Chron. Fordun*, ii.371; *Chron. Bower.*, ii.391.

10. See the account of Roger de Burton, a canon of York, in Raine, *Historical Papers and Letters from the Northern Registers*, pp. 419-20.

11. Fraser, *Northern Petitions*, no. 113.

12. *Historia Anglicana*, i.409-10; *Chron. Angliae*, pp. 239-40.

13. *CCR*, 1377-81, p. 455.

14. PRO E 39/95/13, confirmed by Richard II at Northampton on 1 December. See *Foedera*, III.iii.108-9. The text of the truce of June 1381 is found ibid., III.122-3. See also *Historia Anglicana*, i.446-7, ii.41-2; *Chron. Angliae*, p. 269, and Walker, 'Letters to the Dukes of Lancaster', pp. 269-70.

15. *Anonimalle Chron.*, p. 133. See also *Historia Anglicana*, i.437-8, and *Chron. Angliae*, pp. 269-70, 327-8.

16. *Rot. Parl.*, iii.146; *CPR*, 1381-5 pp. 135-6. For another such incident, see *CPR*, 1381-5, pp. 137-8.

17. *Historia Anglicana*, ii.105; *Westminster Chron.*, pp. 40-3, 50-1, 56-7; *Chron. Knighton*, ii.203.

18. *Westminster Chron.*, pp. 40-3, 56-7; *Chron. Angliae*, p. 357.

19. *CCR*, 1381-5, pp. 476-7; *CCR*, 1385-9, p. 25; PRO E 101/40/6.

20. *Westminster Chron.*, pp.58-9, 104-5; *Chron. Angliae*, pp. 361-2; *Historia Anglicana*, ii.118. Alexander Featherstonhaugh, the keeper of Lochmaben, was prosecuted as a traitor for surrendering the castle to the Scots. Henry Percy was similarly subjected to a sentence of forfeiture for his neglect in permitting Berwick to fall. He was able to regain the castle, but only after purchasing its release for the substantial sum of 2000 marks *CCR*, 1381-5, pp. 476-7; *CDS*, iv., no.331; *CCR*, 1385-9, p. 25.

21. *Westminster Chron.*, pp. 86-7, 100-1; *Historia Anglicana*, ii.111-12. An indenture sealed at Ayton on 7 July included the Scots in the current Anglo-French truce, due to run until 7 October. The Anglo-Scottish armistice was later extended to 1 May. *Foedera*, III.iii.168-9, 170-1; *Rot. Scot.*, ii.64-5.

22. Templeman, 'Two French Attempts to Invade England', p. 227; Nicholson, *Later Middle Ages*, pp. 196-8.

23. *Historia Anglicana*, ii.131-3; *Chron. Knighton*, ii.204-05; *Polychronicon*, ix.60-77; *Chron. Angliae*, pp. 364-5; *Westminster Chron.*, pp. 132-5. The campaign of 1385 is discussed in Goodman, *John of Gaunt*, pp. 103-4; Nicholson, *Later Middle Ages*, pp. 196-7; Nicolas, 'Account of the Army with which King Richard the Second Invaded

Scotland', pp. 13–19; Lewis, 'Last Medieval Summons of the Feudal Levy', pp. 1–26; Palmer; 'Last Summons of the Feudal Army in England', pp. 771–5.

24. *Rot. Scot.*, ii.75; *Foedera*, III.iii.205.
25. *Chron. Bower*, ii.402–3; *Westminster Chron.*, pp. 138–9; *Historia Anglicana*, ii.144; Grant, 'Otterburn War', p. 46.
26. Goodman, *Loyal Conspiracy*, pp. 46–8; Tuck, *Richard II and the English Nobility*, pp. 132–3. The depredations wrought in the west march in the summer of 1388 are reviewed in Summerson, 'Responses to War', p. 159. The truce made in the spring of 1388 expired on 19 June. *Rot. Scot.*, ii.92.
27. The battle is recounted in great detail in several chronicle sources, chief among them Froissart, *Oeuvres*, xiii.200–9.
28. *Foedera*, III.iv.39–42.
29. *Rot. Scot.*, ii.2. An account submitted by Henry Percy earl of Northumberland for the newly reconstituted garrison at Berwick and for Thomas Percy's pay is enrolled at PRO E 101/34/27.
30. *Rot. Scot.*, ii.5.
31. Ibid., ii.14.
32. Ibid., ii.27.
33. Compare the commission of February 1379 with those issued in May 1381 and May 1382; *Rot. Scot.*, ii.36, 42–3.
34. Goodman, *John of Gaunt*, pp. 80–4, 88–91.
35. *Foedera*, III.iii.106–9, 122–3, 156–7; PRO E 364/24 m.7; E 403/496 m.9; Lodge and Somerville, *John of Gaunt's Register*, ii. no.1080; *Rot. Scot.*, ii.29–30; PRO E 39/99/73; E 39/95/4.
36. The expedition of 1384 is discussed in Goodman, *John of Gaunt*, pp. 224–6. In the spring of 1384 Gaunt sealed an indenture with Henry Percy delegating to the earl full authority to defend the marches in his absence. *Rot. Scot.*, ii.62.
37. Goodman, *John of Gaunt*, pp. 104–5.
38. See, for example, PRO E 101/73/42B; *Rot. Scot.*, ii.43, 49, 51–2, 54, 57, 58–9, 65–6, 69 70, 73; PRO E 364/16 mm.1, 2; E 101/39/37; E 101/39/35; E 101/69/239; E 364/32 m.5d; E 101/73/30.
39. *Westminster Chron.*, pp. 50–1.
40. Ibid., pp. 55–6 and note, 56–7, 86–7, 104–5, 132–5.
41. Ibid., pp. 42–3.
42. Goodman, *John of Gaunt*, p. 96; Steel, *Richard II*, pp. 93–4; McKisack, *Fourteenth Century*, pp. 438–40; Tuck, 'Richard II and the Border Magnates', pp. 40–2. For a different view, see Walker, 'Letters to the Dukes of Lancaster', pp. 73–5.
43. Reid, 'Office of Warden', p. 487; *Rot. Scot.*, ii.41; Tuck, 'Richard II and the Border Magnates', p. 41.
44. Storey, 'Wardens of the Marches of England', p. 596; Lomas, *North-East England*, pp. 86–7.
45. Storey, 'Wardens of the Marches of England', p. 601.
46. *Rot. Scot.*, ii.81, 94, 96, 105, 100, 119, 130, 131, 135, 140. The indentures according to which the wardens served are listed in Storey, 'Wardens of the Marches of England', p. 612, notes 1–12.
47. *Rot. Scot.*, ii.19–20. The period during which these men held office (December 1379–March 1381) has been termed a 'short-lived experiment of "gentry" Wardens'. See Walker, 'Letters to the Dukes of Lancaster', p. 74.
48. Storey, 'Wardens of the Marches of England', pp. 595–6. All four were members of the wardens' commissions between March 1380 and March 1386. Their relations with the duke of Lancaster are extensively reviewed in Walker, *Lancastrian Affinity*.
49. *Rot. Parl.*, iii.62, 69.

50. *CCR*, 1377–81, pp. 284–5.
51. *Rot. Parl.*, iii.64.
52. *Rot. Parl.*, iii.80–1, 138, 146, 200, 213, 223, 251; PRO DL 25/99.
53. Professor Dobson is of the opinion that in the two decades after 1378 there occurred 'the most extensive campaign of castle building seen in northern England since the twelfth century'. Dobson, 'Church of Durham and the Scottish Borders', p. 138.
54. PRO C 47/22/11(3); E 364/12 mm.5, 8d; *Chron. Angliae*, pp. 194–5.
55. *Foedera*, III.iii.69–70.
56. *CCR*, 1377–81, pp. 20, 39; PRO C 81/1539.
57. BL MS. Cotton Vesp. F VII, fo.34, printed in *Facsimiles of National Manuscripts of Scotland*, ii. no.45.
58. Rot. Scot., ii.5–6.
59. PRO E 364/11 m.5d; E 364/12 m.5; E 101/603/11; E 101/318/5.
60. PRO SC 1/43(86).
61. PRO SC 8/129(6058). The mariner Thomas Mercer, however, who together with John Mercer had been engaged in aggressive naval operations against England, was still in prison there in June 1379. *Rot. Scot.*, ii.16. The two cases are reviewed in Nicholson, *Later Middle Ages*, pp. 194–5, and Goodman, 'Letter from an Earl of Douglas', p. 70.
62. BL MS. Cotton Vesp. F VII, fo.34.
63. See also PRO SC 1/43(86), and Summerson, 'Early Development', p. 35.
64. *Rot. Scot.*, ii.6, 8, 11–12.
65. PRO SC 1/57(7), printed in *Facsimiles of National Manuscripts from William the Conqueror to Queen Anne*, i. no.32.
66. It was perhaps in retaliation for Musgrave's misconduct that a large gang of Scottish thieves attacked Berwick castle, where they killed its keeper, Robert de Boynton. Raine, *Historical Letters and Papers*, pp. 419–20, and above, p. 70.
67. *Rot. Scot.*, ii.16.
68. In March 1382 Neville obtained a warrant for the seizure of lands and chattels worth 1,000 marks belonging to Musgrave and his son, in partial payment of the debt. PRO C 81/474(2111).
69. PRO C 47/22/11(5). Expenses incurred by the commissioners who met at Lilliot Cross are enrolled at PRO E 101/318/5, 6, 8; BL Egerton Roll 8728; PRO E 364/18 m.8.
70. BL Cotton Ch. XVIII.44.
71. For commissions date May 1378 to July 1380, see *Rot. Scot.*, ii.9, 12, 13, 15–16, 21–2, 25. Expenses relating to march days are found in PRO E 101/318/13, 14, 22; E 364/12 m.9; E 364/13 mm.2d, 3; E 364/14 mm.4d, 5; E 364/16 m.5d. Scottish accounts for the year 1379 are found in *Exch. Rolls*, 1359–79, pp. 602, 605, 621, 622.
72. DCD 2.4 Reg. 4. The earl's intention of respecting the privileges of the see of Durham was given formal expression when he respectfully sought the bishop's grace in the pardon of one of his tenants in 1379. PRO DURH 3/31 m.11.
73. *Chron. Angliae*, pp. 267–70; *Historia Anglicana*, i.437–8.
74. Evidence of Scottish destruction is discussed in Summerson, 'Responses to War', p. 157.
75. *Historia Anglicana*, i.438.
76. *Rot. Parl.*, iii.129. See also below, p. 86.
77. *Rot. Scot.*, ii.20, 26, 30–1; *CPR*, 1381–5, pp. 83–4; PRO SC 8/178(8864). The last of these documents is printed in Fraser, *Northern Petitions*, no.116. See also nos.115, 117.
78. PRO 8/85(4221). In 1382 one of Greystoke's men finally secured from the crown a grant of 40 in aid of his ransom. *CPR*, 1381–5, p. 182.
79. Goodman, 'Letter from an Earl of Douglas', p. 72.
80. Goodman, *John of Gaunt*, p. 76.
81. The people of Northumberland complained bitterly of the great hardship inflicted by

Gaunt's army. *Rot. Parl.*, iii.88; *Historia Anglicana*, i.446–7. Gaunt travelled northward with a series of instructions to negotiate with the Scots, indicating that the royal council itself favoured a diplomatic settlement of the crisis.

82. *Rot. Scot.*, ii.29–30. Accounts relating to the meetings held at Berwick are enrolled at PRO E 364/14 m.7 and E 364/15 m.6. The truce was ratified by Richard II on 1 December.

83. Lodge and Somerville, *John of Gaunt's Register*, ii. nos.1207, 1208, 1210; *Chron. Bower*, ii.403.

84. Lodge and Somerville, *John of Gaunt's Register*, ii. no.1206.

85. *Rot. Scot.*, ii.30–1.

86. PRO C 47/22/3(11); *CCR*, 1377–81, p. 500.

87. *CPR*, 1377–81, p. 580.

88. Lodge and Somerville, *John of Gaunt's Register*, ii. no.439; *CCR*, 1377–81, pp. 431–2.

89. Percy assumed a second debt in respect of a march offence committed in Liddesdale against the Scot, Robert de Blackburn. *Rot. Scot.*, ii.37.

90. *Rot. Scot.*, ii.38–9; PRO E 364/16 mm.2, 5d; E 101/318/29, 31; E 403/484; Lodge and Somerville, *John of Gaunt's Register*, ii. no.573; *Cal. of Inqu. Post Mortem.*, xvi. nos.234, 270.

91. The Anonimalle Chronicler noted the terms of the truce, though he misdated the agreement to 1380. *Anonimalle Chron.*, p. 133.

92. Lodge and Somerville, *John of Gaunt's Register*, ii. no.744.

93. PRO E 39/102/36; *CPR*, 1381–5, pp. 136–7, 137–8. See also Gaunt's order for the distraint of the goods of several merchants of Liverpool, until the matter of a cargo of wine taken from the Scots should be resolved. PRO DL 37/3.

94. In 1383 the duke received 500 marks to help defray the costs of suitably equipping his retinue for a forthcoming meeting. Lodge and Somerville, *John of Gaunt's Register*, ii. no.915.

95. *Rot. Scot.*, ii.41.

96. PRO E 39/102/36.

97. PRO E 101/620/18; E 364/17 mm.1d, 3; E 101/39/30; *Rot. Scot.*, ii.53. See also *Rot. Scot.*, ii.52, orders to the wardens to arrest nine men condemned by a march tribunal, but still at large.

98. PRO C 71/64 m.4; *Foedera*, III.iii.182; *Rot. Scot.*, ii.73; CRO DRC 1/2 fo.133 (Reg. Appleby).

99. DCD 2.4 Reg. 4; PRO KB 27/479 m.32 (Rex). The latter case concerned the goods of Henry Lucher, accused several years earlier at a day of march of adhering to the Scots, participating in the murder of the Englishman Sir John Coupland, attacking the vill of Baremore in Northumberland, and stealing animals and coin from Sir Thomas de Muschamp. Lucher's father David, a former tenant of the earl of Northumberland, had been a known adherent of the Scots. In 1380 Henry Lucher was seeking to exonerate himself of the charges laid against him. *Cal. Inqu. Post Mortem*, xv, no.248.

100. *Rot. Scot.*, ii.65.

101. PRO DURH 3/32 m.4.

102. In 1384, for example, forewarned by the wardens of an impending Scottish attack, Bishop Fordham initiated repairs to several of his fortresses. The following year he was happy to permit these same officials to oversee the proper defence of Durham priory and its estates. PRO DURH 3/32 m.3; DCD 2.4 Reg. 1.

103. *Foedera*, III.iii.305; *Rot. Scot.*, ii.85–6.

104. See Neilson, 'The March Laws', pp. 67–9.

105. 'The Chronicle of Robert de Avesbury', p. 302; *Foedera*, III.i.105. The provisions of the code of 1249 concerning trial by combat are found in Neilson, 'The March Laws', pp. 20–3.

106. *Foedera*, III.iii.108; Lodge and Somerville, *John of Gaunt's Register*, ii. no.1209, *Rot. Scot.*, ii.39–40. Badby had been taken prisoner in late 1380 or early 1381, and managed to win from the king a small pension to assist him in paying off his ransom. *Rot. Scot.*, ii.34.

107. *Rot. Scot.*, ii.50.

108. *Rot. Scot.*, ii.87, 90, 103–4, 111, 129–30; *CPR*, 1391–6, p. 261; PRO E 28/26; *Chron. Bower*, ii.420; *CPR*, 1399–1401, p. 119. See Neville, 'Keeping the Peace', pp. 14–15.

109. Tuck, *Richard II and the English Nobility*, p. 152; Squibb, *High Court of Chivalry*, pp. 17–20.

110. PRO C 81/1053; C 81/1054; *Rot. Scot.*, ii. 60–1, 103–4, 111, 117, 119; PRO C 81/535 (8255); *CPR*, 1391–6, p. 261; *Chron. Wyntoun*, vi.359–62; *Polychronicon*, ix.235; *Brut*, ii.348. The tournaments are discussed in Barker, *The Tournament in England*, pp. 35–6, and Barber, *Tournaments*, p. 36.

111. See, for example, *CPR*, 1401–5, p. 410; *CPR*, 1405–8, p. 101; *CPR*, 1405–8, p. 73; *Foedera*, IV.i.68, 97; IV.ii.89, 100; *Rot. Scot.*, ii.207, 212; PRO E 403/591; E 28/30.

112. See above, p. 53.

113. See, for example, *CPR*, 1385–9, pp. 89, 326, 346, 412, 520; PRO E 28/2/10; *Rot. Scot.*, ii.91, 99. Accounts and other notices of days of march are found in CRO DRC 1/2 fo.133 (Reg. Appleby); PRO E 101/319/30; E 101/319/35. Scottish records are enrolled in *Exch. Rolls*, 1379–1406, pp. 690–1.

114. *Rot. Scot.*, ii.92, 103; *Exch. Rolls*, 1379–1406, p. 239.

115. Nicholson, *Later Middle Ages*, p. 200; Campbell, 'England, Scotland and the Hundred Years War', p. 210; *Foedera*, III.iv.39–42; PRO E 364/23 m.8; E 101/319/38. See also *Historia Anglicana*, ii.182–3; *Polychronicon*, ix.214–17.

116. PRO E 364/31 m.1d.

117. *Foedera*, III.iv.45–6.

118. *Rot. Scot.*, ii.105, 116, 118, 121; *Foedera*, III.iv.62, 74–5, 87, 91.

119. Tuck, 'Richard II and the Border Magnates', pp. 45–6; *PPC*, i.23.

120. The negotiations of 1394–9 and the truces made during that period are reviewed in Tuck, 'Richard II and the Border Magnates', pp. 46–8.

121. *Rot. Scot.*, ii.40, renewed for twenty-eight years in July 1398, *Rot. Scot.*, ii.142. See also Tuck, 'Richard II and the Border Magnates', pp. 49–50; Storey, 'Wardens of the Marches of England', pp. 601–3, 612–13.

122. *Rot. Scot.*, ii.108.

123. Accounts for truce days are enrolled in PRO E 364/31 m.1d (1389); E 364/24 m.7d; E 101/320/3 (1391); E 101/320/10; E 364/28 m.1; E 364/29 m.3d (1394); E 364/29 m.2d; E 101/41/36 (1395). Notices of other sessions of the border tribunals held in 1390, 1391, 1393 and 1396 are found in BL MS Cotton Vesp. F VII fos.28, 32, 36, 37; *CPR*, 1391–6, p. 261; PRO E 28/26.

124. PRO SC 1/43/45; E 30/1631. See also a petition from Percy to Richard II, seeking protection for a shepherd of the Scottish countess of March and her sister to graze sheep in the area of Coldbrandspath. De Fonblanque, *Annals of the House of Percy*, i.161 and note 2. Richard II, interested in befriending George Dunbar earl of March, was more than willing on this occasion to make use of Percy's experience. See Tuck, 'Richard II and the Border Magnates', p. 47.

125. The earl marshal had been appointed to the wardenship in 1389 despite the objections of several members of the royal council. See *PPC*, i.12b–c; Storey, 'Wardens of the Marches of England', pp. 600, 612; Tuck, 'Richard II and the Border Magnates', p. 45.

126. In 1394 the Scottish knight Sir William Inglis briefly captured and occupied the castle of Jedburgh. After its recovery the ousted English keeper, Thomas Strother, challenged Inglis to a duel over which the wardens of the English and Scottish marches presided. 'Annales Ricardi Secundi et Henrici Quarti', pp. 166–7.

127. *Rot. Scot.*, ii.132–3, 142, 143–4, 145, 147.
128. PRO E 364/32 m.1; E 101/320/19; E 364/31 m.1d; E 39/5/27; *Rot. Scot.*, ii.149–50; *Foedera*, III.iv.157.
129. BL MS Cotton Vesp. F VII, fo.38.
130. PRO C 47/22/11(10). The letter should be dated 11 July 1399, rather than 14 July 1398. See *CDS*, v.211. Albemarle had been made warden of the east march in February 1398 and conservator of the truce in July. *Rot. Scot.*, ii.140, 142.
131. See, for example, PRO E 39/91/12; *Foedera*, III.iv.136–7.
132. An exception was the conclusion of a long-standing argument between English and Scottish merchants concerning an incident of piracy in which the Scotsmen Adam Forrester and John Hamilton were awarded compensation. PRO E 101/128/20, 21.
133. *Foedera*, III.iv.136–7.
134. BL Addl MS 9021, fo.100; Summerson, 'Early Development', p. 39.
135. That is, in the truces of November 1380 and November 1381. See *Rot. Scot.*, ii.29–30, 38–9.
136. PRO E 39/1/25; SC 8/218(10867); *CCR*, 1396–9, p. 165.
137. *Rot. Scot.*, ii.143–4.
138. Tuck, 'Richard II and the Border Magnates', p. 50; Tuck, *Richard II and the English Nobility*, p. 202.
139. *Rot. Scot.*, ii.143–4.
140. *Foedera*, III.iv.148–9.
141. Robert Bowes, 'The Order and Form of Days of Truce', in Raine, *History and Antiquities of North Durham*, pp. xxii–vii. See also the treatise by Richard Bell, written *c*. 1605, which drew heavily on Bowes' manuscript: 'A Brief Declaration of the Special Heads, Orders, and Forms of the Laws of Marches of Ancient Used Upon the Borders, by the Lords Wardens of England and Scotland at their Meetings and Days of Trewes', printed in Nicolson and Burn, *History and Antiquities of Westmorland and Cumberland*, i.xxiii–xxxviii.
142. PRO E 39/95/2; *Foedera*, III.iv.150–1.
143. The indenture stipulated that the men were compelled to appear for trial under penalty of £3,000 each.
144. PRO E 39/95/11; *Foedera*, III.iv.151–2.
145. PRO E 39/95/3; *Foedera*, III.iv.152–3.
146. BL MS Cotton Vesp. F VII, fo.33. See also Neville, 'Keeping the Peace', pp. 12–13.
147. BL MS Cotton Vesp. F VII, fo.35.
148. BL MS Cotton Vesp. F VII, fo.32.
149. See above, note 130, and Tuck, *Richard II and the English Nobility*, pp. 201–2.
150. PRO C 47/22/11(10).
151. *Rot. Scot.*, ii.145, 147, 149–50.
152. PRO E 199/95/12.
153. PRO E 39/9/11; E 364/32 m.9d; E 364/34 m.4d; E 28/7/35.
154. In a letter dated before 2 November 1399 Henry IV accused the Scots of committing 'tresgrandz et horribles misprisions'. These offences included an attack on Wark castle. BL MS Cotton Vesp. F VII, fo.80; PRO C 81/601(1853). See also *Historia Anglicana*, ii.242.
155. Henry Percy earl of Northumberland was appointed to the warden's office in the autumn of 1399. *Rot. Scot.*, ii.151, 152; PRO E 404/15/46, 52.
156. BL MS Cotton Vesp. F VII, fos.68, 77, 79, 100; PRO E 364/33 m.3d.
157. PRO JUST 3/169 mm.33, 34d, 37d, 38, 38d, 39d, 42d, 43, 43d.
158. Neville, 'Law of Treason', pp. 7–14.
159. *CPR*, 1381–5, p. 135. The findings of a similar inquest are noted ibid., pp. 137–8.
160. *Rot. Scot.*, ii.48, 49–50.

161. Ibid., ii.50.
162. Ibid., ii.65–6.
163. Neville, 'War, Crime and Local Communities', pp. 211–12.
164. *Rot. Scot.*, ii.79.
165. Ibid., ii.79. See Summerson, 'Early Development', p. 38.
166. *Rot. Scot.*, ii.81. It was in an attempt to limit opportunities for spying and treasonable collusion that the English and Scottish wardens agreed in June 1386 to impose severe restrictions on communication between their subjects. See above, p. 76.
167. PRO E 404/16/695.
168. PRO SC 8/62(3083), cited in Summerson, 'Early Development', p. 36.
169. See above, references at notes 89, 90, 93, 94, 101; *Rot. Scot.*, ii.37.
170. The involvement of the northern noble families in incidents of truce-breaking is discussed at length in Tuck, 'Richard II and the Border Magnates', pp. 29–33; Tuck, 'Northumbrian Society', pp. 33–9; Campbell, 'England, Scotland and the Hundred Years War', pp. 206–7, 212–13; Miller, *War in the North*, pp. 15–17.
171. Neville, 'Law of Treason', pp. 7–13.
172. PRO KB 9/144 m.56; JUST 3/54/1 m.6; JUST 3/176 m.20.
173. PRO C 54/235 m.5.
174. PRO C 47/22/7(67).
175. PRO KB 27/479 m.32d (Rex). See also above, p. 76.
176. Fraser, *Northern Petitions*, ii. nos.116, 117; *Rot. Parl.*, iii.129; *CCR*, 1381–5, pp. 83–4.
177. *CCR*, 1381–5, p. 182.
178. The development of conciliar jurisdiction and the growth of other courts at the expense of the common law during the reign of Richard II are vast subjects. See, for example, *Select Cases before the King's Council, 1243–1482*, pp. xv–xlvi; Baldwin, *King's Council in England*, pp. 262–306; *Select Pleas in the Court of Admiralty*, pp. xv–xl, xlviii–lvii; Squibb, *High Court of Chivalry*, pp. 17–25. During John of Gaunt's period as lieutenant the Chancery of the duchy of Lancaster adjudicated an incident involving the unlawful seizure of Scottish goods by the men of Chester. See PRO DL 37/3 no.54.
179. NRO ZSW 1/101, 102.
180. PRO KB 27/481 m.31d (Rex).
181. *Rot. Parl.*, iii.255–6.
182. The earl's relations with Richard II in 1387–8 are discussed in Tuck, *Richard II and the English Nobility*, pp. 117–18.
183. PRO SC 8/62(3083).
184. PRO C 47/22/7(67).
185. See above, p. 75.
186. Storey, 'The Wardens of the English Marches', pp. 593–615.
187. Steel, *Receipt of the Exchequer*, p. 138.
188. PRO DURH 3/32 m.4.
189. PRO E 101/40/30.
190. Turnbull, *Buik of the Croniclis of Scotland*, iii.394.
191. *Chron. Angliae*, p. 327.

5

Interlude: The Early Lancastrian Years, 1399–1424

The history of late medieval northern England in the early fifteenth century is inextricably bound up with the fortunes of the Percy family, who, according to the chronicler John Harding, 'have the hertes of the people by north and ever had'.[1] Studies of the first years of Henry IV's reign have invariably focused closely on the growing disaffection between the crown and its most powerful northern subject, and on the violent consequences of their disagreement, the Percies' rebellion in 1403. In the area of foreign policy, the machinations of the duke of Albany (regent of the kingdom from 1402 to 1420) to control the Scottish government, first by ousting his rival, the duke of Rothesay, then by preventing the return from captivity in England of his king, James I, have likewise dominated accounts of the relations between the realms. The border lands of northern England and southern Scotland, for several generations already a testing ground for competing claims of the two crowns, throughout the fifteenth century remained crucial in diplomatic relations of Henry IV and Henry V with the Scottish rulers. Since the late fourteenth century they had also become the locus of what has been called a 'war of chivalry' between noble families of either realm, whose campaigns for booty, plunder and ransom only occasionally coincided with royal policies.[2]

The prominent place occupied by the border lands in the context of late medieval politics is reflected, too, in the history of the laws and customs of the marches. By 1399, the legal procedures unique to the border lands were much more than a mere miscellany of practices to which local men gave nodding acquaintance: Edward III's warden–conservators and those of his grandson had erected them into a code of law capable of responding in effective fashion to the many offences peculiar to the frontier region, and the tribunals in which these practices obtained both complemented and supplemented the working of English common law. Despite the difficulties posed by Richard II's attempts to exert firm control over the men who held the office of warden, border legal practices had achieved the status of a system of law, complete with a hallowed and proven tradition, a body of written record, and a legitimate purpose. The fifteenth century by and large witnessed the maturation of border legal practices and principles. Early Tudor monarchs were well aware that the reforms they effected in the legal administration of the north owed much to the process of development and refinement that had occurred under their predecessors, and under Henry VI and Richard III in particular. When an elusive and long-awaited peace between England and Scotland was finally achieved in 1502 one of the most significant aspects of the agreement was the inclusion, among the sealed indentures that collectively constituted the formal record of the treaty, of a comprehensive statement of the laws and customs governing cross-border dispute settlement.[3]

But if the system of border law survived the turbulent political conditions of the fifteenth century, it did so in spite of the policies of the early Lancastrian kings, rather than as a result of any positive efforts on their part. The period 1399–1424 is a difficult one to trace in the history of the law, not least because under Henry IV and Henry V the 'Scottish problem' assumed wholly new dimensions. Both kings were intent on isolating the Scots from their French allies, and both sought to dominate the smaller realm chiefly by reviving the long dormant claim to English lordship over Scotland that previous monarchs had been compelled to admit was doomed to failure. During the reigns of Henry IV and V, negotiations for peace or truce were invariably tied to recognition by the Scots of their subject status. Not surprisingly, the latter were in no wise prepared to make such a submission. One of the most serious consequences of the diplomatic débâcle caused by the early Lancastrians' ill-timed resurrection of Edward I's ambitions was stagnation in the development of the legal procedures that had been so vigorous under their predecessors. The rising of the Percies against Henry IV in the first decade of the fifteenth century further dislocated the smooth functioning of the border tribunals, for the fourteenth century had demonstrated that these courts of law could not operate independent of strong local leadership.

Finally, intense rivalry among border magnates themselves disrupted the effective operation of the law. During the period 1400–1409 the Douglas family clashed in the field with its ancient rivals, the Percies of Northumberland, now joined by the Scottish earl of March, following the latter's defection to the English in 1400. For several years after 1402, prominent Scottish border lords were in English captivity, leaving the courts on the Scottish side of the border poorly led and only minimally organised. The earls of Douglas, Fife and others were joined in captivity in England in 1406 by their king, James I, seized while *en route* to France. Sessions of the border tribunals might have been convened in the absence of the local Scottish lords if Percy himself had not fallen foul of his king in 1403. As a result of these many incidents 'Anglo-Scottish relations were left in topsy-turvy turmoil'.[4] The system of border law, which depended ultimately on a balance of power between the realms and on the ability of both English and Scottish wardens to rise above national and personal quarrels, could not bear the burden of so many stresses. Already in 1411–12, when John of Lancaster, warden of the east march, wrote to the council decrying the state of near anarchy that obtained in the region, he criticised the crown as much for its lack of attention to the integrity of the march tribunals as he did its parsimony in paying his soldiers.[5] His observations still held true a decade and more later.

The precarious existence of the border courts in the early Lancastrian years is most readily apparent in the nature of the written materials that survive in respect of their business. The variety and richness of Exchequer and Chancery records characteristic of the second half of the fourteenth century are nowhere in evidence; in their stead is a patchy collection of mundane and ambiguous references. Almost all are found in the colourless documents that record payments made to royal messengers, and most describe meetings that were fruitless encounters between ambassadors, rather than sessions of the warden-conservators' courts.[6] The stream of petitions to Chancery and the regular issue of commissions of oyer and terminer or commissions to punish violations of the truce with which complaints had formerly been met, and which make it possible to trace the resolution of specific disputes during the reigns of Edward III and Richard II, disappear almost altogether. Even the chroniclers, who had begun to take notice of the march-tribunals in the 1370s – if only to deride the Scots – are, for the most part, silent in respect of the courts in the early fifteenth century.[7] The scanty survival of march-related record materials alone suggests that, for the first time since the reign of Edward I, the effectiveness of the cross-border system of dispute settlement reached a nadir.

Other extant evidence conveys a similar impression. Privy council records of the early fifteenth century indicate that, while Scottish affairs greatly preoccupied the king and his ministers, the crown's interests in promoting legal practices that would facilitate meetings between warden-conservators from the two realms were firmly subordinated to diplomatic efforts designed to secure recognition by the Scots of English overlordship, and to related discussions concerning the military preparedness of the northern counties.[8] The fortuitous survival of a large body of early fifteenth-century correspondence (including a series of letters between the English council and John duke of Lancaster while the latter was warden) has done much to illuminate the difficulties experienced by royal agents in the north.[9] But the letters also chronicle in unambiguous fashion the near collapse of the border courts under Henry IV. His successor, Henry V, promised an extensive investigation of violations of several Anglo-Scottish truces prior to his departure for Normandy in the spring of 1415, but otherwise demonstrated an equal lack of concern to promote the frequent holding of days of march. Indeed, the legislation he enacted beginning in 1414 in respect of truce-time infractions acted as a serious check on the continued growth of border law. It was not until the minority of Henry VI that the English crown awoke to the realisation that, in permitting the days of march to fall into abeyance, the early Lancastrians had created more trouble with the Scots than they had avoided. The minority of the baby king promised to be of long duration, and after 1424 the English no longer enjoyed the diplomatic advantage against Scotland represented by the captivity of its king, James I. Together, these conditions finally created the impetus for restoration of the days of march as normal venues for the resolution of cross-border grievances. There began then a new period of revival and rehabilitation of the procedures that collectively made up border law. As had occurred a century earlier, border practices survived a period of desuetude, and stagnation had the effect of injecting renewed vitality and vigour into the ancient customs of the marches.

Events in England in the summer of 1399 caused a great deal of consternation north of the border; Walter Bower gleefully noted that the conspiracy of the 'three Henries' (Lancaster, Northumberland and Hotspur) succeeded because 'the crowd are moved by easy-going fickleness'.[10] The Scots were quick to take advantage of Lancaster's coup. The belligerence that had been manifested late in the reign of Richard II was given added impetus, and the northerners experienced afresh the terrors of cross-border reiving. A letter sent to the Scots by Henry of Lancaster before his coronation requesting observance of the current truce was answered with only vague assurances from Robert III's regent, the duke of Rothesay.[11] The Scots' true intentions were revealed in an attack launched on the castle of Wark. Its keeper, Sir Thomas Grey, later claimed that the raiders had burned his fortress, carried off goods and chattels valued at 2,000 marks, and set his children and tenants to a collective ransom of £1000.[12] This affront, together with Rothesay's refusal to address him by his royal title, appear to have driven Henry IV to a decision to make war on the Scots.[13] For the time being he was urged by the commons in parliament to bide his time; meanwhile, Sir Robert Umfraville's exploits in the north were ideally suited to the king's needs in these early months of the reign. In a skirmish fought at Fulhope Law he captured several border reivers, including the notorious fugitives Willie Barde and Adam lord of Gordon.[14] In December he appointed commissioners whom he instructed to travel to Kelso early in the new year to treat for truce.[15] Around the same time he wrote again to Robert III, criticising the 'great and horrible' offences committed by the latter's subjects (including the sons of the wardens themselves), but indicating his willingness to send commissioners to discuss the 'pacification' of the borders.[16] But Henry's missive reached the Scottish court too late for Rothesay to do anything about a meeting, and in mid-February Henry openly welcomed the defection of George Dunbar earl of March, thereby committing himself to a renewal of English hostilities against the Scots.[17] Another letter under the seal of Robert III, in which Rothesay blandly reminded Henry that 'you were previously well disposed to reform and redress' English violations of the truce, was ignored.[18] In February a great council warned of continued Scottish raids in the north and of rumours of an invasion; by the late spring commissions of array had been issued and an army ordered to assemble by mid-summer in Newcastle.[19]

Nevertheless, Henry IV did not immediately abandon altogether the possibility of seeking reparation for recent truce-time atrocities. The commission of 10 December 1399 in which Sir Thomas Grey, Master Alan Newark and Jean d'Artois were instructed to travel to Kelso raised afresh the troublesome matter of appropriate meeting places for commissioners from either realm, a diplomatic débâcle that Richard II had thought it well advised to drop.[20] But a series of instructions to these men, undated but probably issued soon after the December commission, suggests that the king had not excluded altogether a session of the border courts: the commissioners were specifically ordered to discover 'if it is the intention of the Scots to make redress for the attempts done since Michaelmas last', and to report to council on the amenability of the warden to the convening of a tribunal.[21] The meeting arranged for 5 January 1400 at Kelso never occurred, but at least one of the king's agents, Alan Newark, considered it worth the effort to travel to the marches.[22]

Henry IV's summoning of a host prevented further *rapprochement* with the Scots over the question of redress and reparation. If, indeed, Henry had considered supporting the continuance of border tribunals, that notion had been abandoned by summer in favour of armed confrontation. When the Scots predictably refused to acknowledge his sudden claim to lordship over Scotland the king marched his army northwards. His costly campaign gained him nothing, and the matter of feudal superiority did little more than aggravate relations between the realms for several years to come.[23] The Scots were interested in nothing less than a peace with England based on the treaty that Robert Bruce had secured in 1328, in which the sovereignty of the smaller realm was acknowledged.[24] Henry IV's refusal to consider those terms had an effect on border law similar to that which had obtained in the early fourteenth century: denial of the sovereign status of Scotland entailed also the refusal to recognise or support a system of law that distinguished the march lands of both realms, and acknowledged their quasi-independence from the normal machinery of the common law. Henry may have deliberately modelled his actions on those of his predecessor, Edward I, whose records of the Great Cause he later had searched, and who had also considered the existence of a body of border law inimical to his feudal interests.[25]

Henry made careful provision for the defence of the region soon after his coronation by restoring Henry Percy earl of Northumberland to the wardenship of the west march, and by renewing the indenture under which Percy' son, Hotspur, had served since 1396 in the east march.[26] The newly won allegiance of George Dunbar earl of March brought with it possession of several important border fortresses.[27] For several months after the failed expedition to Scotland the king took pains to ensure that his officials were regularly paid for their services in maintaining garrisons in key strongholds,[28] but the clause in the wardenial commissions granting the Percies authority to redress violations of the truce was for all intents and purposes a dead letter. A brief armistice was arranged in November, and renewed in December, and the earl of Northumberland was ordered to prohibit all inhabitants of the English marches, under pain of forfeiture, from violating the truce.[29] The king appears to have been more than willing to overlook his own injunctions when he purchased the custody of two Scottish travellers taken 'at sea in the water near the marches of Scotland',[30] but in the border lands themselves, Percy found it advisable to regulate closely all communication between the subjects of either realm. It was perhaps on his advice that, in February 1401, the crown issued commissions designed to prohibit the passage of foodstuffs, grain and cloth into Scotland,[31] and it was certainly on his initiative that six Englishmen were sentenced to death by a wardenial court 'by reason of their treason' shortly thereafter.[32]

Despite a steady exchange of diplomatic delegations throughout the spring and summer of 1401 and the establishment of a brief truce,[33] peace talks did not resume until October.[34] In a large and elaborately attended meeting held at Kirk Yetholm, Henry's determination to win recognition of English lordship over the realm of Scotland once again dominated discussions. The instructions he issued to his ambassadors made no mention of the resumption of the border tribunals, though this might have provided an opportunity for *rapprochement*, as they had so often done before.[35] Indeed, in the midst of the 'undiplomatic language' that was exchanged at Kirk Yetholm, neither side could come to an agreement even about the renewal of truce.[36] Archibald earl of Douglas's request that the current armistice (due to expire in November) be prolonged was refused;[37] he later complained that an agreement he had made with the earl of Northumberland to hold a day of march for the redress of offences committed by both sides had been annulled 'by default of the said earl'.[38] Percy had, in fact, made a written agreement of truce with Archibald Douglas in the summer of 1401, but there is no indication that the meeting had also sought to provide redress for specific incidents of cross-border crime. Henry IV, for his part, held Douglas responsible for the discord expressed at the march day.[39] After the breakdown of the talks at Kirk Yetholm the matter of blame became moot, and soon Douglas resumed hostilities in the eastern march with an invasion of Northumberland. There followed several months of raid and counter-raid, culminating in the battle fought at Homildon Hill in September 1402.[40]

The encounter at Homildon may well have 'wiped out the English reverse at Otterburn',[41] but it ushered in a period of profound distress and dislocation in the marches. Already in the summer of 1402 Henry Percy had hinted that failure to make due payments of the wages owed him as warden was causing 'great peril to the country, displeasure to us and comfort to our enemies'.[42] By the spring of 1403 his demands for prompt remuneration had become more strident,[43] and to those grievances had been added a host of others. These included the complaint that the crown was unfairly favouring the earl of Westmorland in the allocation of the ransoms of Scottish prisoners taken at Homildon Hill,[44] opposition to Henry IV's policy of dealing with the Welsh rebel Owen Glendower, and the impression – not altogether mistaken – that Ralph Neville was gaining an ascendancy in the marches that might overshadow that of the Percy family.[45] The rebellion of the earl of Northumberland in 1403 removed the most experienced and the ablest of the crown's agents in the northern marches, as well as its most capable justice in cross-border dispute settlement. The intermittent holding of days of truce thereafter, and the poor record of restitution and compensation for truce-time atrocities made by both English and Scottish commissioners bore witness to the absence of Percy influence.

The earl of Northumberland was replaced as warden in the west march by Ralph Neville earl of Westmorland, and Hotspur in the east by John duke of Lancaster, the son of Henry IV.[46] The former brought to his position a great deal of experience in border administration and the weight of a major northern landholder, but despite his best efforts, the latter's tenure of office was deeply troubled. The duke was assiduous during his years as warden in ensuring that Henry IV and his council were kept closely informed about the state of the border lands, and his letters provide articulate and invaluable descriptions of the bleak conditions under which he and his fellow northerners laboured in the first years of the fifteenth century. But he awakened only belatedly to the crucial role that regular sessions of the march tribunals might play in the settlement of border-related troubles, and when he eventually did so, he experienced considerable difficulty in convincing the crown of their merits.

Diplomatic discussions with Scotland were resumed in the summer of 1403,[47] but it was not until 1404 that negotiators agreed to a renewal of the truce.[48] A thaw in Anglo-Scottish relations, however, was apparent by mid-summer 1404,

when Henry IV granted licence to Sir Thomas Grey to avenge the raid on Wark
castle by means of a judicial duel, to be held at Carlisle.[49] An indenture sealed in
July at Pontefract made the *rapprochement* more explicit. The agreement provided
for a truce to run until Easter 1405, in accordance with the terms made in 1398
between the dukes of Lancaster and Rothesay.[50] Both sides, however, acknowledged that the earlier truce 'contenet certaine clauses and termes, the which semen
obscure and derke to the understandyng of some men', and each agreed that a day
of truce should be held at which commissioners appointed by the crowns should
'make declaration of the forsaide clauses and termes'. The 'obscure and dark'
clauses no doubt related both to the disagreements concerning appropriate border
meeting places that had divided the parties since the time of Richard II, and the
status of the lands of the earl of March, whose claims to Scottish territory were
maintained despite his defection to the English allegiance.[51] These were issues that
could not be resolved in a single meeting. But the indenture also included provision
for a revival of the border tribunals, where reparation for recent offences might be
adjudicated. Both Henry IV and Albany formally indicated their readiness to abide
by the terms of the agreement forged at Pontefract.[52] The Prince of Wales, too,
expressed his relief at the suspension of hostilities and his opinion that the time for
armistice was well chosen.[53] The day of truce, the first of Henry IV's reign, was
held, as arranged, at Haddenstank.

After such a long period of animosity, it was perhaps predictable that the
meeting should have accomplished very little. The English succeeded in securing
from the Scots payment of certain 'obligations' made to the former warden of the
east march, Henry Percy, but little more.[54] They appear to have offered nothing in
return, and the session broke up with agents of both sides frustrated and angry.
Confidence in the ability of border legal procedures to effect the equitable
resolution of grievances was further eroded in December, when a Scottish ship
was captured by English pirates in Scottish waters, and towed to Lindisfarne. Only
a day after the incident the duke of Albany notified Henry IV of his great concern at
this overt breach of the truce,[55] and within a few weeks the king was bombarded
with a series of demands by Albany and his envoys that the offence be adjudicated
in accordance with the laws of the marches. Albany himself, Henry Wardlaw
bishop of St Andrews, Sir David Fleming and the earl of Crawford all complained
that Robert Umfraville, one of the conservators of the truce, had refused to take
action in respect of the matter, and all warned the king of his sworn obligation to
observe the terms of the current armistice.[56]

Henry IV was too preoccupied with troubles in Wales and Guyenne and with
rumours of the appearance of Richard II north of the border to devote his attention
to what he considered a commonplace occurrence.[57] The duke of Lancaster, warden
of the east march, summoned a conference of march lords, at which Umfraville may
have been asked to defend his complaisance in dealing with the Scots' grievance, but
emphasis in the meeting was laid clearly on the defence of the border region rather
than on maintenance of the truce by means of effective dispute settlement.[58] The earl
of Northumberland, temporarily restored to royal favour and now warden of Berwick

castle, appears to have been alone in arguing the wisdom of tempering belligerent words with a show of goodwill towards the Scots. He succeeded in convincing the king that a day of march should be held for the redress of cross-border grievances, and a meeting was proposed for 24 March 1405. The Scots' attempts to delay the assembly until June were, however, heavily criticised by Lancaster. Although a hastilude held at Smithfield between English and Scottish champions in the late spring presaged a thaw in relations,[59] the meeting never took place.[60] Henry's instructions to envoys dispatched to Haddenstank reveal that recognition of English claims to lands in lowland Scotland remained of much greater importance to him than the restoration of the border tribunals.[61]

By mid-summer 1405 the Scottish baronage and the Douglas family in particular had begun to oppose Albany's ineffectual attempts to repair relations with England. When fresh complaint about the seizure of a Scottish ship was ignored,[62] Albany lost whatever support he had enjoyed at home.[63] The earl of Douglas's younger brother, James, now warden of the east march of Scotland, led an assault against Berwick, leaving the town ablaze. Although Albany hurriedly sent an apology for the offence to Henry IV,[64] Douglas displayed no remorse. In a remarkable letter addressed to Henry he admitted full responsibility for the attack, and informed the king that it had been committed in retaliation for the 'brennyng slachtyr and takyng of prisoners and Scottis schippis', in respect of which repeated requests for redress and compensation had been ignored. He noted astutely that the English wardens, Henry IV and the duke of Albany himself, had demonstrated little interest in adhering to the terms of the current armistice governing the appropriate and lawful settlement of truce-time violations. Until such time as those provisions were observed, there would be no reduction in border violence. Douglas's accusations of English atrocities committed of late against Scottish subjects constituted a lengthy list, probably exaggerated, but not altogether fictitious.[65] Even if only a few were accurate Henry IV had indeed been guilty of losing touch with the extent to which good order in the border lands had degenerated under his wardens.

In July the current truce was extended until Easter 1406,[66] but Douglas's warnings went unheeded. John of Lancaster's letters to the English council continued to stress the need for large sums to pay soldiers and to provide arms and victuals for the garrisons of northern fortresses over the allocation of funds as compensation for cross-border offences.[67] Henry IV's response to his son's repeated requests for money similarly revealed the crown's lack of interest in the revitalisation of the march tribunals. No conservators of the new truce were appointed, and a grant of November 1405 specifically directed that a portion of the revenues generated by a forthcoming clerical tenth from the province of York be delivered to the wardens specifically for the payment of their outstanding wages and those of their soldiers.[68] Neither the Scottish nor the English wardens chose to abide by the truce, and by autumn the Scots were committing fresh assaults against English ships off the coast of Northumberland.[69]

The capture of the young king, James I, in March 1406 greatly altered the balance of power in Anglo–Scottish relations, much as that of David II had done sixty years earlier. For the duration of his reign, Henry IV was able to 'display a certain assurance in his dealings with the Scots';[70] in effect, James's presence in England, together with the continued captivity of important noblemen taken at Homildon Hill, made it possible to avoid addressing in forthright manner the problems of the border lands and to concentrate on troubles elsewhere. In Scotland, Albany's machinations to maintain control of the regency and the royal prerogative meant that border incidents and their resolution were rendered of secondary importance. There settled over the region an uneasy peace, but one that was perpetuated with few interruptions from 1406 until 1413.[71]

John duke of Lancaster remained wary of the Scottish wardens and suspicious of their commitment to the truce. He was beginning, however, to appreciate the consequences of the crown's lack of attention to the conventions that had hitherto brought commissioners from both realms together in the days of march. In the summer of 1406 he wrote to the council a long memorandum, in which he described the many hardships under which he laboured in an effort to maintain a semblance of order in the north: 'the inhabitants of the marches of both realms daily commit armed incursion, robberies, pillages, prises of prisoners, cattle raids, raids on goods and other acts of war'. Neither side, he reported, made any attempt to seek or give redress for these acts; in consequence, the king's lieges were placed in great danger.[72] He recommended that the crown immediately appoint conservators of the truce, but then devoted a large portion of his missive to a plea for the reinforcement of border garrisons. Council's response to the first part of the memorandum was little more than a vague promise to refer the matter to the king.[73] Two years later Lancaster was still requesting extensive financial provision for the defence of key border castles, but in this later report there is apparent a still greater awareness on the part of the warden that defensive preparations alone were inadequate to ensure the security of the region. Echoing in unwitting but uncanny fashion the charges that had earlier been made by James Douglas, he pointed out that the Scots had little reason to offer restitution for the offences they were committing 'because nothing has been assigned or ordained in respect of appointing deputies to make redress for the offences and misprisions done against the truce' on the part of the English.[74]

Lancaster's concerns about the lawlessness of the border region were not overly pessimistic. Although the years 1406–8 saw the increased traffic of Scottish pilgrims to English shrines and some relaxation of trade restrictions against Scottish merchants,[75] it was apparent that disturbances in the border lands were exacting a heavy toll on the inhabitants of the region. Petitions from northern religious houses, great and small, confirm Lancaster's impressions that landed revenues had diminished considerably of late, and there are indications that lay landowners, too, were suffering from a pervasive sense of unease in the borders. The tiny priory of Hexham complained that its church, manors, granges and tenantries were worth almost nothing because of the burning and destruction suffered of late; in despair, its prior sought to make a separate peace with the Scots, only to be condemned as a traitor by the archbishop of York.[76] Similar laments were heard in petitions for favour and compensation submitted by the abbot of Holmcultram, the bishop of Durham, and by the lords of Wark, Otterburn and Harbottle.[77] Local sentiment, moreover, remained widely distrustful of and antagonistic towards the movement of Scottish subjects through the border lands: a petition by the commons in parliament in 1406 complained of the flow of false Scottish coin into the realm, and requested that all those found in possession of such money 'incur the penalty of life and limb'.[78]

Lancaster's calls for the restoration of the cross-border tribunals were finally heeded in 1409. The impetus for the crown's change of heart appears to have been triggered by the seizure of a heavily laden ship by Alexander Stewart earl of Mar, and a retaliatory sea-borne attack on several Scottish vessels by Sir Robert Umfraville.[79] The level of disorder that had for so long been a feature of the border lands was now threatening to spread in uncontrolled fashion to the high seas, and to involve many more Englishmen than the inhabitants of a remote frontier region. A recent attack by Scottish *mediocres* on Jedburgh castle, moreover, was an indication that the brief respite from Scottish harassment in the north had ended.[80] By late spring or early summer envoys sent to Haddenstank to negotiate for the prolongation of the current truce were specifically authorised to address the matter of restitution for English attacks on the Scottish march lands.[81] In November claims arising from recent piratical incidents were heard.[82] Prompted by calls in parliament to make adequate provision for the peace and security of the marches,[83] the redress of border-related offences was again made the subject of discussion by commissioners from England and Scotland in 1410, 1411 and 1412.[84]

It is difficult to assess the success of these officials in making satisfactory and effective settlement of grievances said to have occurred in the marches of either realm. Although the privy council devoted considerable time to a discussion of the allocation of funds to the wardens from the tenths and fifteenths granted in parliament, its members did not make explicit provision for some portion of those monies to be set aside for the purpose of making redress and compensation.[85] Particulars of the accounts submitted by Sir Richard Redman and Master Richard Holm, commissioned as conservators of the truce in 1409, for two journeys to the border region made the following spring, reveal that they were paid only for the expenses they incurred on their travels.[86] If they or their fellows made formal arrangements for the payment of compensation for truce-time offences these obligations have left no trace in extant record. Complaints arising from sea-borne incidents appear to have been adjudicated with greater efficiency, but their resolution was entrusted not to the conservators of the truce, but to special commissioners.[87]

The exclusion of incidents of piracy from the purview of the crown's march officials was perhaps a consequence of the influence now being exercised in the royal council by Henry Prince of Wales, who would, almost as soon as he succeeded his father, make lawlessness on the high seas a matter of close royal interest.[88] But it must also be understood as but one aspect of Henry IV's neglect of the whole subject of law and order in the northern border lands. The indentures of truce sealed during his reign specifically hearkened back to the agreements that had been made in the reign of Richard II at Haddenstank in 1398 and Leulinghen in 1389, neither of which had addressed clearly the question of breaches of the truce done on the high seas. Provision in respect of such offences remained *ad hoc* throughout Henry IV's reign, and was not made the subject of specific legislation and royal policy until that of his successor.[89]

As noted earlier, John of Lancaster's experience as warden of the east march led him to observe a correspondence between the demise of the Anglo-Scottish tribunals and the general level of cross-border crime. By 1408 he was increasingly of the opinion that truces were so poorly kept 'that it would appear that war is about to begin'.[90] With the virtual abandonment of the days of march northerners who had suffered deprivation and bodily harm at the hands of the Scots were denied the opportunity to seek restitution and compensation for their losses, and Lancaster's dire warnings to Henry IV's council were no doubt heavily influenced by widespread disappointment at that loss.

The common-law courts, however, could be used to pursue at least some offenders, and the gaol delivery rolls that survive from Henry IV's reign suggest that plaintiffs found there an acceptable alternative to the border courts for the pursuit of felons who took advantage of the disturbed state of local affairs at the expense of their fellow subjects. The justices of assize who sat in Newcastle, in particular, regularly presided over the trials of suspects accused of colluding in crime with the king's Scottish enemies. Northumberland jurors demonstrated their intolerance of such behaviour in clear and unambiguous terms when they framed indictments that charged suspects not merely with felony, but with the more serious offence of treason. One of the indictments filed against the Northumberland man, Thomas Russell, for example, noted that 'together with others, he treasonably seized William Emson, the king's liege man, at Fawden, led him as far as Cocklaws, and there set him to a ransom of £40'.[91] Thomas Maundore, accused of selling stolen horses and saddles to the Scots, was said to be 'a common thief and traitor to the lord king'.[92] That sessions of gaol delivery were, in some circumstances, the only venues available for the trial and punishment of dangerous cross-border criminals in the reign of Henry IV is suggested by the presence before justices of assize in August 1411 of two men accused of treasonably delivering the castles of Roxburgh and Jedburgh to the Scottish enemy.[93] Elsewhere in the border lands ecclesiastical lords exercised an authority intended to supplement and complement that of the common law in such matters. The deprivation of the prior of Hexham by the archbishop of York in 1408 after the former was found guilty of 'receiving and cherishing' the king's enemies has already been noted.[94] In the liberties belonging to the bishop of Durham and the prior of Tynemouth, too, such felons were pursued by means of the bishop's justices.[95]

The northerners, however, ultimately found their reliance on visitations of the king's justices of assize for the prosecution and punishment of border-related offences to be problematic. Although an act of parliament of 1382 had specifically enjoined twice-yearly sessions throughout the shire towns of the northern circuit,[96] the king's justices still travelled to Newcastle, Carlisle and Appleby only once annually at best, and their visits were fraught with danger.[97] Wardenial commissions continued to include, as they had done since 1399, a clause directing these officials to convene tribunals to make inquiry concerning all those believed to have committed offences in violation of the truce, and to punish them in appropriate fashion.[98] Some of the indentures by which the wardens were engaged similarly made provision for them to retain 'a third part of the prisoners' [ransoms] and other profits of war' devolving from the office,[99] perhaps an oblique reference to revenues derived from the wardenial courts. But there has survived virtually no evidence by which to observe the workings of these courts in the reign of Henry IV. The earl of Northumberland's execution of several march traitors in 1401 has been noted;[100] thereafter the records are silent. Even the few surviving accounts submitted to the Exchequer by the wardens during their tenure of office make no mention of revenues derived from the exercise of their judicial authority.[101] These officials, it would seem, remained important agents of the crown in the defence of the north and in maintaining its readiness for war, but they were compelled to commit the punishment of truce-breakers to other royal officials and to abandon almost altogether English efforts to seek compensation for truce-time atrocities.[102]

The problem of the north was addressed in only piecemeal fashion by Henry IV. In 1410, in an address to parliament Bishop Henry Beaufort identified the poor observance of the Anglo-Scottish truces as one of the most serious causes of disorder in the frontier region.[103] In the same session the commons complained that riots and lawlessness disturbed the king's peace throughout the realm, and noted that the northernmost counties suffered especially from such disturbances.[104] The king promised to appoint a series of commissions of oyer and terminer in an effort to respond positively to the petition, but none was dispatched northwards, and the borderers soon claimed that the justices had so feared the violence of armed men and the king's Scottish enemies that they had been powerless to effect any change there.[105] A petition presented in parliament the following year emphasised anew the twin evils consequent on the demise of the border tribunals and the temerity of the king's justices: responsibility for the indictment of felons in Northumberland had fallen almost exclusively to the coroners and sheriffs, said to be amenable to corruption or easily circumvented by the lords of the numerous northern liberties. The refusal of the king's justices to travel to a county 'so far distant from the law' had virtually suspended the operation of the common law, 'to the great destruction and annihilation of the land'.[106]

These complaints were not exaggerated. In 1410 a Northumberland man notorious for his activities in assisting Scottish ransom-takers was released from custody when justices of gaol delivery ruled that his offences had been committed in the liberty of Hexham, outside the jurisdiction of their commission.[107] For a decade already other cross-border criminals had sought, and won, the assistance of their lords in obtaining pardon for their misdeeds under the terms of the general pardons granted by Henry IV.[108] As in 1410, Henry's response in 1411 to the complaints of the northerners was a promise to appoint justices of oyer and terminer to make inquisition in respect of troublemakers, and a conventional undertaking to see to it that the statutes concerning the common law were observed. Despite their trepidation, justices of assize mustered sufficient courage to travel through the northern counties in the late summer of 1411, but they do not appear to have returned there during the remainder of the reign. Moreover, their commissions did not empower them to deal with the kind of business that had occupied officials at the days of truce in the previous reign. A report by John of Lancaster to the royal council in 1412 stated baldly that the neglect suffered by the inhabitants of the marches in respect of the observance of the armistice was of such long standing that vigorous reform had become utterly necessary to forestall the 'final desolation and destruction' of the region.[109] When Henry IV died in March 1413 very little progress had been made in reducing the lawlessness of the northern frontier lands, and the future of the border tribunals remained uncertain.

Edward Powell's cautious suggestion that 'it would perhaps be too much to speak of a 'crisis of order' in 1413' fundamentally underestimates the mood of pessimism that pervaded the northern border lands at the accession of the new king.[110] Diplomatic relations with Scotland remained tense, and Henry V had good reason to expect the forging of a Franco-Scottish alliance designed to force the release of Scottish prisoners still captive in England (most especially James I) and the escalation of raids into the already impoverished marches of the kingdom.[111] At the first parliament of the reign, convened in May, the chancellor, Bishop Beaufort, once again spoke in general terms of the royal obligation to impose good order on the kingdom and to resist all enemies; the commons were more blunt in reminding Henry of his father's poor record in accomplishing these ideals.[112]

The volatile conditions of the frontier region were not lost on the king, but he considered them to be only one aspect of a plethora of problems that required immediate attention. In the short term it was advisable first to provide for the security and defence of the north. Although the Scots had agreed in 1412 to a suspension of hostilities until Easter 1418,[113] and Henry V intended to abide by the terms of that truce, there was little confidence within the English council in the duke of Albany's ability (or wish) to prevent a resumption of the war by his own border magnates. Plans for the reinforcement of the fensible men at the disposal of the wardens and the renewal of the indentures according to which custodians of key fortresses served under them were discussed, and the commissions empowering the wardens themselves renewed.[114] The Scots, however, seemed amenable to a truce, and by the end of the summer their envoys had made arrangements to renew formal negotiations for an armistice and for the release of James I. The latter remained a matter of discussion and debate – as it would, indeed, until well after the death of Henry V – but a brief truce was proclaimed in September.[115] These talks did not, however, include a resumption of sessions of the cross-border tribunals. Henry V, like his father, was prepared to equip his wardens with all the military authority they needed to defend the marches against Scottish incursions; to this end, he demonstrated impressive far-sightedness in 1416 in restoring Henry Hotpur's son and heir to the Percy family's lands and prominence in the north.[116] But like his father, too, he had little interest in promoting the existence in the marches of a system of law that acknowledged both implicitly and explicitly the independent and equal status of the Scottish kingdom.[117] It was his belief that the common-law courts had functioned as adequate venues for the prosecution of border-related offences in the previous reign. The lack of interest shown in reviving the days of march and the legislation Henry enacted within a year of his accession together signalled his determination to perpetuate the *status quo* established by his predecessor.

Henry was undoubtedly in a position of strength. As long as James I remained in English captivity the Scots were bound to be amenable to diplomatic pressure; dissension north of the border between Albany and his aristocratic opponents over Scotland's demands in ransom negotiations further tipped the balance of power in favour of the English.[118] Henry's tremendous skill in playing a tense game of *Realpolitik* has recently been praised as 'creative', 'innovative' and 'deft'.[119] But Dr Bradley's conclusion that 'what matters is that he was able to confine the war to the border areas and to fight it with local troops'[120] ignores entirely the vital importance that the days of march had assumed in the maintenance of law and order in the north in the course of the later fourteenth century. To the people of the border lands, continually impoverished by and subjected to the terrors of frequent enemy raids, the wardens' authority to seek compensation from the Scots was probably more highly valued than was the military protection they were supposed to ensure. The prosecution of felons at common law afforded the opportunity for Englishmen who suffered loss to revenge themselves against those of their fellows who aided and abetted the enemy, but it was only by means of settlements effected in the cross-border courts that they had any hope of securing material compensation for those losses. John of Lancaster, some years hence, had come to appreciate the esteem in which the people of the north held the days of march. He agreed in 1413 to continue to serve as warden of the east march, hopeful, perhaps, that his calls for a restoration of the courts might be given a more favourable response than they had under Henry IV. He was to be disappointed. Although the commissions in which Lancaster and Ralph Neville were designated wardens continued to stipulate that these officials work for the proper observance of the truce, no conservators were appointed to assist them in the task, and monies paid to Lancaster in the summer of 1413 were assigned specifically to the payment of wages to the warden and his men-at-arms.[121]

Bradley's praise for Henry V's skills in subordinating the problem of the north to the more glamorous pursuit of the French crown echoes similar reassessments by other historians of the king's impressive success in ensuring that the question of public order ceased to be the 'serious political issue' that it had been since the accession of the Lancastrian rulers.[122] While there seems little doubt that by 1422 the crown's image as a champion of law and order throughout the kingdom as a whole had been much enhanced, these assessments also acknowledge, however reluctantly, that Henry's record in northern England in particular was something less than sterling. The king's policies of effecting reconciliation among the garrulous ranks of the aristocracy of the early fifteenth century, then redirecting the belligerence of its members across the Channel were, on the whole, successful in quelling discontent and lawlessness in the Midlands, the south and even in turbulent Wales. But in the north these policies were doomed. The presence of the Scots just across the border required the maintenance of troops – and their unruly commanders – *in situ*. Indeed, the allure of profit and glory in the continental theatre to the fighting men of the borders had the potential to cause more problems in the north than it resolved should too many of them chose to embark for France. The council's generous allocation of funds to border garrisons during the period leading up to the Agincourt expedition was therefore calculated to keep those soldiers content.[123] Though Henry's military preparedness and diplomatic manoeuvrings with the Scots were successful, until 1417 at least, in preventing the large-scale raiding that the borderers had experienced in the previous decade, his actions had very little effect in reducing individual incidents of cross-border crime there or in ameliorating the sense of precariousness that pervaded the northerners' lives.

Henry V's 'campaign' to restore law and order throughout the kingdom began in earnest in the parliament held at Leicester in the spring of 1414.[124] The king was already making preparations for his expedition to France, but the Lollard revolt, an increase in piratical activity and troubles in areas as far apart as Wales, the border region and the Midlands all suggested that while discontent within the realm was so widespread the renewal of war with France was foolhardy and dangerous.[125] The Leicester parliament witnessed an impressive array of legislative activity, including passage of the notorious statute against Lollardy and the revival of commissions of trailbaston designed to suppress disturbances by rioters. In respect of the northern borders, the most significant acts of the assembly were a statute aimed at increasing royal authority in the liberties of Tyndale, Redesdale and Hexham, and another concerned with breach of the truce.[126] Both were promulgated in response to petitions presented by the commons. Both bespoke the determination of Henry V and his counsellors to impose uniformity and procedural regularity in the handling of problems that were, in fact, unique to the border lands. The former soon proved to be a dead letter; the latter had disastrous results.

The statute against outrages in Tyndale, Redesdale and Hexham was intended to address the specific concerns of the people of Northumberland, said to be subjected daily to 'murders, treasons, homicides . . . robberies and other misdeeds' committed by the inhabitants of the liberties. The men of the franchises were also rumoured to give 'shelter and support to many people of Scotland, counselling and comforting them', and to be notorious for colluding with the enemy in incidents of cross-border ransom taking. In Redesdale especially, the sheriff dared not attempt to punish felons 'for fear of death'.[127] The northerners sought remedy for these ills by requesting that felons within the liberties be subjected to the process of outlawry that functioned throughout England, and that the lords of the franchises be compelled more forcefully than they had been to date to ensure the forfeiture and seizure of criminals.

The statute to which Henry V gave his assent undertook to bring these regions more firmly within the purview of the common law. But his compliance was little more than an empty gesture, and it had very little effect on English truce-breakers (and anyone else) who took refuge in the liberties, or on levels of cross-border violence.[128] In 1421 the commons were still lamenting the high levels of disorder in the north generally, and in Tyndale, Redesdale and Hexham especially: thieves and felons known as 'intakers' and 'outputters', they said, remained beyond the jurisdiction of the crown's legal agents.[129] That these unusual terms were employed chiefly in the context of unlawful cross-border activity is clearly illustrated in its frequent use in northern records to describe felons who disposed of stolen goods to the Scottish enemy with a view to sharing with them the profit of the spoils.[130] Despite the legislation aimed against them, intakers and outputters continued to thrive in the northern liberties.

The Statute of Truces, like so many other aspects of Henry V's legislation, has recently been the subject of scrutiny by historians interested in assessing the king's reputation as a ruler who took very seriously his obligation to exercise *bone governance* over his English subjects. These scholars have viewed the statute primarily as a response by the crown to the dangers of piracy in the waters around England. Attacks on the vessels of jurisdictions with which formal truces had been made challenged the authority of the English crown itself. Henry V was no king to brook this kind of challenge: naval incidents created diplomatic rancour, threatened his foreign relations and rendered the seas unsafe for English merchants great and small.[131] The tone of the commons' petition leaves little doubt that its members saw the safeguarding of sea-borne travel as an important goal of the legislation: it referred to incidents in which merchants and travellers were robbed, despoiled and violated 'both on the high seas and in the ports and on the coasts of the sea off England, Ireland and Wales'.[132] The petition also contended that letters of safe conduct were being treated with contempt and their bearers killed, robbed and despoiled; such assaults represented an equally grievous defiance of royal authority.[133] The crown responded to these complaints by agreeing to place in every port a conservator of truces and safe conducts, who would be charged with holding inquests into alleged infractions and authorised to punish by imprisonment and fine (but not by death) all guilty parties. Contravention of the statute was to be deemed high treason, 'done against the king's crown and his dignity', and liable to the severe penalties traditionally imposed for this egregious offence.

The problems associated with the implementation of the new act are also fully appreciated by historians. Henry V never bothered to appoint the port-based conservators; thus, the well regulated inquests promised in the statute were never convened.[134] More onerously, English subjects no longer had recourse to reprisal, for in undertaking such retaliatory actions they now risked prosecution for treason. A petition for repeal of the troublesome legislation was presented in parliament as early as 1415.[135] The following year the crown itself acknowledged the inadequacy of its legislation when it set out procedures according to which victims of breach of the truce or safe conduct might obtain letters of marque. It thus authorised the acts of reprisal it had earlier sought to prevent.[136] In this aspect at least of his programme of reform Henry V failed miserably.

The hardships imposed by the Statute of Truces on the borderers were particularly acute. In the tense atmosphere that had so long characterised the northern marches, subjects of all degrees had for many years depended on the authority inherent in such letters to conduct their business on the perilous roadways that linked the English and Scottish border lands. Because the crown refused to give the wardens the authority to punish as traitors persons who violated safe conducts, pilgrims travelling to English shrines, merchants of England, Burgundy and Flanders and, most important, the king's own ambassadors were now threatened with the loss of what security of movement royal and wardenial letters of protection had provided them. The act's provision for the appointment of conservators of the truce in major port towns must have struck them as particularly ironic. Similar officials, and the special inquests over which they were supposed to preside, had formerly been regular features of Anglo-Scottish indentures of truce, but both had fallen prey to Lancastrian negligence.

The restrictions imposed by the Statute of Truces were felt immediately in the north. In a petition to the royal council in 1414 several English merchants complained that a valuable cargo of salmon had been seized by the Scots in contravention of the current truce. In the absence of a conservator properly authorised to discuss the matter with the Scottish warden and to seek redress on their behalf they requested that they be issued letters of marque that would enable them to arrest the goods, ships and persons of other Scottish traders found in England. The royal council, recognising the futility of the recent legislation, assented to the request.[137] The northern nobleman, Sir John de Clifford, demonstrated a similar mistrust of the act when he sought permission to resolve a border-related dispute not by recourse to an inquest and a jury, but by judicial combat.[138] Significantly, when the commons petitioned in the parliament of 1415 for repeal of the Statute of Truces they identified the inhabitants of the northern marches as those most grievously harmed by the 'mischief' consequent on the legislation.[139]

The borderers' dismay at the crown's refusal to address in satisfactory fashion the legal problems that bedevilled the prosecution of border-related crime was apparently shared by the king's brother, John of Lancaster. Years of ineffective response to his repeated requests as warden of the east march for restoration of the border tribunals had taken their toll, and after a lukewarm reception to his latest report[140] he gladly resigned his office. His place was taken briefly by Edward duke of York,[141] who promptly abandoned the border lands to fight (and die) at Agincourt. York was nevertheless quick to subscribe to his predecessor's astute understanding of the mood of the borderers, and to take up with the royal council Lancaster's dire warnings about the state of the border lands. In a memorandum addressed to the king as he made preparations to assume the office of warden, York requested that a commission be issued granting him authority to meet Scottish commissioners for the purpose of seeking and giving redress for truce-time atrocities, 'lest by negligence anything be done to prejudice your royal estate or your marches'. He further requested that Lancaster (now the duke of Bedford) be present at such a meeting, in order to ensure that English commissioners were well apprised of all outstanding grievances.[142]

York's recommendations for the resumption of days of truce fell on deaf ears. Henry V's only concession to the uneasy state of affairs in the march lands was the appointment, early in May 1415, of a commission of oyer and terminer (headed by York's kinsman and lieutenant, Sir James Harrington) charged with arresting and imprisoning a large gang of notorious northern troublemakers, 'until they have made due reformation of the attempts by the ordinance of the said lieutenant'.[143] The issue of the commission, however, coincided so closely with a planned exchange of royal prisoners of war that it is likely that Henry was motivated more by the need to show goodwill towards the Scots than the will to tackle the problem of cross-border crime.[144] Neither of his intentions was realised: Murdoch earl of Fife was kidnapped *en route* to a meeting planned with ambassadors from Scotland, and Henry found his hands full, on the eve of his departure for France, with a rebellion led by the earl of Cambridge.[145] The commission of oyer and terminer does not appear to have accomplished anything.[146] In a letter written to Albany the king disguised his unwillingness to revive the days of march in words of reproach for what he called the perfidy of the Scots.[147]

The English expedition to France and the establishment of his title to the French crown preoccupied the energies of Henry V for the remainder of his reign, and the problem of the north was left once again to hang fire. The Scots appear to have lost patience with the diplomatic manoeuvrings of Henry's government; the years 1416 to 1422 witnessed a series of truces that were more apparent than real, and both sides raided into the border territories with impunity. The duke of Albany's 'Foul Raid' into the east march in 1417 triggered a retaliatory campaign in lowland Scotland led by Robert Umfraville, in which Scottish farms and villages suffered enormous losses.[148] When a temporary respite to hostilities in the marches was called it came as a consequence of Henry's tactical triumph in securing the temporary allegiance of the most redoubtable of the Scottish border magnates, Sir James Douglas.[149] The king's sudden death at Vincennes in the summer of 1422 signalled an equally abrupt termination of the diplomatic stalemate between the realms; within eighteen months James I had been returned to his people, and Henry's strategies in respect of Anglo-Scottish relations necessarily abandoned. In 1422 it was immediately apparent that, with a long royal minority ahead of it, and however reluctantly, the English government must finally focus serious attention on the problem of the north.

The prospect must have appeared daunting. Possession of the person of James I had generated considerable traffic through the border lands of royal envoys from the two kingdoms, but for every one of these peaceful missions there had occurred a much greater number of illicit cross-border incidents. As in the time of Henry IV, the extant records of the common law suggest not only a deplorable state of affairs; they also reveal the degree to which the northerners were compelled to rely on the machinery of English justice to cope with their peculiar problems. Although there were no agreements for long term truces between 1417 and 1422, the commissions continued to exhort northerners to 'keep the truce' when these were made. They were still prevented, however, by the provisions of the Statute of Truces, from prosecuting truce-breakers. Violence against the Scots, for all intents and purposes, was elevated to the status of lawful harrying of a hated enemy. In the charged atmosphere of the frontier region, even if conservators had been appointed to convene cross-border courts, there is little doubt that efforts to secure compensation for Scottish atrocities would have been futile. When Englishmen sought legal remedy in respect of a host of border-related offences, therefore, they fell back on the one venue that remained to them: the northern sessions of gaol delivery. Even here, they found only limited satisfaction.

The suspension of assize proceedings in 1415,[150] it has been shown, 'disrupted the routine of circuit visitations and consequently the delivery of county gaols', not only in the spring and summer months of that year, but for the remainder of the reign as well.[151] While the winding down of the judicial machinery by no means halted litigation entirely, it shifted a great deal of business both towards Chancery and into the hands of local justices of the peace.[152] The extent to which criminal justice in particular was affected has been the subject of some debate: a paucity of extant record materials from the years 1415–1422 may reveal a real decline in trials for felony throughout the kingdom, or merely an extraordinarily high rate of record loss.[153] If regions as far distant from the locus of war as were the counties of the midland and western circuits did indeed witness a dislocation of the judicial machinery of English law, then the scale of disruption on the northern circuit, and in particular in the border counties, must have been especially acute. The northern shires were traditionally regarded as the least popular of the judicial circuits; in the later 1410s, with the constant threat of Scottish incursions, travel to Newcastle, Carlisle and Appleby appeared to the king's justices at best unappealing, and at worst potentially dangerous. Few assize rolls survive from the reign of Henry V for counties other than Yorkshire, a region that had not suffered a real threat of invasion since the late fourteenth century at least.[154] Gaol delivery rolls survive for the border counties only for the years 1419 and 1421,[155] an indication, perhaps, that judicial activity there may in fact have been significantly reduced.[156]

Nonetheless, when they were able to, the northerners depended exclusively on sessions of gaol delivery for the prosecution of persons accused of unlawful cross-border activity. The justices who sat in Newcastle in 1419 and 1421 presided over cases that had once been the business both of the wardens' courts, and of the tribunals formerly convened with Scottish conservators. Thomas Fletcher of Ryle, for example, was charged with kidnapping several of his countrymen and selling them and their chattels to the Scottish enemy; John Pray of Newcastle was indicted for communicating in illegal fashion with the Scots and selling them wool and worsted cloth in violation of an east march ordinance.[157] There is some indication that northern jurors derived some satisfaction from the fact that accusations of treason, which had been so jeopardised by the provisions of the Statute of Truces, could be heard here in the common-law courts and, moreover, that they made a conscious effort to take full advantage of the severity of the act. At the Newcastle sessions indictments of treason were brought against no fewer than seven suspects involved in a wide variety of incidents that jurors clearly considered triable as treasonable collusion with the enemy.[158]

The people of the marches, however, did not view the common-law courts as completely satisfactory or adequate substitutes for the days of march in the resolution of grievances involving the Scots. While indictments of felony and even treason targeted English subjects who engaged in cross-border criminal activity, they did nothing to address the matter of redress and compensation for wasted lands or loss of goods and chattels. And restitution, as always, was dear to the hearts of most northerners. The petition presented in parliament by the commons of Northumberland, Cumberland and Westmorland in 1421 represented a great deal more than the conventional complaining of a disgruntled people against the great northern liberties; it bore witness to a degree of poverty and deprivation that had been endured for almost a generation.

Henry VI's minority government was surprisingly quick to acknowledge the fact. Although it was conducted in the name of the duke of Gloucester, the influence of John duke of Bedford is immediately apparent in the abrupt reversal of policy with respect to northern affairs that followed the death of Henry V. The experience he had gained as warden of the east march had already made Bedford a valued source of information and advice on march-related issues in the late 1410s;[159] it would not be an exaggeration to suggest that it was thanks largely to his efforts that the system of law peculiar to the northern marches was able to survive at all the desuetude in which it had languished for most of the Lancastrian regime.

The first concern of the minority government was to ensure the security of the northern marches. This was accomplished both by the renewal of the indentures according to which Henry Percy and John Neville served as wardens of the east and west marches respectively,[160] and of peaceful overtures towards Scotland. Neville and Percy were encouraged to redouble their efforts to secure short-term truces for the border lands,[161] and Gloucester's council exerted considerable energy in helping to motivate them by allocating generous payments of the arrears owed to the northern officials for their wages and those of their men-at-arms.[162] Meanwhile, arrangements for the release of James I were put into place. In February 1423 Scottish envoys were granted safe conducts to travel to Pontefract to discuss the matter, and by July the crown's ambassadors had been carefully advised.[163] Instructions issued by the council in February and again in July show that the latter was none too optimistic about a prolonged peace with the Scots: its members were only too aware of the vulnerable position in which the long minority of the baby king would place England.[164] Nevertheless, a truce was achieved in September in which both sides agreed to suspend open hostilities for a period of seven years.[165] The marriage of the Scottish ruler to Joan Beaufort, daughter of the earl of Somerset and a niece of the king, was celebrated in February 1424, and James was back home in Scotland within weeks.

Although the royal marriage was not followed by a firm treaty of peace there were clear signs in the air that the English government was prepared to acknowledge that the long simmering problem of cross-border crime in the north was directly linked to peace and good order in the north and that, finally, it was willing to address the matter in rigorous and systematic fashion. An indenture of truce of 28 March 1424 recalled, in its breadth and depth, those that had been sealed back in the heyday of the later fourteenth century.[166] Both sides agreed to appoint conservators and to restore the arrangements by which malefactors apprehended in the marches of the opposite realm would in future be pursued, arrested and delivered to those conservators for condign punishment. Given the long hiatus during which the business of the border tribunals had been suspended, it was to be expected that the indenture would address in some detail the chronic problem of law and order that had plagued the march lands for almost a generation. The agreement declared that fugitives were to be banned forever from returning to their place of origin; for the time being, full restitution was to be made by both sides for atrocities committed in recent times. Persons unable to make satisfactory compensation out of their goods and chattels were to forfeit their lives. The indenture, in hopelessly optimistic fashion, imposed a moratorium on all acts of reprisal by either side in contravention of the armistice but, more realistically, emphasised that such offences, when they did occur, must be settled by recourse to peaceful negotiation between wardens and conservators. Felons who had switched allegiance in recent years and become the sworn and law-abiding liege men of the enemy king were exempted from all obligation to make reparation for past atrocities, a recognition on the part of both the Scots and the English that several years' worth of border depredations would never be satisfactorily identified or resolved. Those who refused to declare their allegiance, on the other hand, were to be compelled to make restitution.

Clear and unambiguous arrangements were established for the pursuit, across the border line, of persons who committed violations of the truce and their subsequent prosecution in march courts: an initial term of six days was designated for the 'trod', during which no letters of safe conduct were to be required by plaintiffs. Thereafter, the wardens were to make available whatever protections were required to assist foreign plaintiffs to capture fugitive suspects. Perhaps the most significant part of the indenture was that relating to the punishment of offenders charged with cross-border felony: 'if the vassals, liegemen or subjects of one realm commit an offence in the other, it shall be the responsibility of the officials of the realm in which the offence was committed to seize and punish them according to the laws of the realm in which the offence was committed'. This clause represented a clear alteration to a custom that had prevailed since the late fourteenth century. After more than one hundred and fifty years the governments of both realms tacitly acknowledged here the practical difficulties inherent in attempts to resolve cross-border disputes between kingdoms who were at war. Days of march would remain of great significance in the legal process as fora in which the issues of compensation and restitution for offences might be discussed by the warden-conservators, but henceforth the locus for claiming redress became the wardenial courts of each of the realms. The clause in effect cleared the way for renewed recourse to mixed panels of jurors in both English and Scottish tribunals. Because it accorded the common law of both kingdoms equal status it promised both to facilitate the speedy trial of suspects and to enable royal officials to devote the days of march primarily to matters of compensation.

The borderers had not been the subject of such comprehensive royal attention nor of such careful provision in many years. Even before the sealing of the truce expressed its intentions in formal, structured fashion the government took pains to demonstrate its good faith in dealing with the settlement of march-related grievances. As early as February Henry Percy (who was to be appointed one of the new conservators) had been ordered to adjudicate a dispute involving the release of a Scottish prisoner of war.[167] Earlier still, a draft of the wardenial commission issued to Percy on July 1423 suggested that the council had every intention of abiding by the provision later incorporated into the indenture of March 1424 whereby wardens were to exercise full authority in granting letters of safe conduct to Scotsmen of all ranks who wished to travel to the courts of the English marches.[168] That authority was confirmed in the sealed commission issued just two weeks later.[169]

In the late spring and summer of 1424 there were good reasons for the borderers to be optimistic about the future. Tensions with Scotland were, for the time being at least, relatively diffused, and an armistice of seven years' duration – the longest in many years – had been declared. Perhaps most heartening of all recent changes, the new government's apparent interest in reinvigorating the machinery and reviving the personnel of the long dormant border tribunals meant that there was real hope that in future incidents of cross-border reiving by the Scots might occasion tangible compensation and restitution. The remaining years of Gloucester's protectorate were to prove a disappointment in all but one of these respects. Before the year's end the truce was broken when a gang of noblemen from the west march attacked the earl of Douglas's Eskdale lands, and within a mere three years the English council was squabbling with James I over his failure to make timely ransom payments.[170] The gloomy prospect of a lasting peace that had troubled the government's discussions in 1423 was borne out in 1427, when relations with Scotland had degenerated to such an extent that it was deemed advisable to reinforce the border fortresses, and to issue commissions of array in the northern counties.[171] The early years of Henry VI's reign soon witnessed afresh the effects of raiding and destruction in the marches. But in one important respect at least the promise of the years 1423 and 1424 remained real: the duke of Bedford's advice in recommending the revival of the border tribunals had fallen on receptive ears. The courts of the warden-conservators survived the degeneration of Anglo-Scottish relations in the later 1420s and remained, throughout the fifteenth century, vital components of the English crown's *bone governance* in the north.

Notes

1. *Chron. Harding*, p. 378.
2. The term is found in Nicholson, *Later Middle Ages*, p. 194. Alastair Macdonald, however, has recently argued in convincing fashion that the belligerent activities of the Scottish border magnates were part and parcel of a concerted royal policy on the part of Robert III and his advisors. See Macdonald, 'Crossing the Border', pp. 32–5.
3. *Rot. Scot.*, ii.548–51.

4. Nicholson, *Later Middle Ages*, p. 225. The earl of March's quarrel with Albany is discussed ibid., pp. 218–19. The causes of the rebellion of Henry Percy earl of Northumberland are reviewed and debated in Bean, 'Henry IV and the Percies', pp. 212–27; Storey, 'North of England', pp. 135–7; and McNiven, 'Scottish Policy of the Percies', pp. 498–530.

5. BL MS Cotton Vesp. F VII, fo.78, printed in Chrimes, 'Some Letters of John of Lancaster', p. 26. See also below, p. 108.

6. These accounts are enrolled in PRO E 364/34, 35, 37, 41, 43.

7. The importance of the works of the Westminster chronicler, Thomas Walsingham and Henry Knighton for the history of late fourteenth-century Anglo-Scottish relations are reviewed most recently in Goodman, 'Introduction', pp. 6–7. See also Gransden, *Historical Writing in England*, pp. 145, 180. Both acknowledge that Anglo-Scottish relations of the fifteenth century, by contrast, lack a comparable attention by the chroniclers. The exceptions are the works of Adam of Usk and John Harding. See Kingsford, *Historical Literature in the Fifteenth Century*, p. 35 and Riddy, 'John Hardyng's Chronicle', pp. 91–108.

8. See *PPC*, vols. i, ii.

9. This correspondence is found in the large collection BL MS Cotton Vesp. F VII. A few of Lancaster's letters are printed in Chrimes, 'Some Letters of John of Lancaster', pp. 13–27; others are edited in Hingeston, *Royal and Historical Letters*.

10. *Chron Bower*, ii.428. For Henry's attitudes towards Scotland in the early years of his reign, see Tuck, 'Henry IV and Europe', p. 111.

11. BL MS Cotton Vesp. F VII, fo.77, printed in Chrimes, 'Some Letters of John of Lancaster', pp. 13–14, dated 6 October 1399. The text of Henry's letter is lost. The chronology of the early correspondence between Henry IV and Robert III's government adopted here is that of Brown, 'English Campaign in Scotland, 1400', pp. 40–1.

12. PRO C 81/601(1853).

13. Brown, 'English Campaign in Scotland', pp. 41–2; Stones, 'Appeal to History', pp. 80–1; Kirby, *Henry IV*, pp. 99–100. The letter from Scotland, in which Henry was addressed merely as 'duke of Lancaster, earl of Derby and Steward of England', was dated 2 November. See BL MS Cotton Vesp. F VII, fo.70, printed in Hingeston, *Royal and Historical Letters*, i.8–10.

14. *Chron. Harding*, p. 355.

15. *Rot. Scot.*, ii.152–3. Brown says that he also sent a spy 'to report on Scottish war preparations to the council'. Brown, 'English Campaign in Scotland', p. 42.

16. BL MS Cotton Vesp. F VII, fo.96. A first and briefer draft of this letter is found ibid., fo.80, printed in Chrimes, 'Some Letters of John of Lancaster', p. 14.

17. BL MS Cotton Vesp. F VII, fos.68, 82, printed in Hingeston, *Royal and Historical Letters*, i.28–30; *PPC*, i.114–15.

18. BL MS Cotton Vespasian, FVII, fo.82, printed in Hingeston, *Royal and Historical Letters*, i.25–7. In this letter, too, Rothesay continued to avoid addressing Henry as king.

19. *PPC*, i.103–4.

20. Brown, 'English Campaign in Scotland', p. 41.

21. BL MS Cotton Vesp. F VII, fo.85, printed in *PPC*, ii.41.

22. PRO E 364/33 m.3d.

23. Stones, 'Appeal to History', pp. 80–1; Brown, 'English Campaign in Scotland', pp. 44–54; Kirby, *Henry IV*, pp. 103–6.

24. *PPC*, i.122–3; Nicholson, *Later Middle Ages*, p. 219.

25. The records of the Great Cause, and other documents relating to Anglo-Scottish affairs were collected and collated in 1401 by Master Alan Newark at Henry's request. Stones, 'Appeal to History', pp. 82–3.

26. The earl of Northumberland was retained as warden for ten years on 23 October, and

granted a wardenial commission the following month. Hotspur's indenture of 1396 was renewed on 20 October 1399. PRO E 404/15/37, 52; *Rot. Scot.*, ii.151–2.

27. *Rot. Scot.*, ii.153; *PPC*, i.135; *Chron. Bower*, ii.429; *CPR*, 1401–5, p. 428; *Rot. Scot.*, ii.155–6; Douglas, 'Fast Castle and its Owners', p. 63.

28. See, for example, *CPR*, 1399–1401, pp. 406, 453, 456, 539; Devon, *Issues of the Exchequer*, pp. 280–1, 288, 290; PRO E 28/8 *sub* 15 Feb., 11 Mar., 17 Mar., 18 Mar. 2 Hen IV; E 28/9; E 28/10; E 28/11 *sub* 4 Nov. 3 Hen IV; E 28/27; E 101/42/38; E 403/571; E 404/16/695; BL MS Cotton Vesp. F VII, fo.74.

29. *Rot. Scot.*, ii.154, 155.

30. Devon, *Issues of the Exchequer*, pp. 279–80.

31. *CCR*, 1399–1402, pp. 317, 326.

32. PRO E 404/16/695.

33. PRO E 404/16/708; BL MS Cotton Vesp. F VII, fo.120, printed in Hingeston, *Royal and Historical Letters*, i.52–6.

34. It has been argued that negotiations for peace were hampered largely by the earl of Douglas's determination to exclude his rival, the earl of March, from any settlement with England. See Boardman, 'The Man who would be King', pp. 17–18.

35. The instructions issued to Henry's envoys are found in PRO C 47/22/11(14), printed in *PPC*, i.168–73.

36. A unique and invaluable record of the meeting held in October 1401 is preserved in BL MS Cotton Vit. E XI, fos.239–41, printed, with a translation, in Stones, *Anglo-Scottish Relations*, pp. 346–65. See also Stones, 'Appeal to History', p. 82.

37. Stones, *Anglo-Scottish Relations*, pp. 358–61.

38. BL MS Cotton Vesp. F VII, fo.120. Douglas's letter is printed in Hingeston, *Royal and Historical Letters*, i.52–6. Professor Stones notes that it should be dated 1402, rather than 1401. See Stones, *Anglo-Scottish Relations*, p. 347 note 1.

39. BL MS Cotton Vesp. F VII, fo.88, printed in Hingeston, *Royal and Historical Letters*, i.58–65, but misdated here to 1401. The letter belongs more properly to 1402. See below, note 40.

40. *Chron. Adae de Usk*, p. 71. In a letter dated 27 February 1402, Henry IV charged the earl of Douglas with attacking Bamburgh and its environs, 'arrayed for war, with banner or pennon displayed'. BL MS Cotton Vesp. F VII, fo.88, printed (and misdated to 1401) in Hingeston, *Royal and Historical Letters*, i.58–65. See also Wylie, *Henry the Fourth*, i.289–90, and Boardman, 'The Man who would be King', p. 18.

41. Nicholson, *Later Middle Ages*, p. 223. See also Wylie, *Henry the Fourth*, i.337–8.

42. BL MS Cotton Vesp. C XVI, fo.114.

43. Bean, 'Henry IV and the Percies', pp. 221–4; *PPC*, i.203–5.

44. *CCR*, 1399–1402, p. 552; PRO C 81/619(3657, 3658); *CPR*, 1401–5, p. 213.

45. Bean, 'Henry IV and the Percies', pp. 224–6; McNiven, 'Scottish Policy of the Percies', pp. 498–530; Storey, 'North of England' pp. 134–7; Jacob, *Fifteenth Century*, pp. 43–51.

46. *Rot. Scot.*, ii.164, 171; PRO E 404/18/602; E 404/19/131; E 101/69/334–36; E 101/73/46, 47. Warrants to issue their wages from 13 August are enrolled at E 404/18/602 and E 404/19/31.

47. *Foedera*, IV.i.51; *Rot. Scot.*, ii.114, 165; *PPC*, ii.82.

48. Disagreement about the ransom and release of the earl of Douglas and Murdoch of Fife, son of the duke of Albany, kept the two sides apart. Nicholson, *Later Middle Ages*, p. 224.

49. *Foedera*, IV.i.68; Wylie, *Henry the Fourth*, i.397, 399.

50. *Foedera*, IV.i.68–9.

51. Nicholson, *Later Middle Ages*, pp. 224–5.

52. *Rot. Scot.*, ii.168, 169. Commissioners from Scotland were appointed in August, and English envoys in September. *Foedera*, IV.i.56, 71 (the first document should be dated

September 1404, not 1403); *Rot. Scot.*, ii.170. John Mitford, one of the envoys sent to Scotland to receive the oath of the king of Scots for observance of the truce, sought payment for his expenses later that year. See PRO E 28/15 *sub* 30 Oct. 4 Hen IV.

53. Halliwell, *Letters of the Kings of England*, i.64.

54. PRO E 28/16 *sub* 11 Dec. 6 Hen IV.

55. BL MS Cotton Vesp. F VII, fo.70.

56. BL MS Cotton Vesp. F VII, fos.25, 86, 109, 110. Several of the letters are printed in Hingeston, *Royal and Historical Letters*, ii.6–14.

57. Wylie, *Henry the Fourth*, i.269–70.

58. BL MS Cotton Vesp. F VII, fo.110.

59. Safe conducts were issued to Alexander earl of Mar in April 1405. At least one other Scottish knight fought at Smithfield, before the king himself. The event is noted briefly in *An English Chronicle*, p. 43, and in *Incerti Scriptoris Chronicon Angliae*, Henry IV, p. 43.

60. PRO E 28/18 *sub* 26 Feb. 6 Hen IV; BL MS Cotton Vesp. F VII, fo.103.

61. *Foedera*, IV.i.76–7. The commission issued to Henry's envoys reiterated the king's concern that English territorial claims be acknowledged before the settlement of outstanding grievances was discussed. See *Rot. Scot.*, ii.173–4.

62. PRO E 28/20 *sub* 24 Apr. 6 Hen IV.

63. Grant, *Independence and Nationhood*, p. 168; Nicholson, *Later Middle Ages*, pp. 224–5.

64. BL MS Cotton Vesp. F VII, fo.111, printed in Hingeston, *Royal and Historical Letters*, ii.72.

65. *Facsimiles of National Manuscripts of Scotland*, ii. no.liv.

66. *Foedera*, IV.i.84, 90.

67. BL MS Cotton Vesp. F VII, fos.105, 106, 107(i).

68. PRO E 404/21/21.

69. Ramsay, *Lancaster and York*, i.97.

70. Nicholson, *Later Middle Ages*, p. 229.

71. Notices of negotiations for, and extensions of, the truce are found in *Foedera*, IV.i.112–13 (March 1407); *Cal. Signet Letters*, p. 146; *Rot. Scot.*, ii.183 (October 1407); *Foedera*, IV.1.126 (April 1408); PRO E 404/24/413 (November 1408); *Rot. Scot.*, ii.190–2; PRO E 403/599 (April-July 1409); *Foedera*. IV.162 (November 1409); PRO E 404/43 mm.2d, 3; E 101/320/36; E 101/321/2; E 403/65; *Foedera*, IV.1.170; *Rot. Scot.*, ii.194 (February-April 1410); PRO E 39/102/5; *Rot. Scot.*, ii.194 (May 1410); *Foedera*, IV.i.188–9, 191; PRO E 81/651(6890); C 81/1408(12B) (April-May 1411); *Rot. Scot.*, ii.197–9; *Foedera*, IV.ii.12; PRO C 81/653(7002) (September-October 1411); *Foedera*, IV.ii.12 (May 1412); PRO C 81/656(7389–90) (December 1412); *Foedera*, IV.ii.49–50, 66 (January 1413).

72. BL MS Cotton Vesp. F VII, fo.67, printed in *PPC*, ii.91–5. A similar, but briefer, report from the same date is found at fo.93, printed in Chrimes, 'Some Letters of John of Lancaster', pp. 20–1.

73. *PPC*, ii.95. See also Chrimes, 'Some Letters of John of Lancaster', pp. 7–8.

74. BL MS Cotton Vesp. F VII, fo.112(i), printed in Chrimes, 'Some Letters of John of Lancaster', p. 23.

75. Nicholson, *Later Middle Ages*, p. 229.

76. PRO PSO 1/49(167); *CPR*, 1405–8, p. 51; Raine, *Priory of Hexham*, i.xciii.

77. PRO E 179/60/7; Storey, *Register of Thomas Langley*, i.96–7, 134; *CPR*, 1401–5, pp. 182, 372; *CPR*, 1405–8, p. 141. For conditions in Carlisle and the west march, see Summerson, *Medieval Carlisle*, i.396–8.

78. *Rot. Parl.*, iii.600. Manifestations of the profound hostility of the borderers for the Scots in extant legal records and other sources are discussed in Neville, 'Local Sentiment and the 'National' Enemy', pp. 419–37.

79. *Chron. Harding*, p. 365; Ditchburn, 'Piracy and War at Sea', pp. 35–58.
80. *Chron. Bower*, ii.444.
81. PRO E 403/599.
82. *Rot. Scot.*, ii.192; *CPR*, 1408–13, p. 180.
83. *Rot. Parl.*, iii.624.
84. PRO E 403/602; *Foedera*, IV.i.170, 188–9. In November 1412 English commissioners agreed to a truce with Scotland until Easter. *Foedera*, IV. ii.12.
85. *PPC*, i.332–4, 337, 338, 346–7, 349–50, 352; ii.7–18, 30–1, 34–5, 37–40.
86. PRO E 101/320/36; E 101/321/2.
87. PRO E 28/20 *sub* 24 Apr. 6 Hen IV; C 81/655(7287); *Rot. Scot.*, ii.201; *CCR*, 1407–13, p. 288.
88. Allmand, *Henry V*, pp. 319, 329–32.
89. 2 Hen. V, stat. 1, cap. 6. See Ford, 'Piracy or Policy', pp. 66–77; Allmand, *Henry V*, pp. 318, 329–32. See also above, p. 111.
90. BL MS Cotton Vesp. F VII, fo.112(i), printed in Chrimes, 'Some Letters of John of Lancaster', p. 23. Lancaster's years as warden are reviewed in Williams, *My Lord of Bedford*, pp. 11–25.
91. PRO JUST 3/191 m.48.
92. PRO JUST 3/191 m.49. Other accusations of felonious and treasonable collusion with the enemy, including one from Carlisle, are enrolled ibid., mm.45, 47d, 48d, 51, 51d; JUST 3/53/4 m.1. The northern jurors' use of the provisions of the Statute of Treasons of 1352 to charge persons with unlawful collusion with the Scots is examined in Neville, 'Law of Treason', pp. 1–30.
93. PRO JUST 3/191 mm.51, 51d. Jedburgh did, in fact, fall to a Scottish raiding party in May 1409. *Chron. Bower*, ii.444. The suspect accused of delivering it to the Scots was acquitted, but the man charged with having attempted to 'sell' the castle of Roxburgh in 1408 was found guilty of felony and treason and executed.
94. See above, note 76.
95. PRO DURH 3/33 m.32, a letter of Bishop Skirlaw granting a pardon to a felon found guilty before episcopal justices of committing theft and of attempting to carry a man off to ransom in Scotland; and BL Northumberland Papers, microfilm 402, pt. 1, fo.215, a letter from Robert Umfraville warden of the east march to the prior of Tynemouth requesting the release of two 'povres garceons' of Scotland, taken in contravention of the truce.
96. *Rot. Parl.*, iii.139.
97. *Rot. Parl.*, iii.564; Allmand, *Henry V*, p. 311. Professor Storey notes that justices of gaol delivery visited Newcastle only five times between 1401 and 1411. Storey, *Thomas Langley*, p. 140.
98. See, for example, *Rot. Scot.*, ii.146. The clause had been included in commissions granted to the earl of Westmorland in May 1404 and John duke of Lancaster in October 1404, and was still part of the commission in May 1412. *Rot. Scot.*, ii.166, 171, 200–1.
99. See, for example, PRO E 101/43/25 (particulars of the account of John duke of Lancaster, warden of the east march, for the period August 1402–November 1405, in which the indenture of service is cited); E 101/69/335 (indenture of service of Ralph Neville earl of Westmorland, November 1408); E 101/73/46 (indenture of service of John duke of Lancaster, February 1409).
100. See above, p. 100, and note 32.
101. See, for example, PRO E 101/42/38 and E 101/43/25.
102. It is noteworthy in this context that the suspects accused of cross-border offences tried in Newcastle and Carlisle during the reign of Henry IV were indicted by coroners' juries and before justices of the peace.
103. *Rot. Parl.*, iii.622.

104. *Rot. Parl.*, iii.624. The commons also requested that the king order the march lords to remain in the north, prepared to defend the border lands against Scottish incursions and the activities of persons who collaborated with the enemy.

105. *Rot. Parl.*, iii.629–30, a petition from Sir John Bertram for assistance in recovering the manor and castle of Bothal, Northumberland. Bertram complained that he had been visited by Sir Robert Ogle and a gang that included both English soldiers and 'persons of Scotland, all open enemies of the king and his realm'. When two justices of the peace attempted to reason with the rebels on Bertram's behalf they were so vigorously rebuffed that 'they do not dare carry out their office there, for fear of death'. The dispute between Ogle and Bertram is reviewed in Storey, *Thomas Langley*, p. 142.

106. *Rot. Parl.*, iii.662.

107. PRO JUST 3/53/4 m.1; Neville, 'Law of Treason', p. 14.

108. PRO JUST 3/191 m.47d, 48d. See also Neville, 'Common Knowledge of the Common Law', pp. 466 and note 19. The problem of disorder in Northumberland in the reign of Henry IV is also reviewed in Storey, *Thomas Langley*, pp. 140–3 and, more generally, in Dobson, *Durham Priory*, pp. 183–202. For Cumberland, see Summerson, 'Crime and Society in Medieval Cumberland', pp. 111–24.

109. BL MS Cotton Vesp. F VII, fo.78, printed in Chrimes, 'Some Letters of John of Lancaster', pp. 25–7.

110. Powell, 'The Restoration of Law and Order', p. 56.

111. Wylie, *Henry the Fifth*, i.52–7; Nicholson, *Later Middle Ages*, p. 248; Powell, *Kingship, Law and Society*, pp. 136–8.

112. *Rot. Parl.*, iv.3, 4.

113. *Foedera*, IV.ii.12.

114. *PPC*, i.125–35; *Rot. Scot.*, ii.203, 204; Devon, *Issues of the Exchequer*, pp. 323–4; *Rot. Parl.*, iv.17; Wylie, *Henry the Fifth*, i.53.

115. *Rot. Scot.*, ii.206–7; *Foedera*, IV.ii.49–50. The truce was to run until June 1414. The Scots were also included in a truce made with France and its allies, to run until 2 February 1415. *Foedera*, IV.ii.62, 66, 75.

116. Harriss, 'The King and His Magnates', p. 37.

117. In this context it is noteworthy that Henry V, like his father, also had recourse to the by now well used (and well rebuffed) claim to sovereign authority over the smaller kingdom. Although he played this diplomatic card only briefly and half-heartedly in 1416, its association with the king's refusal to acknowledge the validity of the system of border law recalled the policies of Henry IV and, before him, Edward I. The claim to lordship over the Scottish realm is mentioned in *Gesta Henrici Quinti*, p. 138. See also Balfour-Melville, *James I*, p. 66.

118. Grant, *Independence and Nationhood*, pp. 46–7; Nicholson, *Later Middle Ages*, pp. 247–52.

119. Bradley, 'Henry V's Scottish Policy', pp. 177–95.

120. Ibid., p. 195.

121. Devon, *Issues of the Exchequer*, pp. 323–4.

122. Powell, 'Restoration of Law and Order', p. 74. See also Powell, *Kingship, Law and Society*; Allmand, *Henry V*, pp. 306–22, and, for an older view, Bellamy, *Crime and Public Order*, p. 8.

123. PRO E 404/30/151; E 404/31/224; Wylie, *Henry the Fifth*, i.53.

124. Powell, 'Restoration of Law and Order', p. 63.

125. These incidents are extensively discussed in Powell, *Kingship, Law and Society*, pp. 141–228.

126. 2 Hen V, stat. 1, caps. 5, 6.

127. *Rot. Parl.*, iv.21.

128. Allmand, *Henry V*, p. 312; Storey, *Thomas Langley*, p. 140.

129. *Rot. Parl.*, iv.143.
130. The terms and their relationship to the offence of truce-breaking are discussed in Neville, 'Law of Treason', p. 29 note 89.
131. Allmand, *Henry V*, pp. 329–31; Powell, *Kingship, Law and Society*, pp. 170–1; Richmond, 'The War at Sea', p. 112.
132. *Rot. Parl.*, iv.22.
133. Ibid., iv.23.
134. Allmand, *Henry V*, p. 331; Wylie, *Henry the Fifth*, i.331.
135. *Rot. Parl.*, iv.68.
136. *Rot. Parl.*, iv.105; 4 Hen V, stat. 2, cap. 7.
137. PRO E 28/24 no.41 (no specific date assigned).
138. PRO E 28/30 *sub* 13 December 2 Hen V.
139. *Rot. Parl.*, iv.68. See also Storey, *Thomas Langley*, p. 138.
140. BL MS Cotton Vesp. F VII, fo.125, printed in *PPC*, ii.136–9.
141. PRO E 101/73/48; *Rot. Scot.*, ii.210–1.
142. BL MS Cotton Vesp. F VII, fo.119.
143. *CPR*, 1413–16, p. 343.
144. Henry Percy, the son of Hotspur, had been a prisoner in Scotland since the disgrace of his grandfather, the earl of Northumberland. He was to be exchanged for Murdoch of Fife, the son of the duke of Albany, a prisoner in England since Homildon Hill in 1402.
145. The Southampton plot, and the place within it of Fife's capture by Ralph Pudsey, are reviewed in Wylie, *Henry the Fifth*, i.511–43, and Bradley, 'Henry V's Scottish Policy', pp. 181–3.
146. Wylie's erroneous assumption that border tribunals were convened in the years 1414 to 1416 is based on a misunderstanding of entries in the Scottish Exchequer Rolls. The *diebus treugarum* noted there refer to negotiations held by both sides in respect of the release of Murdoch of Fife and James I and the extension of the truce. See Wylie, *Henry the Fifth*, i.328 and note 1; *Rot. Scot.*, ii.212, 213, 214; *Exchequer Rolls* 1406–36, pp. 224, 253.
147. The letter survives only in a copy, included in a formulary of royal letters and writs compiled by William Hoccleve, in BL Add. MS 24062, fo.145r-v.
148. The 'Foul Raid' is described in *Chron. Bower*, ii.449; Wylie, *Henry the Fifth*, iii.89–90. See also a letter of John duke of Bedford describing the incident, in BL MS Cotton Tit. B VI, fo.125. The campaign of harassment led by Umfraville, and an attack into Scotland headed by the Northumberland nobleman, Sir Robert Ogle, are noted in *Chron. Harding*, pp. 381–2; *Chron. Bower*, ii.458–60; *Liber Pluscardensis*, i.353. See also Wylie, *Henry the Fifth*, iii.90; Storey, *Thomas Langley*, p. 153.
149. The complex negotiations involving Douglas, his heir and the still captive James I are reviewed in Wylie, *Henry the Fifth*, iii.286–7; Bradley, 'Henry V's Scottish Policy', pp. 192–3, and Nicholson, *Later Middle Ages*, pp. 250–2.
150. *Rot. Parl.*, iv.147.
151. Powell, *Kingship, Law and Society*, p. 248.
152. Gollancz, 'System of Gaol Delivery', pp. 85–96. In 1421 the delivery of the city gaol of Newcastle-upon-Tyne was undertaken by John Preston and the mayor, John Bywell, acting under commissions of gaol delivery. PRO JUST 3/199 m.24.
153. Powell, *Kingship, Law and Society*, pp. 248–50, and the sources cited there in notes 7–15.
154. The last real fear of assault by the Scots probably occurred in 1388, at the time of the Otterburn campaign. See Summerson, 'Responses to War', p. 159, and Macdonald, 'Crossing the Border', p. 104.
155. Enrolled in PRO JUST 3/53/5 and JUST 3/199.
156. Justices of the peace were active on the northern circuit between 1413 and 1420, as

Powell notes, but their activities in the border shires have left very few traces. What survives is enrolled in PRO JUST 1/1530. See Powell, *Kingship, Law and Society*, p. 249.

157. PRO JUST 3/199 m.23; JUST 3/53/5 m.1.

158. PRO JUST 3/53/1 m.1 (three separate indictments laid against three suspects); JUST 3/199 mm.23, 23d, 24 (two separate indictments). The unusually high incidence of charges of treason in the northern gaol delivery rolls in the years after 1414 in respect of cross-border crime is examined in Neville, 'Law of Treason', pp. 14–22.

159. In 1414, for example, Edward duke of York, newly appointed to the wardenship, had requested that Bedford assist him in proposed negotiations with the Scots so that the English party 'might be well informed of the attempts made against the truce by [the king's] subjects', and in order to assist him to answer allegations of truce violation made by the envoys of Scotland. In 1419 Henry V, preoccupied with French affairs, urged one of his wardens to consult the duke concerning various march matters. BL MS Cotton Vesp. F VII, fos.5, 119, printed in Halliwell, *Letters of the Kings of England*, i. 92; *Cal. Signet Letters*, no. 881.

160. PRO E 404/48/335; E 404/39/60. Percy's first commission of the new reign was dated 3 July 1423, Neville's not until 12 May 1431. *Rot. Scot.*, ii.237–8, 273–4. Storey notes, nonetheless, that indentures engaging both were more than sufficient to authorise their activites in the interval. Storey, 'The Wardens of the Marches', p. 613 notes 7, 8.

161. *Rot. Scot.*, ii.234; PRO E 28/42 *sub* 18 June 1 Hen VI.

162. PRO E 404/39/64; E 404/39/60; E 404/39/65; E 404/39/160; E 404/39/280; E 404/39/ 281; E 404/41/58; *PPC*, iii.7–8, 44, 69, 73–4, 100. In February 1423 Gloucester's government directed that the wardens be preferred above all other creditors in the expenditure of funds raised in a recent subsidy on wool; E 404/39/151; E 28/39 *sub* 1 March 1 Hen VI.

163. The conclusion of the ransom negotiations is reviewed in Ramsay, *Lancaster and York*, i.337–8, 344–5; Griffiths, *Henry VI*, pp. 155–7; Nicholson, *Later Middle Ages*, pp. 258–60.

164. Both sets of instructions noted that the prospect of securing a lasting peace entailed the resolution of many 'arduous and difficult' matters. BL MS Cotton Vesp. F VII, fo.27, printed in *PPC*, iii.139–45; *Foedera*, IV.iv.96–7.

165. *Foedera*, IV.iv.98–9.

166. Ibid., IV.iv.109–11.

167. *CDS*, iv., no.924; *CPR*, 1422–29, p. 78. The defendants, a group of northern noblemen, later complained that Percy had shown 'undue favour' towards the plaintiff, William baron Hilton, and condemned them to 'immoderate and excessive' damages.

168. PRO E 28/42 *sub* 18 June 1 Hen VI; *Rot. Scot.*, ii.237.

169. *Rot. Scot.*, ii.237–8. The commission also reiterated the warden's obligation to welcome into the king's peace Scotsmen who wished to reside in England. This authority, too, was made the subject of one of the clauses of the indenture of March 1424.

170. *PPC*, iii.259–65, 275, 353–4, 356–9; *Foedera*, IV.iv.131.

171. Griffiths, *Henry VI*, p. 157.

6

Restoration and Maturation, 1424–61

The reign of Henry VI is seldom viewed in charitable fashion by historians. If blame for the turmoil in internal politics that erupted in the Wars of the Roses has been variously laid either at the feet of a weak king or those of his 'overmighty' subjects,[1] there has nevertheless been a general consensus that Henry VI singularly failed to exercise his authority in a fashion acceptable to the polity he governed.[2] In the area of foreign policy, assessments of Henry VI's reign have been equally unfavourable: the English government, it is argued, consistently failed to take advantage of disruptions within Scotland and France; beginning in 1453 it suffered the humiliating loss of lands and fortresses that, under Henry's more belligerent predecessors, had symbolised the strength of the English army.[3]

The reign of Henry VI, however, was of great significance and a period of real promise to the inhabitants of the northern border lands, principally because it saw comparatively few periods of open warfare with the Scots. The months between May 1436 and March 1438 were the only period in which there was no formal truce in effect in the region, and widespread raiding by the enemy into the border counties of England occurred only sporadically in the later 1420s, 1430s and 1450s. The virulence of these assaults was by no means negligeable: the laconic comment of the clerk who transcribed the Cumberland gaol delivery rolls that 'no sessions were held there [Carlisle] in the years 1454, 1455 or 1456 because of the rebellion and insurrection of the Scots'[4] is vividly attested in surviving fiscal records of the region.[5] But in comparison with the turbulent years of the fourteenth century, the scale of destruction caused less permanent economic dislocation, and Henry VI's diplomatic discussions with the Scots, undertaken with uninterrupted regularity throughout the reign, prevented a return to the aggressive hostility of the previous century. Most important, the period of relative *détente* between Scotland and England provided the setting in which the renewed interest of the respective governments in the border tribunals reaped tangible results. Days of march were in operation once again in the border lands as early as June 1425; in 1461, when the Yorkist king, Edward IV, demanded that the Scottish government give up the Lancastrian refugees it was protecting, those courts were still functioning as reliable fora for the settlement of cross-border disputes. Henry VI's very ineptness, in fact, proved a boon to the restoration and the subsequent flourishing of the border tribunals, and to the development and maturation of the law administered in them.

The government's wish to facilitate the holding of regular days of march was manifested not only in the clarity of the provisions included in the Anglo–Scottish armistice of 1424, discussed above, but in the equally thorough care it devoted to the role that the wardens should play in future as fully competent conservators of the truce. Thanks to the legacy of K. B. McFarlane, scholarly discussion of the place of the wardens in the governance of northern England has been a staple feature of fifteenth-century studies: in a seminal article published in 1957 Robin Storey showed how the office 'had come to resemble the richer ecclesiastical benefices in that they were regarded largely as sources of revenue';[6] a decade later, in his equally influential book, *The End of the House of Lancaster*, he argued that possession of the office had become 'even more valuable for the opportunity it gave the warden to raise a personal following'. As such, it was 'a classic example of "bastard feudalism"', and, ultimately, a chief contributor to the civil wars of mid-century.[7] Storey's work also examined the abuse, by the fifteenth-century wardens, of 'good lordship' in northern courts of law.[8] Recent studies have confirmed his opinion that interference in the workings of the common law was a much valued perquisite of the wardenship.[9] Yet, in focusing as closely as they do on the machinations of these officials on behalf of their retainers, these scholars have overlooked the tremendously influential role of the wardens in the development of legal principles that were to endure in the border counties well beyond the lifetime of a Richard Neville or a Henry Percy. If the authority and powers of patronage of the wardens were, all too regrettably, subverted by the leaders of noble factions in the north, it was ironically the overweening judicial and political powers inherent in their office that enabled them to carry out lasting reform of the system of border law.

The source of those powers lay, of course, in the commissions granted to the wardens, but they derived also from a new series of instructions issued to them as conservators of the truce sealed with the Scots in 1424. The texts of wardenial commissions of 1423, by which Henry Percy served in the east march, and of 1431, in which Richard Neville was appointed in the west, differed in very few respects from that which had been issued to the earl of Northumberland in 1399.[10] Indeed, despite the oft-discussed struggles between the wardens and the crown in the 1430s over the issue of adequate payment for the office,[11] the substance of the commissions remained essentially unchanged throughout the reign. The same cannot be said of the commissions issued to conservators of the truce: the councils that governed the realm during Henry VI's minority, and after them the king himself, encouraged the expansion of the conservators' duties and responsibilities in a manner that recalled the rapid development of the office under Edward III and Richard II. Behind each alteration in personnel and the increasingly detailed instructions included in the commissions there lay the attempt to refine and reform the conservators' authority so as to encourage recourse to the border courts as fora for the satisfactory and efficient resolution of cross-border grievances.

The indenture of truce sealed at Durham in March 1424 nominated several conservators, including the duke of Gloucester himself and several members of the council established in 1422 to govern the kingdom.[12] Neither the English nor the Scottish envoys can have had any illusions that the likes of Gloucester or the duke of Exeter would occupy themselves with the petty grievances of Scottish plaintiffs; the names of these magnates were included in the list of conservators in order to bestow an aura of authority on the terms of the agreement. The business of the border courts was entrusted, rather, to men familiar with northern conditions and well respected figures of authority. Surprisingly, neither of the wardens was included in the first of the conservators' commissions in July 1425;[13] both were kept occupied in the south with the new royal council. Conciliar interests, however, were well-represented in the persons of Master William Alnwick, keeper of the privy seal, and Ralph Lord Cromwell. Although these men served again as conservators in the north the following year,[14] the council soon found that its concerns were best served by restoring the wardens to the commissions. They acted as the government's chief military and judicial officials in the marches for the duration of the reign.

Gloucester's council made an elaborate show of, and careful preparation for, the day of march that had been announced in the truce of 1424. In July 1425 Thomas Langley bishop of Durham, William Alnwick, Ralph lord Cromwell, John Scrope, Robert Umfraville and William Harrington were granted a commission to 'reform and repair' breaches of the recent armistice; these orders were accompanied by writs commanding the sheriffs of Yorkshire and Northumberland to proclaim the forthcoming meeting, planned for Berwick on 15 August.[15] The tribunal convened none too soon. The earl of Douglas had complained recently of a grievous breach of the truce committed by Robert Tilliol and Thomas Lucy, in which several thousand animals had allegedly been carried off from his Eskdale lands, and men in his allegiance held to ransoms totalling £5000. He claimed that he had offered the raiders £20 to observe the truce, a gift that – perhaps understandably – they had scorned. While assuring the council of his own intention to keep the peace, Douglas made it clear that the incident had generated a great deal of tension in the borders.[16]

The long-awaited day proved something of a disappointment. Conservators from both sides duly convened in Berwick,[17] but a letter sent by Bishop Langley to James I just days after the meeting suggested that the long hiatus since the last day of march had generated antagonism between the agents of the English and Scottish crowns concerning the proper conduct of the sessions.[18] The letter indicated that goodwill on both sides had been sufficient to bring together a mixed jury of eight Englishmen and eight Scots, and each party had made sworn depositions in respect of the questions they had been asked. The conservators recognised from the outset, however, that no progress in matters of reparation and redress for truce-time offences was possible until some agreement had been reached concerning the precise boundary line demarcating English and Scottish territories in the east march, around Berwick and Roxburgh. It was here, Langley reported, that disagreement had disrupted the sessions: while 'thei of our partie observed in every part the fourme of their othe by the whiche the were charged', the Scottish jurors 'observed nought the fourme of the charge yeven unto hem bot were besy and labored in their consytes to maintiengne thair parcialtee'. Langley warned that future days of march were threatened by such intransigence, and dispatched his fellow conservator, Robert Umfraville, to James's court, where he hoped the matter of the boundary line might be clarified, as had been promised in the truce of 1424.

The definitive settlement of the matter of the Anglo-Scottish border line was a recurring and troublesome theme of fifteenth-century diplomatic relations with Scotland. Despite the provision of the Treaty of York of 1237 which had established a line running roughly between the Solway in the west through the Tweed in the east,[19] the thirteenth century had seen both crowns endeavour to extend their territories at each other's expense. The Edwardian conquests of the fourteenth century had further blurred the line; in 1341, it was possible for the earl of Northampton to complain that the Annandale men under his allegiance were being treated – and subjected to prejudice – as 'Scots' by the keeper of the Solway.[20] The lands around Berwick, too, had been the subject of some controversy. Negotiations for the release of James I, which had included discussion of the extent of occupied lands around several key fortresses, had been designed to establish little more than a *modus vivendi* for English soldiers garrisoned in the lowland castles.[21] A satisfactory solution to the squabble was not achieved in 1425, nor indeed was one ever devised. As long as the English remained entrenched in pockets of Scottish soil – that is, until the end of Henry VI's reign – the question of the boundary was doomed to remain unresolved.[22]

The meeting of 1425 nevertheless demonstrated that conservators from the two kingdoms could come together and, more important, that the summoning of the mixed juries mandated in the truce of 1424 was acceptable to both parties. The respective governments of England and Scotland remained optimistic that the satisfactory resolution of cross-border grievances could be achieved, and two further days of march were arranged for June and August 1426.[23] Robert Umfraville apparently found the experience frustrating. Conservators met as planned at Reddenburn, but, he reported, the Scots proved unwilling to begin discussion of outstanding claims against them until a complaint of their own, concerning the alleged theft of several hundred animals, should be addressed.[24] The incident referred to was probably the raid on Eskdale about which the earl of Douglas had written so vehemently the previous year. Although the conservators had agreed to meet two months hence to discuss the allegations anew, Umfraville was pessimistic about the ablity of the days of march to operate in effective fashion. When he threatened to boycott the August meeting the council hurriedly sent the earl of Northumberland northwards, 'to assist and aid you at the said meeting'; furthermore, it authorised payment of a sum of £100 to Umfraville for the expenses he had occurred in attending the June sessions, as well as for disbursements he expected to make in future to Scottish plaintiffs.[25] This march day proved more successful: Umfraville was granted a further £100 in December, in reimbursement for awards made to the Scots in reparation for English atrocities.[26]

Despite their uncertain beginnings, the meetings of 1425 and 1426 demonstrated that the border tribunals were fast becoming key features of Anglo-Scottish diplomacy. At the sessions held in June the Scots proferred written bills of complaint in the manner prescribed by the recent truce agreement; the English conservators were clearly prepared to offer written charges of their own, and attended the day ready to make monetary compensation for English offences. The presence in the royal council of the earl of Northumberland and Richard Neville, wardens of the east and west marches respectively, ensured that border issues remained a matter of concern to, and discussion by, the English government.

When, for example, Garter King of Arms was sent north in the spring of 1427 to remind the Scottish king of his obligation to pay an overdue ransom instalment, he was instructed also to raise with James I the question of cross-border acts of violence. The herald was to propose that the warden-conservators of both realms be assigned full authority to resolve complex claims for restitution and compensation; only those problems that proved particularly intractable should be brought to the attention of councillors 'with suffisant povoir and auctorite to determine the said materes and difficultees'.[27] Despite James's failure to make payment of the ransom monies, another day of march was held in July 1427, where arrangements were made for the release of several Englishmen unlawfully held in Scotland.[28]

The end of Gloucester's protectorate in 1429 was preceded by what has been called 'a major offensive in search of peace' with the Scots, led by Cardinal Beaufort, uncle of James's queen.[29] It was also marked by renewed efforts on the part of both governments to promote days of march in the border lands. The commission issued to envoys sent to Scotland to meet James I included specific instructions that they be prepared to seek, but also to give, redress for violations of the truce,[30] and both crowns indicated their willingness to treat of cross-border incidents by granting commissions enabling their agents to offer restitution to plaintiffs who proved their cases.[31] The peace talks proved fruitless, but discussions concerning the border tribunals were more productive. The result of the negotiations was the drafting of two lengthy and detailed indentures in which commissioners agreed to new procedures to be used at days of march and existing regulations were clarified.[32] The indentures, surprisingly, have escaped the close attention of historians, yet in many respects they should be regarded as the foundations of the fifteenth-century, and later still, the Tudor, system of border law. Each incorporated past practice – including provisions from the indentures of 1398 – but each also established new precedent for the pursuit, punishment and trial of cross-border felons. Both agreements set out the principles that henceforth were to govern the convening of days of march; one included a detailed and sophisticated series of protocols according to which the border sessions would be conducted and cross-border offences defined. Together, the indentures reflected much more than the determination of the English and Scottish governments to address the problem of the border region: they suggest that both crowns were aware of the need to bring their frontier regions into closer contact with current notions of international public law.

The first indenture established procedures to be followed in the determination of border-related incidents, but of some importance, too, were the provisions that touched on the nature of these offences. While the records relating to unlawful cross-border activity had, for some two centuries already, made reference to incidents of larceny, ransom-taking, arson, homicide and reiving, that is, the theft of animals, no attempt had been made since 1249 to list in systematic fashion the kinds of unlawful activities considered liable to trial at border law.[33] The indenture of 1429 made specific mention of homicide, mayhem (*manyheing*), assault, breach of safe conduct, theft of animals and chattels, the unlawful grazing and pasturing of animals, and treason. Clearly, generations of warfare had done little to lessen the borderers' preoccupation with crimes that caused injury to their persons or damage to their property, but the reference to march treason shows that Henry V's legislation respecting truce-breaking had also influenced their definition of unlawful cross-border activity. That category included offences peculiar to the march region, such as illegal ransom-taking and the firing of border castles. Over the course of the long Anglo–Scottish conflict, then, categories of march crime had expanded significantly.

The indenture had much to say about the trial of suspects by panels of mixed jurors. Suspects accused of slaying or attacking persons travelling under safe conduct were to be delivered to the wardens of the opposite realm for punishment 'efter the qualite and the exigent of the trespas' – a return to a system that had not been in effect in the marches since the mid-fourteenth century. The drafters of the agreement devoted considerable attention to the problems that had plagued earlier proceedings, by declaring that all 'traverses' or challenges made by defendants be submitted to a jury of six men, three from each of the east and west marches of England, and three each from the east (together with the middle) and west marches of Scotland.[34] In a provision also reminiscent of early custom, the indenture required that the English jurors be nominated by the Scots, and the Scots by the English, so that neither side might complain of partiality by the other. More remarkable still, the juries were ordered to meet four times a year, 'and oftar gif nede be', to declare on oath whether 'the person billit is gilti or nocht gilti'. Elaborate provision was made in respect of the perennial problem of stolen moveables. Thus, English plaintiffs seeking to recover goods stolen from them by Scottish raiders, then subsequently found in the possession of an English defendant, were to present their claims at a day of march; if found innocent, the person taken with the goods must forfeit the items, then seek recovery for his loss at a future day, in a suit against the Scot who had sold them to him. The same procedure, *mutatis mutandis*, was set out in respect of Scottish plaintiffs. The old scale of compensation, which had mandated both restitution and damages, was apparently abandoned: a person who acquired chattels later found to have been stolen 'sal lose no mar bot that pert of the gude that is fundin with him'. The indenture included a kind of extradition agreement, by which the wardens of each of the marches of either realm might order the arrest of suspects; the latter were required, as they had been in 1398, to produce sureties (*borrowis*) that they would appear at a day of march, 'and gif he find na borrowis . . . he sal be haldin in prison in person'.

The subject of straying animals that had troubled the march day of 1425 was made the subject of another clause. Both sides agreed to implement a system of distraints – known as 'poinds' in the marches – and methods of certifying the value of animals seized in this fashion. These provisions, too, recalled thirteenth-century custom;[35] from 1429, however, such actions were to be governed by the laws of the kingdom in which the offence had occurred. The indenture restricted poinding procedures to the east (and, in Scotland, the middle) marches; a still fluid boundary line in the west marches would greatly have complicated their implementation there.[36] Other clauses included provisions for compelling the men to appear at days of march as jurors, for prohibiting the warden-conservators from 'shooting', or cancelling, the cross-border tribunals 'without a resnabil and ane oppin cause', and for discouraging the needless traversing of suits. A final clause was of great significance: it required that all future days of march be attended by 'sufficient' clerks, charged with recording the business of the courts in parchment indentures. The new provision was more than merely a postcript: it signalled acknowledgement on the part of the authors of the revised code of law of the importance of the written word, and recognition that reliance on written proof, henceforth a hallmark of border legal procedure, necessitated organised and systematic record keeping. In 1429 the border tribunals were on their way to becoming courts of record.

That both the English and Scottish crowns were still much concerned with incidents of piracy is apparent in the text of the second indenture: almost half its provisions touched on offences committed on the high seas. Commissioners from both sides agreed that plaintiffs of either realm must submit, within one month of an alleged incident, 'sufficient records' of their claims for restitution and compensation to the warden-conservators of the opposite side; in the east marches those proofs were to be made to the earl of Northumberland and the chancellor of Scotland, as appropriate, and in the west to Richard Neville (newly created earl of Salisbury) and the Scottish chancellor. Two sessions for adjudicating these plaints were set for the following November, one at Reddenburn in the east, the other at Lochmabenstone in the west. Here, mixed juries consisting of knights, a clerk and an esquire from each kingdom were ordered to make 'full redresse of all swylk attemptatis doo ayeins the tenour of the trewes' of 1424. Resort to sea-borne violence was not ruled out altogether: both sides continued to endorse legal reprisals when they agreed that men adjudged to have been lawfully taken at sea 'be remitted to pay her raunson and thair costs'.

The tribunals planned for November were also to discuss violations of the armistice committed on land. Here, the indenture dealt squarely with the problems that had plagued the sessions of 1425 which, it declared, had been marred by 'favour hate and corruption'; more seriously, suits by either side had been delayed when they had 'fallen in traverses and in doutes'. In order to avoid similar difficulties, the agreement required that all complaints destined for discussion in November be submitted first to a panel of English and Scottish recognitors, who were to reach an accord concerning the disposition of each case and the apportioning of blame for purposes of compensation. Incidents on which no agreement was reached were to be related to the warden-conservators. The lay jurors chosen were all men of local standing: on the English side they included the knights John Bertram and Christopher Curwen and William Lamberton, esquire; the Scots were represented by Sir Thomas Kirkpatrick and Sir Patrick Dunbar and David Hume. The clerics assigned for the task were both men learned in the law: Thomas Oldhall was a bachelor of civil law, while Thomas Roulle was beginning an important career in Anglo-Scottish diplomatic relations. The intention here was clearly to complete the work of reforming the border courts begun in the indenture of 1424. Henceforth, much of the business of the cross-border tribunals was to be undertaken and completed before the sessions themselves convened. The agenda of the days of march, it was hoped, would consist exclusively of the exchange of 'proofs' and the giving and receiving of restitution in respect of incidents that Anglo-Scottish jurors had previously discussed. Negotiation between the warden-conservators was to be confined to acts of violence on which the jurors had failed to reach a consensus. These provisions marked important innovations. The meetings of 1425 had broken down when the Scots had refused to begin discussion of their subjects' transgressions pending resolution of their grievances against the English; the indenture of 1429 sought to ensure that such doubts and delays did not again derail the sessions from their outset.

The matter of 'proofs' was closely addressed in the second agreement; here again, particular care was taken to ensure that accusations of cross-border violence were adequately supported, and that the sums of money requested by plaintiffs in restitution and compensation were justifiable. Men whose claims had been adjudged sound by the panel of Anglo-Scottish jurors were to appear at the November meetings armed with the written record of 'worthy men and credible persons', drawn from their home and from the city, town, borough or port where the offence had occurred. Such evidence was to include a clear statement of the value of the goods taken, authenticated by the seal of an admiral, mayor or bailiffs, as appropriate; likewise, the damages demanded were to be supported by the sworn oaths of these officials. Provision was made for defendants in all such claims to offer proofs 'gretter and of more auctorite' than those of their accusers; should disagreement arise, both parties were required to produce sureties that they would appear at a future day of march.

The provisions of this indenture were sweeping and significant. Although mixed juries had long been familiar fixtures in the courts of the Cinque Ports and in the market towns of England,[37] in the early fifteenth century they were known only as a distant memory, a custom that had once been a prominent feature of Anglo-Scottish border practice, but one rendered obsolete and unworkable by wartime conditions. Similarly, notions of international law, such as those that had for some time already governed the resolution of complaints for restitution and compensation in the mercantile and commercial courts of England and the continent,[38] were largely unknown in the border lands. Here, the concepts that historians have linked with the 'reception of civil law' had been prevented from taking firm root by the simple, but implacable, reality of border conflict: a society mobilised and administered almost entirely on the basis of war was hardly likely to be one in which plaintiffs and defendants from two hostile allegiances might discuss acts of violence in an amicable atmosphere. The border courts of Edward III and Richard II had gone some way towards establishing a *modus vivendi* among the marchers, in that warden-conservators from both sides had succeeded intermittently in making restitution for offences committed by their respective subjects. But the bitterness of the Anglo-Scottish conflict had never been far from their minds, and the days of march over which they presided had not yet achieved the status of wholly impartial or even regularly convened tribunals. That they had been useful at all as fora for the resolution of cross-border offences was a consequence as much of the personal efforts of warden-conservators such as Henry Percy and Ralph Neville as it was a sophisticated jurisprudential policy on the part of the crown and its legal advisors. The early Lancastrian years, moreover, had shown that a crown interested merely in keeping the border lands on a war footing utterly undermined the establishment there of the basis of international accord in matters of cross-border violence.

Gloucester's government was the first in many years to promote vigorously the potential for such accord, even in the midst of continued hostility between the realms, and so to encourage in the border courts the growth of notions of international law that had first influenced the late fourteenth-century warden-conservators. Discussions of the reception of civil law principles in the lay sphere in England have to date emphasised late-medieval developments in the courts of the admiral and those of the marshal and constable.[39] The breadth and depth of the provisions included in the indentures of 1429, however, bear witness to the intrusion into customary border practice of procedures and principles that were familiar to plaintiffs and defendants in those other tribunals, too. The later fourteenth and the early fifteenth centuries saw significant development of the so-called 'sister courts' of admiralty and chivalry in England.[40] But this period also saw the consolidation of tribunals in the border lands that, by the Tudor period, were to be as important, albeit more localised, as those other courts of law. And, just as the law practised in the courts of admiralty and chivalry continued to draw heavily for inspiration on late medieval civil procedure, so, too, did the warden-conservators come to understand that the border law they administered boasted a distinct and particular nature of its own.

The indentures of 1429 were intended to be blueprints for the future, a fact that helps to explain the discrepancies found in the two documents and to reconcile some of their inconsistencies. The relationship between the agreements is not immediately clear. The differences of subject matter and emphasis between them are sufficiently great to reject the argument that one was a first draft, the other a second or revised version. There are, however, some problems relating to the procedures set out in each. Most notably, the first designated the task of sifting though pre-trial bills to panels numbering six jurors, three each from the English and the Scottish marches;[41] the second assigned the responsibility for adjudicating bills to one panel alone, consisting of four English and four Scottish jurors.[42] The matter is rendered more complicated by the fact that both lists included only one name in common, and is further obscured by an examination of royal commissions dated October 1429 for correcting violations of the truce at the forthcoming day of march. These were issued not to the warden-conservators; they appointed as justices three of the individuals named in the indenture lists, but also a further five new men.[43] Another, albeit less problematic, discrepancy between the indentures is found in the provisions relating to the role of the mixed juries: in one text they were to be employed both in the pre-trial stage and in all claims presented at the days of march; in the other the onus of ruling on challenges made at the border tribunals fell to the wardens alone.

These inconsistencies are best explained by viewing the indentures not as consecutive drafts of a single document, but rather as complementary texts embodying both general and specific provisions. The first was the more general, and was intended to be a working plan for all subsequent days of march: it established (with a degree of accord that Richard II would surely have found enviable) fixed sites for the meeting of pre-trial assessors of bills of complaint, at Reddenburn in the east marches and Kirkandrews in the west. A carefully considered schedule of such meetings was set out and, although it must be doubted whether four annual gatherings ever occurred, the inclusion of this clause implies that both sides were in agreement that a competent and reliable system of law was one characterised by clearly defined sessions or terms. The provisions concerning the kinds of offences liable to trial at border law, the procedures established for the adjudication of land and sea offences, and the clause relating to the keeping of written records all point to an attempt by the authors of this agreement to set out a series of guidelines for future consultation. Even the section nominating members of the mixed juries boasted an element of flexibility, for it was followed by another in which arrangements were made for the immediate replacement of these men in the event of their death or incapacity.

The second indenture did not much alter the substance or intent of the first. The composition of the pre-trial jury reflected, perhaps, little more than a belief on the part of all present that a larger body of jurors might obviate the antagonism that had marred the day of march held in 1425. The focus in this document was on the form and nature of the proofs to be presented at the forthcoming sessions of the border courts (scheduled for November). The clearer emphasis on offences committed on the high seas suggests that it was this feature of current practice and these kinds of atrocities that to date had constituted the most serious obstacles to implementation of the provisions embodied in the truce of 1424. Neither indenture, then, was intended either to stand alone or to vitiate the other.

In the years to come both indentures would prove their value as working documents. The changes they effected to practices considered customary in the border lands were profound. Most obviously, neither had anything to say about trial by battle, a method of proof that had hitherto been popular among the people of the frontier and an occasion for ceremony and the ostentatious display of martial splendour. Although royal licences granting authority for northern knights to engage in feats of arms with Scottish opponents had been issued with some regularity during the reigns of Henry IV and Henry V,[44] resort to battle disappeared almost entirely in the marches in the third decade of the fifteenth century. In part this was a reflection of the declining appeal of combat that was evident throughout the English legal community generally,[45] but it was also a consequence of the warden-conservators' recognition that large gatherings of heavily armed borderers too easily degenrated into pitched battle. Beginning in the reign of Henry VI, written proofs and the sworn testimony of mixed juries were the standard procedures for adjudicating claims. Gone, too, were attempts by the warden-conservators to achieve rough parity in the sums each demanded of the other side in restitution and compensation, a feature of border law that had characterised the fourteenth century. The establishment of equal claims had been a useful diplomatic device for bringing together representatives from two hostile allegiances, and in fostering the notion, fundamental to border legal thinking, of a reciprocity of obligation. In the fifteenth century, that notion had become so customary and familiar to both sides that its formal expression was no longer considered necessary.

Negotiations with the Scots preoccupied the English council throughout the early months of 1430 and for most of the following year. Extant records reveal that, despite some posturing, the government was above all interested in winning James I away from the newly reaffirmed Auld Alliance, and that it wished at all costs to avoid war.[46] They suggest also that while both parties were ready to play a shifting game of diplomacy in respect of issues such as the outstanding sums owed on James's ransom and a royal marriage,[47] neither was prepared to jeopardise the new spirit of cooperation that characterised the revitalised border courts. The English council's instructions to the envoys sent to Scotland in 1430 made a brief allusion to the end of a truce as a period in which peace was 'not best kept', but the sharpness of this threat, if threat it was, was blunted by orders to ensure that if an armistice was sealed, discussions about its terms must seek to clarify any 'derknesse or difficulte' that might disturb its observance.[48] In January 1430 the crown commissioned several men to convene a day of march at Newcastle in May,[49] and when it appeared that Anglo–Scottish peace negotiations might disrupt it the warden–conservator, Richard Neville, made it clear that he considered his duty to hold the court the more pressing of his responsibilities.[50]

The tribunal held in 1430, and another arranged for the spring of 1431, demonstrated that the intentions of the English government were genuine.[51] The council further lent its support to the authority of the courts when it ordered two defendants in an alleged incident of piracy to appear before the warden of the east march for resolution of a Scottish complaint.[52] So, too, did James I, when he addressed letters patent to officials in several English ports authorising reprisals in retaliation for an act of Scottish piracy, pending appropriate restitution by the guilty parties.[53] The promise of satisfactory justice in the border courts may, indeed, have been the impetus behind the Scots' acceptance of a five-year extension to the current armistice in December 1430.[54] Far from being a 'modest' truce,[55] the long indenture sealed in Edinburgh included elaborate provisions for the punishment of persons found guilty of committing acts of piracy and of assaulting border fortresses, clauses reforming the current system of extradition for criminal fugitives, and prohibitions against armed raiding and the sheltering of cross-border felons. A long list of conservators was appended to the document, and the English council took pains to ensure that the prorogued truce was widely proclaimed in the north.[56]

No medieval Anglo–Scottish truce was ever observed with exemplary respect, and the 1430s witnessed as many incidents of cross-border violence as had the preceding years. But if surviving records reveal a steady succession of raids, ransom taking and piratical activity, they show equally clearly that the English and Scottish crowns officially continued to endorse the border tribunals as the appropriate fora for the resolution of grievances, and that the warden–conservators were coping with these complaints in satisfactory fashion. The English council issued commissions to punish breaches of the truce on a regular basis throughout the duration of the armistice,[57] and the courts functioned with such evident success that they survived the degeneration of Anglo-Scottish relations and the outbreak of renewed hostilities in 1436. In the decade after 1429 the English council became fully aware that the judicial work of the cross-border tribunals was an integral and crucial aspect of its northern diplomacy, as much as were issues such as the royal marriage or Scotland's relations with France.

The acknowledgement of the new way of thinking on the part of council members is readily apparent in surviving records. Most notably, discussions held on the occasion of visits by Scottish envoys now emphasised the existence of a clear link between the performance of the courts and the general state of relations with the Stewart monarchy. In 1433, when Thomas Roulle travelled to England, he was presented with a series of accusations concerning border reiving, and told that none of the incidents had been properly addressed because James I had failed to nominate conservators of the truce. He was told in no uncertain terms to remind his king that the most recent indenture of armistice had included among its conditions the appointment of such officials and the provision of days of march for the adjudication of grievances.[58] The English envoy, Stephen Wilton, was instructed in 1434 to urge the Scottish ruler to assign a day and place for a session of the border courts lest the Scots be found guilty of 'lachnesse' and 'default' in observing the current truce.[59] In 1436 the relationship between the border courts and the state of Anglo-Scottish war talks was made explicit. When James I complained that English misgovernance of the border lands 'is so fer forth runyn that it is more likly to be lawbours of wer than of pees or trewis', English envoys were urged to promise that the speedy and satisfactory punishment of cross-border felons would proceed apace, and that every effort should be made to win, in return, James's promise to renew the armistice.[60]

The council's keen interest in the days of march was manifested in other ways. One of the conservators, Sir John Bertram, was told in 1433 to assure the inhabitants of the east march that a session of the cross-border courts would be ordered 'withe inne ryzt short tyme'; the same year, two of the conservators were excused attendance in parliament and instructed, instead, to remain in the north to attend to march business.[61] Efforts were made to ensure that some officials were paid for the expenses they incurred in organising sessions of the courts, even as Richard earl of Salisbury was growing increasingly disaffected with the tremendous financial burdens he was carrying in his capacity as warden.[62] More telling still was the scrutiny the council devoted in 1434 to the consequences of its border policy on English foreign affairs generally. Members were asked on this occasion to weigh the benefits to good relations with Scotland promised by two comprehensive clauses in the most recent truce against the potential problems these might create in the already fragile (and fragmenting) Anglo-Burgundian alliance.[63] Meanwhile, discussions about each side's record of performance in providing satisfactory justice in the marches continued to occupy a significant place in negotiations between the English and Scottish governments. Accusations of carelessness and obstruction there were in abundance,[64] but the blustering that characterised these exchanges does not obscure the fact that the border tribunals were being convened on a frequent basis, nor that mixed juries were meeting regularly at traditional sites in the border lands, such as Lochmabenstone, Haddenstank and Reddenburn. In 1434, for example, the warden of the west march petitioned the council for reimbursement of various sums he had offered in redress for English violations of the truce; these had been discussed at two separate days of march convened for 'the reparacion of attemptates doon upon the seid westmarches'.[65]

There are other indications, too, that the border tribunals had assumed the status of fully functional and widely used courts of law. When he agreed to accept a royal offer to act as joint warden of the east and west marches in July 1434, the earl of Salisbury took care to specify that the commissions include his appointment as conservator of the truce. He also requested that 'alle the bookes of the wardein courtes and of the marches concernyng the estmarches' be transferred from the custody of the former warden into his own.[66] Neville's intentions here were both to keep close to hand a clear record of recent and outstanding disputes, and to ensure that careful account be kept of all profits of justice arising from his office. That these might be considerable is apparent in the crown's requirement that the warden–conservators account in Exchequer for fines and forfeitures levied in the border courts.[67] The solemnity of sessions of the border courts was such that the earl of Salisbury felt it necessary to request the loan of a suitably ostentatious horse and carriage from his friend, Prior Wessington of Durham.[68]

The northerners made frequent use of the days of march. A public proclamation issued in November 1433 reminded all who had complaints to make in respect of cross-border offenders that written bills must be submitted to the prior of Coldingham in Scotland well in advance of the sessions, and that English subjects named in Scottish accusations were required to deliver themselves into the custody of the keeper of Berwick, in accordance with the terms of the last truce agreement.[69] A petition sent to Chancery by two English merchants aggrieved in an incident of piracy appears to have been directed to the warden for adjudication, as the official most appropriate to determine the complaint,[70] while even the bishop of Durham, ever the jealous guardian of the privileges of his palatinate, was prepared to assist the warden in the effective execution of border legal procedures.[71]

The brief outbreak of war with the Scots in 1436 did not dampen the confidence of either the English or the Scots in the ability of the days of march to settle grievances arising from incidents of cross-border violence. If attempts to bring together the warden–conservators from the warring realms proved impossible in the midst of open conflict,[72] there was at least agreement that the end of hostilities and the establishment of a new truce should be marked by the appointment of conservators and the reiteration of the principles that now governed the operation of the cross-border courts. Both were achieved in March 1438, when an armistice of nine years' duration was sealed.[73] The border tribunals resumed almost immediately. The resolution of several complaints arising from the unlawful seizure of English goods at sea proceeded smoothly,[74] and, after several years' hiatus, new arrangements were made to assemble a mixed jury to carry out the delineation of the hinterland around the castles of Berwick and Roxburgh, in accordance with one of the provisions of the recent truce.[75] The authority of the warden-conservators in meting out satisfactory justice in their courts was, in fact, so widely acknowledged and respected that the criminous elements of the north began to see advantages in attempting to subvert it. Thus in 1440 a Newcastle man was put to trial on a charge of treason when he used a counterfeited wardenial seal to extort large sums of money 'under false and deceitful premises' from several townsmen.[76]

The truce of 1438 was extended in 1442 for a further seven years.[77] The deeply troubled minority of James II kept the Scottish lords preoccupied at home, while in England Henry VI's assumption of personal rule saw the beginnings of the divisiveness that was soon to degenerate into civil war.[78] Both rulers were content, for the moment, to suspend hostilities indefinitely, and to permit their respective warden-conservators to diffuse tensions created in the marches by sporadic raiding. The decade after 1438 witnessed much hardship in the northern English counties as lay and religious communities struggled to recover from a century and a half of devastation,[79] but also a period of relative quietude. If, on occasion, Henry VI saw fit to issue reminders to his subjects that the current truce must be observed strictly, and to reassure James II of his own intentions to respect the armistice,[80] there were no serious breaches for a full decade, and the border courts functioned with notable efficiency. In 1440 and again in 1448, the sheriff of Cumberland was excused his obligation to render account in Exchequer for the ferme of his county in recognition of business that kept him occupied at days of truce.[81] In 1444 a royal commission directed two conservators in the west marches not only to do justice in respect of violations of the truce, but to discuss with their Scottish counterparts all 'quarrels, arguments, differences and questions' arising from the implementation of current laws.[82] Two years later Henry Percy, warden of the east march, ordered the arrest and imprisonment of the numerous Scottish fugitives said to be hiding in the border lands and their presentation (together with their English accomplices) at forthcoming border tribunals,[83] and in Durham Bishop Robert Neville agreed to appoint a commission of inquiry to examine the claims of Scottish merchants whose vessels were said to have been unlawfully seized in truce time.[84]

Justice in the border courts was often slow in the implementation and, given the tensions between the realms, at times seen to be perverse.[85] Nevertheless, the days of march coped effectively with most incidents of cross-border felony. While the monopoly of the offices of warden in the west march by Richard Neville earl of Salisbury and in the east by Henry Percy lord Poynings has been viewed as a chief contributor to the political dissension that marked the middle decades of the fifteenth century,[86] there is, ironically, good reason to find in the entrenchment in these offices of both magnates and their respective affinities a genuine boon to the continued vitality of the border courts. Violent competition between the followers of the two magnates, and much jockeying for positions of local influence there were, but the rule of the Nevilles in the west and the Percies in the east also provided a great deal of stability in the personnel of the courts. In the decade between 1438 and 1448 Scottish commissioners became well acquainted with a relatively small body of English conservators, including not only the wardens themselves, but local lords such as Thomas lord Dacre, Christopher Curwen, John Bertram, Robert Ogle, Christopher Moresby, Henry Fenwick and William Swynburn, and familiarity no doubt bred at least as much respect as it may have contempt. In 1447 the English council felt sufficiently confident about the good record of the border tribunals to remind James II once again that they were the most appropriate fora for the settlement of disputes between the realms.[87]

The autumn of 1448 saw a brief but savage outbreak of hostilities in which the recent accord generated in the border courts was momentarily forgotten by the governments of either realm. Predictably, English and Scottish chroniclers blamed each other's subjects for the escalation of relatively minor incidents of reiving into virulently destructive raids that reduced the march lands to ruins in the ensuing months.[88] But neither side abandoned diplomatic contact altogether. Envoys began to shuttle back and forth as early as the spring of 1449, and a series of brief truces was forged in the summer.[89] By September Henry VI considered the diplomatic atmosphere sufficiently temperate to request that restitution be made to two English merchants captured at sea and taken to Edinburgh.[90] James II soon indicated his own preparedness to establish afresh a condition of truce, and an elaborate indenture was sealed by commissioners of both realms at Durham in November 1449.[91]

This agreement, though it was to prove no stronger a guarantor of quietude throughout the borders than had its predecessor, was nonetheless an important document in the context of the legal history of the border courts. One scholar has argued that, behind the scenes at the truce negotiations held in Durham, the bishop of Chichester was busy attempting to arrange a permanent peace with the Scots. He notes, too, the 'more cordial attitude' towards Scotland exhibited in the truce agreement.[92] While much of the text reiterated provisions found in the agreements of 1429 and 1438, the dogged repetition of clauses describing the process by which incidents of piracy were to be redressed, fugitives tracked down and punished, and days of march convened suggests that both crowns continued to subscribe to tried and true procedures. The agreement, moreover, effected minor, but important, changes to current practice, further indicating the interest of the two crowns in perfecting the work of the tribunals. Provision was made, for example, for the formal sounding of a trumpet to signal the banishment of offenders who refused to submit themselves to justice. This was a small change of procedure, but one that bestowed on the act an element of ceremony and solemnity. Similarly, a clause that forbade 'infamous persons, rebels, fugitives or traitors' from holding office in the marches or sitting as jurors in border tribunals was more than merely rhetorical: it bespoke consensus on the part of commissioners from both realms about the suitability and rank of the men who acted as conservators and bore witness in court.[93] In making provision for both kings to appoint inquests presided over by members of their royal councils, 'lovers of justice and peace', for the assessment of the warden-conservators' conduct in settling disputes,[94] the agreement revealed a unanimity of opinion on the part of Henry VI and James II about the effectiveness of the days of march that did much to obviate the current atmosphere of animosity.

The enmity displayed by both crowns in 1448–9, however, effected surprisingly little dislocation in the routine convening of the cross-border tribunals. As had occurred a decade earlier, the renewal of truce was accompanied by a royal order that all 'notable men' of the region swear an oath to observe the armistice, and by demonstrations of goodwill on the part of each government. In England, Henry VI made a show of reviewing and amending clauses in the recent agreement, in an attempt better to assure the immunity of Scotsmen wishing to pass into the realm to prosecute claims in the border courts. Henceforth, general safe conducts of unlimited duration were made readily available in each march for small numbers of plaintiffs.[95] More meaningful reform came in the shape of legislation that, in 1451, vested in the chancellor the same powers of redress and restitution exercised by the conservators.[96] The statute satisfied, at one remove, the concerns of several different interest groups. It gave real meaning to the section of the new truce that provided for the close supervision of the work of the warden–conservators by their respective governments. Scottish plaintiffs aggrieved in incidents of breach of truce gained a series of benefits: the act offered them the opportunity to appeal to Chancery if English defendants failed to appear to answer charges.[97] They were given further satisfaction in knowing that the failure of defendants to appear in turn before the chancellor would result in forfeiture, and that in the distribution of forfeited goods they were to enjoy claims superior even to those of the English crown. The legislation once again lifted from acts of lawful reprisal the onus of treason, further freeing the warden–conservators from the jurisdictional constraints imposed on them by Henry V's Statute of Truces of 1414. Finally, in denying the offer of pardon to all persons forfeited in Chancery for contumacy, Henry VI's government gave teeth to the general provisions of the truce concerning the outlawry of persistent offenders, and demonstrated to James II Henry's willingness to treat violations of the armistice with the utmost severity.

James may well have been of the opinion that parliamentary legislation, however accommodating, was only as effective as the English crown's intentions of enforcing it, but, like Henry VI, he was fully prepared to support the resumption of the work of the border tribunals. In the renewed atmosphere of cordiality that accompanied the sealing of the armistice arrangements were made for English envoys to discuss the immediate convening of the courts, and for a thorough investigation of the conduct of the conservators.[98] Both sides affirmed the extension of the truce until August 1454 and agreed, within a fortnight, to hold a day of march at the traditional meeting place of Haddenstank.[99] The English Exchequer was ordered to assign £100 to Henry Percy, warden of the east march, for expenses he expected to incur there.[100] Another series of border sessions was held later that year or early in 1452.[101] Just a few months later, in response to complaints from James II, the royal council issued a stern warning to the wardens that recent breaches of the truce by unruly northern subjects would not be tolerated.[102]

For several months the border lands were once again calm, thanks in part to the preoccupation of the English and Scottish crowns with domestic problems. In

Scotland, James became embroiled in a rebellion led by the kinsmen of the Douglas family, whose leader he had murdered with his own hand; in England, a series of risings similarly kept Henry VI's attentions firmly focused on the increasingly violent rivalry between the dukes of York and Somerset.[103] The renewal of truce and the involvement of the rulers in internal troubles provided an atmosphere of *détente* within which issues that had for some time been left to languish might once again be addressed. The most pressing of these in the years around 1450 were the delineation of territories under English control in the hinterlands of the border fortresses of the east march, and the settlement of an acceptable border line between the realms in the west. Both matters had been the subject of much discussion and discord in the fourteenth century, when Edward III's occupation of lowland Scotland had been at its zenith, and thereafter, when Richard II had been anxious to secure more than merely nominal control over these lands. In the middle of the fifteenth century English ambitions were a great deal more modest. Past territorial claims were by no means forgotten, but Henry VI was interested primarily in securing an acceptable *modus vivendi* for English garrisons in Roxburgh and Berwick and, in the west, in maintaining a strong English presence in the waters of the Solway Firth. It was these questions in particular, then, to which agents of the two crowns now turned their negotiating skills.

The armistice of 1438 had made provision for the appointment of a mixed commission charged with establishing the boundaries around Berwick and Roxburgh within which Englishmen might lawfully pasture their animals and grow the grainstuffs they required without danger of committing breach of truce. Envoys from both realms had soon thereafter met with the intention of carrying out these duties.[104] The exercise, however, had proved unfortunate, and the talks collapsed when one of the commissioners, Sir Robert Ogle, was taken prisoner by the Scots.[105] Special envoys convened again in 1449 in Durham, as final arrangements were being made for the truce that was sealed in November. Here, English commissioners secured a cautious promise that their subjects would enjoy free access to the lands lying around the fortresses in the east; in return, they conceded that 'non Englishman under the payne of forfeiture of al that he may forfett unto the king of England and France shall occupie the batable landes in the westmarches nor bi land nor bi water'.[106] Although no record of precise boundary marking in either area has survived, a general accord reiterating these principles was included in the indenture of truce of 1451.[107] The matter was discussed at negotiations for the extension of the armistice held in May 1453, and still again in 1457.[108]

While the parties representing Henry VI and James II made formal undertakings to assess the claims of each of the crowns to the disputed territories, neither was willing to concede much ground. It was apparent, by now, that the establishment of a clear border line was fraught with such diplomatic baggage that no concord was possible while the two sides remained in a state of war. At each of the negotiations held in 1449, 1451, 1453 and 1457 English envoys linked their discussions – as well as those concerning the general terms of the truce – directly to Henry VI's claim to sovereign authority over the smaller realm.[109] The king's position was, at best, tenuous, but the matter of overlordship had become a time-honoured feature of English relations with Scotland, and Henry was not prepared to abandon it. One scholar has linked the revival of the English position in the 1450s to the rise of the duke of York's influence, and suggests that he was 'anxious to pose as the champion of a nationalist England'.[110] It is probably more accurate, however, to view the claim more broadly, as a keystone of English diplomacy dating back to the late thirteenth century. Certainly, the issue continued to be both 'the main stumbling block to the formulation of a permanent peace' in the late Middle Ages and 'a valuable playing card' for the English.[111] The diplomatic deadlock over the related matter of the Anglo–Scottish border line was broken in the east only with the fall of Roxburgh to the Scots in 1460, and the cession of Berwick by the defeated Lancastrian party in the following year.[112] A satisfactory resolution of the claims surrounding the debatable lands in the west march continued to elude both the Lancastrian kings and their Yorkist successors. These were still a subject of heated diplomatic discord well into the sixteenth century.[113]

The loss of Bordeaux in 1453, signalling the demise of the fortunes of England on the continent, and the beginning of civil war between the Lancastrian and Yorkist factions together proved a tempting series of opportunities for the Scots. In the summer of 1455 James II summarily broke the truce that had been sealed in 1453,[114] and began a siege of Berwick castle, which he called 'our town, long wrongfully detained by the English'.[115]Although the assault was unsuccessful, the English proved powerless to reverse the tide of belligerence that James now encouraged at home. Scottish attacks ravaged Northumberland and the lands around Roxburgh in the summer of 1456, and Berwick was again besieged (albeit unsuccessfully) in 1457.[116] Temporarily frustrated, James agreed to a renewal of truce until 1459, then to its extension until 1463.[117]

Anglo–Scottish relations remained tense for the rest of James's reign, and the fragile peace was broken on more than one occasion; the king of Scots himself was killed in an artillery explosion in July 1460, as his forces attempted to capture Roxburgh castle.[118] The danger posed by the enemy was sufficiently serious to move the English government to increase measures for the defence of the region, and for royal justices to effect the suspension of their activities for most of the period 1455–60.[119] But the damage wrought on the local economy by Scottish inroads was probably not as great as had been suffered in earlier periods of cross-border raiding.[120] Nor, in spite of the rhetoric employed by both sides, was the bitterness that characterised each side's dealings with the other as profound. Throughout the tense months of 1453–4 the government in England, first under Henry VI, then under Richard duke of York, continued to appoint conservators, and to enjoin on them strict observance of the fragile truce.[121] A letter sent to James II in May 1454 by York decried atrocities committed by the Scots, but requested redress for damages in surprisingly conciliatory tones.[122] While there can be little doubt that English demands were made from a position of considerable weakness, the border tribunals and their effective operation remained an integral aspect of diplomatic policy on the part of both the English and the Scots. And, as had occurred earlier in the decade, sessions of the courts were resumed with much relief by either side following the sealing of a truce in June 1457. A long list of conservators was once again included in the terms of the new agreement,[123] and within a month both Henry VI and James II had sent to their respective wardens general letters of safe conduct for all plaintiffs wishing to pursue border-related litigation. The protection they offered was to be made available without prejudice, and was now reinforced. A new provision enabled all who had complaints arising from the wardens' withholding of safe passage to take their grievances to the chancellors of either realm for resolution.[124]

The border tribunals enjoyed a precarious existence between 1457 and 1461, but they survived even the tumultuous events that marked the collapse of the Lancastrian government in October 1459 and the sudden death of James II the following summer. That the warden-conservators were able to convene sessions of the courts was in part a consequence of the Scottish king's astuteness in his dealings with England and the Lancastrians' preoccupations in England. It was very much to James's advantage to promote peace in the border lands, even in the face of English breaches of the truce, for the suspension of hostilities enabled him to devote his close attention to the bitter struggle between the Lancastrian and Yorkist factions. The government of Queen Margaret, anxious to find allies north of the border with which to defeat York and his adherents, had equally good reason to maintain friendly diplomatic ties with the Scots.[125] The borders, then, reaped tangible benefits from the confusion that characterised the troubled last months of Henry VI's reign, but they benefited, too, from the prominence that the border tribunals had by now come to enjoy in the legal administration of the frontier region. A day of march was convened in the summer of 1458,[126] in which both sides demonstrated genuine resolve in their attempts to settle outstanding grievances.

The survival of an indenture of agreement sealed at the conclusion of the sessions held in the east march permits an all too rare glimpse of the business conducted in the northern courts of the late medieval period.[127] Commissioners from both sides, led by Henry Percy lord Poynings and Bishop Spens of Galloway, discussed a wide variety of complaints. Chief among these was the shelter that had been offered by the English to the Scottish rebel, James Douglas, and his kin since 1455.[128] The Scots demanded, and were in turn assured, that Douglas and his adherents should be dealt with in accordance with provisions concerning the extradition of fugitives that had for long been an important aspect of Anglo-Scottish border law. Of equal interest to the Scots was the payment of restitution and compensation for breaches of the recent truce by subjects of the English crown. Bishop Spens presented written evidence and 'autentik instruments' showing that Thomas Stanley and a gang numbering between 500 and 600 men had set afire the toun of Kirkcudbright and laid waste to the surrounding lands, causing £2000 worth of damage, and that a ship sent from Harfleur to the king of Scots had been unlawfully seized by the earl of Warwick. Percy postponed settlement of these and other charges, suggesting that he wished to consult the English council; probably, the sums of money involved were so great that he deemed it advisable to warn his government of the gravity of the claims. Another 'diet' was assigned for 15 January, by which time, Percy promised, all Scottish proofs would have been scrutinised by a jury and all English subjects indicted by those juries compelled to appear to answer the charges.

Issues of a more general nature were also addressed, and commissioners from both sides took advantage of the cautious atmosphere of accord to clarify procedures for the more efficient keeping of the truce in future. More particularly, both acknowledged tacitly that the presence at days of march of armed retainers from two hostile allegiances posed an obvious threat to the peaceful resolution of truce-time complaints. They agreed henceforth to forbid the carrying of 'spere bowe harness or whinhart', on pain of payment of two English nobles (13s 4d). Similarly, persons found guilty of disrupting the tribunals by recourse to violence were liable to fine. The indenture made clear reference to the wardens' authority to impose the death penalty on particularly grievous offenders, including persons who were repeatedly 'filed' for theft.

The important role of mixed panels of jurors was underscored in the reiteration of provisions first made in 1429, which permitted English commissioners to choose Scottish recognitors, and the Scots the English jurors. There was also a new measure that imposed strict monetary penalties and the threat of infamy on all men who violated the secrecy of court proceedings, or who refused to sit as jurors. The problems caused by accomplices who, throughout the marches, sheltered known thieves were acknowledged in the imposition of the heavy fine of £40 on proven offenders, and in a provision that extended liability for restitution of the value of stolen goods to persons who 'distroubled' plaintiffs engaged in the pursuit of suspected thieves. Efforts to obviate differences in the values of the English and Scottish pounds were made in the establishment of a common valuation for such vital border commodities as oxen, cows, sheep and pigs. Finally, the wardens agreed anew to assume ultimate responsibility for the payment of all fines, penalties and damages assessed in the tribunals.

The indenture of 1458 reveals much about the level of sophistication that characterised the days of march by the end of the Lancastrian period. While the regularity of sessions so optimistically and enthusiastically envisaged in 1424 had never been achieved, a near unbroken series of meetings had provided the opportunity for the border magnates of both realms to refine a system of law competent to deal with the most dangerous challenges to truce-time conditions. By the mid-fifteenth century the customs of the marches boasted all the trappings of a distinct and authoritative system of law: a technical language, trial procedures, methods of proof, a scale of fines tailored to suit offences, a system for assessing compensation and damages, and specially empowered justices and juries.

Evidence of the entrenchment of march-related procedures and practices within the legal landscape of the north is found in a variety of record materials. In Scotland, the years 1448 to 1460 witnessed systematic attempts by the crown to define precisely the jurisdiction of the wardens and the business of their courts, in ordinances such as 'the statutis and use of merchis in tym of were' of 1448, and the 'poyntis belangand to the wardane courtis' of 1455/60.[129] A similar, albeit less clearly delineated jockeying for jurisdictional privilege appears to have occurred across the border in England. According to the terms of their commissions the English wardens were to take cognisance of all Scotsmen taken on suspicion of breach of the truce, and of all march–related offences generally. Thus in 1446 Henry Percy ordered the apprehension and detention of several Scots 'until they shall have given surety to appear in the warden's court'.[130] Yet, during the reign of Henry VI justices of assize acting under commissions of gaol delivery continued to preside over the trial of other suspects indicted on charges of march-related treason and felony.[131]

But increasingly the wardens were competing with their common-law fellows for the prosecution and punishment of such offenders. Sessions of gaol delivery convened in the mid-fifteenth century saw far fewer indictments for border-related felony than had their counterparts in the mid-fourteenth, though there is no reason to believe that levels of cross-border crime had abated in the interim. The wardens were, in fact, so active in exercising their authority that in 1453 the commons of Yorkshire were moved to complain of oppression and extortion by them and their agents. In a petition presented to parliament they noted that while the wardens enjoyed unchallenged jurisdiction over breaches of the truce committed anywhere in the marches,

> sumtyme for thaire singuler lucre, and sumtyme for malice that they have borne to certaine persones, [they] have attached, and takes upon theym daily to attache, diverse and many well ruled persones by thaire bodies, as well in Yorkshire as in other places oute of eny of the . . . shires of Northumbr', Cumbr' or Westmerland, or Toune of Newcastell, beryng hem uppon hande that thai were endited in the Wardane Courte; and some of the same persones [they] have put to grete fyne and raunson upon such enditement, and other some of them in sore prison by long tyme have withoute baile or maynpris keped, to the full grete hurte, oppression and importable charge to many of youre true and well ruled Liege people, dwellyng out of eny of the said Shires.[132]

Henry VI's government was sufficiently concerned to order that inquests be held into all such allegations, and the wardens duly punished if found culpable.[133] Northern plaintiffs and defendants, when they experienced the difficulties arising from the overlap of common-law and march-related jurisdictions, turned to the king and his councillors for justice. After her son, William, was killed while executing the office of bailiff of the warden's court in the east march, Isabella Cawood could find no remedy at common law, and sought the assistance of the chancellor.[134] A Cumberland man was indicted in a border tribunal for the homicide of a Scotsman, but when the record of the formal charge was misplaced he sought, and was granted, a royal pardon.[135] Despite the crown's determination to limit the exercise of the wardens' judicial authority to the marches alone, the rapid maturation and expansion of the system of border law during the reign of Henry VI saw these officals compete for business with the justices of assize to a much greater extent than they had done before. In the troubled years of the later 1450s, when Scottish incursions into the border lands were virulent enough to cause the king's justices to avoid the region altogether, the wardens appear to have assumed there the role of sole judicial agents of the crown.

Lamentably, there remain extant few examples of the bills of indictment exchanged in the late medieval days of march, and very little written record of the settlements made there. But the poor rate of survival of border record materials should not be interpreted as evidence that the courts were either irregular or ineffective. In the fifteenth century the English crown did not require that the records of the days of truce be returned to Westminster, and the warden-conservators normally stored them among their own household papers. Border materials, much like the early records of the courts of chivalry and admiralty, were therefore subjected to the same dangers of destruction and loss that beset all such materials. Bills of indictment filed with the conservators, moreover, much like their common–law counterparts, were never intended to be anything more than ephemeral documents. As is well known, the latter survive chiefly as copies in formal enrolments. In fact, well into the sixteenth century, no systematic preservation of any kind was ever ordered in respect of the business conducted in the border courts. The paucity of materials, then, is most accurately interpreted as a consequence of the crown's policy of vesting the administration of the march territories almost wholly in the persons of local magnates.

If fifteenth-century sources arising directly from the work of the courts are lacking, evidence of their vitality is not. The texts of the numerous truces sealed between 1424 and 1461 are of considerable length and of great complexity. The regular restatement of clauses governing the pursuit, apprehension and punishment of fugitives suggests that, with each indenture, efforts were being made to bestow on border procedures the veneer of tradition and custom. Much like the growing emphasis placed on written proofs, the insistence on the part of both English and Scottish commissioners that all alterations to existing provisions be set down in writing and authenticated by wardenial seals and royal ratification suggests that these men were well aware that they were creating a system of law, the respectability and integrity of which was reflected in the extent of its written expression. The reforms effected to current practice likewise reveal that the English and Scottish magnates who were the authors of border law had moved beyond the purely conventional, and that the law they were shaping had reached a stage in which *minutiae* were important, sometimes crucial.

In September 1459, a final indenture of truce made in the name of Henry VI included not only clauses derived from the agreements of 1451 and 1457 – themselves restatements of arrangements made as far back as 1398 – but provisions forged in response to conditions that had influenced the business of the border courts after recent hostilities.[136] The latter attested the vitality and flexibility of a system of law that, given wartime conditions, had to be sensitive to changes in the diplomatic atmosphere and so responsive to alteration and improvement. The former, however, were not merely a tedious repetition of aspirations rendered meaningless by time and the ravages of war. They represented, rather, the affirmation of procedures and principles that had proven effective despite time, and despite the ravages of war. The last of the Lancastrian truces with the Scots set out procedures and principles that, for the most part, were little more than adaptations of what its authors erroneously believed had once been 'customary' practice. More important, it embodied a system of law that bore witness to the esteem in which those authors held tradition, and to the confidence they placed in the ability of the 'ancient laws and customs of the march' to help them overcome the unique problems of the frontier lands. The last years of the fifteenth century were to demonstrate that their confidence was not misplaced.

Notes

1. The literature on the 'causes' of the civil wars is vast. A clear and concise summary of the historiographical debate that surrounds the conflict is found in Pollard, *Wars of the Roses*, pp. 14–19. Pollard's own views of the many causes of the wars are set out on pp. 45–66.
2. Ormrod, *Political Life in Medieval England*, p. 82. See also Carpenter, 'Political and Constitutional History', p. 193; Wolffe, 'Personal Rule of Henry VI', pp. 29–48.
3. Griffiths, *Henry VI*, pp. 160, 240, 250–1, 402. Roxburgh fell to the Scots in 1460 and Berwick was ceded by the Lancastrian party in 1461. Grant, *Independence and Nationhood*, p. 52.
4. PRO JUST 3/213 m.6. The Cumberland gaol deliery sessions of September 1457 had to be moved south to Penrith when the king's justices were still refusing to travel to Carlisle. See also JUST 1/1546 mm.10, 10d, 11, 12, 12d, 13d, 14, 14d, 16, 16d.
5. Summerson, *Medieval Carlisle*, ii. 436–7. More generally, see Macdougall, 'Foreign Relations', pp. 110–1.
6. Storey, 'The Wardens of the Marches of England', p. 606.
7. Storey, *End of the House of Lancaster*, pp. 117, 193.
8. Storey, 'Disorders in Lancastrian Westmorland', pp. 69–80.
9. Summerson, *Medieval Carlisle*, ii.406–8, 437–41; Pollard, *North-Eastern England*, pp. 121–43, 245–65; Griffiths, *Henry VI*, pp. 562–609.
10. *Rot. Scot.*, ii. 152, 237–8, 273–4. For indentures of service sealed with Percy early in the reign, see PRO E 404/39/281; E 404/41/158.
11. Dunning, 'Thomas, Lord Dacre', pp. 195–9; Steel, *Receipt of the Exchequer*, p. 190; Storey, 'Wardens of the Marches of England', pp. 604–5; Griffiths, *Henry VI*, pp. 160–1, 403–4; Summerson, *Medieval Carlisle*, ii. 406–7, 410–1.
12. Thomas duke of Exeter, the earls of March, Warwick, Northumberland and Westmorland. *Foedera*, IV.iv.111; Griffiths, *Henry VI*, pp. 22–3.
13. *Rot. Scot.*, ii.253.
14. Ibid., ii.256.
15. PRO C 81/684(1484); *Rot. Scot.*, ii.253; *Foedera*, IV.iv.117.
16. PRO E 36/190 fo.1, printed in *PPC*, iii.353–4.
17. PRO E 404/41/348.
18. BL MS Cotton Vesp. F VII, fo.42, printed in *PPC*, iii.171–4.
19. Barrow, 'Anglo-Scottish Border Line', pp. 139–61.
20. *CPR*, 1340–3, p. 363.
21. *Foedera*, IV.iv.98–9.
22. The sometimes ambiguous allegiance of English- and Scotsmen living in the occupied lands is reflected in the numerous grants of the king's peace and of letters of

naturalisation by the wardens to persons who could afford to purchase them. On this topic, see Neville, 'Local Sentiment and the 'National' Enemy', pp. 419–37.

23. A commission to correct violations of the truce was issued on 26 May. *Rot. Scot.*, ii.256.

24. PRO E 28/47 *sub* 22 July 4 Hen. VI, printed from a transcript in *PPC*, iii.204–7.

25. BL MS Cotton Cleo. F IV, fo.25, printed in *PPC*, iii.201; PRO E 404/42/297.

26. PRO E 404/43/169.

27. BL MS Cotton Vesp. F VII fos.55–55d, printed in *PPC*, iii.264.

28. BL MS Cotton Cleo. F IV, fo.33d, printed in *PPC*, iii.275. See also *Foedera*, IV.iv.131.

29. Griffiths, *Henry VI*, p. 158; Macrae, 'English Council and Scotland', pp. 415–26.

30. *Rot. Scot.*, ii.65 (February 1429). See also the lengthy answers given by the council to the complaints presented by James I's envoy, Thomas Roulle, in the winter of 1429–30. Although council members complained of the unsatisfactory resolution of several Scottish acts of cross-border violence, they continued to insist that such grievances were best adjudicated in the northern tribunals. BL MS Cotton Vesp. F VII, fo.54, printed in *PPC*, iv.346–50.

31. *Rot. Scot.*, ii.265, 266.

32. *Foedera*, IV.iv.148–9; PRO E 39/92/39.

33. Neville, 'Border Law', p. 339; Neilson, 'The March Laws', pp. 20–1.

34. The indenture included the names of specific jurors: representing the east march of England were Sir John Middleton, William Lamberton and John Fenwick the elder; Sir John Cockburn, David Hume and Alexander Murray stood for the east and middle marches of Scotland. In the west march of England William Martindale, William Stapleton the younger and William 'of Dykis' were jurors; for the west march of Scotland the men nominated were Sim Carruthers, Michael Ramsay and Matthew of Glendenning.

35. See Neilson, 'The March Laws', p. 22.

36. Fifteenth-century negotiations concerning the so-called 'Debatable Lands' in the west marches are discussed below, pp. 141–2, 165–7, 172.

37. Constable, *Law of the Other*, pp. 96–106; *Select Cases concerning the Law Merchant*, i.xxvii; ii.xx–xxi.

38. The procedures that collectively constituted the so-called 'law merchant' in the medieval period are reviewed in *Select Cases concerning the Law Merchant*, i.xxv–xxvi; ii.xxii–xxxiv, xl. For the history of the jurisdiction of the medieval admiralty courts and the procedures used to determine sea-borne incidents of piracy and plunder, see *Select Pleas in the Court of Admiralty*, pp. xi–lvi; *Black Book of the Admiralty*, i.xxxix, lxx–lxxv; *Select Pleas before the King's Council*, pp. xxviii–xxx.

39. For a discussion of the procedures used in the admiralty courts, see the references cited above in note 38. The medieval court of chivalry is examined in Squibb, *High Court of Chivalry*, pp. 1–28, and, more recently, in Keen, 'Jurisdiction and Origins of the Constable's Court', pp. 159–69, and Keen, *Laws of War*, pp. 23–59.

40. The term is Professor Baker's; Baker, *Introduction to English Legal History*, p. 54.

41. See above, note 34.

42. The jurors nominated from England were Sir John Bertram, Sir Christopher Curwen, Master Thomas Oldhall and William Lamberton; the Scottish jurors were Sir Thomas Kirkpatrick, Sir Patrick Dunbar, Master Thomas Roulle and David Hume.

43. The commission relating to the day of march planned for Lochmabenstone was issued to Sir Christopher Curwen, Sir Christopher Moresby, Master Thomas Oldhall and William Beaulieu; that for the day of march to be held at Redden Burn in the east march appointed Sir Robert Ogle, Sir William Elmeden, Master Thomas Cleveland and William Lamberton. Only Curwen, Oldhall and Lamberton were named in the indentures.

44. *Foedera*, IV.i.68, 97, ii.89, 100; *CPR*, 1405–8, p. 101; *Rot. Scot.*, ii.207, 212.

45. Russell, 'Trial by Battle', pp. 154–5.
46. BL MS Cotton Cleo. F IV, fos.48d, 51d, 52; Cotton Vesp. F VII, fo.43; BL Cotton Ch. x.3; BL Add. MS 27401, fos.1–2. They are printed in *PPC*, iv.16, 19–27, 53–4, 68, 73–5 and Macrae, 'English Council and Scotland', pp. 415–26.
47. Macrae, 'English Council and Scotland', pp. 417–21; Griffiths, *Henry VI*, pp. 158–62; Nicholson, *Later Middle Ages*, pp. 290–3.
48. *PPC*, iv.26.
49. *Rot. Scot.*, ii.268–9.
50. BL Add. MS 27401, fo.2, printed in Macrae, 'English Council and Scotland', p. 422.
51. A commission to hold another day of march was issued to several conservators in November 1430. *Rot. Scot.*, ii.272.
52. *CPR*, 1429–33, pp. 105–6. In the summer of 1431 Richard Neville was granted the sum of £200 in payment for expenses incurred in recent Anglo–Scottish peace negotiations, but also for moneys disbursed at the last day of march. PRO E 404/47/326.
53. PRO C 81/693(2323B).
54. *Foedera*, IV.iv.169–71.
55. Griffiths, *Henry VI*, p. 160.
56. *Rot. Scot.*, ii.268–9.
57. *Rot. Scot.*, ii.282–3; *Foedera*, IV.iv.200; PRO E 404/50/168 (August 1433); *Rot. Scot.*, ii.286 (March 1434); ibid., ii.292 (July 1435); ibid., ii.294 (February–March 1436).
58. BL MS Cotton Vesp. F VII, fo.53, printed in *PPC*, iv.169–71.
59. BL MS Cotton Vesp. F VII, fo.58, printed in *PPC*, iv.192–3.
60. BL MS Cotton Vesp. F VII, fo.48, printed in *PPC*, iv.308–15.
61. BL MS Cotton Vesp. F VII, fo.51, printed in *PPC*, iv.172–4.
62. BL MS Cotton Cleo. F IV, fos.69–70, printed in *PPC*, iv.196–7, 203.
63. BL MS Cotton Vesp. F VII, fo.57, printed in *PPC*, iv.193–6. The significance of the collapse of the alliance with Burgundy for Anglo–Scottish relations is reviewed briefly in Grant, *Independence and Nationhood*, pp. 49–50.
64. See, for example, the brisk exchange of letters between the council and James I in respect of a Scottish raid into Berwickshire in July 1433, and a counter-raid led by the English into lowland Scotland, in *PPC*, iv.170–1, 350–1, and another vigorous series of accusations made in the winter of 1435–6; ibid., iv.308–15. See also Nicholson, *Later Middle Ages*, p. 292, and Balfour-Melville, *James I*, p. 221.
65. *PPC*, iv.270.
66. BL MS Cotton Cleo. F IV, fos.79–81, printed in *PPC*, iv.268–77.
67. See, for example, the royal mandate sent to Marmaduke Lumley, warden of the west march, PRO E 101/53/17 (1436–43).
68. DCD Loc. XXV, no.121.
69. *CCR*, 1429–35, pp. 292–3. For the truce of 1431, see *Foedera*, IV.iv.169–71.
70. PRO C 1/28/240.
71. In 1434 the bishop's court recorded a recognisance of 500 marks by various inhabitants of Durham, which forbade one of their numbers from committing breach of the truce. PRO DURH 3/37 m.8d.
72. An attempt made in 1436 to agree to a day and place for sessions of the border courts, for example, proved fruitless. *Foedera*, V.i.27.
73. *Rot. Scot.*, ii.306–10; *Foedera*, V.i.47; PRO C 81/714(4447B).
74. PRO C 81/715(4578B); E 404/56/282; BL Add. MS 4608, no.6, fos.8–9. For the early history of the first of these cases, see above, note 53.
75. *Rot. Scot.*, ii.305; *Foedera*, V.i.50.
76. PRO JUST 3/54/21 mm.1–2. The previous year a court presided over by the mayor and bailiffs of Carlisle upheld the findings of a wardenial court in a case of lawful ransom taking. CRO Ca 3/1/10a (dorse).

77. *Rot. Scot.*, ii.323; *Foedera*, V.i.132. The truce of 1438, due to expire in 1447, was thus extended until 1454.
78. Grant, *Independence and Nationhood*, p. 51; Griffiths, *Henry VI*, p. 402.
79. The evidence for economic dislocation in the north is reviewed in some detail in Griffiths, *Henry VI*, p. 407, and Summerson, *Medieval Carlisle*, ii.411.
80. As occurred, for example, in 1442, when the crown ordered that all notable men of the border counties swear an oath to observe the recently renewed truce. Their names were to be returned to Chancery. *Foedera*, V.i.111–2. See also BL MS Cotton Vesp. F VII, fo.61.
81. PRO E 368/212 m.161; E 368/220 m.205.
82. BL MS Add. MS 4609, no.68, fos.168–9.
83. Alnwick Castle, Northumberland MSS, Box 761, no.22.
84. PRO DURH 3/43 mm.3, 13.
85. See, for example, a petition directed to the chancellor by the Scot, John Battson, who claimed that he had been robbed by the warden while travelling under a safe conduct issued by Richard Neville himself; PRO E 28/77 *sub* 12 July 25 Hen. VI.
86. Storey, *End of the House of Lancaster*, pp. 104–32; Griffiths, *Henry VI*, pp. 406–7; Griffiths, 'Local Rivalries and National Politics', pp. 589–632; Weiss, 'A Power in the North?', pp. 502–4; Pollard, 'Northern Retainers of Richard Nevill', pp. 52–69.
87. BL MS Cotton Cleo. F IV, fo.132, printed in *PPC*, vi.60.
88. *Incerti Scriptoris Chronicon Angliae*, Henry VI, p.35; *Six Town Chronicles of England*, pp. 123–5; *Asloan Manuscript*, i.237; Macrae, 'Scotland and the Wars of the Roses', pp. 124–31; Griffiths, *Henry VI*, pp. 409–10; Summerson, *Medieval Carlisle*, ii.435–6.
89. *Foedera*, V.ii.10–11, 13.
90. BL Add. MS 4610, no.75, fo.123.
91. *Foedera*, V.ii.15–19, 25; *Rot. Scot.*, ii.337–41.
92. Macrae, 'Scotland and the Wars of the Roses', pp. 145–6, 557. See also PRO E 28/79 *sub* 28 November 28 Hen. VI; *PPC*, vi.89.
93. *Rot. Scot.*, ii.339.
94. Ibid., ii.340.
95. Ibid., ii.341–2.
96. *Rot. Parl.*, v. 224–5; 29 Hen. VI, cap. 2.
97. Here again, procedures used in the border courts were being brought into line with those found in the courts of admiralty and chivalry. Plaintiffs who believed themselves aggrieved in these tribunals also had some recourse to the chancellor and the royal council. See *Select Cases before the King and Council*, pp. xxviii–xxx, and Baldwin, *King's Council in England*, pp.280–306.
98. *Rot. Scot.*, ii.344–5, 347.
99. *Rot. Scot.*, ii.349–54; *Foedera*, V.ii.34–8.
100. PRO E 28/81 *sub* 15 July 29 Hen. VI; E 404/67/204.
101. PRO E 404/68/48C.
102. PRO E 28/82 *sub* 4 May 30 Hen. VI; *PPC*, vi.125–7.
103. Nicholson, *Later Middle Ages*, pp. 359–66; Storey, *End of the House of Lancaster*, pp. 94–102; Griffiths, *Henry VI*, pp. 693–8.
104. *Rot. Scot.*, ii.306–7; *Foedera*, V.i.50.
105. BL Add. MS 4608, no.6, fo.8; *Rot. Scot.*, ii.306. See also Wilson, 'Border Incidents from the *Rotuli*', pp. 5–8.
106. Notarial instruments to this effect were dated 14 November 1449; *Foedera*, V.ii.15.
107. *Foedera*, IV.ii.32–3.
108. Ibid., V.ii.51–2, 75–6.
109. PRO E 39/99/85; *Foedera*, V.ii.12–13, 32–4; *Rot. Scot.*, ii.375–6.
110. Macrae, 'Scotland and the Wars of the Roses', p. 165.

111. Pollard, *North-Eastern England*, pp. 220–1.
112. See above, references in note 3.
113. See below, pp. 165–7, 172; Mackenzie, 'The Debateable Land', pp. 109–25; Rae, *Administration of the Scottish Frontier*, pp. 21–2, 176, 181.
114. *Foedera*, V. ii.47–52; *Rot. Scot.*, ii.363–8; PRO E 404/69/158.
115. Nicholson, *Later Middle Ages*, p. 372. In the autumn the Scottish parliament enacted vigorous legislation designed to strengthen the defensive administration of the lowland region. *APS*, ii.44–5. The defence of Berwick was warmly commended by the royal council, but it caused enough of a scare for members to warrant excusing the attendance of the wardens at the forthcoming parliament. PRO E 28/86 *sub* 9 July 33 Hen. VI; *PPC*, vi.247–50. See also Dunlop, *James Kennedy*, p. 157.
116. *Chron. Bower*, ii.516; Dunlop, *James Kennedy*, pp. 163–4, 166, 170–1; McGladdery, *James II*, pp. 96–100; Goodman, 'Anglo-Scottish Marches in the Fifteenth Century', p. 27; Grant, *Independence and Nationhood*, p. 51; Griffiths, *Henry VI*, p. 812; Pollard, *North-Eastern England*, p. 223. The record of the trial in the court of the warden of the Scottish east march of a borderer accused of assisting an English raid is found in *Fourteenth Report of the Royal Commission on Historical Manuscripts*, App., pt. III.10–1.
117. *Foedera*, V.ii.71–9. The truce was again extended, this time until 1468, by an indenture sealed in September 1459. *Rot. Scot.*, ii.393–9.
118. *Asloan Manuscript*, i.230; McGladdery, *James II*, p. 111.
119. Griffiths, *Henry VI*, pp. 812–13, and above, note 4. Although justices of assize were generally willing to venture as far as Yorkshire, even the city of York saw the sporadic cancellation of its assize sessions.
120. Summerson, *Medieval Carlisle*, ii.437.
121. *Rot. Scot.*, ii.361.
122. *Facsimiles of National Manuscripts of Scotland*, i, no.xlii; *Foedera*, V.ii.56.
123. *Rot. Scot.*, ii.382–3. The list included the admirals of either kingdom.
124. Henry VI's letters patent in respect of the English grant of safe conduct are found in *Rot. Scot.*, ii.384–5 (revised and reissued in March 1458; ibid., ii.386–7). Similar letters of James II are preserved in DCD Misc. Ch. 648 (copy at no. 684), with a copy of another such letter in DCD Registrum IV, fo.107d.
125. Pollard, *North-Eastern England*, p. 224; Dunlop, *James Kennedy*, pp. 215–16.
126. *Rot. Scot.*, ii.387–8; PRO C 81/775(10502).
127. SRO SP 6/20.
128. Dunlop, *James Kennedy*, pp. 156–7; Nicholson, *Later Middle Ages*, pp. 368–72.
129. BL Harleian MS 4700, fos.259–62, printed in Neilson, 'The March Laws', pp. 40–6. The parliament of October 1455 enacted a series of statutes designed to clarify the military role of the wardens in the Scottish marches. See Neilson. 'The March Laws', pp. 49–50; *APS*, ii.44–5.
130. De Fonblanque, *Annals of the House of Percy*, i. App., no.37.
131. Numerous cases are enrolled in PRO JUST 3/199, 3/208, JUST 3/54/7, 3/211 and 3/213. They are discussed in Neville, 'Law of Treason', pp. 17–22 and Neville, 'Border Law', pp. 335–56.
132. *Rot. Parl.*, v.267.
133. 31 Hen. VI, cap. 3.
134. PRO C 47/22/7(67).
135. PRO C 81/1461(2631, 2632).
136. *Foedera*, V.ii.86–90, confirmed in February 1460; PRO C 81/777(10765); *Rot. Scot.*, ii.393–9. Commissions to correct violations of the truce done since the last day of march were issued just prior to the truce negotiations, and a session of the border courts duly held; *Exch. Rolls*, 1455–60, p. 498.

7

The Yorkist and Early Tudor Years, 1461–1502

The years of Yorkist rule in England coincided with a dramatic shift in the foreign policy of the Stewart monarchy. Although historians' opinions of James III's efforts to 'resolve Scotland's position in the maelstrom that was European politics' vary from guarded praise to unreserved criticism,[1] most agree that the demise of the Auld Alliance, so long a defining characteristic of Anglo-Scottish relations, lies in the last quarter of the fifteenth century. The loosening of ties with France in turn exerted a profound effect on the attitude of the rulers of England and Scotland towards their respective border territories. While it is true that the problems associated with the frontier region were not ultimately resolved until after the union of the crowns in 1603, the gradual *rapprochement* between the realms begun in the late medieval period was reflected in a growing effort on the part of the Yorkists, then, more vigorously, Henry VII, to impose a modicum of law and order in the region. Beginning in 1462 a series of increasingly lengthy truces signalled the willingness of both crowns to establish an atmosphere of cordial relations; they culminated in the sealing of a comprehensive treaty of peace in 1502, the first since Edward III had been compelled to acknowledge the sovereignty of Scotland in 1328. Incidents of truce-breaking continued to disrupt good relations between the rulers (notably in the mid-1470s) and to jeopardise their efforts to put an end to open hostility. As with diplomatic affairs generally, the achievement of real quietude in the border region was still a long way off in the 1470s and 1480s. The deep mistrust between the peoples of northern England and their lowland neighbours was, moreover, of such longstanding duration that no amount of parchment and sealing wax could easily eradicate it: in 1490, indeed, animosity against the Auld Enemy still ran so high that the English parliament enacted a severely restrictive statute 'Against Scotsmen'.[2] But despite the lingering hostility, the Anglo-Scottish accords of these decades were made in a spirit of goodwill that had not been demonstrated since the 'golden age' of the thirteenth century.

Seldom appreciated by historians, both of England and Scotland, is the place of the cross-border courts in the diplomatic history of the late fifteenth century. The truces of these years were complex documents, replete with the verbiage and elaborate language characteristic of all late medieval 'international' agreements, but they continued to include in detailed and sophisticated fashion – and also to refine – the ways in which the border tribunals should settle grievances arising between the realms. The minutiae of these agreements stand in marked contrast to the rough and ready principles which, in the time of Edward III, had governed meetings between wardens and conservators of the truce. The length alone of the later agreements – running to twenty-nine clauses, for example, in the truce of 1484 –

attest the level of complexity which procedures for the 'reformacion and redress of attemptates done against the truce'[3] had reached. Similarly, the inclusion of discussions for the improvement of procedures as a major item of diplomatic business in meetings between English and Scottish ambassadors reflects the prominent place which the border courts had come to occupy in negotiations for lasting peace. The tremendous expansion of procedural and substantive law that had occurred under the hapless Henry VI bore rich fruit in the reigns of his three successors. By 1502, it was no longer possible for Henry VII or James IV to conceive of the administration of their frontier lands in the absence of wardens, conservators of the truce and, especially, the days of march over which they presided.

The border courts survived intact the tumultuous years of the so-called 'first reign' of Edward IV. That they did so was in no small measure the achievement of the new king's deputy, Richard earl of Warwick, appointed joint warden of the east and west marches in July 1461.[4] Edward IV played a complicated game of diplomacy with the Scots in the early years of his rule, simultaneously threatening open war at their repeated refusal to abandon support for the fugitives, Henry VI and Queen Margaret, conspiring with the Scottish king's enemies to foment rebellion within the realm, and treating with the crown for truce.[5] Defence of the northern frontier against Scottish raids and the disposition of punitive counter-strikes were undertaken by Warwick and another northern magnate, John Neville lord Montagu, appointed warden of the east march in 1463 and the following year granted the earldom of Northumberland forfeited by Henry Percy, third earl.[6] The king's repeated failure to assume leadership of a major offensive against the Scots has been criticised by some historians, as indeed it was by contemporary observers.[7] But as had been the case during the minority of Henry VI, lack of close interest in northern affairs on the part of a monarch could prove advantageous. The first decade of Yorkist rule was marred by a gradual estrangement between Edward and Warwick in matters of foreign policy, but the focus of the earl's frustration lay chiefly in his king's manoeuvrings on the continent.[8] The combination of a shift of Scottish diplomatic interests and the emphasis of English involvement in French and Burgundian affairs proved, in the long run, of great importance to the history of border law and the cross-border tribunals. Preoccupied as he was with matters of international urgency, Edward was content to leave the business of the northern courts to his agents.

The commission of June 1461 by which Warwick was appointed warden of the east and west marches included the authority to treat with the Scots for truce or peace.[9] When the earl's endeavours to defeat Yorkist enemies in the north left him little time for diplomatic sessions with the Scots, similar authority was granted to Sir Robert Ogle, newly raised to the dignity of a peer, and well experienced in the affairs of the region.[10] A truce was eventually sealed in July 1462.[11] Though it was only of brief duration, the Scots' growing awareness of French reluctance to aid the cause of Henry VI smoothed the way for a firmer commitment to armistice with England.[12] A new truce was made in December 1463, and was followed in June 1464 by a significant truce of fifteen years' duration.[13]

The agreement sealed in 1464, like its predecessors, was embodied in a document of great solemnity; the eighteenth-century antiquarian, William Nicolson, unaware of the long history of written agreements that linked the earliest Anglo-Scottish indenture of 1249 with that of 1464, included it among the records that he considered early 'codes' of march law.[14] In respect of the procedures it set out for the apprehension of cross-border fugitives and the resolution of grievances arising from violations of the truce, there was little to distinguish it from the agreement made between Henry VI and James II in 1457. Lack of innovation was, perhaps, predictable. In 1464, after some years of uneasy tension in Anglo-Scottish relations, both sides were content for the time being with a return to official armistice, and a return to the status quo in the matter of cross-border dispute settlement. Provision was made in the new truce for the immediate resumption of days of march, in clauses which appointed a large body of conservators drawn from among the wardens and greater lords of the border lands of either realm. Just a few days after ratifying the agreement Edward IV issued commissions authorising these men to proceed to the prearranged meeting places of Reddenburn (in the east march) and Lochmabenstone (in the west) in July, for the reform of all outstanding disputes 'according to the laws and customs of the said marches'.[15] Implicit in the brevity of the commissions was the understanding that the days of march should be conducted in accordance with practice that had obtained under Henry VI.

Sessions of the border courts resumed with ease, suggesting that the northern lords well appreciated the important role they played in the legal fabric of the frontier region. Even the recent capture of the bishop of Aberdeen and the duke of Albany by English pirates in blatant violation of letters of safe conduct, although it threatened ratification of the truce by the Scots, was not permitted to derail the meetings.[16] Among the bills submitted for adjudication by Scottish commissioners in the east march were two claims for restitution submitted by the prior of Durham, one in the sum of £422, for goods unlawfully carried away from Coldingham Priory by Sir Patrick Home, and another for £58, representing the value of 'divers notable goods' taken by Scottish thieves from the prior's cell at Farne.[17]

The death in 1465 of Bishop Kennedy of St Andrews, long an opponent of the Scottish *rapprochement* with England, removed one of the chief obstacles to good relations between the kingdoms and to the extension of the current truce beyond its initial limit of 1479 for a further forty years, until 1519.[18] The prospect of suspending hostilities for such an unprecedented period undoubtedly bespoke a new interest by the Scots in a formal alliance with England,[19] but peace between the old enemies was by no means a foregone conclusion. It was not long before the accord that underlay the negotiations held in 1465 had dissipated, and breaches of the truce both at sea and in the border lands continued to generate tension between Edward IV and James III. It was not a genuine change of heart or policy on the part of the Scottish crown, nor the inadvertent consequences of Edward's complex machinations with Scottish and continental powers, but rather the dogged work of border officials labouring behind the scenes that kept open the lines of communication. Regular contact between English and Scottish warden-conservators at the days of march ensured that, however the shifting winds of diplomacy and foreign policy might disturb Anglo–Scottish relations, incidents of cross-border crime did not degenerate into open war.

The 1460s and early 1470s saw a period of rare quiet in the northern marches. Although the days of march have left little mark in extant records, the regular issue of commissions to keep the truce, together with payments of arrears to the wardens, sums which included the reimbursement of monies expended in holding 'greet days of trues at our bordours', reveal that they were coping effectively with the requirements of local plaintiffs.[20] The prominence of northern magnates, both lay and ecclesiastical, among the officials appointed as conservators reflected Edward IV's dependence on the local knowledge of these men in the resolution of march-related grievances and the government's abandonment of an earlier policy of combining local expertise with a more broad-based membership.[21] The conservators' commissions of July 1470 included clerics trained in civil law. No provision had been made for them in the lengthy truce agreement of 1464, or in the commission of 1466, suggesting that the absence of expertise in this field had been felt at the sessions of the border tribunals held since the beginning of the new reign. To repeat, while clear evidence of the days of truce for the first decade of Yorkist rule is rather thin on the ground, there is good reason to believe that the courts continued throughout the years 1461–70 to function as the chief fora for the settlement of march offences.

There are other indications that, despite the growing tension between the earl of Warwick and his king, and the consternation caused in the north by the rebellions of Robin of Redesdale,[22] relations with Scotland remained largely untroubled. In the 1460s both the crown and the wardens were busy issuing letters of denisation and naturalisation to numbers of Scotsmen wishing to reside in peace in the border lands.[23] Such letters, it is true, were often sought by foreigners anxious to pre-empt harassment by the English subjects among whom they dwelt.[24] But when viewed in combination with the evidence of a renewal of trade links with the Scots, the frequent exchange of ambassadorial missions, and the issue of letters of safe conduct to merchants and pilgrims,[25] the impression is one of the freer movement of peoples across the border than had been known in the previous reign. The author of a London chronicle probably spoke for many English subjects when, after expressing hope that the Scots would abide by the truce sealed in 1464, he ruefully commented: 'but his ys harde for to tryste unto hem, for they byn evyr founde fulle of gyle and dyssayte'.[26] The later years of Edward IV's first reign, however, suggest that his sentiments were unduly bleak.

The readeption of Henry VI caused much confusion in the administration of the border counties, as it did elsewhere in the kingdom. In 1470, among Edward IV's last acts was the restoration of Henry Percy to the earldom of Northumberland forfeited by his father, and his appointment to the office of warden of the east march.[27] John Neville was given, in exchange for the earldom, the title of marquis of Montagu, but clearly resented his loss both of the lucrative Percy lands and of the warden's office, for later that summer he deserted Edward in favour of the Lancastrian cause.[28] His reward was a return to the office during the brief months of Henry VI's rule.[29] In the west march, Richard duke of Gloucester hardly had time to commence the duties attached to the wardenship, which he had been assigned in October 1470,[30] before Henry's recovery of the throne. The earl of Warwick appears to have assumed afresh the office of warden there.[31] Both Percy and Gloucester, however, were reinstated soon after Edward IV's victories at Barnet and Tewkesbury.[32]

It is hardly surprising that the confused events of the period of Henry's readeption should have left something of a power vacuum in the north; nevertheless, the months between September 1470 and April 1471 were generally quiet. The Scottish king was too busy trying to extricate himself from the consequences of the rule of his own overmighty subjects, the Boyd family, to involve himself in the 'game of musical chairs' unfolding in England,[33] and his borderers had the good sense (or the lack of astuteness) to leave their English neighbours undisturbed. Although Lancastrian refugees were given shelter in Scotland following the battle of Barnet,[34] James III was by now fully committed to recognition of the Yorkist dynasty and quickly acceded to Edward's request for a resumption of the border tribunals.[35] A day of march was planned for late September, at Alnwick. Edward was interested in continuing negotiations begun earlier for a marriage between the royal houses of York and Stewart, and it is significant that the background he chose for such discussions should have been a 'dyet by the grete commissioners of both landes' for the redress of truce-time offences. Safe conducts for Scottish envoys were issued in August, as were commissions appointing English conservators.[36] The importance of the occasion was emphasised when the king ordered officials as far distant from the borders as London and Middlesex to proclaim the forthcoming meeting, and to make strict prohibition against infractions of the truce.[37] The solemnity of the 'ancient' tribunals of the marches clearly provided an appropriate and advantageous venue for heralding the triumph of the Yorkist monarchy.

High in Edward's favour, Henry Percy began preparations for the entertainment of the Scottish envoys and, more generally, for the resumption of his role as representative of the most powerful magnatial family in the northern marches.[38] Much has been made of the rivalry for control of the border lands that is said to have existed between the earl of Northumberland and his fellow warden, Richard duke of Gloucester.[39] The latter's name, it is true, 'appears regularly on a long series of north-country commissions' throughout the 1470s,[40] but for much of the decade it was Percy who undertook the organisation and execution of the day-to-day business of the border tribunals. The duke's advisors and friends, including Ralph Greystoke, Humphrey lord Dacre, William Parr and John Conyers,[41] were regularly appointed to conservators' commissions,[42] and no doubt represented Gloucester's interests in the resolution of cross-border grievances. But these men 'were essentially of the second rank',[43] and discussion concerning the formal exchange of claims for compensation and redress was business most suitably left to the crown's most prestigious subjects. Local plaintiffs were well aware of the fact; so, too, was James III who, when he wrote in 1473 to complain about the depredations of English marchers, directed his letter to his 'richt honorabill and oure entierlie belovet cousing the erle of Nourthumbr'.[44]

Days of truce were held in the 1470s, if not with the regularity that each side had envisaged, then at least with some frequency: commissioners convened at Alnwick in 1471, and again at Newcastle in 1472.[45] As ever, proceedings were punctuated by periods of both cordiality and tension. Thus in April 1473 James III wrote in gracious fashion to Prior Richard Bell of Durham, one of the English conservators, requesting that his envoys be 'favourably treated and conveyed' on their visit to the east march.[46] The infamous incident of the 'bishop's barge', by contrast, strained relations between the crowns and their agents. Discord arose in the summer of 1472, when the Scottish ship, the *Salvator*, was wrecked near Bamburgh, its cargo stolen and one of its passengers, the abbot of Inchcolm held to ransom.[47] The offence was sufficiently serious to attract the attention of Edward IV himself, though the king was slow to accept responsibility in the matter. Eventually, in February 1475, he authorised payment of the sum of 500 marks in compensation to the Scottish merchants.[48]

James III's discontent with Edward's reluctance to settle claims arising from the plunder of the *Salvator* overshadowed another day of march planned for Alnwick in September 1473,[49] but neither side was willing to allow it to disrupt the sessions. The border courts were proving too valuable a venue for the discussion of issues of international importance for their integrity to be jeopardised. The cautious spirit of cooperation kept tempers at bay in the weeks leading up to the September meeting. Early in the summer Henry Percy, warden of the east march, wrote to James III accusing the men of Liddesdale of committing 'gret attemptatis' in violation of the truce.[50] The king promised to raise the matter with his warden–conservators, but countered with charges of his own relating to felons from Tyndale and Redesdale, 'quhilkis daili makes depredacionis and herschippis upon oure liegis'.[51] Both sides, however, agreed to submit their grievances to the warden–conservators at the forthcoming day of truce.

The 'great diet' assembled on 28 September. The result of the deliberations held between representatives of the two crowns was a formal indenture, in which 'remarkable progress' was made both in establishing a schedule for further meetings,[52] and in discussing outstanding claims for compensation and re-dress.[53] In a manner that recalled the optimism that had accompanied the sealing of the indentures of truce early in the reign of Henry VI, the agreement provided for a series of march days to be held within the next few weeks at various locations throughout the marches,[54] where bills of complaint should be exchanged. The culmination of these meetings was to be another great diet held at Kershop Brig in early December, 'which shall be institute by the Wardains [and] such persones of pouer and of gude disposition as they will answer for to thaire prince'. Here, all grievances were to be settled, and written proofs of any new complaints presented. The delicate matter of ships unlawfully seized and persons held to ransom in violation of the truce was noted; by now, both sides were aware that the incident involving the *Salvator* had reached the ears of their respective rulers, but there were other claims that also required resolution.[55] New procedures for the apprehension of suspects accused of committing cross-border homicide were established: such persons – and any one who could be proven to have assisted or received them – were to be delivered by the wardens to the plaintiffs themselves, 'to be justified or raunsoned at the will of the partye compleynyng'. As had by now become customary, fugitives were to be put 'to the kingis horne and declared kingis rebells and not to be reconsalyt onto the tyme that the partie [complaining] be satisfiet'. Provisions limiting the numbers of borderers permitted to accompany the warden-conservators to sessions of the courts (1,000 for the wardens, 500 for their deputies, and 200 for the latter's deputies) and strict prohibitions on the carrying of weapons were aimed at striking a balance between a modicum of good order and a show of strength appropriate to the occasion.

The resolve demonstrated at the Alnwick meeting was not merely empty rhetoric. As early as 4 October James III authorised the payment of expenses relating to one of the meetings planned for later in the month.[56] Although the Scots' demands for redress in the matter of the *Salvator* had not been resolved, other grievances were more quickly addressed. Thus in November Edward IV ordered the payment of silk and woollen cloth worth £200 (representing £911 8s Scots) to a group of Scottish merchants, 'in ful satisfaccion and contentacion' of a long outstanding claim.[57] He further undertook to oversee the arrest and imprisonment of a second band of English pirates who had unlawfully boarded a Scottish ship off the coast of Yorkshire and carried off £200 of salmon and other fish.[58] The tremendous diplomatic value of such awards was fully appreciated by a king anxious to cultivate the goodwill of his Scottish opponent: Edward's grant in fact overruled the findings of his own border commissioners, who had conceded only that the claim to compensation should be submitted to further scrutiny.[59]

In 1473–4 England and Scotland were coming closer to establishing a formal and lasting peace than they had been for almost two hundred years. The diplomatic ambitions of James III, Louis XI and Edward IV had shifted yet again, and the French king was now resisting James's attempts to strengthen the Auld Alliance. Thus rebutted, the Scots king became more favourably inclined towards friendly relations with England. Edward IV, for his part, was making preparations for an invasion of France, and was anxious to affirm the existing truce with his northern neighbour.[60] But if issues of international strategy and diplomacy combined to thaw relations between the English and Scottish crowns, both also knew that the ancient enmity that still heavily influenced the lives of the borderers for so long was not an obstacle easily overcome. Edward and James both recognised that the days of march had an important role to play in containing border hostilities, and that it was in their interests that the courts be seen to be functioning effectively and impartially. The English commitment to supporting and facilitating the business of the days of march was given concrete expression in the parliamentary session of May 1474, in a statute that threatened severe measures against English subjects who committed breach of the truce.[61] It was also made abundantly clear in the text of an indenture sealed in October 1474, which reaffirmed the current truce. That agreement was accompanied by a treaty of marriage, in which Edward's daughter, Cecilia, was betrothed to Prince James, son and heir of the Scottish king.[62]

The thorough integration of the cross-border courts into the business of Anglo-Scottish diplomacy is clearly demonstrated in a lengthy series of instructions issued by Edward to Alexander Legh, sent north in the spring of 1475 to discuss the ongoing problem of breaches of the truce.[63] The mission was ordered in response to several complaints by the Scottish king; more generally, it was also designed to assuage James's concerns that provision be made for the proper functioning of the days of march while Edward conducted his continental campaign.[64] The projected invasion of France by a large English army would remove from the border lands the crown's most important and influential subjects, including the earl of Northumberland and the duke of Gloucester, and James was concerned about the threat to the stability of the frontier represented by the absence of these figures of authority. He had little reason to doubt the ability of Gloucester's deputies in the west march, who had been active in conducting the business of the days of march since 1471, but he must have been sceptical of Edward's recent appointment of the untried and unfamiliar prior of the Hospital of St John of Jerusalem, Robert Multon, as warden in the east during Percy's absence.[65] Legh's embassy, coupled with Edward's reassurance that Multon would be suspended from office upon Percy's return, indicate that the king was aware of the Scottish crown's concerns, and anxious not to jeopardise the cordiality established between them in 1474.[66]

One of James's complaints in 1475 related to the plunder of two Scottish ships, one of them his own. Edward instructed Legh to assure James that due consideration would be given to the matter as soon as written evidence relating to the quantity and value of the goods allegedly stolen should be delivered to English conservators.[67] He was also ordered to consult with Percy and Gloucester about the incidents, and to convey Edward's regret at the failure of his representatives to resolve the matter satisfactorily. An equally vigorous response was prepared to James's claim that the English wardens had failed to appear at a day of march arranged in the indenture of 1474. Legh was instructed to inform the Scots – and the duke of Gloucester himself – that a special session was being organised for 8 May at South Berwick, for the exchange of 'complayntes and prouffes', to address the matter of sea-borne violations of the truce. Proclamations had been ordered inviting plaintiffs to submit their grievances to Gloucester as admiral; he in turn was to arrange with his Scottish counterpart for the review of Scottish bills of complaint, copies of which Legh now held. Legh was to remind the duke of his duty to issue letters of safe conduct for the meeting. He was further ordered to inform the English wardens that the days of march must be held 'withoute faile', as had been promised. The absence of the earl and the duke from the region was no excuse for laxness in this all-important obligation: Legh was told to urge them to make provision for their deputies to convene the sessions every fifteen days 'at convenyent places over alle the Marches for due reformacion to be made'. He was to bring with him to the Scottish court representatives appointed by the wardens, who together were to do their utmost to assure James that Edward 'hath so ordeigned and disposed for the rule of the Marches in his absence that he trusteth ther shalbe of his parte no cause of trouble ne breche geven to the hurt or derogacion of the trewes'.[68]

Admonition of Gloucester's less than satisfactory record of observing the truce may well have coloured the tone of Edward's instructions.[69] But his strategy of appeasing the Scottish king's concerns for the good order of the border lands was well received, and the years 1475–9 proved generally peaceful. Occasional violations of the truce disturbed the quiet: in 1477, for example, Gloucester was told to provide redress to the tenants of the Scottish lord, Sir John Carlill, for the depredations they had suffered at the hands of English thieves.[70] The king continued, however, to demonstrate an interest in the resolution of cross-border grievances by intervening personally in the awarding of compensation to some plaintiffs. Thus in May 1475 he ordered that Sir John Colquhoun of Luss be granted £6 13s 4d of English money in restitution for goods lost to the English privateer, Lord Grey of Codnor.[71] In 1477, when the Scottish merchant, Thomas Yare, complained that he had not yet been paid the £200 promised him more than two years earlier in reparation for stolen cargo, the king undertook to summon the recalcitrant debtors to explain to the royal council their failure to abide by the award.[72] Collectively, these manifestations of good intent on the part of the English crown helped to maintain order and a rare sense of stability in cross-border relations. As late as the winter of 1479–80, when the tenor of Anglo-Scottish diplomacy was once again shifting ominously, the wardens and the courts over which they presided were providing satisfactory remedy to aggrieved Scottish plaintiffs.[73]

The accord between Edward IV and James III did not last very long: by the early months of 1480 the English king was preparing to make 'rigorous and cruel werre' on the Auld Enemy.[74] The causes of this abrupt reversal in Anglo-Scottish diplomacy were numerous and complex; chief among them were Edward's fears of a renewal of the old alliance between Scotland and France and his wish to safeguard his own interests on the continent.[75] The king himself, however, cited issues and problems closer to home as the source of his increasingly hostile dealings with the Scots. Instructions issued to Alexander Legh late in 1479 or early in 1480 contained a number of grievances. Some were of recent date; thus Edward complained of the failure of the Scots to finalise the marriage agreed to in 1474, although regular instalments of Cecilia's dowry had been paid over. Others were of a more traditional nature: Legh was told to warn the Scots that the English would no longer tolerate the unlawful occupation of the key border fortresses of Berwick, Coldingham and Roxburgh, nor James's repeated refusal to perform homage to Edward 'as he oweth to doo and as his progenitours have doon in tyme passed'. But Legh's instructions devoted particular attention, too, to the problem of cross-border violence and to the Scottish crown's alleged carelessness in ensuring that the truce was duly observed. Edward drew a strong contrast between the goodwill demonstrated by the English in the payment of 'grete and notable soumes of money' for his daughter's dowry and recent depredations committed by ungrateful Scottish marauders 'ayeinst all honour lawe of armes and good conscience'. He noted a recent incident in which his warden, Henry Percy, had been taken prisoner, together with several of his attendants, and Sir Robert Lisle murdered; this, he charged, had occurred with the knowledge and support of the Scottish warden. Legh's instructions were well calculated to justify a war of aggression, but the emphasis on border-related incidents demonstrates how closely the state of the frontier lands and the integrity of truce agreements had been woven into the fabric of Anglo-Scottish relations.

The war against Scotland brought little satisfaction to Edward who, in fact, never bothered to lead the army he had mustered; instead, assaults on lowland castles and the defence of northern England against Scottish incursions were left to his brother, Richard duke of Gloucester.[76] The bitterness of the conflict was reflected in the speed with which both sides commenced raiding each other's territories. In the spring of 1480 the earl of Angus penetrated deep into the east march; Gloucester was assiduous in retaliating with punitive expeditions of his own.[77] Extensive preparations for a concerted assault on Scotland, including the appointment of Gloucester as lieutenant-general in the north,[78] and the arraying in 1481 of armies by both the duke and James III destroyed the atmosphere of cooperation that was essential to the proper functioning of the border courts. In Scotland, the wardens were strictly commanded to summon their courts not in order to deal with allegations of cross-border reiving, but rather to punish anyone whose trespasses or treasons threatened the security of border castles and vills.[79] In similar fashion, Gloucester's commission as lieutenant emphasised the necessity for the duke to limit the exercise of his judicial authority to matters of military discipline, and to the encouragement of defections to the English allegiance of as many Scotsmen as possible.[80]

If the border courts could not survive the open enmity displayed by both crowns in the war of 1480–4, the tribunals were nonetheless never far from the minds of either the English or the Scots. In June 1482 a formal alliance was made between Edward IV and James III's estranged brother, the duke of Albany, the purpose of which was to establish the latter on the throne as a puppet king.[81] The prizes promised the English – cession of Berwick, Liddesdale, Eskdale, Annandale and Lochmaben, and recognition of English overlordship – have often been cited by historians. Less well noted, however, is another clause in the agreement between Edward and Albany that touched on depredations committed during truce time, and the related matter of days of march. In the treaty, which established a truce to run until February 1483, commissioners for both parties swore to ensure that

if any persone or persones belonging to the oone or the othre of the parties aforesaide doo or attempte by way of fete, hostilitie, robberye or otherwise any thing contrary to the wele and prouffit of any of the othre partie, that restitution and amendis shall be made unto the harme takers of and upon the goodis and persones of suche as have doon it with as good maner and diligence as it hath bene at eny tyme best used, when treux have be kept bitwene both reaumes.

The indenture included a further clause appointing the earls of Northumberland and Angus keepers of the truce in the east and middle marches, with Gloucester and Albany himself performing these duties in the west.

Edward's designs on a wide swathe of territories in lowland Scotland, and his demand for Albany's homage when the latter was duly installed on the throne, clearly recalled the heyday of English power over the smaller kingdom in the late thirteenth and again in the mid-fourteenth centuries. But it is significant that in contrast to his predecessors, Edward I and Edward III, Edward IV in no way envisaged the suppression of the border courts as an immediate consequence of that relationship. A schedule attached to an indenture of February 1483, which renewed the alliance with Albany, specifically noted that the inhabitants of any lands newly occupied by the English should be subject to the governance of the warden-conservators and their courts.[82]

The scheme between the English crown and the duke of Albany came to naught, and Edward's death in April 1483 signalled an end to the war with Scotland. The accession of the duke of Gloucester to the English throne brought with it a host of new diplomatic concerns, both in respect of Anglo–Scottish relations and of English ambitions on the continent.[83] The success of the campaign into Scotland which he had led in the summer of 1482 made Richard reluctant to abandon the war, but James was determined to return to the peaceable conditions of the years 1474–9 and, ultimately, to the search for an enduring peace. Once again, the border courts came to provide an appropriate setting for the discussion of matters of international importance. Anxious to resume formal contact with the English as soon as possible, James set about making arrangements for the appointment of a new warden–conservator in his west march (to replace Albany), and to subdue the 'masterfull trespassours' who, since 1480, had been encouraged by their lords to wage war on their English neighbours.[84] In England, Richard III renewed the commission of Edward IV that had appointed the earl of Northumberland warden in the east march,[85] retaining for himself the wardenship of the west.

Negotiations between the crowns for a day of march began late in the summer of 1483 and eventually bore fruit a year later.[86] The meeting was marked by a show of ceremony led by Richard himself, who was present in Nottingham to receive the Scottish ambassadors,[87] and concluded with the sealing of an indenture of truce for three years, and a formal marriage alliance between James's son and heir and Richard's niece, Anne de la Pole.[88] The suspension of hostilities effected in September 1484 has been viewed by both English and Scottish historians as 'less convincing than its predecessor of 1474'; similarly, there is agreement among them that the motives of the two kings were 'suspect'.[89] Genuine amity may indeed have been lacking in the talks, and the establishment of a three-year truce certainly fell short of the long armistice provided in the agreement of 1474. Yet both Richard and James, and the former in particular, also demonstrated considerable foresight when they insisted that the indenture of truce include careful provision for a return to the traditional laws and customs of the marches, the resumption of cross-border tribunals and the exchange of fugitives and outlaws responsible for committing violation of the truce. The agreement concluded with a long list of conservators, and a new clause in which all such officials solemnly swore to observe current practice in the punishment of march offenders. Clearly, both kings intended that the border courts assume immediately the task of coping with incidents that might all too easily rupture the fragile peace.

In September 1484 'current practice' recalled procedures established in the reigns of Richard's predecessors, Edward IV and Henry VI, but the truce also included some changes. Most obviously, the castle of Dunbar was in English hands (where it would remain until late 1485 or early 1486)[90] and provision was made for the inclusion of the town and its inhabitants within the purview of the laws and customs of the marches. The tendency of border lords to collude in incidents of truce-breaking was specifically noted, and arrangements made for the strict prohibition and punishment of such abuses of authority. This clause must have been particularly pleasing to King Richard, whose northern subjects had suffered heavy losses when the earl of Angus had violated the armistice in 1480. The sealing of the indenture of 1484 was also the occasion for the appointment of Humphrey lord Dacre as Richard's lieutenant in the west march.[91] Retention of the office in his own hands while he was king would have represented a conflict of interests, an impression that Richard was anxious to avoid giving in the new atmosphere of Anglo–Scottish accord.

A spirit of cautious cooperation similarly lay behind inclusion in the agreement of a clause that enjoined the rulers of the two realms to advise each other, by means of formal letters and through the persons of heralds, of any grievances concerning the conduct of their respective conservators, and to authorise inquests into allegations of abuse. Together, these provisions signalled the growing awareness on the part of the kings of England and Scotland that their 'overmighty subjects' represented a challenge to the effectiveness of the border tribunals and, ultimately, to international relations generally. The tremendous influence of the warden-conservators in the border region had not, of course, escaped the attention of previous monarchs, Yorkist, Lancastrian or Stewart, and in England the previous years had seen experiments in both the separation and the coordination of the offices of warden and conservator designed to prevent abuses of power and authority. But it was a concern that had not to date been clearly addressed in the negotiations for the governance of the border lands held between the realms. The agreement of 1484 thus marked a significant development in the wardens' office: henceforth, it would be firmly separated from that of the conservators. Responsibility for undertaking the arrest and prosecution of border criminals, as distinct from the military duties of the wardenial office, remained with the important landholders of the frontier region, men who had intimate knowledge of, and experience with, the problems peculiar to the marches. In England these included the families of Ridley, Salkeld, Musgrave and Cartington; in Scotland those of Scott, Hume, Kerr and Rutherford.[92] But the judicial duties of the conservators in respect of the border courts would be kept quite distinct from the military responsibilities attached to the wardenial office.

The resumption of the border courts was not left to chance. Two days after the indenture of truce had been sealed another formal agreement set out dates and sites for forthcoming days of march.[93] In the west marches sessions were planned for Lochmabenstone on 14 October and 18 November; conservators from the east and middle marches (the latter in Scotland alone) were ordered to convene on 18 October and 1 December at Haddenstank and Reddenburn. Complaints originating in the area around English-held Dunbar were to be brought to that town on 10 October. Provision was also made for the issue of letters of safe conduct to ensure that plaintiffs from both sides of the border were able to travel unmolested to the sessions.

If Richard III remained less seriously committed to peace than was James III, he was nevertheless assiduous in providing for the regular convening of the border tribunals that played so vital a role in maintaining law and order in his northern lands. The business conducted at the days of march held in 1484 has left little trace in extant record, but the conservators appear to have been successful at least in encouraging cordial discourse between the kingdoms. In January 1485 envoys from England and Scotland discussed ways of improving the safety of ships and merchandise plying the waters between the ports of either realm, as had been provided in the recent truce,[94] and in April safe conducts were issued from both kings to conservators bound for Lochmabenstone and other traditional meeting places for the purpose of holding days of march.[95] The sessions no doubt helped to prepare the ground for negotiations intended to address the particulars of the marriage of Prince James to Anne de la Pole, to which the Scots agreed in May.[96] Those discussions, of course, never took place, for the summer of 1485 witnessed the landing in Milford Haven of an army led by Henry Tudor, and the abrupt end of the reign of Richard III.

Richard's belligerent attitude towards the Scots, first as duke of Gloucester, then as king, has frequently been noted by historians and contrasted sharply with the overtures for an Anglo-Scottish peace offered him by James III.[97] While there is little reason to query the unanimity of opinion that scholars have achieved nor to doubt the enthusiasm with which Richard embarked on his military campaigns against the Auld Enemy, it is also true that the work of these historians has too often overlooked the energies Richard directed towards keeping the peace in the northern marches. Perhaps better than any of his Plantagenet, Lancastrian or Yorkist predecessors, Richard III's dealings with Scotland demonstrated a shrewd use of the twin strategies of armed force and diplomacy. If the war fought against the Scots between 1480 and 1484 was, indeed, 'Gloucester's war',[98] then it is equally accurate to point out that the retainers who fought with him were prepared, when appropriate, to lay down their swords and to discuss in peaceful fashion with the enemy the business of reparation for atrocities committed in times of truce. The success of the border courts depended heavily on the willingness of both Richard III and James III to recognise that, no matter how grandiose their respective strategic ambitions, the problems of the frontier they shared could not be ignored. Richard's astuteness in acknowledging the importance of the 'problem of the north' was manifested in the support he lent to the effective functioning of the border courts, an attitude that in no wise derogated from his determination to wage war on the Scots. That shrewdness was also apparent in the interest he demonstrated in resolving, by diplomatic as well as military means, the difficult matter of the Anglo-Scottish boundary in the west marches.

Of the many gifts of land and office given by Edward IV to his brothers, none was more significant in the context of Anglo-Scottish border relations than the palatine lordship bestowed on the duke of Gloucester in the parliament of January 1483.[99] The grant was unusual in several respects: it gave the duke title to a vast array of estates and privileges both in Cumberland and in regions of south-west Scotland promised to England by the duke of Albany in the Treaty of Fotheringhay, the wardenship of the west march as a hereditary office, and authority over a liberty 'as large . . . as the Bischopp of Duresme hath within the Bisshoprike of Duresme'. The separation of the office of warden from the crown marked the final stage in the medieval development of this key office and signalled a profound alteration in the governance of the border lands, similar in nature to the transformation of the Welsh marches that had occurred in the previous decade with the creation of a council there.[100] Richard's accession as king, however, compelled him to address the problem of the north from a different perspective. The council of the north, created in 1484 and granted broad judicial authority over all manners of trespass and felony, was intended to bring reform to the administration of the region as a whole.[101] Equally important were the steps the king took to resolve the troubles associated with the governance of the marches in particular. In the east the occupation of Dunbar by an English garrison and the recapture of Berwick had enlarged the extent of the English march, and led to the inclusion in the indentures of September 1484 of provisions intended to facilitate the exchange of written bills of complaint and the settlement of English and Scottish claims to compensation throughout these new territories. In the west, the question of the 'Debatable Lands', long a source of contention between the realms, remained unresolved. Competing claims to territories there had recently been complicated by the undertaking made in 1482 by the duke of Albany to cede much of south-western Scotland to England should he manage to wrest the throne from James III.

Neither Edward nor Richard can have set much store by these grandiose promises. Although the Scottish lands were mentioned in the franchise created for Gloucester,[102] in the 1480s (as indeed in the 1460s and 1470s) the interests of both parties lay primarily in the area between the Rivers Sark and Esk where these joined the Solway Firth. One of Edward IV's early acts had been to establish a claim to the land by assigning a custodian of the ferry that crossed the Solway.[103] By 1474 the focus of competing claims had become the revenues derived from the fishery of the Esk waters, lucrative in their own right, but increasingly a symbol of sovereignty to both crowns. A commission headed by Bishops Booth and Story of Durham and Carlisle was appointed in February of that year to treat with the Scots 'in friendly fashion' about usage and custom in the area, presumably by means of a mixed jury of English and Scottish borderers.[104] James, however, was not prepared to concede defeat or to relinquish a claim that would prejudice his interest in the west march, nor Edward to allow the matter to drop. An indenture sealed in December made arrangements for another formal meeting in respect of the fishgarth, this one to be dominated by arbitrators drawn not from the border lands (whose views were obviously irreconcilable), but from lords whose interests lay elsewhere. An inquest composed of local jurors of either allegiance was to be held to 'fynyssh and determine' the debate that troubled the region.[105]

A decade later the question of the Esk fishery was still a matter of contention,[106] and the English and Scottish crowns remained deadlocked. The envoys who negotiated truce terms in 1484 agreed only to prohibit their respective subjects from erecting buildings and the sowing or planting of lands lying 'within the boundes of Batable Lands'.[107] A satisfactory resolution to the problem of the border line was still a long way off: although the two sides continued to argue their claims throughout the remainder of the fifteenth century, it was not until the reign of Elizabeth I that the Anglo-Scottish boundary running through the Debatable Lands was finally settled.[108] Richard III, however, was instrumental in linking the specific question of the border line to larger diplomatic issues and, more directly, to the business of the days of march. From 1484 onwards, the commissions appointing conservators of the truce directed these officials to discuss the fishgarth on the Esk and the claims of their respective crowns to the Debatable Lands whenever they convened the cross-border courts.[109] Despite the intractability displayed by the rulers of both kingdoms, disagreement over the establishment of a firm border line never degenerated into open war, nor did it disrupt the process by which mixed panels of English and Scottish recognitors came together to resolve claims arising from cross-border grievances. Richard III, then, proved adept at making use of the tradition of the days of march as convenient venues for the discussion of a variety of border-related issues.

Henry VII, too, knew a good thing when he saw it. Although early Tudor policy towards Scotland ranged from the belligerent to the cordial between 1485 and 1502, and despite his alterations to the office of warden of the marches (discussed below), Henry never wavered in his support of the border courts. Indeed, more thoroughly than ever before they became integral to the royal administration of the frontier region and to the king's policy of maintaining peaceful relations with the Auld Enemy. Henry's motives were, of course, in large part self-serving: in the early years of his reign he was preoccupied with establishing his own position in England and could not afford to risk open war with the Scots. But like his predecessor, he was also shrewd enough to see that the border courts constituted a valuable avenue of contact both with the northern nobility (a significant proportion of which was Yorkist in sympathy) and with the Scottish magnates whose interests must also be preserved. Under Henry VII the consolidation of the days of march as permanent features of the legal administration of the north was completed.

Anglo-Scottish relations in the first years of Henry's reign were dominated by the Scots' continued calls for the surrender of Berwick, and increasingly vociferous opposition of the Scottish border magnates to peace with England.[110] But officially at least, the crowns remained on good terms. By the winter of 1485–6 negotiations for an extension of the current truce were under way, and an agreement of three years' duration was sealed in London in July.[111] Although he came to demonstrate profound hostility towards Henry in the early 1490s, the young James IV was, at the outset of his reign, amenable to continued peace. Between 1488 and 1491 there were a series of truces in effect in the border lands.[112] Formal diplomatic encounters with the Scots were supplemented with a steady stream of commissions that authorised conservators to treat for the redress of violations of the armistice.[113] Like his predecessor, Henry VII established a direct link between the business conducted in the border courts and discussions of the problematic fishery on the River Esk. His interest in promoting the tribunals was more than merely casual: included within the commissions were clauses that specifically instructed his conservators to seek ways in which the current laws governing the apprehension and punishment of border felons might be clarified, amended and improved. Whatever his suspicions of the Scottish crown's role in the domestic troubles he experienced during the first years of his rule, Henry VII sought to ensure that the days of march continued to function effectively.

The work of the border courts in this period has left tantalisingly few traces in extant record materials from England: there survives from 1488, for example, a warrant for a safe conduct issued to John lord Maxwell, warden of the west march of Scotland, dated December 1487, to attend a forthcoming day of march; English conservators had been appointed the previous October.[114] Around the same time Henry Percy earl of Northumberland excused Sir Robert Plumpton's attendance at a session of the border tribunals in the east march, at the latter's request.[115] Scottish sources, however, reveal that sessions were held with some regularity throughout the years 1486 to 1491. The treasurers' accounts include frequent payments in various sums made to Scottish conservators in reimbursement either of expenses they incurred in travelling to the meetings, or of monies paid over in compensation to English plaintiffs.[116] Records of the Scottish parliament, too, suggest that during the early years of his reign James IV was assiduous in making provision for the appointment of wardens, and in endowing them with the judicial authority they required to implement verdicts returned in the courts.[117]

But while sessions of the border tribunals were convened and bills of complaint exchanged in customary fashion, it is apparent that royal support for peaceable Anglo-Scottish relations ran counter to the wishes of the borderers themselves. In 1487–8 tentative plans for a three-fold marriage alliance among members of the English and Scottish royal families were abruptly terminated when the Scottish parliament refused to separate its demands for the restoration of Berwick from the marriage proposals.[118] The following year a group of Scottish magnates opposed to peace attempted to discredit the enemy by forging a royal commission that purported to grant licence to Englishmen of all ranks to violate the truce and initiate an invasion of the smaller realm.[119] By 1491 the king of Scots found it necessary to issue 'scharp' warning to others of his border magnates, reminding them of their sworn obligation to observe the truce with England and to attend the days of march provided for in armistice agreements,[120] but he proved unable to prevent the pirate, Andrew Wood, from committing depredations against the English at sea.[121]

The English were no more inclined towards friendly relations with their neighbours. In the 1480s and early 1490s anti-Scottish sentiment in the northern counties was so pronounced that some Scots found it wise to purchase letters of denisation and naturalisation so as to avoid harassment; in the city of York Englishmen whose antecedents were suspect found themselves accused of being

Scots and compelled to defend their good names.[122] In May 1490 Henry VII responded to the discontent of his northern subjects by ordering a strongly worded proclamation. Noting that great numbers of Scottish persons were said to be roaming about the border shires 'to the grette hurte inquietacion and often disturbaunce of his pore true and feithfull subgettis' there, he commanded the deputy warden to round up all persons not known to local men as householders or servants and to drive them out of the realm.[123] Antagonism towards the Scots was still running high in the border lands eighteen months later, when Henry's fourth parliament enacted a statute 'Against Scotsmen'. The preamble began with a weary recitation of the king's efforts to maintain the truce, but noted that such agreements were 'ever under their surest promyse broken and not kept'. It concluded that 'it is better to be with theym at opyn werre than under such a feyned peas', and the act went on to order the expulsion from England and Wales, within forty days, of all non-denizen Scottish men and women.[124] The precarious position of Scottish subjects in the border lands in this period is well illustrated in the fate of the Scot Thomas Meburn, who was hanged without benefit of formal presentment or trial at a day of march in the summer of 1491.[125]

Against a background of such overt hostility it is something of a wonder that the days of march were able to function at all. The courts, however, did survive the efforts of local troublemakers to jeopardise them. More remarkably, they continued to conduct business even after Anglo-Scottish diplomatic relations degenerated in the years 1492–7. A change in James IV's formerly pacific attitude was apparent by the spring of 1491, when the Scottish parliament formally approved a renewal of the Auld Alliance; it was made explicit several months later, when the estates ratified a treaty directed against Henry VII.[126] In 1495 James welcomed at his court the pretender to Henry's throne, Perkin Warbeck, and in 1496 and 1497 led Scottish armies across the border with the intent of overthrowing the Tudor dynasty and wresting Berwick from English hands.[127] Henry weathered this 'sword-rattling' from the north,[128] remaining committed to an eventual peace with Scotland. Thus in the spring and autumn of 1492 conservators from England met with their Scottish counterparts at Coldstream to settle grievances arising from recent incidents of border-related violence.[129] In November, around the same time as he set his seal to a treaty of peace with Charles VIII of France, Henry's agents were again at Coldstream, concluding negotiations for an extension of the truce until April 1494.[130] As had become customary the text of the truce included the names of the Anglo-Scottish border landowners appointed as conservators, a schedule for the convening of days of truce in the east and west marches, and the assignation of a day the following summer at which the thorny problem of piracy might be fully addressed.[131]

Formal contacts between Henry and James were continued through the spring of 1493, and both set their seals to a new truce – this one to run until 1501 – that summer.[132] In a gesture that was far more shrewd than has been acknowledged,[133] Henry insisted that the indenture of abstinence include a clause in which he accepted full responsibility – and liability – for a series of attacks committed by English privateers in violation of the armistice. He undertook to deliver to several Scottish merchants the handsome sum of 1,000 marks of English gold, in compensation for the atrocities, and further agreed to renounce any claims that he or his subjects might have against Scottish offenders. The king, moreover, proved as good as his word. In just over a month he had assigned the promised money to his agents, seen it delivered it to the Scottish treasurer, and received formal acquittance from James for the entire sum.[134] These were not the actions of a ruler manifesting 'great anxiety' about an opponent;[135] they were the coolly considered measures of a king confident that he could win over his enemy with patience and calculation. The animosity of his northern subjects, likewise, could be overcome with some guile: although he bowed to local opinion by enacting the statute against Scotsmen in 1491, Henry continued to accept into the English peace any Scot who agreed to take an oath of allegiance to his crown,[136] and to appoint conservators to punish violations of the truce 'according to the laws and customs anciently observed in those parts'.[137] A meeting held at Coldstream in the spring of 1494 demonstrated that accord in the matter of border grievances was possible even amidst the fragile peace that then obtained: the inquest convened there returned a verdict of guilt against a gang of English reivers and ordered that Henry's conservators make redress to the plaintiff. The goodwill of both parties was further attested when all solemnly swore that similar violations of the truce would not be permitted to threaten on-going discussions concerning the fishery on the Esk.[138]

The ambitions of the pretender to Henry's throne, Perkin Warbeck, represented too great an opportunity for James IV to overlook. From Warbeck's arrival in Scotland in the late summer of 1495 until 1496 royal support for the Yorkist impostor rendered cordial relations between the crown untenable, even for a ruler as patient as Henry VII had been. James was probably not convinced of the veracity of Warbeck's claims to royal descent, but there is little doubt that 'it suited his policy to appear to do so'.[139] For his part, Henry was not prepared to resume negotiations for peace of any kind with the Scots as long as they gave shelter and assistance to the pretender. Official diplomatic discussions between the realms were therefore suspended. The summer of 1496 saw the renewal of open warfare in the border lands and the movement of small but ruthless armies through Northumberland and the Scottish lowlands.[140] The deep animosity of their respective rulers, however, did not prevent the local magnates from carrying on the administration of march law, and, in despite of war, business proceeded much as usual. The Scottish treasurer's accounts reveal that commissioners met at least once in 1495, and again in 1496.[141] That the courts should have ridden such a stormy period in Anglo-Scottish relations is eloquent testimony to the important role they played in the governance of the frontier region.

The outbreak of rebellion in Cornwall caused Henry VII to turn his efforts away from the north and, ultimately, to seek a return to cordial relations with the Auld Enemy. Peace with Scotland had become a matter of concern not only to England, but also to its continental allies,[142] and once Scottish support for Warbeck had disappeared (as it had by the summer of 1497) there was no longer any need to endanger the security of the north, or to spend money on its defence, by perpetuating animosity against James IV. As early as September 1496 English ambassadors were making overtures for peace at the Scottish court;[143] these bore fruit a year later at Ayton, with the sealing of an abstinence of seven years' duration.[144] The agreement was notable for the attention it devoted to procedures according to which suspects accused of committing march-related offences should be apprehended, kept under safe custody pending arraignment at days of march and guilty persons punished in condign fashion. Both rulers had come to appreciate the place of the courts not only within the larger context of Anglo-Scottish relations, but, equally important, within their respective realms. The depredations of cross-border felons threatened much more than the disruption of conditions of armistice: networks of criminal gangs also represented a challenge to royal authority that neither Henry nor James was willing to brook. The indenture of 1497 represented, then, something more than an agreement by both kings to observe a long period of truce. It signalled their continued determination to make use of the days of march in the normal legal administration of their respective frontier regions.

The truce of Ayton initiated a long series of diplomatic encounters between representatives of England and Scotland which culminated in 1502 in a comprehensive treaty of peace and a treaty of marriage between James IV and Margaret Tudor.[145] The period of *rapprochement* provided both kings with a valuable opportunity to observe the border courts at work. Surviving record materials reveal that Henry and James kept a close eye on the cases that were brought to the attention of their respective conservators, and that each demonstrated a keen interest in effecting improvements to the procedures employed in the settlement of grievances.

Despite his relief at the renewal of peaceful relations with Scotland, Henry adopted a stern attitude in respect of depredations committed by Scottish offenders during the months of open war between 1495 and 1497. Envoys sent north to Ayton to negotiate the truce were ordered to remind the Scots that it was they who had first violated the truce, and to emphasise his wish to obtain satisfactory resolution of all claims arising from the assaults made against his northern subjects. Accordingly, they were to arrange a day of march at which inquests should be held and compensation made to English plaintiffs.[146] In December 1497 Pedro de Ayala, ambassador of Ferdinand and Isabella of Spain, was named an arbiter in the matter of all such claims, an appointment aimed not only at ensuring that discussions for reparation did not destroy good relations between the English and Scottish courts, but at giving weight to Henry's demands.[147] Instructions issued to Norroy King of Arms soon thereafter similarly bespoke the English crown's resolve that English complaints be favourably addressed: they asked that James undertake to amend forthwith all 'murders and roberies' committed by his subjects in recent years.[148]

While Henry's demands for recognition of the validity of his plaints were vociferous, they were tempered by his willingness to admit that his own subjects were not without blame in causing disorder in the marches. In a sharply worded precept sent to the sheriff of Northumberland in the autumn of 1498, the king denounced the unlawful cross-border activities of a gang of northern criminals, and ordered them to appear before the warden's lieutenants in the east march to answer for 'certayne murdres and slaughters nowe lately by theym doon upon certayne Scottyshmen'. He further condemned the families who reset and sheltered the felons, and ordered that all persons of the surnames of Hedle, Rede, Melbourne, Charlton, Fenwick, Robson, Cressop, Wilkinson and Whelpdale be banished from the kingdom if they failed to surrender the culprits.[149] The same period saw the king issue commissions that, in accordance with the terms of the truce sealed at Ayton, encouraged his conservators to explore with their Scottish counterparts ways in which border legal procedures might be made to function more efficiently and effectively.[150]

James IV, though he was careful not to accept unnecessary responsibility for his subjects' misconduct, was as desirous as Henry to portray himself as a staunch supporter of the truce of Ayton. In the spring of 1500, when discussions between officials of the English and Scottish marches in the matter of cross-border reiving into Eskdale were faltering, the king wrote to his agents ordering them to appoint a date by which time all differences must be resolved and compensation for any assaults proven against Scottish offenders duly handed over. Justice was swift on this occasion: within three weeks suspects had been rounded up, sureties for their appearance at the proposed day of march secured and sworn, and the summons of a mixed panel of jurors organised.[151]

The treaties of peace and marriage of January 1502 were drawn up with appropriate fanfare and celebration. Although a recent assessment of their significance argues that tension between James IV and Henry VII remained palpable,[152] both sides publicly set great store in the 'real, whole and firm peace, friendship, league and confederation' which each swore to observe forever,[153] and although the amity did not survive the death of Henry VII in 1509, the nuptials of James and Margaret ushered in a decade of formal peace the likes of which had not been known since the thirteenth century. The determination of both kings to give tangible expression to their respective commitment to peace was made evident in the round of diplomatic negotiations that produced the treaties of peace and marriage. A third agreement was sealed on the same occasion, less widely publicised or acclaimed than the others, but of considerable significance to future relations between English and Scottish borderers. Its several clauses set out in considerable detail the procedures that would henceforth govern the apprehension and punishment of cross-border offenders.[154] The indenture represented, in many respects, the culmination of a century and a half of negotiation, experimentation and refinement. It was the last agreement of its kind made by Henry VII, who clearly intended it to serve as a working document for the years to come.

The indenture opened with a clause that required the wardens, their lieutenants or deputies to advise officials in the opposite march, within ten days, of the arrest of fugitive felons, and of the charges laid against them. Failure to comply with this provision was to result in the immediate punishment and removal from office of the recalcitrant. Suspects of either allegiance apprehended on a charge of homicide were to be brought to a day of march; if convicted there by a mixed panel of English and Scottish jurors they were to be surrendered to the appropriate official – the English warden if the victim had been a Scot, the Scottish warden if the victim had been English – for condign punishment, interpreted here as the penalty of death. Limited raids of reprisal were permitted, but only in cases in which a satisfactory resolution had not been achieved within six months, but such reprisals must by no means threaten the integrity of the peace. Incidents of violence at sea were to be dealt with according to the elaborate procedures established in 1464; that is, by mixed juries of recognitors in trials held before the wardens, conservators and admirals of both kingdoms. Here, too, reprisals were permitted, though these were strictly controlled. Both crowns undertook to supervise closely the workings of the days of march, and to make provision for the regular appointment as conservators of local lords and men learned in civil law. Both also promised to amend within their respective marches the legal procedures required to ensure the effectiveness and efficiency of the border courts and, ultimately, the preservation of peace and amity in the frontier region.

The alliance forged in 1502 may well have been 'brittle',[155] but as a blueprint for the future the agreement concerning the days of march secured more than merely nominal recognition. Royal commissions issued to conservators in February 1502, April 1506 and April 1507 suggest that incidents of cross-border lawlessness continued to require the attention of Henry VII's agents.[156] But surviving records of serious disruption in the years 1502–9 are quite astonishingly few, and there is little evidence of the period of 'anarchy' said by one historian to have characterised the region in the later years of the reign.[157] In 1504 Thomas lord Dacre, the warden's lieutenant in the east march, was joined by no less a personage than King James IV himself in a judicial raid designed to punish gangs of cross-border thieves whose activities were disturbing the area.[158] It has been argued that the king's cooperation with the English lieutenant was a thinly veiled attempt by James to assert jurisdiction over the Debatable Lands that were still a matter of contention between the realms.[159] James may very well have participated in the raid with such a design in mind, but the accounts submitted to the Scottish treasurer after the expedition, which included expenses incurred in hawking, playing cards and feasting, reveal that both king and lieutenant found something other than questions of justice to occupy themselves. Moreover, friendly relations with the Scottish court were a hallmark of Dacre's tenure of office from 1486 down to 1509,[160] a state of affairs that was quite unprecedented in the history of the wardenship. The murder of the Scottish warden of the middle march, Robert Kerr, towards the end of Henry's reign certainly cast a pall over the amity between the crowns, but at least one of the culprits was delivered to Scottish officials in accordance with the procedure set out in the agreement of 1502; his brother was also surrendered and two other felons outlawed.[161] The heyday of cross-border reiving was by no means a thing of the past in the early sixteenth century, but Henry VII's attention to the work of the border courts, together with the provisions he made for the efficient dispatch of officials sufficiently authorised to apprehend and punish offenders, ensured that incidents of violence never escalated into open war.

Much of the credit for maintaining good relations with the Scots must be given to the reforms Henry effected to the office of warden; reforms that complemented and supplemented the refinements he made to the substance and procedure of border law. As noted above, Edward IV had envisaged a profound change in the office when he included it in his grant of a hereditary regality to his brother, the duke of Gloucester. The king's reforms were nullified by Gloucester's assumption of the crown, but further changes occurred, and, as Professor Storey notes: 'Far from enhancing the wardenship of the west march, Richard diminished its standing'.[162] He appointed in place of the warden a royal lieutenant, a policy that Henry VII perpetuated after 1485 by reserving the office of warden to himself and assigning Thomas lord Dacre his lieutenant.[163] A similar alteration to the nature of the warden's office was made in the east march following the death of Henry Percy fourth earl of Northumberland in 1489: the king's sons, Prince Arthur and, in 1495, Prince Henry, were appointed warden-general in the east and middle marches, with Thomas earl of Surrey as lieutenant.[164] Still further changes were to come: in 1500 the office of lieutenant (variously referred to as that of vice warden or deputy warden) was assigned in commissions made up of several northern gentry.[165] The effects of this series of experimentations have been much discussed by scholars interested in the origins of the Tudor Council of the North,[166] and need not be examined afresh here. Less frequently considered, however, were the consequences of these changes on the general question of law and order in the north. Surviving record materials, though they are of a scanty nature, suggest that while Henry's reforms brought few tangible benefits to the administration of justice in the marches, they do not appear to have hampered the crucial role played by the wardens-lieutenants in maintaining law and order in the region.

Henry VII's motives for effecting sweeping change to the office of warden of the marches were heavily influenced by a determination to reduce the tremendous financial burden associated with it. At the same time, as Professor Storey has noted, he 'also realized the danger of granting the wardenship for long periods, on terms that permitted the wardens to keep their own armies', and his indefinite grants were intended to minimise the threat to the stability of the north, and to royal authority generally, inherent in the office.[167] The king accomplished these goals first by assigning the office to men drawn from the ranks of the gentry, rather than persons of magnatial background, thus avoiding the problems historically associated with 'overmighty subjects'. The salaries paid to the lieutenants were dramatically reduced – to a mere £153 6s 8d per annum for the west, and £114 13s 4d for the east and middle marches.[168] The heavy cost of defending the frontier was thus shifted from the Exchequer to the local nobility. Finally, by detaching custody of the fortresses of Carlisle and Berwick from the office and cutting the cost of keeping garrisons in them, the crown pared down the financial burden of the wardenship even further, and simultaneously reduced the size of the armies at the disposal of the lieutenants.[169] In many respects, then, the reign of Henry VII saw an unmistakable decline in the wardenship from its heyday in the mid-fifteenth century.

Scanty though they may be, surviving record materials nevertheless do not suggest that there was a concurrent diminution of the judicial powers wielded by the lieutenants, either in their capacity as presidents of the cross-border tribunals or in the courts through which they exerted their authority within the English marches proper. Only too aware of the central role they played in maintaining a semblance of law and order in the turbulent society of the border lands, the first Tudor monarch (and, indeed, his successors) had no wish, and no reason, to lessen his lieutenants' authority in this sphere. Indeed, Henry VII may even have tolerated, perhaps even approved of, some encroachment by them on the jurisdiction of the justices of the peace and assize. The peace commissions of the three border shires were both smaller and issued less frequently during the years 1485–1509 than they had been under the Yorkist kings, leading one scholar to comment that the king 'seemed to be especially uninterested in these northern counties'.[170]

The loss of assize records relating to the northern circuit for the period after 1460 and of evidence concerning the early work of the Council of the North is especially regrettable in that it renders impossible an accurate assessment of the lawlessness of the region in general.[171] It also makes it very difficult to appreciate how great was the competition between the common-law and the wardenial courts, an aspect of northern judicial administration that, as seen earlier, characterised the second half of the fourteenth and the fifteenth centuries. The wardens' tribunals are glimpsed only occasionally in the Yorkist and early Tudor periods, as in 1471–2, when the earl of Northumberland's bailiff rendered account for items carried from Alnwick to Morpeth 'to the warden's court held there', and for expenses incurred in keeping under lock and key various prisoners destined for trial there.[172] In 1498 a gang of felons from Tyndale and Redesdale was ordered to appear before the lieutenant of the east march for arraignment, though it must be wondered if the 'murderers and thieves' mentioned in the royal writ responded to the summons with any alacrity.[173] In the absence of reliable record, conclusions concerning the place of the wardenial courts can be tentative at best. But it is appropriate to remember here that the commissions by which the early Tudor lieutenants were appointed bestowed on these officials the same extensive judicial authority that their Yorkist and Lancastrian predecessors had exercised.

The lay liberties of the north appear to have caused Henry VII as much a judicial headache as they had his royal predecessors. It may be that, as has been suggested in respect of the west march in the 1450s, the lieutenants assumed rough-and-ready jurisdiction over a wide variety of criminal and trespassory offences that, outside the franchises, lay clearly within the purview of the king's justices.[174] Several years ago Rachel Reid convincingly challenged Gaillard Lapsley's assertion that the authority exercised by the medieval wardens had the consequence of eclipsing entirely the workings of the common law in the border counties of Northumberland, Cumberland and Westmorland.[175] Nevertheless, her assumption that the wardenial powers were clearly marked off from those of justices of the peace or of assize is difficult to support. The absence of complaints in parliament similar to that made in 1453, to the effect that the wardens were extending their authority beyond the marches, suggests that they had learned to confine their activities to those territories that lay closest to the Anglo-Scottish border line. But there is little reason to believe that, within the marches proper, they had stopped competing with common-law justices for the prosecution of persons accused of committing cross-border offences. That competition had begun as early as the reign of Edward III, and was probably still a feature of the legal administration of the northern shires a hundred and fifty years later. Indeed, long after the death of Henry VII, the crown considered it necessary to issue a strong reminder to one of its wardens that he had 'no authority to meddle in any causes, except by Scots or Englishmen'.[176]

In the late fifteenth century the lords of the lay liberties of the frontier region – Cockermouth, Tyndale, Redesdale – were often also recipients of wardens' and lieutenants' commissions; the most obvious example was the lord of the franchise created in Cumberland in 1483 for Richard duke of Gloucester. The lines between the authority they exercised as lords of liberties and that inherent in the office of warden must have been all too easily blurred, rendering well-nigh impossible a clear distinction between their functions as justices of common law and of border law. In 1489, when he assumed control over the lands and offices that had belonged to Henry Percy fourth earl of Northumberland, including the wardenship of the east march,[177] Henry VII required that the bailiff of Tyndale undertake a recognisance of £500 to perform assiduously the duties of his position; these included the prohibition of communication of any kind between English and Scots.[178] The same sort of oath must have been required of the bailiff during Percy's tenure of office, before whose court border felons and violators of the truce would have been arraigned and tried. In the 1490s the liberties of Tyndale and Redesdale were notorious for their lawlessness,[179] but the commissions issued to the king's lieutenants ensured that elsewhere at least these officials continued to exercise broad judicial authority over subjects whose criminal activities involved the Scottish enemy.

In the ecclesiastical franchises the jurisdictional lines were much more firmly drawn. The liberty of Hexham, although it lay within the marches, was jealously controlled by the archbishop of York; so much so that when in 1487 he claimed authority over the persons of two borderers convicted of high treason, Henry VII was quick to reassure Archbishop Rotherham that 'we ne woll nor have attempted anythyng against the privileges and franchises of your lordshipp'.[180] The palatinate of Durham lay firmly outside the marches, its felons subject to the jurisdiction of the episcopal courts. Although the earlier fifteenth century had seen Bishop Langley cooperate with the warden in the punishment of border felons from the east march, he did so purely out of courtesy.[181] When one such offender sought sanctuary within the cathedral precincts in 1478 Edward IV had to remind the prior that persons guilty of high treason must be surrendered to the royal courts for punishment,[182] though some cross-border felons clearly preferred the refuge offered by the church to the wardens' justice.[183] A series of presentments made before Durham justices of the peace in 1471–2, and sessions of gaol delivery held in the bishopric in 1472–3 included no indictments for march-related offences.[184] The absence of such cases implies, albeit indirectly, the existence of courts convened under the authority of the warden, Henry Percy, for earlier in the fifteenth century, and certainly in the fourteenth, criminal society in Durham counted its fair share of Scottish felons and victims.[185]

Henry VII, like his Yorkist and Lancastrian predecessors, never intended that the lieutenants' tribunals should replace the courts of common law in the north. Yet, despite the substantial changes he wrought to the office of warden, he was careful to preserve in his commissions to those officials all the judicial authority they required to apprehend and punish border felons within the confines of the marches. To have done otherwise would have been to threaten the very security of the frontier region. However serious were the difficulties that bedevilled their implementation, the ancient laws and customs of the marches continued to perform a vital function in the context of Anglo–Scottish relations generally, and the warden and lieutenants had become deeply entrenched in the administrative structure of the region. A recent study of early Tudor policy towards the border lands argues that the crown did as little as it could to keep the peace in the north, for as little expense as possible.[186] This assessment underestimates the attention that Henry VII paid to the tenor of Anglo–Scottish relations, as well as his appreciation of the broader implications of peace with the Auld Enemy. Henry VII could afford to dispense with the system of border law and its agents as little as he could his common law and his common lawyers. The achievement of the first Tudor was not so much in accepting that the northern border lands must be accorded special treatment within the polity that was England – for the Plantagenet kings had demonstrated such astuteness long before the sixteenth century – but in acknowledging that the way towards *bone governance* in the north was one which took into account, and made allowance for, the problems unique to a frontier.

Notes

1. Wormald, *Court, Kirk and Community*, p. 6. See also Grant, *Independence and Nationhood*, pp. 52–3; Macdougall, *James III*, pp. 92–7, 113–20; Macdougall, 'Foreign Relations', pp. 104–11; Nicholson, *Later Middle Ages*, pp. 478–9, 487; Ferguson, *Scotland's Relations with England*, pp. 38–9.
2. Hen. VII, cap. 6; see also below, p. 168. The hostility of the English towards the Scots is discussed in Neville, 'Local Sentiment and the 'National' Enemy', pp. 419–37. Scottish animosities in respect of the English are noted in Macdougall, 'Foreign Relations', p. 111, and Macdougall, *James III*, p. 117.
3. BL MS Cotton Vesp. C XVI, fo.122, printed in Dunlop, 'Redresses and Reparacons', pp. 351–3.
4. *Rot. Scot.*, ii.402; PRO E 404/71/943; E 404/72/3/33.
5. The tortuous Anglo-Scottish diplomacy of Edward IV in the years 1461–71 and the moves of the regent, Mary of Gueldres, to counter it, are reviewed and assessed in Ross, *Edward IV*, pp. 45–8, 49–57, 112, and Scofield, *Life and Reign of Edward the Fourth*, i.214, 244–5, 308–11, 328–30, 349–50, 388–90, ii.17–18. Scottish diplomacy is discussed in Macdougall, *James III*, pp. 57–61, 92.

6. PRO E 404/72/3/33; *Rot. Scot.*, ii.407–8; *CPR*, 1461–67, pp. 332, 340–1.
7. Ross, *Edward IV*, pp. 52–6, 62–3; *Three Fifteenth-Century Chronicles*, p. 221; *Rot. Parl.*, v.497–9. See also the sources cited in Ross, *Edward IV*, p. 62n.
8. Ross, *Edward IV*, p. 104.
9. *Rot. Scot.*, ii.402.
10. *Rot. Scot.*, ii.404; *Foedera*, V.ii.105; Pugh, 'Magnates, Knights and Gentry', p. 117.
11. *Paston Letters and Papers*, ii.279; *Three Fifteenth-Century Chronicles*, pp. 159, 175.
12. Ross, *Edward IV*, pp. 56–7; Scofield, *Edward the Fourth*, i.310; Dunlop, *James Kennedy*, pp. 238–9; Ramsay, *Lancaster and York*, ii.301.
13. *Rot. Scot.*, ii.409; *Foedera*, V.ii.118 (1463); *Leges Marchiarum*, pp. 36–61 (truce, June 1464); *Rot. Scot.* ii.412 (ratification of truce by Edward IV, 3 June 1464).
14. *Leges Marchiarum*, pp. 36–61. Nicolson's collection of march codes was in turn based on a compilation by the Tudor antiquary, Richard Bell. CRO MS copy of Richard Bell's *History of the Borders*.
15. *Rot. Scot.*, ii.413–14.
16. *CPR*, 1461–71, pp. 348–9; Dunlop, *James Kennedy*, pp. 244–5. Dunlop corrects the dating of the incident, noted also in Scofield, *Edward the Fourth*, ii.335–6. Dunlop, however, is erroneous in her statement that 'there is no evidence that the tryst [arranged in the truce of 1464] was kept'.
17. DCD Registrum Parvum III, fo.123d. The outcome of Prior Burnby's claims is not known, but it seems likely that they were ignored. By 1461 the Scottish border lord, Patrick Home, had set his sights and ambitions on securing control of the priory of Coldingham and its possessions. See Dobson, 'Last English Monks on Scottish Soil', pp. 1–25.
18. *Foedera*, V.ii.136–7; *Rot. Scot.*, ii.419–20.
19. Grant, *Independence and Nationhood*, p. 52; Scofield, *Edward the Fourth*, i.390.
20. *Rot. Scot.*, ii.420 (October 1466); PRO C 81/1503(4405); E 404/74/1/59; E 404/74/1/127 (July and November 1468); *Rot. Scot.*, ii.422–3 (July 1470).
21. Compare, for example, the conservators of the truce appointed by the duke of Gloucester in the 1420s, and those named in the commission issued in October 1466. The former included nobles whose lands and influence lay outside the north, such as Ralph lord Cromwell, Thomas duke of Exeter, Robert de Willoughby and Walter Hungerford; the latter the northern luminaries Richard earl of Warwick and Salisbury, John earl of Northumberland, Ralph Greystoke, Henry Fitzhugh, John Scrope of Bolton, Thomas Lumley, Robert Ogle, Henry Neville, James Strangways, Robert Constable, Robert Claxton and Roger Thornton.
22. Ross, *Edward IV*, pp. 127–8; Scofield, *Edward the Fourth*, ii.488–97.
23. *CPR*, 1461–7, pp. 55, 191, 459, 518, 542; *CPR*, 1467–77, pp. 84, 159; PRO C 81/1497(4132); C 81/810(2028); C 81/818(2443); C 81/1499(4239); C 81/826(2811). Few such letters survive in extant form; for examples granted by the earls of Warwick and Salisbury late in the reign of Henry VI, see CRO D/Lons/L5/1 no.C58; D/AY 1/132. The repetitive and formulaic nature of the documents, which were copied out with spaces left blank for the name of the beneficiary and the conditions of his naturalisation, suggests that they were issued with some frequency.
24. Neville, 'Local Sentiment and the 'National' Enemy', pp. 430–3.
25. These links are discussed in Macrae, 'Scotland and the Wars of the Roses,', pp. 368–72. See also *CPR*, 1461–7, pp. 93, 163, 271, 468; PRO C 81/1499(4228); CDS, iv. nos.1338, 1340, 1343, 1347, 1358, 1361.
26. 'Gregory's Chronicle', p. 224. John Harding expressed a similarly pessimistic opinion of the Scots' reputation in his chronicle. See Gransden, *Historical Writing in England*, pp. 274–87, and Kennedy, 'John Hardyng and the Holy Grail', pp. 188–91.
27. *CPR*, 1467–77, p. 206; PRO E 39/99/91; *Rot. Scot.*, ii.422–3.

28. Ross, *Edward IV*, pp. 163–5; Scofield, *Edward the Fourth*, i.517–18, 534, 539; Pollard, *North-eastern England*, p. 311.
29. *Rot. Scot.*, ii.425.
30. PRO E 101/71/950; *Rot. Scot.*, ii.423–4.
31. Storey, 'Wardens of the Marches of England', p. 608.
32. *Rot. Scot.*, ii.428–9; Pollard, *North-eastern England*, p. 312.
33. Nicholson, *Later Middle Ages*, pp. 475, 476.
34. Ross, *Edward IV*, p. 168.
35. Macdougall, *James III*, p. 92; Nicholson, *Later Middle Ages*, p. 476.
36. *Rot. Scot.*, ii.429–30; *Foedera*, V.iii.6–7; PRO E 404/75/1/25; C 81/1503(4405).
37. *Foedera*, V.iii.6.
38. *Percy Bailiffs' Rolls*, p. 6. Percy's pivotal role in assisting Edward IV to regain the throne in the spring of 1471 is critically examined in Pollard, *North-eastern England*, pp. 312–14. For a different point of view, see Weiss, 'A Power in the North?', pp. 506–7.
39. Pollard, *North-eastern England*, pp. 326–7; Scofield, *Edward the Fourth*, ii.5; Kendall, *Richard III*, pp. 153–4; Bean, *Estates of the Percy Family*, p. 133. Ross, however, argues forcefully that in the 1470s Percy's apparent subordination to Gloucester 'was essentially private rather than official'. Ross, *Edward IV*, p. 199. See also Hicks, 'Dynastic Change', pp. 81–8; Reid, *King's Council in the North*, pp. 43–4.
40. Ross, *Richard III*, p. 24. See also Pollard, *North-eastern England*, p. 316.
41. Pollard, *North-eastern England*, pp. 329, 258; Ross, *Richard III*, pp. 48–9, 239 (Table 2).
42. See, for example, *Rot. Scot.*, ii.430–1, 433, 434, 437, 438–9; *Foedera*, V.iii.33–4. In 1474 and 1475 Parr was acting as Gloucester's lieutenant in the marches. PRO E 404/75/3/63; E 404/76/1/86.
43. Ross, *Edward IV*, p. 200.
44. PRO E 39/102/22, printed in *CDS*, iv. App., no.24. The letter is discussed below.
45. For the meeting held in 1471, see above, references in notes 36–8. The day of march convened in 1472 was mentioned in a meeting of the border tribunals held in 1473. PRO E 39/152, discussed below.
46. DCD Loc. XXV, no.101.
47. Lesley, *History of Scotland, from the Death of King James*, p. 39; *Rot. Scot.*, ii.434–5; Nicholson, *Later Middle Ages*, p. 477. Macdougall dates the incident to March 1473; Macdougall, *James III*, p. 116.
48. *Rot. Scot.*, ii.445; *APS*, ii.106; PRO E 39/52; E 39/99/96; E 39/1/32; Nicholson, *Later Middle Ages*, pp. 477–8; Macdougall, *James III*, p. 116.
49. *Rot. Scot.*, ii.436–7; *Foedera*, V.iii.33; PRO E 39/5/14; Pollard, *North-eastern England*, p. 234.
50. PRO E 39/102/22, printed in *CDS*, iv. App., no.24. The earl's letter to James does not survive, but Percy's allegations are noted in this document, a response by James III to Northumberland's grievances. The letter was misdated by Bain; it belongs more appropriately to the year 1473. See Nicholson, *Later Middle Ages*, p. 476n.
51. A second letter, undated but written around the same time, defended the Scots' sheltering of the Lancastrian rebel, Robert de Vere, earl of Oxford, on the grounds that the royal safe conduct under which he claimed refuge in Scotland had not yet expired. PRO E 39/96/28, printed in *CDS*, iv. App., no.25.
52. Nicholson, *Later Middle Ages*, p. 477.
53. PRO E 39/52; *Foedera*, V.iii.34–5.
54. The schedule was as follows: Newbiggin on 20 October, Reddenburn on 28 October, Gamelspath on 5 November, 'Bell' (Belford?) on 9 November, and Lochmabenstone on 25 November.
55. A separate day was set aside for the resolution of grievances relating to incidents of piracy. It was planned for 8 January 1474, and was to be presided over by the admirals of

either realm and at least one 'notable person of gude knawlage, auctorite and disposicioun to the bordour'.

56. *Treasurer Accts*, i.45.
57. PRO E 39/102/21, printed in *CDS*, iv. App., no.23. See also ibid., no.1412.
58. *CPR*, 1467–77, p. 409.
59. The complaint was to be examined afresh at the meeting of admirals scheduled for January 1474. PRO E 39/52.
60. Ross, *Edward IV*, pp. 205–13; Macdougall, *James III*, pp. 113–15.
61. *Rot. Parl.*, iv.163; 14 Edw. IV, cap. 4.
62. *Rot. Scot.*, ii.445–50; *Foedera*, V.iii.49–52. The treaty and its significance in the context of Anglo-Scottish peace negotiations are discussed in Macdougall, *James III*, p. 117; Scofield, *Edward the Fourth*, ii.102–4, and Nicholson, *Later Middle Ages*, pp. 478–9.
63. BL MS Cotton Vesp. C XVI, fos.121–6. The instructions are closely examined and edited in Dunlop, 'Redresses and Reparacons', pp. 340–53.
64. Edward's preparations for the expedition against France, planned for July 1475, and the disappointing results of the 'great enterprise' itself are extensively reviewed in Ross, *Edward IV*, pp. 216–38.
65. *Rot. Scot.*, ii.442.
66. *CPR*, 1467–77, p. 545.
67. Dunlop, 'Redresses and Reparacons', pp. 346–7, 352.
68. Dunlop, 'Redresses and Reparacons', p. 353.
69. This is the interpretation of the instructions proposed by Pollard, *North-eastern England*, pp. 233–5.
70. BL MS Cotton Vesp. C XVI, fo.127, printed in Halliwell, *Letters of the Kings of England*, i.147–8. The incident is mentioned in a letter of Edward IV to his almoner and ambassador, Alexander Legh.
71. PRO E 39/92/33. Colquhoun's grievance had been one of the matters discussed between Legh and James III earlier that spring. See Duncan, 'Redresses and Reparacons', p. 352.
72. BL MS Cotton Vesp. C XVI, fo.127. Yare's complaint had been the subject of a commission of inquiry in October 1475. *CPR*, 1467–77, p. 409.
73. A document of April 1480 makes reference to a recent day of truce, when several Englishmen received 'a certane some of mone' in compensation for a Scottish assault. *Acts of Council*, 1478–95, p. 49. Another day of truce held shortly before the outbreak of war in 1480 is mentioned in the instructions issued by Edward IV to Alexander Legh. PRO E 39/102/25, discussed below.
74. PRO E 39/102/25, printed in *CDS*, iv., App., no.28 (instructions issued to Alexander Legh). The document should be dated to the period between November 1479 and May 1480. See Macdougall, *James III*, p. 143; *CDS*, v.125.
75. Edward's concerns with the diplomatic *rapprochement* between James III and Louis XI are reviewed in detail in Macdougall, *James III*, pp. 143–4. The English king was determined to prevent a renewal of Scoto-French amity, but he was equally intent on ensuring the continued payment of a rich pension granted him by Louis.
76. The war of 1480–4 is discussed in Macdougall, *James III*, pp. 140–55, 168–70; Ross, *Edward IV*, pp. 278–93; Pollard, *North-eastern England*, pp. 237–44; Nicholson, *Later Middle Ages*, pp. 490–507, and Ross, *Richard III*, pp. 44–7. See also Reid, 'The Merkland Cross', pp. 216–27.
77. Macdougall, 'Richard III and James III', p. 159; Macdougall, *James III*, p. 145; Ross, *Edward IV*, p. 45; Pollard, *North-eastern England*, pp. 237–8.
78. *CPR*, 1476–85, pp. 205, 213–14; Ross, *Edward IV*, p. 279.
79. *APS*, ii.143–4.
80. *Rot. Parl.*, vi.204–5.

81. The expression is Ross's, *Edward IV*, p. 287. See also Macdougall, *James III*, pp. 152–3, and Scofield, *Edward the Fourth*, ii.338–9. The Treaty of Fotheringhay is found in *Foedera*, V.iii.127–8.

82. *Foedera*, V.iii.128.

83. Macdougall, 'Richard III and James III', pp. 165–6; Macdougall, *James III*, p. 208; Ross, *Richard III*, pp. 191–209.

84. *APS*, ii.165.

85. Nichols, *Grants, etc. from the Crown during the Reign of Edward the Fifth*, pp. 19–20; *CPR*, 1476–85, p. 462.

86. See the correspondence between Richard and James in the period August 1483 to August 1484, Horrox and Hammond, *British Library Harleian Manuscript 433*, iii.47–51, 105–7. Some of the correspondence is also printed in *Letters and Papers Richard III and Henry VII*, i.51–3, 59–62, and Ellis, *Original Letters*, i.111–13. The letters are discussed in Macdougall, 'Richard III and James III', p. 166, and Macfarlane, *William Elphinstone*, p. 132. Richard's instructions to Northumberland Herald, dated April 1484, are found in Horrox and Hammond, *British Library Harleian Manuscript 433*, iii.71.

87. Laing, 'Minutes of the Proceedings of the Commissioners at Nottingham', pp. 35–48. This collection of documents includes the text of a lengthy oration in praise of peace delivered by the Scottish ambassador, Archibald Whitelaw.

88. *Foedera*, V.iii.150–3 (truce), 153–5 (marriage alliance). The truce was proclaimed by Richard just days after the sealing of the indenture, and by James in October. Ibid., V.iii.156; Horrox and Hammond, *British Library Harleian Manuscript 433*, ii.26.

89. Macdougall, *James III*, p. 214; Grant, 'Foreign Affairs under Richard III', pp. 117, 123; Pollard, *North-eastern England*, p. 242; Ross, *Richard III*, p. 193; Ramsay, *Lancaster and York*, ii.525–6.

90. Macdougall, *James III*, p. 217.

91. *CPR*, 1476–85, pp. 485–6.

92. See, for example, *Foedera*, V.iii.152–3.

93. Ibid., V.iii.155.

94. *Rot. Scot.*, ii.466–7.

95. *Foedera*, V.iii.162–3; PRO C 47/22/11(53).

96. *APS*, ii.170.

97. See references above in notes 76, 89. See also Conway, *Henry VII's Relations*, p. 4.

98. Pollard, *North-eastern England*, p. 242.

99. *Rot. Parl.*, vi.204–5. See also Storey, 'Wardens of the Marches of England', p. 608; Ross, *Edward IV*, p. 202.

100. Ross, *Edward IV*, pp. 193–8; Williams, *Council in the Marches*, pp. 6–10; Griffiths, 'Wales and the Marches', pp. 161–2.

101. The ordinances drawn up for the regulation of the new council are found in Horrox and Hammond, *British Library Harleian Manuscript 433*, iii.107–8, 114–15. They are discussed in Reid, *King's Council in the North*, pp. 59–70, and Brooks, *Council of the North*, pp. 11–12.

102. *Rot. Parl.*, vi.204. The Scottish territories included within the new liberty were Liddesdale, Eskdale, Ewesdale, Annandale, Wauchopedale, Clydesdale and the west march of Scotland. Gloucester was said to have 'subdued' them to such an extent already that they were 'at this tyme not inhabite with Scots'.

103. PRO C 81/787(518); *CPR*, 1462–7, p. 56. See also Graham, 'Debateable Land', p. 38. Another grant of 'custody of the passage of the water of Sulwath' was made in April 1464; *CPR*, 1461–7, p. 374.

104. *Rot. Scot.*, ii.450–1.

105. PRO E 39/99/88 and E 39/96/27, printed in *Foedera*, V.ii.53.

106. Still another commission, appointed in August 1475, had proven incapable of resolving the issue of the boundary line. See *Rot. Scot.*, ii.452. More generally, see Mack, *Border Line*, pp. 101–4.
107. *Foedera*, V.iii.155.
108. Sixteenth-century surveys of the border line in the west march are reviewed in Mack, *Border Line*, pp. 8–41 and Mackenzie, 'Debeateable Land', pp. 109–25. Two of the surveys are printed in Hodgson, *History of Northumberland*, III.ii.171–248.
109. See, for example, *Rot. Scot.*, ii.478, 479, 482 (1487); PRO C 82/34(1488); *Rot. Scot.*, ii.491 (1489); PRO C 82/65; Campbell, *Materials for a History of the Reign of Henry VII*, ii.504, *Rot. Scot.*, ii.493 (1490); *Rot. Scot.*, ii.496, 498–9 (1491); *Foedera*, V.iv.51 (1492); PRO C 82/114; C 82/164; *Rot. Scot.*, ii.513 (1493); PRO E 36/254 pp. 1–4, printed in *CDS*, iv., App., no.34; *Rot. Scot.*, ii. 513–14 (1494); *Reg. Sec. Sig.*, i. no.192 (1498).
110. Conway, *Henry VII's Relations*, pp. 8–41; Chrimes, *Henry VII*, pp. 70–1, 87–8, 279; Nicholson, *Later Middle Ages*, pp. 518–20.
111. PRO E 39/93/10; *Rot. Scot.*, ii.473–7. See the important correction of Rymer's errors in dating this and other documents relating to Anglo-Scottish truces made during the reign of Henry VII in Conway, *Henry VII's Relations*, pp. 10, 22–3, 147.
112. PRO E 39/5/2, *Rot. Scot.*, ii.480–2 (28 November 1487); PRO C 82/45, *Rot. Scot.*, ii.488–90 (October 1488); *Rot. Scot.*, ii.503–5 (December 1491).
113. *Rot. Scot.*, ii.478, 479, 482, 491, 493, 494, 497, 498–9, 500.
114. PRO C 82/33; *Rot. Scot.*, ii.479.
115. Stapleton, *Plumpton Correspondence*, pp. 56–7.
116. *Treasurer Accts.*, i.96, 172, 173, 178, 183.
117. *APS*, ii.214, 226.
118. *APS*, ii.181–2; Conway, *Henry VII's Relations*, pp. 10–11; Macfarlane, *William Elphinstone*, pp. 141–4.
119. *APS*, ii.201, 202.
120. *APS*, ii.226. More generally, see Nicholson, *Later Middle Ages*, pp. 519–20; Summerson, *Medieval Carlisle*, ii.471–2.
121. *Reg. Mag. Sig.*, ii, no. 2040; *APS*, ii.227; Macdougall, *James IV*, pp. 226–7; Conway, *Henry VII's Relations*, pp. 30–1; Nicholson, *Later Middle Ages*, p. 549; Macfarlane, *William Elphinstone*, pp. 140, 144–5.
122. Neville, 'Local Sentiment and the 'National' Enemy', pp. 433–4. See also *Letters and Papers Henry VIII*, App., no.36; and Howden, *Register of Richard Fox*, p. 29.
123. PRO C 66/570 m.21d; *CPR*, 1485–94, p. 322.
124. 7 Hen. VII, cap. 6.
125. Raine, *Sanctuarium Dunelmense*, p. 19.
126. *APS*, ii.224; *Treasurer Accts*, i.cix–cx; Macdougall, *James IV*, p. 91.
127. These events are reviewed in Macdougall, *James IV*, pp. 125, 130–6; Arthurson, 'King's Voyage into Scotland', pp. 1–22; Conway, *Henry VII's Relations*, pp. 40–1, 99–115; Chrimes, *Henry VII*, pp. 88–91; Storey, *Henry VII*, pp. 81, 85; Nicholson, *Later Middle Ages*, pp. 550–3.
128. Wormald, *Court, Kirk and Community*, p. 6.
129. *Treasurer Accts*, i.199; PRO E 39/5/15; *Foedera*, V.iv.48.
130. PRO E 39/99/78; *Foedera*, V.iv.50–1.
131. Days of march were planned for Coldstream, Norham and Lauder, a meeting to discuss the disputed fishery on the Esk River was scheduled for 8 August, and the sessions appointed for the resolution of maritime offences set for 1 August at Haddington and Berwick.
132. *Foedera*, V.iv.62; *Rot. Scot.*, ii.508–12.
133. See, for example, Conway, *Henry VII's Relations*, p. 40; Nicholson, *Later Middle Ages*, p. 549.

134. PRO C 82/329; E 39/102/32; E 39/99/71. James's commission to his treasurer, the abbot of Cambuskenneth, directing the latter to travel to Wedderburn to receive the money, was dated 31 July; E 39/99/54.
135. Conway, *Henry VII's Relations*, p. 40.
136. See, for example, *CPR*, 1485–94, pp. 127, 345, 376, 381; *CPR*, 1494–1509, pp. 74, 110, 116, 136.
137. *Rot. Scot.*, ii.513 (November 1493); *Foedera*, V.iv.73; *Rot. Scot.*, ii.515 (May, December 1494); *Rot. Scot.*, ii.516, 518–19 (May 1495). A warrant authorising a safe conduct for Scottish conservators travelling to Northumberland for the 'diet' to be held on 6 August was issued in May 1495; PRO C 82/331.
138. PRO E 36/254 pp. 1–4 (copy), printed in *CDS*, iv. App., no.34.
139. Nicholson, *Later Middle Ages*, p. 551. See also Macdougall, *James IV*, pp. 118–19, 132.
140. Nicholson, *Later Middle Ages*, pp. 551–2; *Treasurer Accts*, i.cxliv–clviii.
141. *Treasurer Accts*, i.268, 270.
142. Chrimes, *Henry VII*, pp. 272–84; Storey, *The Reign of Henry VII*, pp. 84–8.
143. See the series of diplomatic instructions issued to Bishop Fox of Durham in PRO SP 58/22 and BL MS Cotton Vesp. C XVI, fos.147–50, printed in *Letters and Papers Richard III and Henry VII*, i.104–11. See also Conway, *Henry VII's Relations*, p. 110.
144. *Rot. Scot.*, ii.526–30.
145. *Foedera*, V.iv.168–70, 172, 184. The numerous ambassadorial discussions that preceded the sealing of the treaties of 1502 are reviewed in Conway, *Henry VII's Relations*, pp. 115–16 and Mackie, *James IV*, pp. 90–101.
146. *Rot. Scot.*, ii.524. A similar commission was issued in July 1495; *Rot. Scot.*, ii.530–1.
147. *Rot. Scot.*, ii.526; *Foedera*, V.iv.120. Ayala had been sent to the Scottish court in the summer of 1496, where he befriended *James IV*. See Mackie, *James IV*, pp. 84, 88–9; Macdougall, *James IV*, pp. 282–4.
148. BL MS Cotton Vesp. C XVI fos.119–199v.
149. PRO C 66/582 m.6(17)d; *CPR*, 1494–1509, p. 160. The criminous activites of the surnames of the northern liberties are reviewed in Robson, *English Highland Clans*, pp. 69–75.
150. *Rot. Scot.*, ii.531 (July 1498); *Rot. Scot.*, ii.543, *Foedera*, V.iv.139–40, PRO C 82/206 (July 1500).
151. *Acts of Council*, 1496–1501, pp. 408, 411.
152. Macdougall, *James IV*, pp. 248–54.
153. *Rot. Scot.*, ii.556–7.
154. PRO E 39/93/12; *Rot. Scot.*, ii.548–51; *Foedera*, V.iv.170–2.
155. Macdougall, *James IV*, p. 251.
156. *Rot. Scot.*, ii.544–6, 566; *CDS*, iv. no.1744.
157. Robson, *English Highland Clans*, pp. 67–75.
158. *Treasurer Accts*, ii.451–5.
159. Macdougall, *James IV*, p. 251.
160. Ellis, *Tudor Frontiers*, p. 156.
161. *Letters of James the Fourth*, no.171; Buchanan, *History of Scotland*, ii.246–7; Holinshed, *Chronicles*, v.464–5.
162. Storey, 'The Wardens of the Marches of England', p. 608. See also Storey, 'North of England', p. 137.
163. PRO E 101/72/1062; *Rot. Scot.*, ii.472. This first appointment was made for one year only. Subsequent commissions assigning Dacre to the office of lieutenant in the west march 'during the king's pleasure' were granted in August 1487, July 1488, February 1497 and December 1498; *Rot. Scot.*, ii.479; PRO C 82/40; *CPR*, 1494–1509, p. 116; *Rot. Scot.*, ii.532. Richard III's appointment of Humphrey lord Dacre as his lieutenant in the west march is enrolled in *Rot. Scot.*, ii.485–6.

164. *CPR*, 1485–94, p. 314; *Rot. Scot.*, ii.501–2; *Foedera*, V.iv.79.
165. *CPR*, 1494–1509, pp. 200, 213, 442, 487; PRO C 82/227; C 82/276; Reid, 'Office of Warden', pp. 495–6. Dacre was reappointed sole lieutenant in 1504, and given the more prestigious title of warden general. *CPR*, 1494–1509, p. 379.
166. Reid, *King's Council in the North*, pp. 61–91; Brooks, *Council of the North*, pp. 10–3. Changes to the office under Henry VII are also examined in the context of the Dacre ascendancy in north-western England in Ellis, *Tudor Frontiers*, pp. 48–9.
167. Storey, 'The Wardens of the Marches of England', pp. 608–9. See also Ellis, *Tudor Frontiers*, pp. 48–9, 260.
168. Ellis, *Tudor Frontiers*, p. 49.
169. Storey, 'The Wardens of the Marches of England', p. 608.
170. Storey, *English Justices of the Peace*, p. 38. See also Ellis, *Tudor Frontiers*, p. 53, where note is made of the 'shortage of substantial gentry' in the north.
171. The problem of disorder in the north during the reign of Henry VII constitutes a notable gap in surveys of early modern crime and criminality. Historians are able to make only general comments on the subject. See, for example, Chrimes, *Henry VII*, pp. 185–93; Bellamy, *Criminal Society*, pp. 1–7; Ellis, *Tudor Frontiers*, p. 56; Summerson, *Medieval Carlisle*, ii.469–70, 530.
172. *Percy Chartulary*, p. 6; *Percy Bailiff's Rolls*, p. 6.
173. PRO C 66/582 m.6(17)d; *CPR*, 1494–1509, p. 160.
174. Summerson, *Medieval Carlisle*, ii.439.
175. Reid, 'Office of Warden', pp. 483–4; Lapsley, 'Problem of the North', pp. 440–6.
176. *Letters and Papers Henry VIII*, xii(1). no.595. See also ibid., xviii(i). no.964. The first memorandum noted further that 'some reform is necessary of the laws of the marches, and there are no books of them . . .'.
177. James, 'Murder at Cocklodge', p. 81.
178. *CDS*, iv. no.1556.
179. In 1498 Bishop Fox of Durham issued a resounding condemnation of the 'infamous and blatant thieves of Tyndale and Redesdale', and of the lords who refused to bring them to justice. A gang of such felons later sought the bishop's absolution. See *Depositions and Other Ecclesiastical Proceedings*, pp. 37–41, 42–3; Tuck, 'War and Society', p. 51.
180. Hodgson, *History of Northumberland*, III.ii.41.
181. PRO DURH 3/37 m.8d, a recognisance in which several of the bishop's tenants undertook to prevent one of their fellows from committing breach of the truce.
182. DCD Loc. XXV no.87.
183. Thus in the autumn of 1503 Edmund Coke was granted sanctuary after confessing to the homicide in self defence of a Scot. In 1508 the Scot James Elwald sought sanctuary after admitting that he had committed burglary. *Sanctuarium Dunelmense*, pp. 37–8, 54.
184. PRO DURH 19/1/1, edited in *Durham Quarter Sessions Rolls*, pp. 1–65.
185. Incidents of march-related crime involving Scottish suspects and victims are found scattered throughout the surviving common-law records of county Durham, classified under various headings in the Durham Cathedral Dean and Chapter Muniments collections known as Locelli IV and V.
186. Ellis, *Tudor Frontiers*, esp. pp. 260–72.

Conclusion

The Legal and Social Contexts of Anglo–Scottish Border Law in the Later Middle Ages

In the spring of 1475, at Warkworth castle, Henry Percy warden of the east march set his seal to a certificate which attested that one William Jonson 'formerly of Scotland' had sworn an oath of allegiance to Edward IV, and ordered that the king's new subject henceforth enjoy royal protection.[1] Around the same time a panel of eight Yorkshiremen assembled in a formal tribunal to declare John Richardson a true liegeman of the king of England, notwithstanding recent rumours in which it was 'noysed yat he shuld be a Scottesman and borne in Scotland'.[2] The Englishman, Robert Brown, too, came to the attention of his betters in the little vill of Selby in the North Riding, but his actions landed him in trouble when he was charged with receiving in his home 'Scottes and othir suspect peple'.[3] In the xenophobic atmosphere that characterised northern society in the 1470s association of any kind with the Auld Enemy was viewed as suspicious, potentially dangerous, and worthy of censure.

Anti-alien sentiment was a widespread feature of late medieval English society, though its focus was by no means confined to the Scots. The opinion of John of Salisbury that the Welsh were 'rude and untamed'[4] was echoed three centuries later, when the author of the *Libelle of Englyshe Polycye* warned of the natural tendency of the Welsh to rise in rebellion.[5] The Irish fared little better in contemporary opinion: to Gerald of Wales they were an irascible, rude and irreligious people; even their saints 'appear to be of a vindictive temper'.[6] Some 300 years after him, the epithets 'wild' and 'savage' were frequently associated with the Gaelic-speaking peoples of the island.[7] Enmity against the French, expressed in parliamentary legislation, literature and song throughout the period of the Hundred Years War, was so widespread that it hardly requires comment here. The sense of a distinctly 'English' identity, as measured against the 'foreignness' or 'otherness' of various peoples, has long been a subject of interest to medieval scholars, and few historiographical traditions have been better served than that which seeks to understand the interaction of the Anglo-Norman and the Gaelic cultures of medieval Britain. On the one hand there is an abundance of literature on the exchange of ideas and institutions between differing cultures in localised areas: the English lordship in Ireland and its hinterland, Wales and the Welsh marches, the border lands lying between England and Scotland;[8] on the other, a stream of historical inquiry that seeks to understand the meeting of contrasting cultures in the broader context of the British 'imperial' tradition.[9] While similarities among all three frontier cultures have been noted, the proliferation of studies especially of the latter kind has led to a sometimes bewildering variety of opinion about the successes and failures that attended the interaction of the Anglo-Norman people of England and their Celtic neighbours. Predictably, unanimity of opinion has proven elusive. Moreover, the recent tendency of some historians to associate their inquiries into the medieval origins of the modern British state with controversial questions of national sentiment will ensure that the field remains hotly debated.[10]

Among the more fruitful consequences of historiographical inquiry into the nature of the British polity has been the attention paid to the notion of frontiers and, more particularly, to definitions of the term 'marches' in the later Middle Ages. There can be no doubt that the term was familiar to, and well understood by, all medieval Englishmen. At its simplest it designated a distinct geographical territory, even when the physical limits of that region shifted in their size and location. In Ireland the marches consisted of a strip of territory that lay between English dominated lands and areas controlled by Gaelic lords. By the fourteenth century the extent of English occupation had diminished considerably, and the marches became more clearly defined as the region lying between the 'land of peace' (the Pale), and the rest of the island, the 'land of war'.[11] In Wales the process of delineating the boundaries between *pura Wallia* – the land of the Welsh-speaking people – and English held territories was at once more complex and more decisive. At the time of the Edwardian conquest of the late thirteenth century, when medieval observers wrote about 'the marches' (though they also employed the singular form of the term), they had in mind a series of forty-odd lordships that had been brought under the rule of Anglo-Norman lords, were subject however notionally to the English crown, and were administered by a hybrid of English and Welsh law known as the Law of the March.[12]

The Anglo-Scottish frontier, too, was a matter of some ambiguity, albeit to a lesser extent than its Irish and Welsh counterparts. Here, after the year 1237, the marches were confined to – though not contiguous with – the northernmost shires of Northumberland, Cumberland and Westmorland. As in the case of Wales and Ireland, contemporaries often referred to them by way of contrast or exclusion. An early fourteenth-century challenge to English common-law procedure, for example, was based on ancient claims to damage and plunder peculiar to the marches of Northumberland alone, while in 1453 an act of parliament made it clear that counties other than those situated on the border lay well beyond the limits of the marches.[13] The defeasance in 1237 of Scottish claims to the northern shires saw the establishment of a relatively stable frontier with Scotland along the Solway-Tweed line, one that, with the notable exception of Berwick and its hinterland, remained largely unchanged throughout the Middle Ages.[14] But it was the eruption of war with Scotland in 1296 that ultimately worked to delineate the marches of either realm: in England they became, and throughout the fourteenth and fifteenth centuries remained, the front line of defence against the Auld Enemy. Included within the confines of the northern marches were the coastal lands lying between Berwick and Newcastle, as well as Coquetdale, Redesdale, North Tyndale, South Tyndale and most of the county of Cumberland.[15]

If Englishmen were conscious of the existence in the northernmost parts of a frontier that set the region apart from the rest of the kingdom, they were nonetheless ambivalent about the way in which it should most effectively be governed. In the late thirteenth and early fourteenth centuries the crown's view was that the kingdom of the Scots, newly conquered, should be administered by English officials alone; although the measures included in an ordinance of 1305 were not as harsh as those which had been imposed on Wales twenty years earlier, the Scots were left in no doubt that they were 'a conquered country, occupied by foreign garrisons and governed by the foreign officials of a foreign king'.[16] The conquest transformed the border castles of Berwick, Roxburgh, Lochmaben and Carlisle from distant outposts of the English realm into frontier fortresses, and the border lands into a vast military front. The effects of this transformation were manifest even to the most casual observer: among other changes wrought by war was the proliferation throughout the march lands of pele towers and bastles that had no counterparts elsewhere in the kingdom.[17] The impact of war on northern border life left its mark in equally telling fashion on the language of the borderers: terms such as 'outputters', 'grithmen', 'trucebreaker', 'reiver' and 'blackmail', virtually unknown south of the Tweed, became common currency among the people of the marches and required no elaboration.[18]

In the opinion of Edward I there was no longer any room, after 1296, for a distinct system of law that explicitly acknowledged the existence of a buffer zone between two separate and independent realms. Earlier still, from the time of his involvement in arbitrating rival claims to the Scottish throne the king did his best to ensure that the ancient laws and customs of the marches were suppressed altogether. In so doing he imposed on the march lands, as he had done with respect to the Scottish kingdom itself, the 'assumption of superiority and indeed "naturalness" of *English* law' about which Professor Davies has written so extensively.[19]

The failure of the English crown to sustain its domination of Scotland became patent in the aftermath of Bannockburn, when Robert Bruce secured his hold over the throne of the smaller kingdom. Although Edward III attempted once again to establish an English presence in lowland Scotland, it became clear by the 1340s that the garrisoning of the march fortresses and the military preparedness of the region to resist Scottish assault were to be chief components of the royal administration of the north. The existence of a now permanent war front clearly required an adjustment to the way in which the marches were governed. In the middle of the fourteenth century, therefore, the crown began to devote serious and careful consideration to the conditions and problems unique to the northern marches. The other border lands of the realm proved instructive in this respect, both in terms of the similarities they shared with the north and with respect to the contrasts they represented.

The analogies between the Anglo-Scottish and the Anglo-Irish marches were plentiful and striking. Native Ireland, like Scotland, boasted distinct systems of government and taxation and its own parliament. Just as there was a unity to the realm of Ireland that set it apart from England, so, too, did distinct systems of taxation, common law and representative institutions – not to mention the existence of a sovereign prince – distinguish Scotland from its larger neighbour.[20] In each of the marcher territories of Ireland and Scotland, then, English officials confronted fiscal, tenurial and administrative traditions that were not predisposed to be receptive to their own, and which required subtle but important adjustments to the machinery of governance.

Another condition of Anglo–Scottish border society found also in Ireland was the presence of 'chieftains' or nobles whose rank and status combined to make them powerful spokesmen for their respective peoples. In Ireland and the Irish marches these local notables were of both Gaelic and Anglo–Irish descent, but no matter their origins the English crown learned after bitter and prolonged warfare that to ignore them was to jeopardise the very existence of its authority in the island.[21] In northern England the crown dealt not with Gaelic-speaking lords, but with the thoroughly English families of Percy, Umfraville, Lucy, Clifford and Neville. Yet as early as the reign of King John, and frequently thereafter, it was made aware of grievances peculiar to noblemen whose interests were at odds with those of their fellows living in the populous and prosperous south.[22] The broad grants of royal authority made to baronial lords both in the march lands of Ireland and the north of England were as much an admission of the crown's inability to exercise firm control over the great men of the region as they were judicious delegations of administrative duties. Professor Lydon's observation that the crown's dependence on local lords 'meant that the government had to tolerate a degree of independence which in other circumstances would have been intolerable'[23] is as appropriate in the context of the Anglo–Scottish border lands as it is in the Irish theatre.[24]

The Welsh marches, too, offered a model upon which the English crown might draw in devising a workable administrative system for the northern parts. The fourteenth-century kings looked on the region and its native lords as unstable and potentially dangerous elements within the realm of England, but they drew on the achievements of their thirteenth-century predecessors and applied in the northern context some of the lessons Henry III and Edward I had learned in Wales. Despite the marked independence of the Welsh marcher lords from the crown in matters of jurisdiction and administrative authority, by the fourteenth century the landed interests of the greatest of these magnates lay firmly in England, and they were deeply entrenched within the English political community.[25] So, too, were the chief families of the north. Like the FitzAlan earls of Arundel and the Mortimer earls of March, the Umfravilles, Percies and Lucys were capable of exerting a tremendous influence on behalf of the crown. Not least among their strengths was their ability, through networks of tenurial and feudal *familiares*, to keep the king in touch with local attitudes towards the policies of the central government. John of Lancaster's detailed reports to his brother, Henry IV, in the early fifteenth century were but one manifestation of a tradition already old of close contact between the crown and the men to whom it entrusted the governance of its most distant parts.[26]

Like the lordships of the Welsh marches, a region often referred to as 'a land of compact territorial blocks',[27] the estates of the northern families tended to be more geographically concentrated than those found south of the Tweed. The most obvious of these conglomerations were the lands held by the medieval bishops of Durham,[28] but by the later fourteenth century the Percy family had accumulated a large block of territory in Northumberland, and the Neville earls of Westmorland had begun to eclipse Cliffords, Dacres and others as the chief landholders in Cumberland.[29] The grave dangers associated with the concentration of power in a relatively small territorial basis are as familiar to historians as they were to the late medieval kings of England, though their advantages are less often emphasised. The ability of the lords of Chirk or Alnwick to summon an armed host at short notice and to prevent forays by Welsh raiders or Scottish reivers from escalating into full-blown invasions must have offset many a royal concern about the wisdom of trusting to the loyalty of its great border lords. Contemporary chroniclers, too, although seldom sympathetic to the authority of the 'overmighty' subjects of the march lands, were more than happy to praise them when their authority was effectively used against an aggressive enemy.[30]

The most significant of the many features that set all the march lands of medieval Britain apart from the core region of the kingdom was the extensive authority of resident magnates to wage war and make peace. The institution of the truce was in no way unique to the frontier regions of the British Isles; indeed, as one of several distinct 'conditions' of war it was well known wherever English armies operated, and by 1400 had been carefully defined and refined.[31] But the tenor of Anglo-Gaelic agreements to suspend open warfare was of a particular nature. In continental campaigns truces were almost universally regarded as preliminary to peace. According to the theorist, Honoré Bonet, a state of armistice promised 'hope of peace, for during the truce ways and means of reconciling and pacifying the two sides are sought',[32] and it was with a view to securing treaties of peace and alliance that English ambassadors of the fourteenth and fifteenth centuries negotiated with the princes of western Europe.[33] Truces made by the border magnates with the Irish, Welsh and Scottish border lords were of a different nature altogether: here they were established above all to diffuse tensions between aggrieved parties after particularly violent armed encounters, or to provide a respite during which native and English lords might discuss claims arising from raids and forays – the so-called 'love days' of the Welsh and Irish marches, and the days of truce of the northern border lands.[34] For the most part, the crown remained deeply uneasy in respect of the exercise of these powers, and only begrudgingly conceded that the prerogative to make peace was one that belonged *de rigueur* to its greatest marcher subjects.

Royal attitudes in respect of truce-making authority with the Scots shifted dramatically with the fortunes of war in the course of the fourteenth century. While English overlordship of Ireland and Wales throughout the century was undisputed, Scotland was by no means a dominion in this same sense, securely held and subject to the English crown. The period of the Wars of Independence, in particular, saw Edward I and Edward II strictly limit the authority of local men to make truces with the Scots. It could not have been otherwise: to allow their northern agents free reign to treat with the Scots as equals would have made a mockery of the image so carefully fostered by the English crown of the Scots as rebellious vassals, and would have undermined the legitimacy of its 'just war' against them.[35] Thus it was his keen awareness of the intricacy of this political stance that compelled Edward II to treat Andrew de Harcla's treaty with Robert Bruce in 1323 as a grievous arrogation of the royal prerogative.[36] The earl's offence was not that he had presumed to treat with the Scots – for wardenial commissions had granted this authority to his predecessors – but rather that he had bestowed on his agreement with Bruce the trappings and the solemnity of a treaty.[37] After 1328 the lines between 'private' and 'public' war, and between 'private' and 'public' truces, became more fluid in the north, as they had been for some time already in Wales and Ireland. Harcla's real misfortune lay in the fact that he embarked on his negotiations with Bruce at a particularly sensitive period in Anglo–Scottish relations.[38] Conditions thereafter dictated that the crown abandon its reluctance to endow wardens with the authority to make temporary peace with the Scots. Moreover, private agreements aimed at staving off destruction and depredation became a regular, if tiresome, feature of life in the Anglo–Scottish border lands in the fourteenth century: they were made by the bishops of Durham and Carlisle and (not altogether successfully) by townships and hamlets.[39] If, during the period of the Wars of Independence it had been dangerous to undertake private truces without royal approval,[40] by the reign of Edward III royal vigilance had relaxed, and the endeavours of various northerners to negotiate localised armistices were regarded with a more benign eye.[41] Despite the enduring differences between the relationship of Wales and Ireland to England on the one hand, and Scotland on the other, then, the authority to make and to suspend war was a prerogative that the crown, however reluctantly, was compelled to share with its great subjects.

If similarities between the Anglo–Scottish lands and the marcher regions of Ireland and Wales disposed the English government to consider the problems of all three border regions with some unity of purpose, there were nevertheless conditions that, after 1296, set the counties of Northumberland, Cumberland and Westmorland apart. These required that the later medieval kings devise a wholly novel approach to routine matters of law and administration, one that took into account the special needs of the north without compromising the crown's traditional prerogatives. The efforts of the government to balance both aims collectively made of the Anglo–Scottish marches a region quite unlike any other.

The most telling of the many features that rendered the north unique was the proximity of a 'national' enemy. In 1331, although he was preparing to lead an expedition to Ireland in order to discipline restive native chiefs, Edward III would have been hard pressed to consider the Gaelic Irish the sworn enemy of the English; in 1395 his grandson, Richard II, could still envisage 'a future in which the native lords might form part of a polity that took in all the powerful elements in the island'.[42] More than a hundred years later, the crown was still determined that Ireland beyond the Pale remain an 'integral part' of the English polity.[43] Royal attitudes towards the Welsh were mixed in the fourteenth century: in the late 1310s the government considered it prudent to keep the fortresses of Caernarvon and Pembroke well garrisoned and provisioned, but at the same time there are discernible the beginnings of a long process of accommodation and cooperation between the native and the English peoples.[44] One hundred and thirty years later, when parliament introduced a tax on aliens, there was no question in the mind of Henry VI of including the Welsh among the 'foreigners' targeted by the legislation, despite their reputation in England for lawlessness and disorder.[45] No such ambiguity attended English royal opinion of the Scots. From 1296 down to the end of the Middle Ages the people of Scotland were vilified by the Plantagenet, Lancastrian, Yorkist and Tudor monarchs alike. Official attitudes were in turn reflected and amplified in poetry, song and chronicle, and everywhere, but especially in the north, the Scots were treated as a bitter national enemy.[46] The presence of hostile peoples hard by the limits of the kingdom of England itself was bound to render infinitely complex the normal machinery of English administration. As a consequence of crucial aspects of diplomatic and political history the crown and its advisors were forced in the northern marches to adapt institutions of government, law and finance to a degree that they were never required to do either in Ireland or in Wales.

Among the myriad features that distinguished English administration in the north, three in particular are noteworthy: the importance of trial by combat as a method of proof in legal causes, the development of the office of warden of the marches, and, perhaps most significant, the body of custom known as border law. Trial by battle remained a part of the northern legal fabric long after it had fallen out of favour elsewhere in the realm. The lists provided the opportunity for belligerent northern plaintiffs and defendants to engage in carefully regulated warlike encounters with the Scottish enemy without the dangers consequent on unrestrained raids of plunder and retaliation. The later fourteenth-century kings were mindful of the current of public opinion expressed in parliament that decried the practice, but against these criticisms they weighed the value of trial by combat in the context of Anglo-Scottish diplomatic relations. In the end, Richard II not only condoned judicial combat, he actively promoted the ceremonialisation of the duel as an integral aspect of dispute settlement in the marches.[47] Although the crown regularly reminded its officials that royal permission was a prerequisite of northern feats of arms it did not otherwise attempt to curb this traditional and popular method of proof.

In the later fourteenth century the office of warden of the marches was unique to the northern border lands. Many of the military and diplomatic duties attached to the office were replicated in other frontier regions, including the negotiation of armistices, the supervision of hostage exchanges, the arbitration of parleys at love days, and the summoning of local hosts for the defence of a locality against raiders. In the Irish and Welsh marches these duties were shared by a variety of officials. In the former the justiciar acted on behalf of the crown in concert with sheriffs, seneschals, keepers of the peace and several local lords acting under special commissions.[48] In the latter, where marcher families jealously guarded their traditional regalian rights and privileges, they were most often performed by the heads of the great territorial lordships within their respective lands, but also occasionally by agents appointed in royal commissions.[49] In the Anglo–Scottish border lands, however, from the early years of the fourteenth century virtually all these responsibilities fell to the wardens (and later the warden-conservators) alone. The tremendous development of the office is perhaps most strikingly attested in a comparison between the brief commission by which Robert de Clifford was appointed in 1309 and the much more complex agreement by which Henry Percy earl of Northumberland served as warden of the east march beginning in 1457: the former consisted of only a single clause, the latter of more than a dozen.[50] The commission of 1309 granted Clifford authority merely to array the fensible men of the northern parts and to lead them to the border; that of 1457 bestowed 'all the powers necessary to the military governor of a frontier district',[51] that is to say extensive military, judicial, administrative and fiscal authority. Nowhere in the Irish or Welsh marches was such extensive authority concentrated for such extended periods in the hands of a single official.

The warden was not, of course, an agent of the royal machinery of the common law, and Rachel Reid was justified, many years ago, in stressing that the northern counties remained, throughout the later medieval period, firmly within the purview of the English legal system.[52] But the crown itself was only too aware of the shortcomings of writ-based procedures in a region whose inhabitants' lives were so heavily influenced by the proximity of a national enemy. Chief among these was the inability of the common law to offer redress and reparation for offences committed by subjects of another allegiance. Equally worrisome – and more annoying – was the fundamental problem posed by the reluctance of royal justices to travel the dangerous roads of the northern circuit. The combination of geographical, political and diplomatic factors that set the northern march lands apart from their Irish and Welsh counterparts compelled the crown to bestow on the office of the warden an unusual mix of judicial powers, one that was not required elsewhere. The process of shaping the unique features of the warden's authority was lengthy and piecemeal, suggesting that successive kings gave considerable thought to the task. The experimentation and innovation effected by Edward III and Henry VI in particular demonstrate that the kings sought to build on the achievements of their predecessors while avoiding their mistakes.

Among the more important of the judicial powers vested in the office of warden and, later, warden-conservator, were those of ensuring that truces sealed with the Scots were properly observed, that breaches of the armistice were investigated and amended, and that the perpetrators of such offences were punished.[53] In these respects they exercised an authority comparable to that of the thirteenth-century keepers of the peace, whose duties had similarly included the maintenance of peace and good order in the shires and coastal regions of the kingdom,[54] and to those exercised contemporaneously by the keepers of the peace in Ireland.[55] Indeed, in the course of the fourteenth century, as the English keepers of the peace were steadily 'transformed' into judicial agents, it was the Irish keepers who came to serve as models for the crown in the elaboration of the wardens' office: in both regions, 'the keepers' judicial powers sprang naturally from their police and military authority'.[56] At first, the expansion of the wardens' duties within the marches so closely paralleled similar developments in Ireland that it is difficult not to see in them a concerted effort on the part of the crown to respond to the local conditions of the two regions with uniform solutions.[57] Thus in the marches of both lands the keepers and wardens had the power to compel the men of the region to remain on their lands in moments of acute border tension,[58] and to offer the king's peace to any who wished to accept it;[59] similarly, both were on occasion granted extraordinary commissions to enquire into a variety of unlawful activities by the borderers.[60]

From the middle years of the fourteenth century, however, there is apparent a growing differentiation between the powers exercised by the Irish keepers of the peace and those attached to the wardens' office. Most significant of these was the power to terminate indictments, which the crown granted only rarely and for limited purposes to the Irish keepers,[61] but which belonged as a matter of course to the wardens from the second decade of the fourteenth century. Conditions in the northern shires required a relaxation of the stringent practice that elsewhere in the English realm – and in most of Ireland – reserved the resolution of legal causes to the normal machinery of the common law. Scottish miscreants, whether they crossed the border in large numbers in organised raids or individually as free-booting felons, were outside the king's allegiance and, in turn, beyond the reach of the king's common-law judges. The damage they inflicted on English suspects, especially in ransoms extorted from hapless prisoners snatched out of their homes and farmsteads, was considerable, but English plaintiffs were poorly served by lawyers ill trained in notions of 'international' law or the rules governing conditions of war. Moreover, Englishmen who consorted in crime with the Scots, although liable to trial before justices of assize when they could be apprehended, found it all too easy to evade royal agents by seeking refuge in one of the many northern liberties or, more ominously, going over to the allegiance of the king of Scots.[62] In either circumstance they removed themselves from the grasp of the common lawyers, and thus bedevilled the attempts of English plaintiffs to secure satisfactory resolution of their causes.

The ever-increasing authority bestowed on the wardens was deliberately fashioned to meet circumstances peculiar to the northern marches. Their military powers granted them broad authority to deal with most, if not all the offences committed by the fighting men they commanded as keepers of the royal fortresses of Berwick, Newcastle and Carlisle, and as captains of the armed hosts sent across the border by royal decree to harry the Scots and to carry war into the smaller realm. As conservators of the truces they were authorised to hear and determine indictments laid in respect of a large number of offences deemed breaches of the armistice, wherever these were committed in the north. In periods of acute tension in the border lands, virtually any act involving the Scots directly or indirectly was thus considered. The warden–conservators also exercised punitive powers far in excess of their common-law brethren sitting as justices of the peace: they were not restricted to the imposition of fines or prison sentences, but might also punish offenders with the penalty of life and limb. Here again, the tremendous level of royal trust implicit in the appointment of wardens is noteworthy. In terms of the judicial authority they exercised by virtue of their office, the warden–conservators of the fourteenth and the fifteenth centuries far surpassed the justices of the peace; they might even be said to have approximated those of the great palatine lords of the realm. It is small wonder that Henry IV was caught so inexorably on the horns of a dilemma when, early in his reign, he learned of the revolt of the Percy family in Northumberland. Open rebellion and treason were offences that no king could afford to tolerate, but the repeated pardon of Percy family members was the price that Henry had to pay in order to keep them in the key position that was the wardenship of the east march.

Just as the unique conditions of the border lands necessitated the ministrations of officials endowed with extraordinary judicial authority, so, too, did they demand access to a body of law designed to suit those conditions. The common law of England was as much a feature of every day life in Northumberland, Cumberland and Westmorland as it was elsewhere in the kingdom: the northern assize circuit, although it was regarded as the least desirable of all the judicial circuits by ambitious lawyers, was nevertheless an integral part of the legal administration of the realm. Justices of the peace here, too, witnessed the same processes of experimentation and refinement in their office in the course of the fourteenth century as did their more southerly brethren. But as the kings of England quickly learned after 1237, the substantive and procedural rules of the common law were ill-equipped to cope with the problems attendant on the establishment of an artificial political boundary. After 1296 these proved even less capable of providing satisfactory resolution to a host of legal causes arising from war. Professor Barrow has remarked of the medieval laws and customs of the marches in general that they were 'a way of enforcing the kind of law already familiar and acceptable to individuals north and south of the Border when, because of that border, the individuals' customary courts lacked the competence to act'.[63] So, indeed, they were for most of the thirteenth century; so they became again from the middle of the fourteenth, when it became obvious to the crown that Edward I's attempt to suppress them had been ill founded. In the 1340s, as in the 1240s, the English crown found the machinery of the common law in the marches defective in so many respects that, even in the face of the enmity engendered by war, it was willing to revive and promote the old laws and customs. More important still, it was prepared to confront the possibility that these might compete with the common law. Edward III had very little choice in the matter, and he knew it.

A distinct body of law and custom was not, of course, unique to the northern parts: in the later medieval period a 'loose assemblage . . . of native Welsh law, local custom, feudal convention, and English common law' flourished in the Welsh marches, 'a plural law, drawing on two (at least) legal traditions and catering for two peoples'.[64] Ireland, too, had its own law of the march, 'a hybrid system' that, although denounced by some contemporaries as barbaric,[65] and condemned outright in 1366,[66] nevertheless survived attempts by the English crown to suppress it. The law of the northern marches was, like its Gaelic cousins, an amalgam of local custom and English common law; its provisions for parleys, lawful ransom-taking and schemes of compensation constituted 'a mixed law for a mixed people'.[67] There were some striking similarities of procedure and practice among all three: for example, all included provision for the appointment of sureties on behalf of both plaintiffs and defendants, and for the recourse to mixed juries in the determination of guilt and innocence.[68] More generally, all had recourse to formal arbitration as a legitimate method of dispute settlement (and indeed may have helped to promote its use elsewhere in England).[69] But alone among the sometimes bewildering variety of custom and practice that collectively made up the laws of all three frontier societies, those of the later medieval Anglo–Scottish marches boasted more than a passing claim to systematic codification, as well as to regular review and reform. Here again, the background of war against which the laws were developed and refined demanded no less.

Beginning in the sixteenth century, antiquarians demonstrated great interest in the origins of the laws and customs of the Anglo–Scottish marches: among the earliest collections of treaty and truce texts compiled and deliberately preserved for purposes of reference was that of Richard Bell, clerk to Lord Henry Scrope (d. 1592) and to the latter's successor in the east march, Thomas lord Scrope.[70] Long before this, however, the principle had taken firm root that written texts of indentures of truce and treaties represented formal statements – in effect, 'codes' – of the laws and customs that obtained in the marches. The compilation of 1249 was made in the same age that produced the systematic examination of English law and custom attributed to Bracton, and the same age that witnessed the earliest expressions by the Welsh of their distinct legal status. The reduction to written form of customs and practices the origins of which were believed to lie in the distant northern past was in this sense entirely typical of the age.[71] But the codification of 1249 was not an isolated effort, and the sense of authority and legitimacy bestowed on written versions of the laws remained strong in the north throughout the medieval period. It was, in fact, precisely because no such codification had been attempted in recent memory that in 1343 the borderers requested written protocols of march law and custom to guide the newly revived office of the conservator in the proper maintenance of the truce.[72]

From the middle of the fourteenth century representatives of the crowns of England and Scotland devoted a great deal of time and effort in their diplomatic negotiations to the substance of the law and its workings, and consciously sought to identify and amend deficiencies in its execution.[73] The authoritative voice attributed to these written compilations is nowhere more strikingly attested than in the survival of dozens of truce texts dating from the later fourteenth through the fifteenth centuries. The length of these agreements, as well as their sheer weight in numbers, stand in marked contrast to the paucity of written records that survive with respect to Welsh and Irish march laws.[74] Northern border law was, moreover, a living law: sensitive, certainly, to the tenor of diplomatic relations between the warring realms of England and Scotland, but subject to conscientious alteration, refinement and improvement. Each time they set their seals to a new indenture of truce in which changes were effected to the practices governing cross-border dispute settlement, the agents of the two crowns implicitly enacted afresh a new 'code' of border law, intended to serve as a point of reference in future causes. When they did so, they gave formal expression to a shared belief that this body of custom was both amenable to, and deserving of, dispassionate review and amendment. Tudor statesmen, acting under the aegis of a monarchy whose hallmark has been described as 'political centralization, administrative uniformity, and cultural imperialism',[75] tirelessly generated a plethora of documents intended to bring order and coherence to the chaotic border region. They saw in the little tracts and treatises they compiled on such varied matters as the form and order of days of truce, the proper conduct of wardenial ambassadors, and the correct 'filing' of bills[76] the first systematic attempts to impose uniformity and rationality on a bewildering array of custom, practice and tradition. In reality, they accomplished little that was innovative. 'Order' and 'cohesion' in the border lands of the Anglo-Scottish marches was a chimera that the men of Tudor England chased in vain. The achievement belonged, rather, to their medieval predecessors, who fully appreciated the unique problems of the frontier and who managed, despite them, to construct from that bewildering array a workable system of law.

Notes

1. Alnwick Castle, Northumberland MSS, Box 761, no.24.
2. *A Volume of English Miscellanies*, p. 35. In another part of the kingdom the Oxfordshire justice of the peace, Humphrey Forster, wrote to the chancellor on behalf of the brother of one of his tenants, who had been 'atached for a Scot'. He assured the chancellor that the brothers had been born only two miles from the home of Sir James Strangways, 'whiche is fifty myle from Scotland and more', and asked that the plaint be given favourable remedy. PRO SC 1/46(280).
3. *A Volume of English Miscellanies*, p. 25.
4. Cited in Gillingham, 'Beginnings of English Imperialism', p. 397. Other twelfth-century opinions of the Welsh are noted in Davies, *Conquest, Coexistence, and Change*, pp. 14–15, 66, 70, 127–8, 173, 175–8.
5. *The Libelle of Englyshe Polycye*, p. 40.
6. Wright, 'The Topography of Ireland', p. 111.
7. Lydon, *Lordship of Ireland*, pp. 283–90; Lydon, 'The Middle Nation', p. 10; Davies, *Domination and Conquest*, pp. 116–18. The growth and development of English prejudices towards the Celtic peoples in the Middle Ages are discussed in Jones, 'England against the Celtic Fringe', pp. 155–71; Jones, 'The Image of the Barbarian', pp. 396–7, and Snyder, 'The Wild Irish', pp. 691–4, 710–3.
8. The literature here is vast. In addition to the sources cited in notes 7 and 9, for Anglo-Irish relations in the Middle Ages see Frame, 'Military Service in the Lordship of Ireland', pp. 101–26; Frame, *English Lordship in Ireland 1318–1361*; Frame, 'War and Peace', pp. 118–41; Frame, 'English Officials and Irish Chiefs', pp. 748–77; Frame,

'Power and Society in the Lordship of Ireland', pp. 3–33; Brand, 'Ireland and the Literature of the Early Common Law', pp. 95–113; Murphy, 'The Status of the Native Irish after 1331', pp. 116–28; Simms, 'Bards and Barons', pp. 177–97. Anglo-Welsh contacts are discussed in Davies, *Lordship and Society*; Davies, 'Law and National Identity', pp. 51–69; Davies, 'Colonial Wales', pp. 3–23; Walker, 'Cultural Survival in an Age of Conquest', pp. 35–50; Jones, 'Government and the Welsh Community', pp. 55–68. The history of Anglo-Scottish border relations is dominated by the work of Barrow, including 'Anglo-Scottish Border', pp. 21–42; 'The Pattern of Lordship and Feudal Settlement in Cumbria', pp. 117–38; *The Anglo-Norman Era in Scottish History* (Oxford, 1980); 'Wales and Scotland', pp. 302–19; 'Frontier and Settlement', pp. 3–21. See also Tuck, 'Northumbrian Society', pp. 22–39, and Tuck, 'War and Society in the Medieval North', pp. 33–52.

9. Davies, *Domination and Conquest*; Davies, 'Frontier Arrangements', pp. 77–101; Davies, *The British Isles 1100–1500*; Davies, 'The English State and the 'Celtic' Peoples', pp. 1–14; Davies, 'Race Relations in Post-Conquest Wales', pp. 32–56; most recently, see Professor Davies's vigorous series of presidential addresses delivered to the Royal Historical Society, 'The Peoples of Britain and Ireland 1100–1400 I. Identities, II. Names, Boundaries and Regnal Solidarities, III. Laws and Customs'. See also Richter, 'Political and Institutional Background to National Consciousness', pp. 37–55; Frame, *Political Development*; Frame, 'Les Engleys nées en Irelande'', pp. 83–103; Grant and Stringer, *Uniting the Kingdom?*, pp. 3–110. For the late medieval period, see also Ellis, *Tudor Frontiers*; Ellis, 'Nationalist Historiography', pp. 1–18; Ellis, 'Tudor State Formation', pp. 40–63; Gillingham, 'Beginnings of English Imperialism', pp. 392–409.

10. See, here, the historiographical review of recent literature and the debates it has sparked in Ellis, *Tudor Frontiers*, pp. 8–16, 251–7.

11. Frame, 'War and Peace', pp. 118–41; Hand, *English Law in Ireland*, p. 34. See also Ellis, *Reform and Revival*, p. 51; Davies, 'Frontier Arrangements', pp. 81–2.

12. Davies, 'Frontier Arrangements', pp. 81–2; Davies, *Lordship and Society*, pp. 15–33; Mann, 'The March of Wales', pp. 1–13.

13. PRO JUST 3/53/2 m.4/1d; *Rot. Parl*, v.267.

14. Barrow, 'Anglo-Scottish Border', pp. 21, 23.

15. The boundaries of the Scottish marches are reviewed in Rae, *Administration of the Scottish Frontier*, pp. 1–20.

16. Barrow, *Robert Bruce*, p. 135.

17. Richard Lomas notes that around 1166 there were between sixteen and twenty fortified castles in Northumberland; by the late sixteenth century the county had become 'densely fortified' with castles, pele towers and keeps numbering well over 130. Lomas, *North-East England*, pp. 70–2. See also Hugill, *Borderland Castles and Peles*, and Bates, 'Border Holds of Northumberland'. For the west march, see Curwin, *Castles and Fortified Towers*, and Graham, *Barony of Gilsland*.

18. For the terms 'outputter' and 'trucebreaker', see Neville, 'Law of Treason', p. 28 note 89. For 'grithmen' – fugitives from justice, many of them march men – see *Rot. Scot*, ii.629. An early use of the term 'reiver' is found in an indenture of truce of 1386; *Foedera*, III.iii.205.

19. Davies, *Domination and Conquest*, p. 115; Davies, 'Law and National Identity', pp. 51–69.

20. Davies, 'Frontier Arrangements', 98–9; Frame, 'Les Engleys Nées en Irelande', pp. 83–103.

21. Frame, 'English Officials and Irish Chiefs', pp. 748–77; Frame, 'Power and Society', pp. 7–33.

22. Holt, *The Northerners*; Fryde, *Tyranny and Fall of Edward II*, pp. 70–4; Tuck, 'Emergence of a Northern Nobility', pp. 1–17; Tuck, 'Northumbrian Society', pp. 22–39; Tuck, 'Richard II and the Border Magnates', pp. 127–52.

23. Lydon, *Ireland in the Later Middle Ages*, p. 49.
24. Compare Lydon's comments here with those made some years earlier by Edward Miller in respect of the forces maintained by the wardens of the northern marches: 'these subsidized private armies . . . helped to make the great northern families the over-mighty subjects *par excellence* of late medieval England and a danger to internal peace'. Miller, *War in the North*, p. 13.
25. Davies, *Lordship and Society*; Davies, *Conquest, Coexistence and Change*, pp. 395–97; Frame, *Political Development*, pp. 199–200; Griffiths, 'Wales and the Marches', pp. 151–2.
26. The regular and detailed correspondence between Edward III and his chief agent in Ireland in the 1340s and 1350s, for example, is reviewed in Frame, 'Thomas Rokeby', pp. 8–13. I wish to thank Professor Frame for permitting me to read his article before its publication.
27. Davies, *Lordship and Society*, p. 403; Davies, 'Frontier Arrangements', pp. 82, 90.
28. Throughout the later Middle Ages, moreover, the bishops of Durham had a crucial role to play in the defence of the border region. See Storey, *Thomas Langley*, pp. 144–7, and Lapsley, *County Palatine of Durham*, pp. 303–7.
29. Tuck, 'Emergence of a Northern Nobility', pp. 15–16; Tuck, 'War and Society', pp. 49–50; Given-Wilson, *English Nobility in the Late Middle Ages*, pp. 105–6, 127, 132–5, 162, 174.
30. See, for example, the favourable review of the young Henry Percy by the Westminster chronicler, who noted that the warden's five armed encounters with the Scots kept the enemy at bay following the withdrawal of Richard II's army in 1385. *Westminster Chron.*, pp. 138–9. The monk of Westminster was generally critical of Richard's governance of the realm.
31. Keen, *Laws of War*, pp. 104, 207; Fowler, 'Truces', p. 18.
32. Coopland, *The Tree of Battles of Honoré Bonet*, p. 190.
33. Fowler, 'Truces', pp. 185–6.
34. Examples of truces made between the Welsh marcher lords and the native princelings are discussed in Davies, 'Frontier Arrangements', pp. 85–7; Davies, *Lordship and Society*, pp. 219–20. For Ireland, see Frame, 'War and Peace', pp. 136–8; Frame, *English Lordship in Ireland*, pp. 38–9; Hand, *English Law in Ireland*, pp. 35–6.
35. Barrow, *Robert Bruce*, pp. 11–12, 60, 73–4, 78–9; Prestwich, *Edward I*, pp. 374–5, 475–6.
36. See above, pp. 18–19.
37. Whitton, 'La Sainteté des traités', pp. 446–8.
38. Edward II had only recently crushed his enemy, Thomas of Lancaster, who himself had been in treasonable conspiracy with the Scots. See McKisack, *Fourteenth Century*, p. 67; Fryde, *Tyranny and Fall of Edward II*, pp. 123–4.
39. The arrangements made in the decade of the 1310s between the bishop of Durham and Robert Bruce, designed to safeguard episcopal lands from raids and forays are well known and have been extensively discussed in Scammell, 'Robert I and the North of England', pp. 385–403. See also Lapsley, *County Palatine of Durham*, pp. 39, 119, 121–2, 272. Similar agreements concerning lands in Cumberland are reviewed in McNamee, 'Buying Off Robert Bruce', pp. 77–89; Fryde, *Tyranny and Fall of Edward II*, pp. 121–2.
40. Thus, in April 1319 Pope John XXII reminded the archbishop of York and the bishop of Carlisle that negotiations for a truce with the Scots should be undertaken only with the king's permission, on pain of excommunication. The same year the abbot of Holm Cultram obtained special licence to engage in truce talks, as did the people of Pickering and Ripon in Yorkshire in 1319–20, and the men of Bamburgh, Northumberland and Cumberland in 1322. Private truces were again made by men of the northern marches in 1327 and 1328. See Raine, *Historical Papers and Letters from the Northern Registers*,

pp. 285–6; *Rot. Scot.*, i.205; PRO SC 8/8(364); *CCR*, 1318–23, p. 597; *Chron. Lanercost*, pp. 230, 237–8, 258; PRO SC 8/71(3549); *Chron. Melsa*, ii.357; *CPR*, 1327–30, p. 233; Fraser, *Northern Petitions*, pp. 177–8.

41. In 1343 Bishop Bury of Durham purchased a truce for £160; five years later he again paid £168 13s 4d to the Scots for a 'good peace or truce'. The people of Carlisle and Bamburgh castle won similar respites in 1376–7. The abbot of Holm Cultram, however, considered it wise to seek a formal pardon for presuming to treat with the Scots for truce in 1385. The English were in a state of open war with Scotland at this time. PRO DURH 3/29 m.13d; Kitchen, *Richard D'Aungerville of Bury*, pp. 159–60; Hardy, *Reg. Pal. Dunelm.*, iii.159–60 (Register of Bishop Bury); *Chron. Lanercost*, p. 332; Raine, *History and Antiquities of North Durham*, pp. 346–7; PRO SC 8/20(994); *CPR*, 1385–9, p. 71.

42. Frame, *English Lordship in Ireland*, pp. 196–202; Frame, *Political Development*, p. 216.

43. Ellis, 'Crown, Community and Government', p. 192; Ellis, *Reform and Revival*.

44. Davies, *Conquest, Coexistence and Change*, pp. 412–30; Walker, *Medieval Wales*, pp. 163–4.

45. *Rot. Parl*, iv.415; v.6; *CPR*, 1436–41, pp. 409–11. See also Giuseppi, 'Alien Merchants in England', pp. 91–2; Griffiths, *Henry VI*, p. 168; Jones, 'Government and the Welsh Community', pp. 55–68.

46. Neville, 'Local Sentiment and the 'National' Enemy', pp. 419–37.

47. Neville, 'Keeping the Peace', p. 15.

48. Frame, 'War and Peace', pp. 133–4; Frame, 'English Officials and Irish Chiefs', pp. 754–70; Frame, 'Judicial Powers of the Medieval Irish Keepers of the Peace', pp. 308–26.

49. Davies, *Lordship and Society*, pp. 254–63.

50. *Rot. Scot.*, i.76; ii.377–8.

51. Reid, 'Office of Warden', p. 483.

52. Ibid., pp. 483–4.

53. All three powers were included in wardenial commissions from the late 1310s. See, for example, *Rot. Scot.*, i.180.

54. Harding, 'Origins and Early History of the Keepers of the Peace', pp. 88–99.

55. Frame, 'Judicial Powers of the Medieval Irish Keepers of the Peace', pp. 310–11; Otway-Ruthven, *History of Medieval Ireland*, pp. 180–1; Jones, 'Violence, Criminality, and Culture Disfunction', pp. 29–47.

56. Frame, 'Judicial Powers of the Irish Keepers of the Peace', p. 314.

57. The substance of several of the ordinances of Kilkenny of 1351 resembles in many respects the powers granted to the northern wardens in their commissions. Some were re-enacted in 1366 as the Statutes of Kilkenny. See *Statute Rolls of the Parliament of Ireland*, i.394–7, and Hand, 'The Forgotten Statutes of Kilkenny', pp. 299–312.

58. This power was understood within the terms of the wardenial commissions that authorised them to 'do all and everything required to repulse and destroy our enemy and for the defence and salvation of our lands'. *Rot. Scot.*, i.130.

59. Frame, 'War and Peace', pp. 133–6. The power to accept men into the king's peace was granted to Henry Percy by special commission in 1327, but it became a standard feature of the wardens' commissions in 1335. *CPR*, 1327–30, p. 20; *Rot. Scot.*, i.318.

60. In 1352, for example, a royal commission ordered the wardens of the west march to arrest and punish 'thieves, plunderers and other evildoers' in the region; another issued in 1372 authorised the wardens of both marches to investigate the illegal export of fleeces and sheep across the border. *CPR*, 1350–4, p. 336; *CPR*, 1370–4, p. 244. Irish examples are cited in Frame, 'Judicial Powers of the Medieval Irish Keepers of the Peace', p. 315.

61. Ibid., p. 319.

62. The strains imposed on the English judicial system by the northern liberties and the proximity of the border line itself are clearly illustrated in surviving common-law

records. See, for example, the record of several sessions held before justices of the peace in Northumberland in 1364, and several incidents concerning the flight of fugitives noted in a roll of gaol delivery from the same period, PRO JUST 1/661; JUST 3/145 m.24.

63. Barrow, 'Frontier and Settlement', p. 20.

64. Davies, *Conquest, Coexistence, and Change*, p. 285; Davies, *Lordship and Society*, p. 162. See also Davies, 'The Law of the March', pp. 1–30.

65. MacNiocaill, 'The Interaction of Laws', p. 112; Nicholls, *Gaelic and Gaelicised Ireland*, pp. 47–8. See also Otway-Ruthven, *History of Medieval Ireland*, pp. 278–9.

66. Otway-Ruthven, *History of Medieval Ireland*, p. 292. The Statutes of Kilkenny forbade recourse to 'March or Brehon law which by right ought not to be called law but bad custom'. *Irish Historical Documents 1172–1922*, p. 53.

67. Davies, *Lordship and Society*, p. 162.

68. See, for example, Hand, *English Law in Ireland*, p. 160; MacNiocaill, 'The Interaction of Laws', pp. 107–8, 116; Davies, *Lordship and Society*, p. 160; Davies, 'The Law of the March', pp. 3–4; Davies *Conquest, Coexistence, and Change*, pp. 285–6.

69. Recent studies of arbitration in secular matters suggest that extra-judicial settlements increased in number in the fourteenth century, and that they remained a crucial feature of late medieval and early modern law. See, for example, Powell, 'Arbitration and the Law', pp. 49–69.

70. CRO MS copy of Bell's treatise. Part of the work was printed in Nicolson and Burn, *History and Antiquities of Westmorland and Cumberland*, i.xxiii–xxviii, lv–lvi.

71. Davies, 'The Peoples of Britain and Ireland 1100–1400 III. Laws and Customs', pp. 5–6.

72. PRO SC 1/42(19).

73. See, for example, *Rot. Scot.*, ii.268–9.

74. Davies, 'The Law of the March', 3–6; Davies, 'Fragmented Societies', pp. 98–9. The rarity of record materials relating to Irish marcher law is a theme that runs through virtually all scholarly discussions of the subject: see, for example, Nicholls, *Gaelic and Gaelicised Ireland*, pp. 48–9; Hand, *English Law in Ireland*, pp. 34–6; Jones, 'Violence, Criminality, and Culture Disjunction', pp. 30–1.

75. Ellis, 'Tudor State Formation', p. 62.

76. See, for example, the several compilations noted in 1592 by William Fielding in his search through Henry lord Scrope's wardenial papers. *Border Papers*, i.474, 778, 782.

Bibliography

Manuscript Sources

Public Record Office, London

CHANCERY

C 47	Miscellanea
C 49	Chancery, Parliamentary and Council Proceedings, Henry III–1650
C 54	Close Rolls
C 66	Patent Rolls
C 71	Scottish Rolls
C 81	Warrants for the Great Seal, Series I
C 82	Warrants for the Great Seal, Series II
C 145	Inquisitions Miscellaneous
C 260	Chancery Files (Tower and Rolls Chapel Series), *Recorda*
C 269	Chancery Files (Tower and Rolls Chapel Series), *Certiorari*: Ecclesiastical

DUCHY OF LANCASTER

DL 25	Ancient Deeds, Series L
DL 34	Ancient Correspondence and Diplomatic Documents
DL 36	Cartae Miscellaneae
DL 37	Chancery Rolls

PALATINATE OF DURHAM

DURH 19/1	Miscellanea
DURH 3	Cursitor's Records

EXCHEQUER

Exchequer of Pleas

E 13	Plea Rolls

Treasury of the Receipt

E 28	Council and Privy Seal Documents
E 30	Diplomatic Documents
E 36	Books
E 39	Scottish Documents

Queen's Remembrancer

E 101	Various Accounts
E 199	Sheriffs' Accounts
E 159	Memoranda Rolls
E 179	Subsidy Rolls

Lord Treasurer's Remembrancer
E 364   Foreign Accounts
E 368   Memoranda Rolls

Exchequer of the Receipt
E 403   Issue Rolls
E 404   Writs and Warrants for Issue

RECORDS OF JUSTICES ITINERANT

JUST 1   Assize Rolls
JUST 2   Coroners' Rolls
JUST 3   Gaol Delivery Rolls

COURT OF KING'S BENCH

KB 9   Ancient Indictments
KB 26   *Curia Regis* Rolls
KB 27   *Coram Rege* Rolls

SPECIAL COLLECTIONS

SC 1   Ancient Correspondence
SC 8   Ancient Petitions

STATE PAPER OFFICE

SP 58   State Papers, Scotland incl. Borders, Transcripts

British Library

Additional Manuscripts 4608, 4609, 4610, 9021, 24062, 27401
Cotton Charter XVIII
Cotton MSS Cleopatra F IV
               Faustina A VI
               Titus A XIX
               Titus B VI
               Vespasian C XVI
               Vespasian F VII
               Vitellius E XI
Egerton Roll 8728
Harleian MS 4700
Northumberland Papers (microfilm)

Cumbria Record Office (Carlisle)

DRC 1/1, 2   Episcopal registers
D/AY/1   Aglionby Papers
D/Lons/L5   Lonsdale Records
Ca3/1   Carlisle City Records; Court Rolls
MS of Richard Bell's *History of the Borders*

Archives of the Dean and Chapter, Durham Cathedral

Locelli IV, V, XXV
Miscellaneous Charters
Regalia
Registrum I
Registrum II
Registrum III
Registrum IV
Registrum Parvum I (=BL MS Titus B VI)
Registrum Parvum II

Alnwick Castle, Northumberland

Northumberland MSS; Percy Family Letters and Papers

Northumberland Record Office

ZSW 1   Swynburn MSS

Scottish Record Office

SP 6   Treaties with England

National Library of Scotland

NLS Adv. MSS 7.1.9   Advocates' MSS

Printed Primary Sources

'An Account of the Army with which King Richard the Second Invaded Scotland in the Ninth Year of his Reign, A.D. 1385', ed. H. Nicolas, *Archaeologia Aeliana* 22 (1829), pp. 13–19.

Acta dominorum concilii. Acts of the Lords of Council in Civil Causes. Vol. II: A.D. 1496–1501, ed. G. Neilson and H. Paton, Edinburgh, Scottish Record Office, 1918.

The Acts of the Lords of Council in Civil Causes, A.D. 1478–A.D. 1495, ed. T. Thomson, London, Record Commission, 1839.

Acts of the Parliaments of Scotland, ed. T. Thomson and C. Innes, 12 vols in 13, Edinburgh, Record Commission, 1814–75.

'Adae Murimuth Continuatio Chronicarum', in E. M. Thompson, ed., *Adae Murimuth continuatio chronicarum. Robertus de Avesbury De Gestis Mirabilibus Edwardi Tertii*, London, Rolls Series, 1889.

Ancient Petitions relating to Northumberland, ed. C. M. Fraser, Durham, Surtees Society, 1966.

Anglo-Scottish Relations 1174–1328. Some Selected Documents, ed. E. L. G. Stones, Oxford, Oxford University Press, 1965.

'Annales de Burton', in *Annales monastici*, ed. H. R. Luard, 5 vols, London, Rolls Series, 1864–9.

'Annales Ricardi secundi et Hernici quarti', in *Johannis de Trokelowe et Henrici de Blaneforde monachorum S. Albani, necnon quorundam anonymarum, Chronica et Annales*, ed. H. T. Riley, London, Rolls Series, 1866.

The Anonimalle Chronicle 1333 to 1381, ed. V. H. Galbraith, Manchester, Manchester University Press, 1970.

The Asloan Manuscript, ed. W. A. Craigie, 2 vols, Edinburgh, Scottish Text Society, new ser., 1923–4.

John Barbour, *The Bruce*, ed. W. W. Skeat, 2 vols, Edinburgh, Scottish Text Society, 1894.

The Barony of Gilsland. Lord William Howard's Survey, taken in 1603, ed. T. H. B. Graham, Kendal, Cumberland and Westmorland Antiquarian and Archaeological Society, Extra Series, 16, 1934.

The Black Book of the Admiralty, ed. T. Twiss, 4 vols, London, Rolls Series, 1871–6.

The Border Papers. Calendar of Letters and Papers relating to the Affairs of the Borders of England and Scotland preserved in Her Majesty's Public Record Office, London, ed. J. Bain, 2 vols, Edinburgh, Scottish Record Office, 1894–6.

Robert Bowes, 'The Order and Form of Days of Truce', in J. Raine, ed., *The History and Antiquities of North Durham*, London, J. B. Nichols and Sons, 1852, pp. xxii–xxvii.

British Library Harleian Manuscript 433, ed. R. Horrox and P. W. Hammond, 4 vols, London, Richard III Society, 1979–83.

The Brut or The Chronicles of England, ed. F. W. D. Brie, Oxford, Early English Text Society, 1906–8.

George Buchanan, *The History of Scotland*, trans. J. Aikman, 4 vols, Glasgow, Blackie, Fullarton, 1827–9.

The Buik of the Chroniclis of Scotland, or a metrical version of the history of Hector Boece, by William Stewart, ed. W. Turnbull, 3 vols, London, Rolls Series, 1858.

Calendar of Chancery Warrants preserved in the Public Record Office, A.D. 1244–1326, London, Public Record Office, 1927.

Calendar of Documents relating to Scotland preserved in Her Majesty's Public Record Office, London, ed. J. Bain, 4 vols, Edinburgh, Scottish Record Office, 1881–8.

Calendar of Documents relating to Scotland preserved in the Public Record Office and the British Library, vol. 5 (Supplementary), ed. G. G. Simpson and J. D. Galbraith, Edinburgh, Scottish Record Office, n.d.

Calendar of Inquisitions Miscellaneous (Chancery) preserved in the Public Record Office, 7 vols, London, Public Record Office, 1916–68.

Calendar of Inquisitions Post Mortem and other analogous documents preserved in the Public Record Office, 14 vols, London, Public Record Office, 1904–54.

Calendar of Signet Letters of Henry IV and Henry V, ed. J. L. Kirby, London, HMSO, 1979.

Calendar of the Close Rolls preserved in the Public Record Office, London, Public Record Office, 1892–.

Calendar of the Fine Rolls preserved in the Public Record Office, London, Public Record Office, 1911–49.

Calendar of the Patent Rolls preserved in the Public Record Office, London, Public Record Office, 1893–1916.

Chronica monasterii de Melsa, a fundatione usque ad annum 1396, auctore Thomas de Burton, abbate, ed. E. A. Bond, 3 vols, London, Rolls Series, 1866–8.

The Chronicle of John Hardyng, ed. H. Ellis, London, F. C. and J. Rivington, 1812.

The Chronicle of Lanercost 1272–1346, ed. H. Maxwell, Glasgow, James Maclehose and Sons, 1913.

'The Chronicle of Robert de Avesbury', in E. M. Thompson, ed., *Adae Murimuth Continuatio Chronicarum. Roberti de Avesbury de Gestis Mirabilibus Regis Edwardi Tertii*, London, Rolls Series, 1889.

Chronicon Adae de Usk A.D. 1377–1421, ed. E. M. Thompson, New York, AMS Press, 1980.

Chronicon Angliae, ab anno domini 1328 usque ad annum 1338, auctore monacho quondam sancti Albani, ed. E. M. Thompson, London, Rolls Series, 1874.

Chronicon Galfridi le Baker de Swynbroke, ed. E. M. Thompson, Oxford, Clarendon Press, 1889.

Chronicon Henrici Knighton, vel Cnitthon, monachi Leycestrensis, ed. J. R. Lumby, 2 vols, London, Rolls Series, 1889–95.

Compota thesaurariorum regum Scotorum. Accounts of the Lord High Treasurer of Scotland, ed. T. Dickson and J. Balfour Paul, 11 vols, Edinburgh, Scottish Record Office, 1877–1916.

Councils and Synods. Vol. II. A.D. 1205–1313, ed. F. M. Powicke and C. R. Cheney, 2 vols, Oxford, Clarendon Press, 1964.

Depositions and Other Ecclesiastical Proceedings from the Courts of Durham, ed. J. Raine, Durham, Surtees Society, 1885.

Documents Illustrative of the History of Scotland 1286–1306, ed. J. Stevenson, 2 vols, Edinburgh, Scottish Record Office, 1870.

The Douglas Book, ed. W. Fraser, 4 vols, Edinburgh, 1885.

Durham Quarter Sessions Rolls 1471–1625, ed. C. M. Fraser, Durham, Surtees Society, 1991.

Edward I and the Throne of Scotland, ed. E. L. G. Stones and G. G. Simpson, 2 vols, Oxford, Oxford University Press, 1978.

An English Chronicle of the Reigns of Richard II, Henry IV, Henry V, and Henry VI. Written before the year 1471, ed. J. S. Davies, London, Camden Society, 1861.

Facsimiles of National Manuscripts from William the Conqueror to Queen Anne, ed. H. James, 4 vols, Southampton, Ordnance Survey Office, 1865–8.

Facsimiles of National Manuscripts of Scotland, ed. C. Innes, 3 vols, Southampton, Ordnance Survey Office, 1867–72.

Foedera, conventiones, litterae, et cujuscunque generis acta publica . . ., ed. T. Rymer, 20 vols, London, J. Johnson, 1727–35.

Foedera, conventiones, litterae, et cujuscunque generis acta publica . . ., ed. T. Rymer 10 vols, facsimile of the Hague edition, Jean Neaulme, 1739–45.

Foedera, conventiones, litterae, et cujuscunque generis acta publica . . ., ed. T. Rymer, 4 vols in 7 parts, London, Record Commission, 1816–69.

Fourteenth Report of the Royal Commission on Historical Manuscripts, London, Historical Manuscripts Commission, 1896.

Jean Froissart, *Oeuvres*, ed. K. de Lettenhove, 25 vols in 26, Brussels, V. Devaux et cie., 1867–77.

Gerald of Wales, 'The Topography of Ireland', in T. Wright, ed., *The Historical Works of Giraldus Cambrensis*, London, H. G. Bohn, 1863.

Gesta Henrici Quinti, ed. F. Taylor and J. S. Roskell, Oxford, Clarendon Press, 1975.

Grants, etc. from the Crown during the Reign of Edward the Fifth, ed. J. G. Nichols, London, Camden Society, 1854.

Historical Papers and Letters from the Northern Registers, ed. J. Raine, London, Rolls Series, 1873.

Ralph Holinshed, *Chronicles of England, Scotland, and Ireland*, 6 vols, London, J. Johnson et al., 1807–8.

Illustrations of Scottish History from the Twelfth to the Sixteenth Century, ed. J. Stevenson, Glasgow, Maitland Club, 1834.

Incerti Scriptoris Chronicon Angliae de Regnis Trium Regum Lancastrensium, Henrici IV, Henrici V, et Henrici VI, ed. J. A. Giles, London, D. Nutt, 1848.

Irish Historical Documents 1172–1922, ed. E. Curtis and R. B. McDowell, Dublin, Methuen, 1943.

Issues of the Exchequer; being a collection of payments made out of His Majesty's revenue, from

King Henry III to King Henry VI inclusive, ed. F. Devon, London, Record Commission, 1837.

Joannis de Fordun Scotichronicon cum Supplementis et Continuatione Walteri Boweri, ed. W. Goodall, 2 vols, Edinburgh, Robert Fleming, 1759.

Johannis de Fordun Chronica Gentis Scotorum, ed. W. F. Skene, 2 vols, Edinburgh, Edmunston and Douglas, 1871–2.

Johannis de Trokelowe et Henrici de Blaneforde monachorum S. Albani, necnon quorundam anonymarum, Chronica et Annales, ed. H. T. Riley, London, Rolls Series, 1866.

John of Gaunt's Register, ed. E. C. Lodge and R. Somerville, 2 vols, London, Camden Society, 1937.

Leges Marchiarum or Border Laws, ed. W. Nicolson, London, Timothy Goodwin, 1705.

John Lesley, *The History of Scotland, from the Death of King James I, in the year MCCCCXXXVI, to the Year MDLXI*, ed. T. Thomson, Edinburgh, Bannatyne Club, 1830.

Letters and Papers, Foreign and Domestic, of the Reign of Henry VIII, ed. J. S. Brewer *et al.*, 21 vols, London, Public Record Office, 1862–1910.

Letters and Papers Illustrative of the Reign of Richard III and Henry VII, ed. J. Gairdner, 2 vols, London, Rolls Series, 1861–3.

The Letters of James the Fourth, 1505–1513, ed. R. L. Mackie, Scottish History Society, 1953.

Letters of the Kings of England, ed. J. O. Halliwell, 2 vols, London, Henry Colburn, 1848.

The Libelle of Englyshe Polycye, ed. G. Warner, Oxford, Clarendon Press, 1926.

Liber Pluscardensis, ed. F. J. H. Skene, 2 vols, Edinburgh, W. Paterson, 1877–80.

'The March Laws', ed. G. Neilson, *Stair Society Miscellany*, vol. 1, Edinburgh, Stair Society, 1971, pp. 11–77.

Materials for a History of the Reign of Henry VII from Original Documents Preserved in the Public Record Office, ed. W. Campbell, 2 vols, London, Rolls Series, 1873–7.

'Minutes of the Proceedings of the Commissioners at Nottingham, in September M.CCCC.LXXXIV', ed., D. Laing, *The Bannatyne Miscellany*, vol. II, Edinburgh, Bannatyne Club, 1836, pp. 35–48.

Northern Petitions Illustrative of Life in Berwick, Cumbria and Durham in the Fourteenth Century, ed. C. M. Fraser, Durham, Surtees Society, 1981.

The Original Chronicle of Andrew of Wyntoun, ed. F. J. Amours, 6 vols in 7, Edinburgh, Scottish Text Society, 1903–14.

Original Letters Illustrative of English History, ed. H. Ellis, 3rd ser., 2 vols, London, Richard Bentley, 1846.

The Parliamentary Records of Scotland in the General Register House, Edinburgh, ed. W. Robertson, London, Record Commission, 1804.

Parliamentary Writs and Writs of Military Summons, ed. F. Palgrave, 2 vols, London, Record Commission, 1827–34.

Paston Letters and Papers of the Fifteenth Century, ed. N. Davis, 2 vols, Oxford, Clarendon Press, 1971.

Percy Bailiffs' Rolls of the Fifteenth Century, ed. J. C. Hodgson, Durham, Surtees Society, 1921.

The Percy Chartulary, ed. M. T. Martin, Durham, Surtees Society, 1911.

'A Plea Roll of Edward I's Army in Scotland, 1296', ed. C. J. Neville, *Miscellany of the Scottish History Society*, vol. XI, Edinburgh, Scottish History Society, 1990, pp. 7–133.

Plumpton Correspondence, ed. T. S. Stapleton, London, Camden Society, 1839.

Polychronicon Ranulphi Higden monachi Cestrensis, ed. J. R. Lumby, 9 vols, Rolls Series, 1865–6.

The Priory of Hexham, ed. J. Raine, 2 vols, Durham, Surtees Society, 1864–5.

Proceedings and Ordinances of the Privy Council of England, ed. H. Nicolas, 7 vols, London, Record Commission, 1834–7.

Proceedings Before the Justices of the Peace in the Fourteenth and Fifteenth Centuries, Edward III to Richard III, ed. B. Putnam, London, Butterworth, 1938.

The Register of Richard Fox Lord Bishop of Durham 1494–1501, ed. M. P. Howden, Durham, Surtees Society, 1932.

The Register of Thomas Langley, Bishop of Durham, 1406–1437, ed. R. L. Storey, 6 vols, Durham, Surtees Society, 1956–70.

Registrum episcopatus Glasguensis: munimenta ecclesie metropolitane Glasguensis, a sede restaurata seculo ineunte XII, ad reformatam religionem, ed. C. Innes, 2 vols, Edinburgh, Maitland Club, 1843.

Registrum magni sigilli regum Scotorum. The Register of the Great Seal of Scotland, ed. J. M. Thomson *et al.*, 9 vols, Edinburgh, Scottish Record Office, 1882–1912.

Registrum palatinum Dunelmense. The Register of Richard de Kellawe, Lord Palatine and Bishop of Durham 1314–1316, ed. T. D. Hardy, 4 vols, London, Rolls Series, 1873–5.

Registrum secreti sigilli regum Scotorum. The Register of the Privy Seal of Scotland, ed. M. Livingstone *et al.*, 4 vols, Edinburgh, Scottish Record Office, 1908–52.

Richard D'Aungerville of Bury. Fragments of his Register and Other Documents, ed. G. W. Kitchin, Durham, Surtees Society, 1910.

Roberti de Avesbury De Gestis Mirabilibus Regis Edwardi Tertii, ed. E. M. Thompson, London, Rolls Series, 1889.

Rotuli Parliamentorum; ut et petitiones, et placita in parliamento, 7 vols, London, Record Commission, 1783–1832.

Rotuli scaccarii regum Scotorum. The Exchequer Rolls of Scotland, ed. J. Stuart and G. Burnett, 23 vols, Edinburgh, Scottish Record Office, 1878–1908.

Rotuli Scotiae in turri Londonensi et in domo capitulari Westmonasteriensi asservati, ed. D. MacPherson *et al.*, 2 vols, London, Record Commission. 1814–19.

Royal and Historical Letters During the Reigns of Henry IV, ed. F. C. Hingeston, 2 vols, London, Rolls Series, 1860.

Sanctuarium Dunelmense et Sanctuarium Beverlacense, ed. J. Raine, Durham, Surtees Society, 1837.

Scalacronica; The Reigns of Edward I, Edward II and Edward III as Recorded by Sir Thomas Gray, ed. H. Maxwell, Glasgow, James Maclehose and Sons, 1907.

Select Cases before the King's Council, 1243–1482, ed. I. S. Leadam and J. F. Baldwin, London, Selden Society, 1918.

Select Cases concerning the Law Merchant, ed. C. Gross and H. Hall, 3 vols, Selden Society, London, 1908–32.

Select Pleas in the Court of Admiralty. Vol. I: The Court of the Admiralty of the West (A. D. 1390–1404) and the High Court of Admiralty (A.D. 1527–1545), ed. R. G. Marsden, London, Selden Society, 1984.

Six Town Chronicles of England, ed. R. Flenley, Oxford, Clarendon Press, 1911.

Statute Rolls of the Parliament of Ireland, ed. H. F. Berry and J. F. Morrissey 4 vols, Dublin, Irish Record Office, 1907–39.

Statutes of the Realm, from original records and authentic manuscripts, ed. A. Luders *et al.*, 11 vols in 12, London, Record Commission, 1810–28.

Thomae Walsingham quondam monachi S. Albani Historia Anglicana, ed. H. T. Riley, 2 vols, London, Rolls Series, 1863–4.

Three Early Assize Rolls for the County of Northumberland, saec. XIII, ed. W. Page, Durham, Surtees Society, 1891.

Three Fifteenth-Century Chronicles, ed. J. Gairdner, London, Camden Society, 1880.

The Tree of Battles of Honoré Bonet, ed. G. W. Coopland, Cambridge MA, Harvard University Press, 1949.

Vita Edwardi Secundi Monachi cuiusdam Malmesberiensis, ed. N. Denholm-Young, London, Thomas Nelson and Sons, 1957.

A Volume of English Miscellanies Illustrating the History and Language of the Northern Counties of England, ed. J. Raine, Durham, Surtees Society, 1890.

The Westminster Chronicle 1381–1394, ed. L. C. Hector and B. Harvey, Oxford, Clarendon Press, 1982.

'William Gregory's Chronicle of London', in *The Historical Collections of a Citizen of London*, ed. J. Gairdner, London, Camden Society, 1876.

'Ypodigma Neustriae, a Thome Walsingham, quondam monacho S. Albani, conscriptum', in *Chronica Monasterii S. Albani*, ed. H. T. Riley, 12 vols, London, Rolls Series, 1863–76.

Secondary Sources

Acheson, E. (1992), *A Gentry Community: Leicestershire in the Fifteenth Century, c.1422–c.1485*, Cambridge, Cambridge University Press.

Allmand, C. (1992), *Henry V*, Berkeley and Los Angeles, University of California Press.

Arthurson, I. (1987), 'The King's Voyage into Scotland: The War that Never Was', in D. Williams (ed.), *England in the Fifteenth Century: Proceedings of the 1986 Harlaxton Symposium*, Woodbridge, Boydell Press, pp. 1–22.

Baker, J. H. (1971), *An Introduction to English Legal History*, London, Butterworth.

Baldwin, J. F. (1913), *The King's Council in England during the Middle Ages*, Gloucester MA, Peter Smith.

Balfour-Melville, E. W. M. (1954), *Edward III and David II*, London, Historical Association.

Balfour-Melville, E. W. M. (1936), *James I, King of Scots, 1406–1437*, London, Methuen and Co.

Barber, R. (1989), *Tournaments*, New York, Weidenfeld and Nicolson.

Barker, J. R. V. (1986), *The Tournament in England, 1100–1400*, Woodbridge, Boydell Press.

Barrow, G. W. S. (1980), *The Anglo-Norman Era in Scottish History*, Oxford, Clarendon Press.

Barrow, G. W. S. (1973), 'The Anglo-Scottish Border', in *The Kingdom of the Scots*, London, Edward Arnold, pp. 139–61.

Barrow, G. W. S. (1989), 'Frontier and Settlement: Which Influenced Which? England and Scotland 1100–1300', in R. Bartlett and W. Mackay (eds), *Medieval Frontier Societies*, Oxford, Clarendon Press, pp. 3–21.

Barrow, G. W. S. (1975), 'The Pattern of Lordship and Feudal Settlement in Cumbria', *Journal of Medieval History*, 1, pp. 117–38.

Barrow, G. W. S. (1988), *Robert Bruce and the Community of the Realm of Scotland*, 3rd edn, Edinburgh, Edinburgh University Press.

Barrow, G. W. S. (1981), 'Wales and Scotland in the Middle Ages', *Welsh History Review*, 10, pp. 302–19.

Bates, C. J. (1891), *The Border Holds of Northumberland*, London, Society of Antiquaries.

Bean, J. M. W. (1958), *The Estates of the Percy Family 1416–1437*, Oxford, Oxford University Press.

Bean, J. M. W. (1959), 'Henry IV and the Percies', *History*, 44, pp. 212–27.

Bean, J. M. W. (1957), 'The Percies and their Estates in Scotland', *Archaeologia Aeliana*, 4th ser., 35, pp. 91–9.

Bellamy, J. G. (1973), *Crime and Public Order in England in the Later Middle Ages*, London, Routledge and Kegan Paul.

Bellamy, J. G. (1984), *Criminal Society and the Law in Late Medieval and Tudor England*, New York, St Martin's Press.

Bellamy, J. G. (1970), *The Law of Treason in England in the Later Middle Ages*, Cambridge, Cambridge University Press.

Black, R. (1975), 'A Historical Survey of Delictual Liability in Scotland for Personal Injuries and Death', *Comparative and International Law Journal of Southern Africa*, 8, pp. 46–70.

Blair, C. H. H. (1950), 'Wardens and Deputy Wardens of the Marches of England towards Scotland in Northumberland', *Archaeologia Aeliana*, 4th ser., 28, pp. 13–95.

Boardman, S. (1992), 'The Man who would be King: the Lieutenancy and Death of David, Duke of Rothesay, 1378–1402', in R. Mason and N. Macdougall (eds), *People and Power in Scotland: Essays in Honour of T. C. Smout*, Edinburgh, John Donald, pp. 1–27.

Bradley, P. J. (1989), 'Henry V's Scottish Policy: a Study in *Realpolitik*', in J. S. Hamilton and P. J. Bradley (eds), *Documenting the Past: Essays in Medieval History presented to George Peddy Cuttino*, Woodbridge, Boydell Press, pp. 177–95.

Brand, P. (1981), 'Ireland and the Literature of the Early Common Law', *Irish Jurist*, new ser., 16, pp. 95–113.

Brooks, F. W. (1966), *The Council of the North*, London, Historical Association.

Brown, A. L. (1974), 'The English Campaign in Scotland, 1400', in H. Hearder and H. R. Loyn (eds), *British Government and Administration: Studies Presented to S. B. Chrimes*, Cardiff, University of Wales Press, pp. 40–54.

Campbell, J. (1965), 'England, Scotland and the Hundred Years War', in J. R. Hale, J. R. L. Highfield and B. Smalley (eds), *Europe in the Late Middle Ages*, Evanston, IL, Northwestern University Press, pp. 184–216.

Carpenter, C. (1992), *Locality and Polity: A Study of Warwickshire Landed Society, 1401–1499*, Cambridge, Cambridge University Press.

Carpenter, C. (1995), 'Political and Constitutional History Before and After McFarlane', in R. H. Britnell and A. J. Pollard (eds), *The McFarlane Legacy: Studies in Late Medieval Politics and Society*, New York, St. Martin's Press, pp. 175–206.

Cheney, C. R. (1972), *Notaries Public in England in the Thirteenth and Fourteenth Centuries*, Oxford, Clarendon Press.

Chrimes, S. B. (1972), *Henry VII*, Berkeley and Los Angeles, University of California Press.

Chrimes, S. B. (1939), 'Some Letters of John of Lancaster as Warden of the East Marches towards Scotland', *Speculum* 14, pp. 3–27.

Clanchy, M. T. (1985), 'Literacy, Law and the Power of the State', in *Culture et idéologie dans la genèse de l'état moderne*, Rome, L'Ecole française de Rome, pp. 25–34.

Clayton, D. J. (1990), *The Administration of the County Palatine of Chester 1442–1485*, Manchester, Manchester University Press.

Constable, M. (1994), *The Law of the Other: Changing Concepts of Citizenship, Law, and Knowledge*, Chicago, University of Chicago Press.

Contamine, P. (1976), 'The War Literature of the Late Middle Ages: The Treatises of Robert de Balsac and Béraud Stuart, Lord of Aubigny', in C. T. Allmand (ed.), *War, Literature and Politics in the Late Middle Ages*, Liverpool, University of Liverpool Press, pp. 102–21.

Conway, A. (1972), *Henry VII's Relations with Scotland and Ireland 1485–1498*, New York, Octagon Books.

Coopland, G. W. (1923), 'The Tree of Battles and Some of its Sources', *Revue d'histoire du droit*, 5, pp. 173–207.

Curwin, J. F. (1913), *The Castles and Fortified Towers of Cumberland, Westmorland, and Lancashire North-of-the-Sands*, Kendal, Cumberland and Westmorland Antiquarian and Archaeological Society, Extra Series, 13.

Davies, R. R. (ed.) (1988), *The British Isles 1100–1500: Comparisons Contrasts and Connections*, Edinburgh, John Donald.

Davies, R. R. (1974), 'Colonial Wales', *Past and Present*, 65, pp. 3–23.

Davies, R. R. (1987), *Conquest, Coexistence, and Change: Wales 1063–1415*, Oxford, Clarendon Press.

Davies, R. R. (1990), *Domination and Conquest: The Experience of Ireland, Scotland and Wales 1100–1300*, Cambridge, Cambridge University Press.

Davies, R. R. (1993), 'The English State and the "Celtic" Peoples 1100–1400', *Journal of Historical Sociology*, 6, pp. 1–14.

Davies, R. R. (1989), 'Frontier Arrangements in Fragmented Societies: Ireland and Wales', in R. Bartlett and W. Mackay (eds), *Medieval Frontier Societies*, Oxford, Clarendon Press, pp. 77–100.

Davies, R. R. (1984), 'Law and National Identity in Thirteenth-Century Wales', in R. R. Davies, R. A. Griffiths, I. G. Jones and K. O. Morgan (eds), *Welsh Society and Nationhood: Historical Essays presented to Glanmor Williams*, Cardiff, University of Wales Press, pp. 51–69.

Davies, R. R. (1970–1), 'The Law of the March', *Welsh History Review*, 5, pp. 1–30.

Davies, R. R. (1978), *Lordship and Society in the March of Wales 1282–1400*, Oxford, Clarendon Press.

Davies, R. R. (1984), 'Lordship or Colony?' in J. Lydon (ed.), *The English in Medieval Ireland*, Dublin, Royal Irish Academy, pp. 142–60.

Davies, R. R. (1994), 'The Peoples of Britain and Ireland 1100–1400 I. Identities', *Transactions of the Royal Historical Society*, 6th ser., 4, pp. 1–20.

Davies, R. R. (1995), 'The Peoples of Britain and Ireland 1100–1400 II. Names, Boundaries and Regnal Solidarities', *Transactions of the Royal Historical Society*, 6th ser., 5, pp. 1–20.

Davies, R. R. (1996), 'The Peoples of Britain and Ireland 1100–1400 III. Laws and Customs', *Transactions of the Royal Historical Society*, 6th ser., 6, pp. 1–23.

Davies, R. R. (1974–5), 'Race Relations in Post-Conquest Wales', *Transactions of the Honourable Society of Cymmrodorion*, pp. 32–56.

De Fonblanque, E. B. (1887), *Annals of the House of Percy, from the Conquest to the Opening of the Nineteenth Century*, 2 vols, London, R. Clay and Sons.

Dickinson, W. C. (1960), 'Surdit de Sergaunt', *Scottish Historical Review*, 39, pp. 170–5.

Ditchburn, D. (1992), 'Piracy and War at Sea in Late Medieval Scotland', in T. C. Smout (ed.), *Scotland and the Sea*, Edinburgh, John Donald, pp. 35–58.

Dobson, R. B. (1992), 'The Church of Durham and the Scottish Borders, 1378–88', in A. Goodman and A. Tuck (eds), *War and Border Societies in the Middle Ages*, London, Routledge, pp. 124–54.

Dobson, R. B. (1973), *Durham Priory 1400–1450*, Cambridge, Cambridge University Press.

Dobson, R. B. (1967), 'The Last English Monks on Scottish Soil. The Severance of Coldingham Priory from the Monastery of Durham 1461–78', *Scottish Historical Review*, 46, pp. 1–25.

Douglas, W. (1820–1), 'Fast Castle and its Owners: Some Notes on their History', *Proceedings of the Society of Antiquaries of Scotland*, 55, pp. 56–83.

Duncan, A. A. M. (1988), '*Honi soit qui mal y pense*: David II and Edward III', *Scottish Historical Review*, 67, pp. 113–41.

Duncan, A. A. M. (1978), *Scotland: The Making of the Kingdom*, Edinburgh, Oliver and Boyd.

Duncan, A. A. M. (1954), 'A Siege of Lochmaben Castle in 1343', *Transactions of the Dumfriesshire and Galloway Natural History and Archaeological Society*, 3rd ser., 31, pp. 74–7.

Dunlop, A. I. (1950), *The Life and Times of James Kennedy, Bishop of St. Andrews*, Edinburgh, Oliver and Boyd.

Dunlop, D. (1990), 'The "Redresses and Reparacons of Attemptates": Alexander Legh's Intructions from Edward IV, March-April 1475', *Historical Research*, 63, pp. 340–53.

Dunning, R. W. (1968), 'Thomas, Lord Dacre and the West March towards Scotland, ?1435', *Bulletin of the Institute of Historical Research*, 41, pp. 95–9.

Ellis, S. (1986), 'Crown, Community and Government in the English Territories, 1450–1575', *History*, 71, pp. 187–204.

Ellis, S. (1986), 'Nationalist Historiography and the English and Gaelic Worlds in the Late Middle Ages', *Irish Historical Studies*, 25, pp. 1–18.

Ellis, S. G. (1986), *Reform and Revival: English Government in Ireland, 1470–1534*, Woodbridge, Boydell Press.

Ellis, S. G. (1995), *Tudor Frontiers and Noble Power: The Making of the British State*, Oxford, Oxford University Press.

Ellis, S. (1995), 'Tudor State Formation and the Shaping of the British Isles', in S. G. Ellis and S. Barber (eds), *Conquest and Union: Fashioning a British State, 1485–1725*, New York, Longman, pp. 40–63.

Emden, A. B. (1957–9), *A Biographical Register of the University of Oxford to A. D. 1500*, 3 vols, Oxford, Oxford University Press.

Ferguson, W. (1977), *Scotland's Relations with England: A Survey to 1707*, Edinburgh, John Donald.

Ford, C. J. (1979), 'Piracy or Policy: The Crisis in the Channel, 1400–1403', *Transactions of the Royal Historical Society*, 5th ser., 29, pp. 63–77.

Fowler, K. (1971), 'Truces', in K. Fowler (ed), *The Hundred Years War*, London, Macmillan, pp. 184–215.

Frame, R. (1993), ' "Les Engleys nées en Irelande": The English Political Identity in Medieval Ireland', *Transactions of the Royal Historical Society*, 6th ser., 3, pp. 83–103.

Frame, R. (1982), *English Lordship in Ireland 1318–1361*, Oxford, Clarendon Press.

Frame, R. (1975), 'English Officials and Irish Chiefs in the Fourteenth Century', *English Historical Review*, 90, pp. 748–77.

Frame, R. (1967), 'The Judicial Powers of the Medieval Irish Keepers of the Peace', *Irish Jurist*, new ser., 2, pp. 308–26.

Frame, R. (1989), 'Military Service in the Lordship of Ireland 1290–1360: Institutions and Society on the Anglo–Gaelic Frontier', in R. Bartlett and W. Mackay (eds), *Medieval Frontier Societies*, Oxford, Clarendon Press, pp. 101–26.

Frame, R. (1990), *The Political Development of the British Isles 1100–1400*, Oxford, Oxford University Press.

Frame, R. (1977), 'Power and Society in the Lordship of Ireland 1272–1377', *Past and Present*, 76, pp. 3–33.

Frame, R. (1996), 'Thomas Rokeby, Justiciar of Ireland: Service on Two Frontiers', *Peritia*, 10, pp. 1–23.

Frame, R. (1984), 'War and Peace in the Medieval Lordship of Ireland', in J. Lydon (ed.), *The English in Medieval Ireland*, Dublin, Royal Irish Academy, pp. 118–41.

Fryde, N. (1979), *The Tyranny and Fall of Edward II 1321–26*, Cambridge, Cambridge University Press.

Gillingham, J. (1992), 'The Beginnings of English Imperialism', *Journal of Historical Sociology*, 5, pp. 392–409.

Giuseppi, M. S. (1895) 'Alien Merchants in England in the Fifteenth Century', *Transactions of the Royal Historical Society*, new ser., 9, pp. 75–98.

Given-Wilson, C. (1987), *The English Nobility in the Late Middle Ages: the Fourteenth-Century Political Community*, London, Routledge and Kegan Paul.

Gladstone, R. (1916–19), 'The Early Annandale Charters and their Strange Resting Place', *Transactions of the Dumfriesshire and Galloway Natural History and Antiquarian Society*, 3rd ser., 6, pp. 137–46.

Gollancz, M. (1936) 'The System of Gaol Delivery as Illustrated in the Extant Gaol Delivery Rolls of the Fifteenth Century', MA thesis, University of London.

Goodman, A., (1987) 'The Anglo-Scottish Marches in the Fifteenth Century: A Frontier Society?', in R. A. Mason (ed.), *Scotland and England 1286–1815*, Edinburgh, John Donald, pp. 18–33.

Goodman, A. (1992), 'Introduction', in A. Goodman and A. Tuck (eds), *War and Border Societies in the Middle Ages*, London, Routledge, pp. 1–29.

Goodman, A. (1992), *John of Gaunt: The Exercise of Princely Power in Fourteenth-Century Europe*, New York, St Martin's Press.

Goodman, A. (1985), 'A Letter from an Earl of Douglas to a King of Castile', *Scottish Historical Review*, 64, pp. 68–75.

Goodman, A. (1971), *The Loyal Conspiracy: The Lords Appellant under Richard II*, Coral Gables, FL, University of Miami Press.

Graham, T. H. B. (1925), 'Border Tenure', *Transactions of the Cumberland and Westmorland Antiquarian and Archaeological Society*, new ser., 25, pp. 86–95.

Graham, T. H. B. (1912), 'The Debateable Land', *Transactions of the Cumberland and Westmorland Antiquarian and Archaeological Society*, new ser., 12, pp. 33–58.

Gransden, A. (1982), *Historical Writing in England. Vol. II: c. 1307 to the Early Sixteenth Century*, London, Routledge and Kegan Paul.

Grant, A. (1993), 'Foreign Affairs under Richard III', in J. Gillingham (ed.), *Richard III: A Medieval Kingship*, New York, St Martin's Press, pp. 113–32.

Grant, A. (1984), *Independence and Nationhood: Scotland 1306–1469*, London, Edward Arnold.

Grant, A. (1992), 'The Otterburn War from the Scottish Point of View', in A. Goodman and A. Tuck (eds), *War and Border Societies in the Middle Ages*, London, Routledge, pp. 30–64.

Grant, A. and Stringer, K. (eds), (1995), *Uniting the Kingdom? The Making of British History*, London, Routledge.

Griffiths, R. A. (1968), 'Local Rivalries and National Politics: The Percies, the Nevilles, and the Duke of Exeter, 1452–55', *Speculum*, 43, pp. 589–632.

Griffiths, R. A. (1981), *The Reign of King Henry VI*, Berkeley and Los Angeles, University of California Press.

Griffiths, R. A. (1972), 'Wales and the Marches', in S. B. Chrimes, C. D. Ross and R. A. Griffiths (eds), *Fifteenth-century England 1399–1509*, Manchester, Manchester University Press, pp. 145–72.

Hand, G. J. (1967), *English Law in Ireland 1290–1324*, Cambridge, Cambridge University Press.

Hand, G. J. (1966), 'The Forgotten Statutes of Kilkenny: A Brief Survey', *Irish Jurist*, new ser., 1, pp. 299–312.

Harding, A. (1960), 'The Origins and Early History of the Keepers of the Peace', *Transactions of the Royal Historical Society*, 5th ser., 10, pp. 85–110.

Harriss, G. L. (1985), 'The King and His Magnates', in G. L. Harriss, ed., *Henry V: The Practice of Kingship*, Oxford, Oxford University Press, pp. 31–51.

Hicks, M. A. (1978), 'Dynastic Change and Northern Society: The Career of the Fourth Earl of Northumberland, 1470–89', *Northern History*, 14, pp. 78–107.

Hill, R. M. T. (1972), 'Belief and Practice as Illustrated by John XXII's Excommunication of Robert Bruce', in G. J. Cuming and D. Baker (eds), *Popular Belief and Practice*, Cambridge, Cambridge University Press, pp. 135–9.

Hodgkin, T. (1908), *The Wardens of the Northern Marches*, London, John Murray.

Hodgson, J. (1820–58), *A History of Northumberland*, 3 pts in 7 vols, Newcastle-upon-Tyne, Thomas and John Pigg *et al.*

Holdsworth, W. (1966), *A History of English Law*, 7th edn, 16 vols, London, Methuen and Co.

Holt, J. C. (1971), *The Northerners: A Study in the Reign of King John*, Oxford, Oxford University Press.

Hugill, R. (1970), *Borderland Castles and Peles*, Newcastle-upon-Tyne, Graham.

Jacob, E. F. (1993), *The Fifteenth Century 1399–1485*, Oxford, Oxford University Press.

James, M. E. (1965), 'The Murder at Cocklodge 28th April 1489', *Durham University Journal*, 57, pp. 80–7.

Jewell, H. M. (1994), *The North-South Divide: The Origins of Northern Consciousness in England*, Manchester, Manchester University Press.

Jones, J. G. (1974), 'Government and the Welsh Community: the North-east Borderland in the Fifteenth Century', in H. Hearder and H. R. Loyn (eds), *British Government and Administration: Studies presented to S. B. Chrimes*, Cardiff, University of Wales Press, pp. 55–68.

Jones, W. R. (1971), 'England against the Celtic Fringe: A Study in Cultural Stereotypes', *Cahiers d'histoire mondiale*, 13, pp. 155–71.

Jones, W. R. (1971), 'The Image of the Barbarian in Medieval Europe', *Comparative Studies in Society and History*, 13, pp. 376–407.

Jones, W. R. (1980), 'Violence, Criminality, and Culture Disfunction on the Anglo–Irish Frontier: The Example of Armagh, 1350–1550', *Criminal Justice History*, 1, pp. 29–47.

Keen, M. (1984), 'The Jurisdiction and Origins of the Constable's Court', in J. Gillingham and J. C. Holt (eds), *War and Government in the Middle Ages: Essays in Honour of J. O. Prestwich*, Cambridge, D. S. Brewer, pp. 159–69.

Keen, M. (1962), 'Treason Trials under the Law of Arms', *Transactions of the Royal Historical Society*, 5th ser., 12, pp. 85–103.

Keen, M. H. (1965), *The Laws of War in the Late Middle Ages*, London, Routledge and Kegan Paul.

Kendall, P. M. (1956), *Richard III*, New York, W. W. Norton and Co.

Kennedy, E. D. (1989), 'John Hardyng and the Holy Grail', *Arthurian Literature*, 8, pp. 185–206.

Kingsford, C. L. (1913), *Historical Literature in the Fifteenth Century*, New York, Burt Franklin.

Kirby, J. L. (1970), *Henry IV of England*, London, Constable.

Lapsley, G. T. (1924), *The County Palatine of Durham*, Cambridge MA, Harvard University Press.

Lapsley, G. T. (1901), 'The Problem of the North', *American Historical Review*, 5, pp. 440–6.

Lewis, N. B. (1958), 'The Last Medieval Summons of the Feudal Levy, 13 June 1385', *English Historical Review*, 73, pp. 1–26.

Lomas, R. (1992), *North-East England in the Middle Ages*, Edinburgh, John Donald.

Lydon, J. (1973), *Ireland in the Later Middle Ages*, Dublin, Gill and Macmillan.

Lydon, J. F. (1972), *The Lordship of Ireland in the Middle Ages*, Toronto, University of Toronto Press.

Lydon, J. F. (1984), 'The Middle Nation', in J. Lydon (ed.), *The English in Medieval Ireland*, Dublin, Royal Irish Academy, pp. 1–26.

Macdonald, A. (1995), 'Crossing the Border: A Study of the Scottish Military Offensives against England c. 1369 – c. 1403', Ph.D. thesis, University of Aberdeen.

Macdougall, N. (1977), 'Foreign Relations: England and France', in J. M. Brown (ed.), *Scottish Society in the Fifteenth Century*, London, Edward Arnold, pp. 101–11.

Macdougall, N. (1982), *James III: A Political Study*, Edinburgh, John Donald.

Macdougall, N. (1989), *James IV*, Edinburgh, John Donald.

Macdougall, N. (1986), 'Richard III and James III: Contemporary Monarchs, Parallel Mythologies', in P. W. Hammond (ed.), *Richard III: Loyalty, Lordship and Law*, London, Richard III and Yorkist History Trust, pp. 148–71.

Macfarlane, L. J. (1985), *William Elphinstone and the Kingdom of Scotland 1431–1514*, Aberdeen, University of Aberdeen Press.

Mack, J. L. (1924), *The Border Line*, Edinburgh, Oliver and Boyd.

Mackenzie, W. M. (1951), 'The Debateable Land', *Scottish Historical Review*, 30, pp. 109–25.

Mackie, R. L. (1958), *James IV*, Edinburgh, Oliver and Boyd.

MacNiocaill, G. (1984), 'The Interaction of Laws', in J. F. Lydon (ed.), *The English in Medieval Ireland*, Dublin, Royal Irish Academy, pp. 105–17.

MacQueen, H. L. (1993), 'The Kin of Kennedy, "Kenkynnol" and the Common Law', in A. Grant and K. J. Stringer (eds), *Medieval Scotland: Crown, Lordship and Community: Essays presented to G. W. S. Barrow*, Edinburgh, Edinburgh University Press, pp. 274–96.

MacQueen, H. L. (1991), 'The Laws of Galloway: A Preliminary Survey', in R. D. Oram and G. P. Snell (eds), *Galloway: Land and Lordship*, Edinburgh, Scottish Society for Northern Studies, pp. 131–43.

Macrae, C. (1939), 'The English Council and Scotland in 1430', *English Historical Review*, 54, pp. 415–26.

Macrae, C. (1939), 'Scotland and the Wars of the Roses: The Diplomatic Relations of England and Scotland, 1435–1485', D.Phil. thesis, University of Oxford.

Mann, K. (1996), 'The March of Wales: A Question of Terminology', *Welsh History Review*, 18, pp. 1–13.

Mason, J. (1929), 'Sir Andrew de Harcla, Earl of Carlisle', *Transactions of the Cumberland and Westmorland Antiquarian and Archaeological Society*, new ser., 29, pp. 98–137.

McGladdery, C. (1990), *James II*, Edinburgh, John Donald.

McIntire, W. T. (1939), 'The Fords of the Solway', *Transactions of the Cumberland and Westmorland Antiquarian and Archaeoloical Society*, new ser., 39, pp. 152–70.

McIntire, W. T. (1939), 'Historical Relations between Dumfriesshire and Cumberland', *Transactions of the Dumfriesshire and Galloway Natural History and Archaeological Society*, 3rd ser., 21, pp. 70–89.

McKisack, M. (1991), *The Fourteenth Century, 1307–1399*, Oxford, Oxford University Press.

McNamee, C. (1992), 'Buying Off Robert Bruce: An Account of Monies paid to the Scots by Cumberland Communities in 1313–14', *Transactions of the Cumberland and Westmorland Antiquarian and Archaeological Society*, 92, pp. 77–89.

McNiven, P. (1979–80), 'The Scottish Policy of the Percies and the Strategy of the Rebellion of 1403', *Bulletin of the John Rylands Library*, 62, pp. 498–530.

Miller, E. (1960), *War in the North: The Anglo-Scottish Wars of the Middle Ages*, Hull, University of Hull Press.

Moore, M. F. (1973), *The Lands of the Scottish Kings in England*, London, Allen and Unwin.

Murphy, B. (1967), 'The Status of the Native Irish after 1331', *Irish Jurist*, new ser., 2, pp. 116–28.

Neville, C. J. (1988), 'Border Law in Late Medieval England', *Journal of Legal History*, 9, pp. 335–56.

Neville, C. J. (1994), 'Common Knowledge of the Common Law in Later Medieval England', *Canadian Journal of History*, 29, pp. 461–78.

Neville, C. J. (1994), 'Keeping the Peace on the Northern Marches in the Later Middle Ages', *English Historical Review*, 109, pp. 1–25.

Neville, C. J. (1991), 'The Law of Treason in the English Border Counties in the Later Middle Ages', *Law and History Review*, 9, pp. 1–30.

Neville, C. J. (1996), 'Local Sentiment and the "National" Enemy in Northern England in the Later Middle Ages', *Journal of British Studies*, 35, pp. 419–37.

Neville, C. J. (1995), 'War, Crime and Local Communities in the North of England in the Later Middle Ages', in J. Drendel (ed.), *La Société rurale et les institutions gouvernementales au Moyen Age*, Montreal, CERES Press, pp. 207–19.

Nicholls, K. (1972), *Gaelic and Gaelicised Ireland in the Middle Ages*, Dublin, Gill and Macmillan.

Nicholson, R. (1965), *Edward III and the Scots*, Oxford, Oxford University Press.

Nicholson, R. (1978), *Scotland: The Later Middle Ages*, Edinburgh, Oliver and Boyd.

Nicolson J. and Burn, R. (1777), *The History and Antiquities of Westmorland and Cumberland*, 2 vols, London, W. Strachan.

Ormrod, W. M. (1995), *Political Life in Medieval England, 1300–1450*, New York, St Martin's Press.

Ormrod, W. M. (1990), *The Reign of Edward III*, New Haven, Yale University Press.

Otway-Ruthven, J. (1968), *A History of Medieval Ireland*, London, Ernest Benn Ltd.

Packe, M. (1983), *King Edward III*, London, Routledge and Kegan Paul.

Palmer, J. N. (1968), 'The Last Summons of the Feudal Army in England (1385)', *English Historical Review*, 83, pp. 771–5.

Payling, S. (1991), *Political Society in Lancastrian England: The Greater Gentry of Nottinghamshire*, Oxford, Oxford University Press.

Pease, H. (1913), *The Lord Wardens of the Marches of England and Scotland*, London, Constable.

Pollard, A. J. (1990), *North-eastern England during the Wars of the Roses*, Oxford, Clarendon Press.

Pollard, A. J. (1976), 'The Northern Retainers of Richard Nevill, Earl of Salisbury', *Northern History*, 11, pp. 52–69.

Pollard, A. J. (1988), *The Wars of the Roses*, New York, St Martin's Press.

Pollock F. and Maitland, F. W. (1968), *The History of English Law Before the Time of Edward I*, 2nd edn, 2 vols, Cambridge, Cambridge University Press.

Powell, E. (1983), 'Arbitration and the Law in England in the Late Middle Ages', *Transactions of the Royal Historical Society*, 5th ser., 33, pp. 49–69.

Powell, E. (1989), *Kingship, Law and Society: Criminal Justice in the Reign of Henry V*, Oxford, Clarendon Press.

Powell, E. (1985), 'The Restoration of Law and Order', in G. L. Harriss (ed.), *Henry V: The Practice of Kingship*, Oxford, Oxford University Press, pp. 53–74.

Prestwich, M. (1988), *Edward I*, Berkeley and Los Angeles, University of California Press.

Prestwich, M. (1989), 'England and Scotland during the Wars of Independence', in M. Jones and M. Vale (eds), *England and her Neighbours, 1066–1453: Essays in Honour of Pierre Chaplais*, London, Hambledon Press, pp. 181–97.

Pugh, T. B. (1972), 'The Magnates, Knights and Gentry', in S. B. Chrimes, C. D. Ross and R. A. Griffiths (eds), *Fifteenth-century England 1399–1509*, Manchester, Manchester University Press, pp. 86–128.

Putnam, B. (1950), 'Shire Officials: Keepers of the Peace and Justices of the Peace', in J. F. Willard, W. A. Morris, J. R. Strayer and W. H. Dunham (eds), *The English Government at Work, 1327–1336*, vol. III, Cambridge MA, Medieval Academy of America, pp. 185–217.

Putnam, B. (1929), 'The Transformation of the Keepers of the Peace into the Justices of the Peace 1327–1380', *Transactions of the Royal Historical Society*, 4th ser., 12, pp. 19–48.

Rae, T. I. (1966), *The Administration of the Scottish Frontier: 1513–1603*, Edinburgh, Edinburgh University Press.

Raine, J. (1852), *The History and Antiquities of North Durham*, London, J. B. Nichols and Sons.

Ramsay, J. H. (1892), *Lancaster and York*, 2 vols, Oxford, Clarendon Press.

Reid, R. C. (1939), 'The Merkland Cross', *Transactions of the Dumfriesshire and Galloway Natural History and Antiquarian Society*, 3rd ser., 21, pp. 216–27.

Reid, R. R. (1921), *The King's Council in the North*, London, Longmans, Green and Co.

Reid, R. R. (1917), 'The Office of Warden of the March; its Origin and Early History', *English Historical Review*, 32, pp. 479–96.

Reynolds, S. (1984), *Kingdoms and Communities in Western Europe 900–1300*, Oxford, Clarendon Press.

Richmond, C. F. (1971), 'The War at Sea', in K. Fowler (ed.), *The Hundred Years War*, London, Macmillan, pp. 96–121.

Richter, M. (1978), 'The Political and Institutional Background to National Consciousness in Medieval Wales', in T. W. Moody (ed.), *Nationality and the Pursuit of National Independence*, Belfast, Appletree Press, pp. 37–55.

Riddy, F. (1993), 'John Hardyng's Chronicle and the Wars of the Roses', *Arthurian Literature*, 12, pp. 91–108.

Robson, R. (1989), *The English Highland Clans: Tudor Responses to a Medieval Problem*, Edinburgh, John Donald.

Rose, R. K. (1984), 'The Bishops and the Diocese of Carlisle: Church and Society on the Anglo-Scottish Border 1292–1395', Ph.D. thesis, University of Edinburgh.

Ross, C. (1974), *Edward IV*, Berkeley and Los Angeles, University of California Press.

Ross, C. (1981), *Richard III*, Berkeley and Los Angeles, University of California Press.

Russell, M. J. (1980), 'Trial by Battle and the Appeals of Felony', *Journal of Legal History*, 1, pp. 135–64.

Saul, N. (1986), *Scenes from Provincial Life: Knightly Families in Sussex 1280–1400*, Oxford, Clarendon Press.

Scammell, J. (1958), 'Robert I and the North of England', *English Historical Review*, 73, pp. 385–403.

Scofield, C. L. (1967), *The Life and Reign of Edward the Fourth*, 2 vols, New York, Octagon Books.

Scott, W. W. (1993), 'The March Laws Reconsidered', in A. Grant and K. J. Stringer (eds),

Medieval Scotland: Crown, Lordship and Community: Essays presented to G. W. S. Barrow, Edinburgh, Edinburgh University Press, pp. 114–30.

Simms, K. (1989), 'Bards and Barons: The Anglo-Irish Aristocracy and the Native Culture', in R. Bartlett and W. Mackay (eds), *Medieval Frontier Societies*, Oxford, Clarendon Press, pp. 177–97.

Smith, L. B. (1980), 'The Statute of Wales, 1284', *Welsh History Review*, 10, pp. 127–54.

Snyder, E. D. (1920), 'The Wild Irish: A Study of Some English Satires against the Irish, Scots and Welsh', *Modern Philology*, 17, pp. 687–725.

Squibb, G. D. (1959), *The High Court of Chivalry: A Study of the Civil Law in England*, Oxford, Clarendon Press.

Steel, A. (1954), *The Receipt of the Exchequer, 1377–1485*, Cambridge, Cambridge University Press.

Steel, A. (1941), *Richard II*, Cambridge, Cambridge University Press.

Stones, E. L. G. (1969–70), 'The Appeal to History in Anglo-Scottish Relations between 1291 and 1401: Part II', *Archives*, 9, pp. 80–3.

Storey, R. L. (1954), 'Disorders in Lancastrian Westmorland: Some Early Chancery Proceedings', *Transactions of the Cumberland and Westmorland Antiquarian and Archaeological Society*, new ser., 53, pp. 69–80.

Storey, R. L. (1966), *The End of the House of Lancaster*, London, Barrie and Rockliff.

Storey, R. L. (1989), *English Justices of the Peace 1461–1509*, Gloucester, Alan Sutton.

Storey, R. L. (1972), 'The North of England', in S. B. Chrimes, C. D. Ross and R. A. Griffiths (eds), *Fifteenth-Century England, 1399–1509*, Manchester, Manchester University Press, pp. 129–44.

Storey, R. L. (1968), *The Reign of Henry VII*, New York, Walker and Co.

Storey, R. L. (1961), *Thomas Langley and the Bishopric of Durham 1406–1437*, London, SPCK.

Storey, R. L. (1957), 'The Wardens of the Marches of England towards Scotland, 1377–1489', *English Historical Review*, 72, pp. 593–615.

Summerson, H. (1982), 'Crime and Society in Medieval Cumberland', *Transactions of the Cumberland and Westmorland Antiquarian and Archaeological Society*, new ser., 82, pp. 111–24.

Summerson, H. (1989), 'The Early Development of the Laws of the Anglo-Scottish Marches, 1249–1448', in W. M. Gordon and T. D. Fergus (eds), *Legal History in the Making. Proceedings of the Ninth Legal History Conference, Glasgow, 1989*, London, Hambledon Press, pp. 29–42.

Summerson, H. (1993), *Medieval Carlisle: the City and the Borders from the Late Eleventh to the Mid-Sixteenth Century*, 2 vols, Kendal, Cumberland and Westmorland Antiquarian and Archaeological Society, Extra Series, 25.

Summerson, H. (1992), 'Responses to War: Carlisle and the West March in the Later Fourteenth Century', in A. Goodman and A. Tuck (eds), *War and Border Societies*, London, Routledge, pp. 155–77.

Templeman, G. (1949), 'Two French Attempts to Invade England During the Hundred Years War', in F. Mackenzie, R. C. Knight and J. M. Millner (eds), *Studies in French Language, Literature and History, presented to R. L. Graeme Ritchie*, Cambridge, Cambridge University Press, pp. 225–38.

Tough, D. L. W. (1928), *The Last Years of a Frontier: A History of the Borders during the Reign of Elizabeth I*, Oxford, Oxford University Press.

Tuck, J. A. (1986), 'The Emergence of a Northern Nobility, 1250–1400', *Northern History*, 22, pp. 1–17.

Tuck, J. A. (1995), 'Henry IV and Europe: the Search for Recognition', in R. H. Britnell and A. J. Pollard (eds), *The McFarlane Legacy: Studies in Late Medieval Politics and Society*, New York, St Martin's Press, pp. 107–25.

Tuck, J. A. (1971), 'Northumbrian Society in the Fourteenth Century', *Northern History*, 6, pp. 22–39.

Tuck, J. A. (1968), 'Richard II and the Border Magnates', *Northern History*, 3, pp. 27–52.

Tuck, J. A. (1973), *Richard II and the English Nobility*, London, Edward Arnold.

Tuck, J. A. (1985), 'War and Society in the Medieval North', *Northern History*, 21, pp. 33–52.

Van Caenegem, R. C. (1988), *The Birth of the English Common Law*, 2nd edn, Cambridge, Cambridge University Press.

Walker, D. (1984), 'Cultural Survival in an Age of Conquest', in R. R. Davies, R. A. Griffiths, I. G. Jones and K. O. Morgan (eds), *Welsh Society and Nationhood: Historical Essays presented to Glanmor Williams*, Cardiff, University of Wales Press, pp. 35–50.

Walker, D. (1990), *Medieval Wales*, Cambridge, Cambridge University Press.

Walker, D. M. (1990), *A Legal History of Scotland. Vol. II: The Later Middle Ages*, Edinburgh, W. Green and Son.

Walker, S. (1990), *The Lancastrian Affinity 1361–1399*, Oxford, Clarendon Press.

Walker, S. K. (1991), 'Letters to the Dukes of Lancaster in 1381 and 1399', *English Historical Review*, 106, pp. 68–79.

Webster, B. (1958), 'The English Occupation of Dumfriesshire in the Fourteenth Century', *Transactions of the Dumfriesshire and Galloway Natural History and Archaeological Society*, 3rd ser., 35, pp. 64–80.

Weiss, M. (1976), 'A Power in the North? The Percies in the Fifteenth Century', *Historical Journal*, 19, pp. 501–9.

Whitton, J. B. (1936), 'La Sainteté des traités: *Pacta sunt servanda*', *Revue de droit international*, 18, pp. 440–80.

Williams, E. C. (1963), *My Lord of Bedford 1389–1435*, London, Longmans.

Williams, P. (1958), *The Council in the Marches of Wales under Elizabeth I*, Cardiff, University of Wales Press.

Wilson, S. C. (1930), 'Border Incidents: A Prisoner', *Transactions of the Hawick Archaeological Society*, pp. 32–4.

Wilson, S. C. (1920), 'Border Incidents from the *Rotuli*', *Transactions of the Hawick Archaeological Society*, pp. 5–8.

Wolffe, B. (1972), 'The Personal Rule of Henry VI', in S. B. Chrimes, C. D. Ross and R. A. Griffiths (eds), *Fifteenth-century England 1399–1509*, Manchester, Manchester University Press, pp. 29–48.

Wormald, J. (1981), *Court, Kirk and Community: Scotland 1470–1625*, Toronto, University of Toronto Press.

Wright, W. A. R. (1976), 'The *Tree of Battles* of Honoré Bouvet and the Laws of War', in C. T. Allmand (ed.), *War, Literature and Politics in the Late Middle Ages*, Liverpool, University of Liverpool Press, pp. 12–31.

Wylie, J. H. (1884–98), *History of England under Henry the Fourth*, 4 vols, London, Longmans, Green and Co.

Wylie, J. H. (1968), *The Reign of Henry the Fifth*, 3 vols, New York, Greenwood Press.

Index

224